THEMATIC GUIDE TO
MODERN DRAMA

Susan C. W. Abbotson

GREENWOOD PRESS
Westport, Connecticut · London

Library of Congress Cataloging-in-Publication Data

Abbotson, Susan C. W., 1961–
   Thematic guide to modern drama / Susan C. W. Abbotson.
      p. cm.
   Includes bibliographical references and index.
   ISBN 0–313–31950–2 (alk. paper)
   1. Drama—20th century—Themes, motives. 2. Drama—19th century—Themes, motives.   I. Title.
   PN1861.A235 2003
   809.2'04—dc21   2002035216

British Library Cataloguing in Publication Data is available.

Library of Congress Catalog Card Number: 2002035216
ISBN: 0–313–31950–2

First published in 2003

Greenwood Press, 88 Post Road West, Westport, CT 06881
An imprint of Greenwood Publishing Group, Inc.
www.greenwood.com

Printed in the United States of America

The paper used in this book complies with the
Permanent Paper Standard issued by the National
Information Standards Organization (Z39.48–1984).

10 9 8 7 6 5 4 3 2 1

For a wonderful mother and friend
Joan Mary Abbotson
For all the help and encouragement received
through the years
"Haply I may remember"

Contents

Introduction

It is difficult to define modern drama beyond considering the period in which a play was written. Beginning toward the end of the nineteenth century with the work of dramatic pioneers Henrik Ibsen, August Strindberg, and George Bernard Shaw, there was a decided break from the moralistic, often sensational, melodramatic fare that dominated much of the nineteenth century. These playwrights introduced realism to the stage, and added to the concept of the "well-made play" with its tidy denouement, the possibility of the more open-ended "discussion play" on which many later playwrights would build. Shaw's book, *The Quintessence of Ibsenism* (1891), did much to facilitate the initial change, bring Ibsen to critical attention, and awaken theatergoers to the possibilities of socially conscious drama.

Both Shaw and Ibsen felt that "well-made plays" with their meticulous plotting and pat denouements were artificial. Plays in which a discussion, often unresolved, superseded the plot, were preferable because they allowed audiences to judge events for themselves, thus making them an active part of the theatrical experience rather than merely passive viewers. From this change in the way plays were considered have grown increasingly more experimental theater forms and concepts of theatrical expression, often in reaction against the constraints of realism. Therefore, alongside realism, we find expressionism, absurdism, agit-prop, epic theatre, and the relative extremes of metatheatrical postmodern works. All fall under the general rubric of *modern drama*.

The focus of this volume is to offer the reader a sense of the numerous themes that weave their way through modern drama, and to highlight the variety of thought that exists in response to them. Although presentational differences may be noted and briefly explained, due to constraints of space they are not dwelt upon unless they are indicative of a play's theme. This emphasis on theme rather than form helps to assimilate the insights and experiences of a variety of modern dramatists from the last hundred and more years. Whereas greater emphasis is given to American dramatists with whom more students are more familiar, many playwrights from other parts of the world are considered, to give a wider picture of how these chosen themes impact humanity at large.

The "Themes" of the book's title are broad. Many are the common concerns of artists throughout literary history, including social attitudes toward death, religion, women, or ambition. Specific events that have impacted many people and commonly feature in modern drama are also covered, such as the Holocaust and slavery. Some themes incorporate specific character relationships, such as those between siblings, couples, or parents and children, others more general relationships between people, such as those generated by a sense of community, growing up, or aging. Themes also cover specific areas of concern from the past century, including attitudes toward work, illness, war, and substance abuse, as well as the particular ethnic mix of the United States, with chapters on African Americans, Asian Americans, Jewish Americans, Latin Americans, and American Indians. Each theme is developed with a focus on its universal conflicts and dilemmas, as well as considering more specific social, moral, and political issues to which it can be related. Each chapter tries to consider people from varied walks of life in terms of ethnicity, gender, and opportunity, to give as wide a response as possible.

Thirty-three themes are arranged alphabetically in this volume. They can be read sequentially, but each is presented independently. Certain themes naturally overlap and complement each other; any discussion of marriage, for instance, will include reference to courting and attitudes toward women, just as any discussion of African Americans might touch on the heritage of slavery or the relationship between parents and children. Undue repetition is avoided by using different plays to illustrate each theme. This approach will, hopefully, help readers understand the vast scope of modern drama, and to facilitate this understanding, each chapter begins with a broad discussion of the social, cultural, and/or dramatic impact and importance of its particular theme. While many of these plays relate to more than one theme, each has been chosen for the chapter in which it appears because that chapter's theme is a central concern of the play.

Each theme is explicated through three plays that have been chosen because they display contrasting views. Sometimes these views are contradictory, or they may just approach the theme from differing perspectives. A brief summary of each play is given to familiarize readers with the basic plot, and the discussion considers what the action, language, and semiotics of the plays reveal about the central characters and the apparent beliefs of the playwrights who have created them. Woven throughout is a consideration of how the plays reflect and comment on the theme under discussion. Following each essay is a selected list of further suggested readings related to the theme.

This thematic approach will hopefully enrich the reader's understanding of the vast scope of modern drama, by putting these plays in context with one another and showing how the same theme has been developed in a variety of directions. While only a small fraction of the entire output of modern drama could be discussed within this volume, one hundred plays are discussed, which offer a good representative sample, and they are supplemented with examples for further reading. Plays familiar to most high school and college readers—particularly ones that are more accessible to the inexperienced reader—have taken precedence over more obscure works.

Teachers and librarians should find this volume useful in identifying appropriate dramatic works for a theme unit. The book's format also facilitates comparison and contrast of differing approaches to any particular theme. The suggested reading lists at the close of each chapter offer alternative plays featuring that chapter's theme, as well as sociological studies related to the theme, and, where available, approachable introductions to the playwrights and/or plays that have been under consideration. In addition, the index allows for easy identification and access to specific plays and playwrights that may be under study.

Despite the imbalance of output (since drama has been dominated by white male playwrights for many years), as many plays as possible by women and members of various cultural groups have been included. Although no play is discussed more than once, a number of important playwrights, including Henrik Ibsen, George Bernard Shaw, Anton Chekhov, Eugene O'Neill, Arthur Miller, Clifford Odets, Tennessee Williams, August Wilson, Brian Friel, and David Henry Hwang, have more than one play under discussion. These separate discussions can be combined to develop an understanding of the breadth of the particular playwright's concerns.

The dates given in the heading for each chapter are those of the plays' first known professional production, which may differ from their date of publication, and for some plays may not have been in English. Many of the plays under discussion have been anthologized in various collections and are readily available, but the bibliographical data for the editions consulted for this volume appear in the suggested reading list for each chapter.

Absurdity of Life

Waiting for Godot by Samuel Beckett (1953)
The Bald Soprano by Eugène Ionesco (1950)
The Birthday Party by Harold Pinter (1958)

The Theater of the Absurd grew as a response to what critics saw as the collapse of moral, religious, political, and social structures in the twentieth century. The primary aim of its plays was to point out the absurdity of life. Though it incorporated a diverse group of playwrights, each with his or her own set of beliefs, many influenced by the dadaist and surrealist movements, in general, they agree that human life and endeavor had become so essentially illogical, and language such an inadequate form of communication, that the only refuge was laughter. In absurdist plays, all truth becomes relative, and life is reduced to an illusion, to highlight the absurdity and hopelessness of the world. Martin Esslin defines the movement as striving to "express its sense of the senseless-ness of the human condition and the inadequacy of the rational approach by the open abandonment of rational devices and discursive thought." His expla-nation continues, "The Theatre of the Absurd has renounced arguing *about* the absurdity of the human condition; it merely *presents* it in being" (*Theatre of the Absurd,* 6), which separates this theater movement from existentialism, just as experience is different from theory.

Samuel Beckett's *Waiting for Godot* is generally considered to be at the forefront of the absurdist movement. Beckett conveys a sense of the hopeless-ness and absurdity of modern life in his depiction of two men passing time, as they vainly wait for the title character to arrive. The play is not a story about life, but rather the condition of living, being itself a metaphor for what Beckett saw as the mental state of twentieth century life. The apparent simplicity of the play is deceptive, for the text can be read at multiple levels and is densely filled with visual and linguistic symbolism, drawing on Freudian psychology, Christian mythology, and various philosophical outlooks. Beckett calls the play a "tragicomedy," through which he wants to suggest that since life is so tragic and impossible to comprehend, laughter might be the only sane response to it.

Eugène Ionesco's *The Bald Soprano* has even greater elements of burlesque humor than Beckett, as Ionesco exposes the inanities within commonplace behavior and thought. The "well-made play" is parodied as being conventionally predictable and innately stereotypical in character and plot. Feeling that the absurdity of modern existence cannot be communicated intellectually, Ionesco makes his audience sense and feel it through the experience of a play that mocks those who believe in causality, and exposes the meaninglessness and irrationality of people's lives and relationships in its presentation of characters whose inability to communicate leads them to dehumanize themselves and others. Although the experimental nature of his plays allies him to the surrealists, his work is not fully surreal in that it is never entirely divorced from reality. Likewise, his allegiance to existentialism is only partial, in that he would agree with Albert Camus and Jean-Paul Sartre that modern existence is meaningless, irrational, and absurd, but, unlike them, does not feel that such notions can be communicated through traditional literary modes.

The Birthday Party is less overtly comedic than Beckett or Ionesco, despite some entertaining wordplay. A sense of menace and violence fills Pinter's play and remains unrelieved by the close. Pinter underlines this with tense, quick-fire sequences of dialogue, though we learn as much from the silences and gestures as from what characters say. Pinter's dialogue ensures that we recognize how inadequate a form of communication language has become for these people, as they cannot make themselves understood to one another on even the simplest level. The idea that life is an illusion is conveyed by the fact that we are never allowed to be sure who any of the characters are, how they relate to each other, what it is they may have done, or what will happen to them.

In *Waiting For Godot*, Vladimir and Estragon (or Didi and Gogo, as they call each other) are two tramps waiting for a local landowner, Godot, to meet with them, and possibly change their lives. They pass the time conversing, arguing, and dreaming, diverted by two visits, one in each act, from Pozzo and Lucky, a sadistic master and submissive slave, whose relationship is inextricably and unpleasantly connected. A boy enters near the close of each act to announce that Godot will not come that day, and the tramps continue to wait.

The play challenged most theatrical expectations of its time with its illogical plot, purposeless action, virtually nonexistent set, and repetitive language, which frequently contradicts the action. Estragon complains, "Nothing happens, nobody comes, nobody goes" (41), but this is untrue, for although there is minimal plot and little character development, the play is never static; rather, it is filled with conflicts, mock conflicts, verbal exercises, comic routines, and mishaps. The play's humor, often bawdy, comes from farcical stage action, wordplay, and defeated expectancy (where we are tricked into expecting one thing and given another). Its seriousness is conveyed by extended philosophical monologues, and the layered symbolism of all we see and hear. Characters exchange hats as easily as they exchange roles, depicting the fluidity of identity, and boots fail to fit, just as lifestyles or religions might. A bare tree takes on varying significance as the denatured tree of life, the site of a crucifixion that forever changed the world, or, as it grows leaves, the possibility of progress.

Survival creates the action of the play, as we witness how humanity survives the empty existence Beckett sees as life. Vladimir and Estragon tell stories, contemplate suicide, eat carrots and radishes, pull their boots on and off, and somehow keep going. "We always find something," Estragon tells Vladimir, "to give us the impression we exist" (69). These two, representative of humankind in general, continue to sustain themselves through their endless inventiveness and refusal to finally despair, though they remain forever on a knife edge between despair and hope. They have different temperaments, concerns, strengths, and weaknesses, yet they complement each other to form a whole that holds them together despite the occasional argument.

Pozzo and Lucky also complement each other, but, in contrast to the tramps, they are bound together by a rope rather than the sustaining bond of friendship between Vladimir and Estragon, and their relationship is exploitative and destructive, with Lucky dancing and spouting empty rhetoric at Pozzo's tyrannical whim. In act 1 Lucky carries Pozzo's luggage, but also the whip with which he allows his master to beat him, suggesting that Lucky is complicit in his own subjugation. Pozzo may represent the ruthless capitalist against Lucky's hardworking, but ineffectual proletariat.

Pozzo initially seems rich and powerful, but reappears in act 2 in severely reduced circumstances, having lost much of his earlier self-certainty along with his sight. He represents those people who, with forced optimism, blind themselves to the illusory nature of both power and permanence in this world. When by act 2 Lucky has been struck dumb and Pozzo blind, it becomes symbolic of their moral and emotional limitations. Pozzo has throughout debunked faith, which blinds him to possibility, suggesting the reduction of life without Christian principle. While Vladimir and Estragon show the potential in working together when their combined efforts allow Pozzo to rise, Pozzo and Lucky are unable to learn this lesson, doomed to live in unhappy inequality.

The play suggests that life is a process of interminable waiting, bracketed by birth and death. Whether Godot is seen as God with a diminutive suffix, or an oblique reference to a character named Godeau from Honoré de Balzac's comedy *Le Faiseur*, who strongly influences the action but never appears on stage, the name signifies that thing for which we wait. Ascertaining Godot's identity runs contrary to the play's intention to portray the uncertainty of life by repeatedly defeating our expectation of discovering who he is. What may be more important is the probability that Godot's arrival would be a disappointment if it ever occurred, for it is the waiting that defines life. Since the only certainties are birth and death, it is up to the individual to make the best of what happens in between. The more people communicate with others, the better life will be, but the problem is that people, by nature, are poor communicators. Beckett's language is filled with linguistic tricks to convey the difficulties of communication. His characters find it impossible to say exactly what they mean, because there is no real meaning, and they speak in repetitious cycles, non sequiturs, and incomplete sentences that reflect this.

Beckett's work idiosyncratically combines elements of two contrasting philosophies: "determinism," which insists that human action is not free but determined by external forces acting on the will, and "existentialism," which insists that the individual is free and a responsible agent who determines his or her own development. The result is a total confusion, which is what Beckett sees as the reality of life. The search for salvation has become increasingly problematic in a modern world that questions even the concept of salvation. In Lucky and Pozzo this leads to despair, but Vladimir and Estragon maintain hope, which is sufficient to sustain them. Thus, the play is not hopeless: Vladimir and Estragon's lives, despite their apparent meaninglessness, become meaningful to them in their persistence in the face of hopelessness and refusal to be destroyed.

As a typical absurdist drama, there is little plot to *The Bald Soprano;* the action contradicts the words just as the words continuously contradict the action, so we are never sure of anything. We meet the Smiths, who have a number of confusing conversations, and are joined by a possibly married couple, the Martins, for dinner. All four continue in increasingly nonsensical debates, momentarily interrupted by a fire chief in search of a fire, and end in a hostile standoff, before the Martins assume the identities of the Smiths and the play begins again from where it started.

Despite its "slice of life" setting—the husband smokes a pipe and reads the paper while his wife darns socks in their cozy home—*The Bald Soprano* disrupts this apparent normalcy by having a clock strike seventeen. This temporal confusion continues throughout the play, but becomes the least of our worries, as Mr. and Mrs. Smith, the play's stereotypical middle-class couple, embark upon a disconcerting dialogue of information they must already know, such as what they had for dinner and descriptions of their children. Ionesco parodies a middle class whose lives have become spiritually and intellectually empty. The Smiths's speech has ossified into a patois of ready-made expressions and platitudes devoid of any real meaning and is a reflection of their entire existence, which has been dehumanized by its senseless banality and inflexibility. This disintegration of language is one of the play's central themes. As the two make absurd declarations regarding the nature of grocers, yogurt, and doctors, we see how their mechanical language has taken them close to the realm of idiocy. By the close of the play their constantly frustrated efforts to communicate with one another are reduced to subhuman sounds, as both couples are forced to recognize their inability to articulate anything that makes sense.

A confusion regarding reality permeates the entire play, no more evident than in the Smiths's discussion of the obituary of Bobby Watson, supposedly dead for two years. Their speech becomes filled with contradictions and patently bizarre information, such as declarations that each member of the potentially deceased's family was named Bobby Watson. Lying behind this is Ionesco's fear of human interchangeability, the inevitable conclusion of a group of people no longer differentiated by individuality in their efforts to assimilate into society. When people refuse to think for themselves, they can no longer be themselves. This means they can become anyone, but that is tantamount to being no one—and so the Smiths and the Martins become indistinct and interchangeable by the play's end, just as the Watson family became.

Mounting evidence of this lack of individuality comes with the entrance of the Martins, who, despite initially seeming not to know each other, come to a conclusion that they are husband and wife, until interrupted by Mary, the maid, who claims to be Sherlock Holmes, and suggests that they are mistaken. The nonexistence of an inner life in these characters is what prevents the forging of any meaningful relationships. Their inability to know for sure who they are and what their relationship might be is tragic. Unable to truly communicate, people become condemned to isolation; assertions of love and marriage are as empty as their linguistic attempts to connect. The characters' relationships are as nonsensical as their conversations, which insist that acts such as a man bending down to tie his shoelaces or reading a newspaper are extraordinary, but view as ordinary the most fantastic stories told to them by the fire chief.

In his belief that life is intrinsically nonsensical, Ionesco also ridicules what he sees as a misleading faith in causality. After the doorbell rings three times, but no one is there, Mrs. Smith ridiculously reasons, "Experience teaches us that when one hears the doorbell ring it is because there is never anyone there" (23). When causality cannot even make sense of daily events, it should surely be abandoned when exploring the more important problems and mysteries of life. This speaks to the heart of absurdist belief—that reason, logic, and rational principles of discourse are inadequate when it comes to looking at and certainly trying to understand the world in which we live. The fourth time the bell rings, the fire chief enters, looking for a fire that began three days earlier yet is timed to start in "three-quarters of an hour and sixteen minutes" (37). Such absurdity continuously obfuscates rather than enlightens and the relationships and re-actions become as unpredictable as they are ridiculous. The fire chief stays to tell complex and absurd tales, while Mary, who we learn has fought fires in the past, recites a repetitive poem about fire until she is pushed offstage. But after the fire chief departs, the conversation becomes even more bizarre, filled with gratuitous truisms about the nature of their environment; senseless as-sertions about merits of varied, unconnected objects and actions; and surreal-istic proverbs, including "Take a circle, caress it, and it will turn vicious" (38). Initially naturalistic in utterance, the dialogue becomes increasingly aggressive and all four end up screaming and shaking their fists at each other until they run out of words and all they can do is grunt at one another as the stage grows dark, before it returns to its opening dialogue, only with the Martins replacing the Smiths on stage.

The Bald Soprano is not a negative play, despite its parody and ridicule of the middle class. Ionesco does not see the future as hopeless, but uses his writing to shock that middle class out of what he saw as its dangerous and complacent beliefs in rationality, logic, and traditional ideas of causality and reality. He saw these as reducing rather than expanding our humanity, and called for a more imaginative existence that would better complement the wonderful absurdity he saw as life.

In *The Birthday Party*, Meg and Petey run a spurious boarding house, at which Stanley, an unemployed pianist, has lodged for the past year, perhaps in hiding. To his concern, Goldberg and McCann, two imposing men, come to stay, and grow increasingly threatening toward Stanley, who may or may not be hiding from criminals, who may or may not be these two men. The characters throw Stanley a birthday party, with games like blindman's buff, casting an incongruous air of normalcy over the violence that takes place. Stanley has a mental breakdown, attacks Meg and their neighbor Lulu, and, the next day, is taken away by the mysterious visitors, as Meg and Petey settle back into their routine as if nothing has happened.

Pinter's characters habitually lie and disguise their true intentions, while attempting to assert themselves over others. However, no one is able to achieve the complete domination each craves, indicating that life is uncertain even for people like Goldberg and McCann. Everyone's uncertainty is emphasized by the ominous pauses that fill their speech. Words are constantly deployed to have double meanings, such as when Lulu tells Goldberg he is "empty," referring to both his glass and his moral state. One can only half-guess at the significance of most speeches or actions. This vagueness draws audiences into the play, forcing them to explore its suggestions and share its encounters alongside the actors. Pinter's repetitive, short sentences reflect natural conversation, showing how mundane lives progress in their little routines—a mundanity that becomes safer and more attractive next to the violence that results when those routines are disrupted.

McCann and Goldberg create a mounting tension, as their covert threats become more open, beginning with verbal violence—they accuse Stanley of every possible crime—and building to physical violence. Their quick-fire speech echoes that of Vaudeville routines, which only makes their words more absurdly threatening. At one point Goldberg quite seriously asks Stanley why the chicken crossed the road. Pinter does not use humor to alleviate tension, but to emphasize the unreality of the situation. Against this, Stanley loses his capacity for speech and is silent for the rest of the play. The final act seems anticlimactic, with Meg apparently unaware of the violence around her, Petey safely staying on the sidelines, and Lulu the only one declaring outrage, although the possibility that she spent the night with Goldberg deflates this.

The play's unsettling vision of paranoia begins when we understand that Stanley has been hiding for a year, waiting for someone to arrive to punish him. Why, we are never certain, just as we never learn the cause of his estrangement from his parents. That his offenses are never clearly stated carries the suggestion they are so terrible as to be unspeakable. This is the end of the line, and he has nowhere left to hide, which is why he cannot run from McCann and Goldberg. It is possible he hides not from criminals but from his own guilt, and just projects his fears onto these visitors. The vagueness of the fiction encourages the audience to become caught up and find its own fears and impulses mirrored in those of the characters.

The inability to communicate is central to the play, as these characters are helpless to defend themselves because they cannot make themselves understood by each other. At the start, Meg and Petey go through the rhythm of a conversation without apparently understanding a word the other says, as they repeat questions, and make comments indicating no awareness of what the other has said. Another time, Lulu and Goldberg have a simultaneous conversation with Meg and McCann, in which everyone becomes incomprehensible. Words have become meaningless for these people—some kind of incomprehensible code they are unable or unwilling to break—and one wonders if they prefer it this way, as ignorance becomes a kind of bliss.

To further underline the desire to hide from reality, problems of identity abound in the play, beginning when Meg asks Petey to identify himself. We are also kept in the dark as to the real names, identities, and backgrounds of Goldberg and McCann. It is not that we are given no information, but that we are presented with conflicting stories—both answer to a variety of names, and McCann could be anything from a career criminal to a defrocked priest. Is Stanley a criminal or a concert pianist? Despite Meg's working-class persona, she reminisces about growing up in wealth. All this uncertainty forces the audience to question the very notion of identity and how it is formed; what allows us to know who anyone truly is? Pinter plays with the effect that names, jobs, and backgrounds have on how we view people, suggesting the impossibility of ever really knowing someone else.

McCann and Goldberg may represent dangers present in the modern world, waiting to steal a person's comfort, sanity, and even life. Stanley's fear seems to be what finally silences him, and renders him virtually paralyzed. But all of these characters are afflicted with doubts and uncertainties, unsure of what the truth might be, or even if any exists. Meg seems unsure of her relationship to Stanley; one moment mothering him, the next trying to seduce him. Meanwhile, Stanley asserts a responsibility for Meg and Petey, which he apparently betrays by living with them and placing them in danger.

Goldberg and McCann are total contradictions, Goldberg with his lectures about traditional values, and McCann with his possible stint as priest, balanced against the strong suggestion that they are gangsters. Goldberg also finds it difficult to complete his assertions, indicating an uncertainty over those beliefs, but also that they may be an insincere attempt to mask his evil purposes. With Goldberg representing Judaism, McCann Catholicism, Meg motherhood, and Stanley the arts, these characters suggest the way in which traditional values have failed modern society. Pinter offers nothing with which to replace these values, and all his play finally offers is an extended metaphor for the randomness, danger, and incomprehensibility of modern life; we are all of us stumbling in the dark as in a giant game of blind man's buff. With luck we will fare better than Stanley, but there are no guarantees.

FURTHER SUGGESTED READING

Albee, Edward. *The Zoo Story; The Death of Bessie Smith; The Sandbox; Three Plays.* New York: Coward-McCann, 1960.

Beckett, Samuel. *Waiting For Godot.* London: Faber and Faber, 1965.

Blocker, Gene. *The Metaphysics of Absurdity.* Washington: University Press of America, 1979.

Bradby, David. *Beckett*, Waiting for Godot. New York: Cambridge University Press, 2001.

Esslin, Martin. *The Theatre of the Absurd.* Rev. Ed. Garden City, NY: Doubleday, 1969.

Genet, Jean. *The Balcony.* New York: Grove, 1958.

Gordon, Lois. *Harold Pinter: A Casebook.* New York: Garland, 1990.

Hayman, Ronald. *Eugène Ionesco.* New York: Ungar, 1976.

Ionesco, Eugène. The Bald Soprano *and Other Plays.* Trans. Donald M. Allen. New York: Grove, 1982.

Lazar, Moshe, Ed. *The Dream and the Play: Ionesco's Theatrical Quest.* Malibu: Undena, 1982.

Mayberry, Bob. *Theatre of Discord: Dissonance in Beckett, Albee, and Pinter.* Rutherford, NJ: Fairleigh Dickinson University Press, 1989.

Pinter, Harold. *The Birthday Party.* London: Methuen, 1959.

Schleuter, June, and Enoch Brater. *Approaches to Teaching Beckett's* Waiting for Godot. New York: MLA, 1991.

African American Experience

A Raisin in the Sun by Lorraine Hansberry (1959)
Fences by August Wilson (1985)
Wedding Band by Alice Childress (1966)

The African American experience, despite being centuries old, has had a relatively recent appearance in American literature, especially drama. Despite an
African American tradition of minstrel shows and melodrama, with a few notable exceptions it was not until the surge of interest in African American
culture, thought, and experience during the 1960s that serious plays by and
about African Americans reached mainstream theaters. Since then an increasingly vibrant Black Theater movement has pursued African American themes
and even attempted to create and inculcate African American forms that utilize
aspects of African performance to create a unique blend.

All three plays in this chapter consider African American experiences prior
to the turbulent civil rights movement in the sixties. Each portrays African
American life accurately and realistically, challenging stereotypes by the very
complexity of their characters. Facing the African American experience un-
flinchingly, pointing out its strengths and weaknesses, they try to explain past
behaviors and offer hope for a potentially greater future given the positive
qualities their characters exhibit.

As with most ethnic groups in America, African Americans face what W.E.B.
Du Bois called a "double-consciousness." Affected by two very different cultures, they find themselves unable to ignore either culture without sacrificing
a part of their identity. An effective value system for African Americans becomes problematic as they seek a balance between African tradition and American experience. This double-consciousness creates some of the apparent
contradictions within Lorraine Hansberry's *A Raisin in the Sun,* such as the
conflict between Mama's matriarchal rule (African) and Walter's patriarchal
expectations (American). Hansberry never asks us to take sides, but rather to
consider the potential within each tradition.

Hansberry's racial commentary is subtle throughout the play, but color is integral to its plot, which takes its title from Langston Hughes's poem about the way in which the dreams of African Americans are constantly deferred in a society constantly antagonistic to their advancement. *A Raisin in the Sun* depicts a middle-class African American family trying to advance itself in American society, and much of its plot was drawn directly from Hansberry's own experience when her family tried to settle in a white neighborhood. While growing up, Hansberry also experienced the tension between wanting to assimilate and maintaining pride in one's own culture. Her play anticipated many of the mounting concerns for African Americans and women of its day.

August Wilson's *Fences* has a similar focus on the family, set during the same period, when African Americans were becoming more vocal in demanding their rights. But Wilson explores different social tensions than Hansberry, with his central relationship between a father and his sons rather than a mother and her children, and the depiction of a more working-class family. Wilson offers a skeptical consideration of those African American roads to instant success via sports or entertainment, and through the character of Troy suggests the qualities best suited to African American success; it is unsurprising that Troy was largely modeled on Wilson's own stepfather, whom he much admired.

Alice Childress's *Wedding Band*, set farther South, looks at American anti-miscegenation laws, which tried to prevent romantic interracial relationships, and the effect they had on people's lives. These laws were regularly enforced during the nineteenth century and remained accepted social policy well into the twentieth. They were grounded in disturbing beliefs regarding racial superiority and inferiority. *Wedding Band* depicts tragic events that take place during the flu epidemic of 1918, but the lack of tolerance between white and African American cultures it addresses remains a contemporary issue.

A Raisin in the Sun relates a defining period in the lives of the Younger family: Beneatha comes to a better understanding of her ethnicity, Walter learns how to be a man, his wife, Ruth, rediscovers hope, and Mama learns to be less controlling. Mama's dream has been to relocate to a better neighborhood, but they face racist opposition from local whites, led by Karl Lindner.

The differences between Beneatha's two boyfriends, Joseph Asagai and George Murchison, are important, as is her choice between them. While Asagai is the complete African, George is the assimilated American. Despite his social standing, George is not a character to emulate for two reasons: first, because he refuses to recognize the equality of women, wanting Beneatha as his "little woman"; and second, because he fails to acknowledge the importance of his African heritage, dismissing it as irrelevant. He knows facts about Africa but has lost touch with its spirit and strength. Because of his wealth he is satisfied with the status quo and selfishly refuses to change. Such individual selfishness thwarts African American development as a whole. George may have wealth, but he has no real identity of his own and he lacks the vibrancy we see in Asagai's firm, ethnic identity.

Asagai is not just showing the rich tradition of Africa to Beneatha, but also to the audience. In the fifties, when this play was first produced, his sophistication would have been at odds with many people's narrow perception of Africans as savages. Yet we should recognize that Asagai is unable to recognize the "American aspects" of Beneatha's character, for his experience is entirely African. Asagai cannot accept Beneatha's drive for independence, though he admires her spirit. In his own way he wishes to dominate her as much as George does. Beneatha needs to find her own identity, which lies between the Americanness of George and the Africanness of Asagai.

Asagai wants to take Beneatha to Africa, but his impulse is selfish. Beneatha's home is in America, and America needs her spirited contributions. Beneatha will not find herself in Africa, because she is also American, though she is right to suggest that African Americans need a better understanding of Africa as a part of their heritage. Beneatha and Walter's pride in their African roots is important, but they also need to have pride in their American-born family and recognize what their strength has achieved in six generations.

Initially, Ruth seems prematurely aged and tired, ready to give in and accept the meager life she has. She has borne a large burden, nurturing and providing for her family with little reward. But Ruth's dormant strength returns as she refuses to give up the house Mama buys. We learn that this has been her dream as much as Mama's, and she is able to reinforce Mama's slipping spirit. The Youngers live in a ghetto neighborhood and their desire to move is valid—the kids chase rats in the street, and the apartment is not only cramped but infested with cockroaches. A better home will allow them more room to grow. The urgency of this move is emphasized by the discovery that Ruth is pregnant.

Mama's key attributes are her strength and her clear sense of direction. The combined strength of her and her husband has brought the family this far. Hansberry recognizes that African American progress cannot happen overnight but will be a lengthy process. Equality will take generations of struggle—each generation contributing a little bit to the progress. Mama's plant, which she so doggedly preserves, underlines both her desire to grow and her refusal to give in. It also represents her dream: to have a house with a garden. The "Scarlett O'Hara" hat Travis gives Mama indicates her achievement: by owning property, she has become akin to the mistress of the plantation, rather than one of the slaves working there.

Walter erroneously believes that life is money, but Mama knows that freedom is more important, having been closer to a generation that had none. Walter needs to respect the past, and his parents' achievements, but it is now his turn to achieve, and Mama must allow him the freedom to develop his own self-respect, for it is Mama's self-respect that provides the roots of her strength. Mama allows Walter real control—not when she gives him money, but when she lets him decide what to do about the house.

Awkward and soft-spoken, by himself Karl Lindner seems to offer little threat. However, we should recognize the larger community and power behind him. His discomfort ensures that we realize that what he asks is wrong. Even he seems to realize this, but he cannot surmount his own prejudice. He uses platitudes to mask what he is doing, but no one is ultimately fooled. His commentary on empathy is ironically something of which he himself is incapable. How is the Youngers's hardworking background any different from that of the residents of Clybourne Park? How can Lindner be anything other than a full-fledged racist?

Walter's instinct to eject this man from his home is right and this action will be more empowering than the money he got from Mama. Walter begins his second confrontation with Lindner sheepishly, but draws strength as he continues—partly from within himself and his own pride, and partly from his family and a recognition of the dignity he owes them for their sacrifices. It is at this moment that we see the man in Walter. Now he can give orders to others and expect them to follow those orders, since he has finally earned their respect.

One aspect of the play that has drawn criticism is its lack of black solidarity, with the inclusion of such unhelpful characters as Willy Harris and Miss Johnson. While Willy runs off with Walter's money, Miss Johnson's appearance as a gossipy, unhelpful neighbor suggests the inability of many blacks to assist each other. Miss Johnson is motivated by jealousy, not wanting the Youngers to rise above her, and Beneatha is right to compare her to the Ku Klux Klan: both are destructive to black development in America.

Although the Youngers get their house, it would be a mistake to see this as a happy ending. Hansberry purposefully leaves us uncertain as to what will happen next. What indignities might the Youngers be forced to suffer in Clybourne Park, where it is clear they are not welcome? What will Beneatha decide to do with her life, and will gender restrict her choices? What these stage characters have achieved so far is only a fragment of what they will need to ensure true equality in society for both African Americans and women.

Fences introduces us to the masculine world of the Maxsons. Troy, the father, makes mistakes but takes responsibility for his actions in a way Wilson asks the entire African American community to consider. His wife, Rose, mostly supports him, though she has trouble accepting his infidelity, although it is a weakness for which he pays. Troy tries to teach his sons Lyons and Cory what he has learned to help them survive in a world antagonistic to African American advancement. They expect success too easily and initially reject his message of hard work, but by the play's end develop new respect for their father.

The house and its setting are expressions of its owner, Troy, surrounding him with the elements that make up his life: home, baseball, garbage, porch, and his fence. Their permanence gives us a strong sense of Troy's solidity of presence. He has built onto his family's home a "sturdy porch" to facilitate his storytelling sessions, and set up a bat and ball in the yard as a permanent reminder of his thwarted potential. The perennial garbage cans remind us of how he makes his living as a garbage collector, and he is building a fence to satisfy his wife and to keep his family safe. Troy's home is as much under siege by antagonistic opposition as ancient Troy found herself to be, and he is right to beware of any "Greeks bearing gifts"—be they loans or scholarships—for he lives in a world where he must forever be wary of white exploitation and unfairly weighted laws.

The concept of the fence is a central image of the play. The trick with fences, Wilson insists, is to build one that will protect rather than separate. Such a fence provides supportive boundaries rather than divisive restrictions, but its construction will not be easy. Troy completes his fence just before he drives Cory away, but it has a gate by which his son can one day return. Cory thinks he has broken free of his father on leaving home; however, he only swaps one set of rules for another. He has exchanged the African American ethos of his father for the white-dominated ethos of the Marine Corps. It will be better for him to reclaim the former and reenter his father's house, which he accomplishes by the close of the play as he declares his intent to quit the Marines and begins to understand his father's legacy.

It is useful to read Troy's life as a metaphor for the enduring, life-affirming African American spirit, which is the legacy he hands his children. After a harsh upbringing that had no cushioning from the hardships of life, Troy spent time in jail for killing a man (an action that could easily be taken as self-defense, given the circumstances). His captivity in jail represents the tribulations of slavery that he needs to get beyond. Troy is subsequently allowed to develop white skills (playing baseball), but not allowed to compete in white circles (baseball leagues remained segregated at his peak). After release from jail he is left with only the basest jobs from which to choose. His two sons seek paths to riches through music and sports, which are apparently easy, but deceptive. Troy is rightly suspicious of both (standing in the way of Cory's sports scholarship and refusing to listen to Lyons's band), because in each area the tendency was toward exploitation, and most African American participants gained meager rewards for the talents they exhibited. Troy refuses to consider such deceptive possibilities and through hard work makes a solid niche for himself, ensuring that his spirit lives on after he is dead.

The song that Troy sings about Old Blue is one he learned from his father, and it shows a generational bond that is undeniable. Cory and Raynell (an illegitimate child for whom Troy takes responsibility), end up singing that same song and through it, recognize something of their heritage. Just as Troy has many characteristics of his father, so is Cory very similar to *his* father. Their mutual lack of patience, their stubbornness, their desire for control, and their inability to openly express love may not be attractive qualities, but they are family traits that each generation needs to recognize and accept. They are also traits that form the bedrock of their ability to be so hardworking, determined, and responsible.

The final scene of the play occurs after Troy's death on the morning of his funeral. Despite the sad circumstance, it remains a scene of hope. Troy's presence remains strong. Lyons, having survived a stint in jail for cashing other people's checks, like his father, who did jail time for murder, has found new direction from being so restricted. Raynell, tending her garden, indicates a future growth. And Cory comes to a new understanding of his patrimony by beginning to acknowledge his father's spirit in him and is able to attend his father's funeral. The most lasting significance of that hardwood fence becomes truly apparent as Troy tells us when he is building it: "How you know how long I'm gonna be here, nigger? Hell, I might just live forever" (60). And in a way he does, through his enduring values and his offspring.

Wedding Band tells of the deforming pressures that antimiscegenation laws have on the relationship of Herman, a German American, and Julia, who is African American. Unable to marry, and trying to avoid discovery of their illegal relationship, Julia grows tired of changing apartments and being alone, as she waits for Herman to save up sufficient funds to pay back a loan from his mother and relocate them to the North where they can marry freely. Before this happens, Herman is struck by flu while at Julia's house, and to hide the relationship, medical treatment is delayed, resulting in his death.

Prior to the Civil War, many white slaveowners had relations with women slaves, but their offspring were legally slaves. After slavery was abolished, an obsession with the preservation of "pure" bloodlines developed, largely to ensure that land stayed in white families and could not be inherited by people of "mixed" race. This was supported by state law in forty states, even into the 1960s. Consequences for breaking these laws were harsh, from hefty fines to extended jail sentences, depending on the seriousness of the relationship. In South Carolina, where this play is set, intermarriage was forbidden between whites and African Americans, American Indians, mulattos, and mestizos, and the minimum penalty was a fine of $500 and/or a twelve-month jail sentence.

Herman and Julia display a domestic intimacy and devotion that insists theirs is a lasting love and not some brief infatuation; she even buys his socks. The title refers to the wedding band Herman gives Julia on the tenth anniversary of their secret relationship, but she cannot wear it on her finger. They are held apart by an unfair law, and the social stigma their relationship invokes. Mattie's man, October, a cook in the Merchant Marines, writes in his letter to Mattie that there are "two things a man can give the woman he loves . . . his name and his protection" (90). Herman can give neither to Julia, and, ironically, October can give neither to Mattie. Mattie has a previous husband she cannot divorce, and, because they are not legally married, she cannot claim October's allowance to pay her rent. Julia's generous gift to Mattie of her ring and her tickets to New York near the close of the play indicates a bond between these women in their mutual poverty and predicament, a bond that also offers Julia a release from her loneliness.

When Herman falls ill, Julia's first thought is to fetch him a doctor, but she is prevented by her African American neighbors and Herman's family, because of the social and legal ramifications of making their relationship public. She fears to take him to a doctor in case the trip should make him worse and she be blamed. His family refuse to take him until dark to avoid being seen. They patronize and insult Julia, and Herman's mother declares that she (the mother) is "as high over [her] as Mount Everest over the sea. White reigns supreme" (120), as she reclaims Herman and takes him home. Angry at her own powerlessness, Julia lets loose ten years of resentment over the way she has been treated, and vows to have no more to do with whites. When Herman returns with a ticket for her to head North, planning to join her later, she initially rejects his offer, holding him responsible for the whole history of African American exploitation and restriction. But her anger subsides when she realizes how ill he is. This time they lock the door against his mother's interference, and Herman dies in Julia's arms, a gesture that triumphantly affirms Julia's moral right to be with her love.

Before the invention of antibiotics, flu was often fatal, and calling a doctor would have been a matter of life and death for Herman, who might have been saved by earlier medical intervention. But if his relationship with Julia had been discovered, everyone would have suffered: Julia would have faced a fine and/or a prison sentence, Fanny a loss of reputation for allowing the relationship to take place under her roof, and Herman's whole family a stigmatization that would have affected their social and business life. Fanny and her tenants were also reluctant to suffer from being quarantined, which would have taken away their chance to earn money. These people are not villains for waiting to call a doctor, as much as victims of a society that allows such unfairness to exist.

Julia's African American neighbors are as disturbed by her affair as Herman's mother, although for different reasons. At worst, they assume Herman is just using Julia, and at best they see his choice as foolish because he cannot protect his partner. Fanny urges Julia to leave him before her reputation is destroyed, Lula cannot even imagine being intimate with a white man, and Nelson points out that if the genders were reversed in such a coupling the man would soon be lynched. The Bell Man, a local white peddler, shows a common response on discovering that Julia is seeing Herman, by assuming she is a prostitute.

The play's secondary characters create the cultural atmosphere that influences the action. They voice social attitudes of the time, as well as depict other problems that came from living in a racist culture. Through Nelson, an African American soldier who goes to fight for a country that still denies him equal rights, we get a sense of a growing African American discontent and unrest. His anger at the discrimination he constantly faces contrasts with the obsequiousness toward white people that we hear is displayed by Greenlee, who used to work in Herman's bakery. Nelson's mother Lula and Mattie both scrabble against poverty to raise children alone. Even Herman's mother struggles to maintain a hard-won social status at a time when anyone of German descent was vilified because of the war.

Aiming for authenticity, Childress allows characters of both races to display pettiness, intolerance, and materialism. Mattie and Lula share stereotypical views of white men that border on racism. The children play games with racist references toward the Chinese, and Fanny makes anti-Semitic remarks. Fanny is also snobbish, materialistic, and a selfish opportunist. Even Herman and Julia are not without their flaws, for Herman delays their move North for selfish reasons, reluctant to give up his business, while Julia is harsh in accusing him of racism. Herman has nursed her when sick, paid her debts and expenses, and shown nothing but high regard for her. Yet Herman's own father had been a member of the Ku Klux Klan and taught his son to recite bigoted speeches at their meetings, and Julia is disturbed by Herman's refusal to hate his father. Nevertheless, they possess sufficient dignity to seem heroic as they struggle against great odds in their search for happiness, and their dilemma draws attention to an uncomfortable aspect of American race relations.

FURTHER SUGGESTED READING

Carter, Steven R. *Hansberry's Drama: Commitment and Complexity.* Urbana: University of Illinois Press, 1991.

Childress, Alice. *Wedding Band. In 9 Plays by Black Women.* Ed. Margaret B. Wilkerson. New York: NAL, 1986: 73–133.

Du Bois, W.E.B. *The Souls of Black Folk.* New York: Random House, 1994.

Hansberry, Lorraine. *A Raisin in the Sun/The Sign in Sidney Brustein's Window.* New York: NAL, 1966.

Jennings, LaVinia Delois. *Alice Childress.* New York: Twayne, 1995.

Kennedy, Stetson. *Jim Crow Guide to the USA.* Westport, CT: Greenwood, 1973.

Nadel, Alan, Ed. *May All Your Fences Have Gates: Essays on the Drama of August Wilson.* Iowa City: University of Iowa Press, 1994.

Nemiroff, Robert, Ed. *To Be Young, Gifted, and Black: Lorraine Hansberry in Her Own Words.* Englewood Cliffs, NJ: Prentice-Hall, 1969.

Patterson, Lindsay, Ed. *Black Theater.* New York: Dodd, Mead, 1971.

Shannon, Sandra. *The Dramatic Vision of August Wilson.* Washington, DC: Howard University Press, 1995.

Wilson, August. *Fences.* New York: Plume, 1986.

Wolfe, George. *The Colored Museum.* New York: Grove Wheatland, 1985.

Aging

Sweet Bird of Youth by Tennessee Williams (1956)
I'm Not Rappaport by Herb Gardner (1984)
Arsenic and Old Lace by Joseph Kesselring (1941)

Modern Western culture has a disturbing tendency to idolize the young and reject the elderly, and a number of modern dramas have turned their attention to the issue of aging, both positively and negatively. Many comedies produced in the first half of the twentieth century featured stereotypes, such as the absent-minded or mean-spirited elderly person, as comic relief or as foil to a main character, but these representations rarely considered the actual condition of aging, and its social and psychological effect on people. Some modern playwrights, like Tennessee Williams, display a vivid fascination with youth that underscores their own fear of aging. Others approach the idea of age more optimistically, pointing out how valuable older people can be, while acknowledging the ways in which Western society sadly tends to ignore and marginalize the elderly.

Williams's *Sweet Bird of Youth* explores ways in which people try to resist aging and the tremendous importance they place on youth. It introduces us to a group of desperate people who hope to conquer time, and so be able to maintain their youthful looks, hopes, and ambitions. By and large, all fail. Williams relates their failure in a series of sexual and religious metaphors, poetically reinforced by an innovative series of cyclorama images—pictures projected onto the backdrop of the stage—and snatches of music complementary to the action, as well as the use of special lighting and costumes to highlight characters' dreams and evasions. The central characters, Heavenly and Chance, are beaten by time into shadows of their former selves. The Princess may find her film career revitalized, but her youth is gone and she remains fearful of her future. Boss Finley has the Heckler who tells the truth at his rally severely beaten and he is silenced, but Heavenly's collapse and the public ridicule by his mistress, Miss Lucy, saying he "is too old to cut the mustard" (60), imply that his day is also past.

I'm Not Rappaport by Herb Gardner considers many of the problems of aging—issues of health and safety; the fear of losing one's independence, sight, and mind; and the inevitable loss through death of those nearest to you. Gardner asks his audience to view the inherent condition of old age in all of its challenges, difficulties, and possible triumphs through the comic interaction of two octogenarians, Nat and Midge, who pass the time on a bench in Central Park. Beneath the humor, we see a serious demand that the elderly be treated with respect and dignity, and be valued as social assets rather than ignored or shut away out of sight. These men are not saints, but they try to be good citizens and maintain an involvement in the life that surrounds them, but that constantly threatens to pass them by. Nat suggests that people ignore the aged because they fear getting old themselves, but he insists that old people are worthwhile; they are survivors of life, with immense knowledge, and should be treasured rather than told that they are unnecessary.

Arsenic and Old Lace by Joseph Kesselring, written during the privations of World War II, is intentionally escapist. Its production caused a controversy regarding whether or not insanity and murder were appropriate topics for comedy. Kesselring had intended it as a melodrama, but in rehearsal the play took on life as a farce. Melodrama and farce are closely connected, since both place situation over character; use fast, physical action and exaggeration; and tend not to ask an audience to think too deeply. While melodrama is played for thrills, farce goes for laughs. Thus, aging takes on an even more humorous bent as two spinster sisters do away with old gentlemen who answer their advertisement for lodgers. Yet beneath the comedy is the serious issue of what becomes of the elderly when they find themselves alone and unable to look after themselves, which should make us question whether the sisters' actions might be considered in some ways defensible.

In *Sweet Bird of Youth*, Chance, a failed actor turned gigolo for older women, has returned to his hometown, with aging actress Alexandra Del Largo, hiding from her public under the alias of Princess Kosmonopolis. He has come to try to reconnect with his true love, Heavenly, whose father, Boss Finley, had stood in the way of their marriage. Since Chance's absence Heavenly was discovered to have venereal disease and forced to have a hysterectomy, and Boss has vowed to get even by castrating Chance. Meanwhile, Boss has been trying to revitalize his political career, backed by an ultraconservative youth movement he has created. We watch as all of Chance's plans fail: his attempt to blackmail Princess into getting him a movie contract, his attempt to win back Heavenly, and his attempt to beat back the clock. As the play closes, Princess discovers that her comeback film has been a success and returns alone to Hollywood, while Boss's henchmen close in on Chance.

For all of his desire to stay young, ironically, Chance's youth was a time of frustration, without the money or fame he desired. His only advantage was his looks, but he felt past his prime even by twenty-three when he left the Navy on a medical discharge. He recently put his watch in hock, but cannot escape the passage of time. He is fearful of his thinning hair, and ravages what looks he retains with excessive drugs, alcohol, and cigarettes, which he consumes to calm his panic and escape from reality. Princess warns him about his bleak future, and Aunt Nonnie warns him that he must forget about trying to turn the clock back—he is caught in the middle of an unhappy life with no way out. He blames time, but it is really his own weakness that has brought him to this juncture. His expectation that he could make it on looks alone was wrong, just as his tendency to set impossible goals he could never attain must always leave him defeated.

Chance talks of loving Heavenly, but one wonders how much this love is a figment of his youthful fantasy. That he had not known of her illness and operation, and because neither speak nor touch on their one brief meeting during the play, suggest that his regard is more a creation of his own need to idealize love rather than honest affection. Prior to being driven away, he had slept around, and was in and out of Heavenly's life. By the close he sees the truth of what he has become and realizes that he has lost his race with time. In defeat, he waits for Boss's men to castrate him and speaks directly to the audience, not asking for pity but a recognition "of me in you, and the enemy, time, in us all" (111). He asks that we recognize our own secret desire for immortality and youth, as well as the impossibility of ever recovering that youth, which Williams sees as a troubling contradiction of human existence.

Heavenly is no less defeated, for all the possibility her name suggests and the way Boss has her dress in white to project an image of youthful innocence and virginity. She began sleeping with Chance at fifteen, and a nude picture he took of her has been all around town. She sees the doctor as having "cut the youth out of my body, made me an old childless woman" (65), an act akin to castration, and since then has viewed herself as tantamount to dead. An empty shell, she has little of the vitality Chance recalls, and can only swoon at the hypocrisy of which she has become a part, distressed at the truth the Heckler tries to force her father to admit. She is as much a victim of her father's brutality as the Heckler, and has no strength with which to fight back.

Princess seems the stronger, at least on the surface. She insists on preserving the appearance of youth, especially since she sees it as integral to her success as an actress. But her image on screen is a fantasy, and not the desperate woman we see drinking, smoking hash, and sleeping with Chance in an effort to regain some semblance of youth by association. Like Chance, she abuses alcohol and drugs to escape the truth of her advancing age, and hysterically refuses to allow anyone to mention death in her presence. She asks Chance to make her believe "that we're young lovers without any shame" (42), but they are neither young, in love, nor guilt free. She declares herself triumphant as she hears of her movie's success, but cannot hide the fact that she is ultimately as doomed as Chance, and as incapable of love.

A central image of the first act is the double bed that dominates the stage, and this indicates the way these characters use sex as a means to holding on to youth. Chance, Princess, Heavenly, and Boss all associate sex with youth, and the fact that each is (or soon will be) physically or psychologically castrated, implies that youth has been lost to each of them. The significance of the play taking place on Easter Sunday sets up the hope of resurrection most of these characters maintain—be it for a film career, political office, or love—but this is a fallen world, imbued with original sin. These people have long since lost their innocence, and the chance of resurrection for such sinners is negligible. Instead of rising, we only see them fall deeper into shame, despair, or deceit. It is only through their destruction that they may finally atone for the social ills of which they are the product.

In *I'm Not Rappaport,* Nat Moyer and Midge, both in their eighties, sit and chat on a bench in Central Park. Nat enjoys fabricating stories to see how long he can string his audience along. While each sympathizes with the other for being old, both struggle to maintain dignity as age reduces their lives physically, socially, and economically. Having worked past retirement age as a building supervisor, Midge is about to lose his job and apartment, so Nat impersonates a union lawyer to keep him there. Nat faces up to a young thug, Gilley, who asks for daily protection money from the elderly. He gets hurt, but feels happy he fought back. However, his daughter is worried about him and insists that he be more closely supervised. To dissuade her from this plan he invents a love-child he plans to live with in Israel. Both men watch a drug dealer, the Cowboy, threaten a young woman, Laura, who owes him money, and the two elderly men try to help the young woman. Nat pretends to be a mafioso to get the Cowboy to back down, but the Cowboy is not fooled and attacks Midge, who tries to defend Nat, sending him to the hospital. Midge gets out to find a broken-spirited Nat whose stories have all backfired, but Midge encourages him to start a new fabrication to raise both their spirits, and to pass the time.

The two main characters tell us a lot about what it is like to be old—about glaucoma and cataracts in the eyes, weakening hearts, and when falling down carries the risk of broken bones as the body wears out. They paint a picture of the elderly kept hidden away in retirement homes as if they were criminals. They scrape to get by on a social security check, living limited lives, with poor food, high doctor bills, and, worst of all, people not wanting to listen to them. We see this when the head of Midge's building's tenant committee, Mr. Danforth, jogs by and speaks to Midge. Danforth talks about himself, ignoring what Midge tries to tell him, even though he ironically teaches "Communication Arts." He is unconcerned about whether Midge can do the job; he just sees him as old and unnecessary. Nat is right to mock him for taking pleasure in collecting antiques, yet viewing old people as "bad souvenirs, they talk too much. Even quiet, they tell you too much; they look like the future and you don't want to know" (47). The battered bench beside the isolated path on which the two men sit acts as an effective metaphor for the aged: so often left beaten and alone. What Gardner does is invest Nat and Midge with such spirit that the audience cannot help but see the wrongness in this.

The play's title, recalling an old Vaudeville routine Nat enjoys, attests to both Nat's vitality and the question of identity raised in the play, in terms of the limited identity society tends to allow the aged. It is this homogenization of the elderly against which these two rebel. The Jewish Nat seems more out-going, and since his bypass surgery has developed the tendency to fictionalize his life to spice it up. He finds it encourages people to notice him, and invigorates his life. An activist in spirit, it has been a long time since his days as a union organizer, having waited tables for most of his life, and finally being forced into retirement for talking too much. Good-hearted, he helps where he can without a thought, refusing to accept what he sees as unfair situations. Yet for all of Nat's apparent vibrancy contrasted with Midge's reticence, Midge has lived the fuller life, with his five wives and variety of jobs. Nat has lived quietly, never having approached the girl he loved, but settling for a long and com-fortable marriage with someone else, now dead.

Yet against this simple background Nat weaves wonderful stories of his life as an undercover agent, a tempestuous lover with an illegitimate child, and a movie star, throwing in his impersonations of a union lawyer and a mafia boss along the way. These engaging stories are told partly as a diversion to pass the time and partly as an attempt to escape a mundane reality, but also in the hopes of helping others. His attempts to keep Midge his job, to stop Gilley from shaking them down, to prevent his daughter from restricting him, and to help Laura get rid of her drug pusher all fail. Indeed, Nat's interference tends to make most matters worse, but we should understand that his stories remain a necessity, for without them he is nothing but a sad, old man, stripped of spirit. The stories are his means of escape. His friend Midge realizes this, which is why he insists that Nat keep telling his tales. They also help Midge lead a more interesting life.

Midge is a near-blind, African American building superintendent, who con-stantly worries about getting into trouble. He hides from his tenants in hopes that no one will recall that he still works there and decide to fire him, taking away his chance to earn a living. He is fiercely proud of the independence his job affords him, but he only maintains it because he has not asked for a raise in fifteen years, and he does the night shifts no one else wants. Both he and Nat have regrets from past things they did or did not do, but while it irks Nat to live in the past and be pushed to the social periphery, Midge seems satisfied to accept whatever society demands, preferring not to make a fuss and so draw attention to himself. But eventually, both men gain spiritual strength from their attempts to stand up for themselves and others, even if they are physically damaged in the process.

Nat demonizes his daughter, Clara, as insensitive to his needs, but she has suffered from her father's beliefs, and offers alternative insight into the child who does not wish to limit the parent's liberty but who genuinely fears for his safety. For all of Nat's criticism, Clara turns out to be caring and sensitive to her father's need for independence, pointing out the reality that sometimes the aged need greater supervision. She offers him options to live with her, go to a senior residence, or stay home but visit the senior center and allow her to keep an eye on him. This is not to shut him away or ignore him, but to ensure that he is safe. That he finally accedes to her demands is only fair given the anguish he has put her through by pretending to have another daughter with whom he intends to live.

In *Arsenic and Old Lace*, Abby and Martha Brewster live in an old house in Brooklyn, New York, and have been poisoning elderly lodgers to send them to peaceful rest and then burying them in the cellar. Their nephew, Teddy, who lives with them, thinks he is Teddy Roosevelt. His brother, Mortimer, a theater critic, seems relatively sane, and he proposes to Elaine, the Reverend's daughter whom he has been dating. Finding their latest victim while looking for a manuscript, Mortimer is horrified to discover his aunts' secret, and decides to blame Teddy for the corpses and prevent them from killing anyone else. He goes to review a play and another brother, Jonathan, arrives with his plastic surgeon, Dr. Einstein, and plans to set up criminal operations in his aunts' house. He, too, is a murderer and has a corpse, which gets muddled with the sisters' latest murder until everyone realizes the truth. Jonathan tries to kill Mortimer, but is prevented from doing so by the arrival of Policeman O'Hara, who has come to talk to Mortimer about a play O'Hara has written. Other officers arrive in search of O'Hara, and Jonathan is caught. The police refuse to believe anything they are told about corpses, but Teddy is committed to a mental institution and the sisters choose to accompany him there and leave the house to Mortimer. Before they leave they appear to claim one last victim in Mr. Witherspoon, to top their nephew Jonathan's total of murders.

Insanity obviously runs in the Brewster family. Mortimer is so fearful of this that he calls off his marriage to Elaine, until the sisters tell him he is not a blood relative, but the son of a servant they took pity on. Martha and Abby's father had been something of a crazy scientist, making a fortune with his medicines, but often killing people as he tested them out, and we suspect, burying his corpses in the cellar, too. Teddy thinks he is Teddy Roosevelt, and Jonathan is a psychotic who attacks people for suggesting that he looks like Boris Karloff, and has twelve murders to his credit. Martha and Abby seem pleasant enough, but surely they must be crazy to do what they do.

The ladies' project began after a lodger, a lonely old man with no family left, died of a heart attack, and they noticed how peaceful he looked. They decided to bring that same peace to others in the same position, and give each a Christian burial in their cellar, with services appropriate to each victim's faith. If Mr. Gibbs, whom Mortimer prevents them from killing, is any indication of the type they have "helped," it becomes hard to criticize what they do. He is miserable, distrusting, and bitter, and hates his life, living alone in a hotel. The sisters, too, clearly have no ethical qualms or doubts, not viewing themselves as criminals, but seeing what they do as a form of charity. In contrast to Jonathan, whose spree of indiscriminate murders also numbers twelve and who is thoroughly unpleasant, the sisters have good reasons for killing, treat their corpses with the utmost respect, and seem like pleasant, sweet old ladies.

In their late sixties, Abby and Martha are the epitome of what society views as the ideal elderly. They are churchgoing, friendly, generous, and discreet. They bother no one; perform numerous good works, giving toys to children and tending the sick and needy; and seem to be on good terms with everyone in the community. Friendly with judge and police, they doubt they would be charged even if their acts were discovered, and the determination of the police to not even investigate accusations against them seems to support this. Determinedly anachronistic, they keep their house as a relic from the Victorian age. Teddy's belief that he is President Roosevelt, in office at the start of the century, contributes to this anachronistic atmosphere, as does the sisters' reluctance to use electricity. Reverend Harper loves to visit their home, seeing it as a refuge from the harsher modern life outside and the sisters as full of old-fashioned virtue and good manners. The irony, of course, is that these old ladies are, in fact, serial killers: they could never tell a lie, but they have killed eleven people, and are about to kill another as the curtain goes down, just to show their nephew, Jonathan, that they have a higher score of corpses. What is even more ironic is the way the audience is led to applaud their efforts.

Aside from the suggestion that what they do could be seen as a mercy to those they "help," Kesselring's presentation of two determined old ladies, who for all their pleasantries are apparently not as toothless as they might seem, must surely make audiences reconsider their often dismissive assessment of old people in general.

FURTHER SUGGESTED READING

Gardner, Herb. *I'm Not Rappaport*. Garden City, NY: Doubleday, 1986.

Griffin, Alice. *Understanding Tennessee Williams*. Columbia: University of South Carolina Press, 1995.

Gurney, A. R. *Later Life*. New York: Plume, 1994.

Howe, Tina. *Pride's Crossing*. New York: TCG, 1998.

Keith, Jennie. *Old People as People: Social and Cultural Influences on Aging and Old Age*. Boston: Little, Brown, 1982.

Kesselring, Joseph. *Arsenic and Old Lace*. New York: DPS, 1942.

Roudané, Matthew C., Ed. *The Cambridge Companion to Tennessee Williams*. New
    York: Cambridge University Press, 1997.
Ryff, Carol D., and Victor W. Marshall, Eds. *The Self and Society in Aging Processes*.
    New York: Springer, 1999.
Williams, Tennessee. *Sweet Bird of Youth, A Streetcar Named Desire, The Glass Me-
    nagerie*. Harmondsworth, U.K.: Penguin, 1962.

Ambition and Fame

Golden Boy by Clifford Odets (1937)
The Great White Hope by Howard Sackler (1967)
Pygmalion by George Bernard Shaw (1913)

The concepts of ambition and fame are ones that have often troubled modern dramatists, especially those who have felt pulled by the former and restricted by the latter. Because ambition can be viewed both positively and negatively, dramas have reflected the consequences of both too little and too much ambition, as well as showing the damage caused by those ambitious for the wrong things. Ambition has been depicted by modern playwrights as striving for a variety of rewards beyond mere fame, including professional, competitive, pecuniary, or critical success. However, most agree that little is deemed worthwhile by society at large unless it brings in, or reflects the acquisition of, large amounts of money. This concentration on material success at the risk of demeaning the spirit is the aspect of fame and ambition that has most captivated modern dramatists.

Golden Boy by Clifford Odets and *The Great White Hope* by Howard Sackler are alike in that both consider the problems of ambition in men who each achieve greatness, but at a loss to themselves. They differ largely because of the central characters' ethnicity, ability, and character, and how these influence their development. In many ways the story of *Golden Boy* is a deeply personal one for Odets. Like his character, Joe Bonaparte, Odets saw himself as an artistic, sensitive individual whose dual search for self-actualization and financial success held him in an unresolvable bind. Odets was torn between the commercial possibilities of screenwriting in Hollywood and the artistic fulfillment of playwriting; for Joe the conflict is between the fame and fortune of a boxing career, and the spiritual fulfillment he gains from playing his violin.

Based in part on the history of Jack Johnson, who became the first African American heavyweight champion in 1908, Howard Sackler's *The Great White Hope* is an epic presentation of the victory, exile, and defeat of Jack Jefferson, told in nineteen short scenes that take place in eight countries across two continents in the years preceding World War I. Sackler mixes dialogue and direct address, as various characters act as a chorus, commenting on the action. The speech of Jack and other African Americans is rendered in black dialect of the period, but to ensure that this not be read as indicative of a lack of intelligence, what they say is as profound, and often as poetic, as anything we hear uttered by whites. Jack, especially, is capable of clever manipulation, as when he defuses the Salvation Army protest against his bar in Chicago, and prevents a riot. Race complicates matters throughout, but the play is also about the wages of success and individualism on a more universal level, showing the dangers and ultimate compromises into which people can be led by their desire to be the best, for whatever reason.

George Bernard Shaw's *Pygmalion* is a story of more limited ambition, but it is ambition nonetheless that inspires Henry Higgins to take Liza Doolittle on as a student, and ambition that leads Liza to agree. Because they are more limited in scale, they suffer less as a result, but the motivation behind their desires is still rooted in selfishness. Higgins dallies with the life and future of Liza on a mere whim, not realizing how what he does leaves her unfit for both her own society and his. The play is based on the Pygmalion myth, in which King Pygmalion sculpts a statue, Galatea, with which he falls in love, and whom the goddess Aphrodite brings to life out of pity on the king. Shaw uses this myth to explore the dangers and problems that arise when one human being tries to exert too much control over another. Higgins irrevocably changes the lives of Liza and her father, and does so without obtaining the clear consent of either of them beforehand.

Liza is not without ambition herself, for it is she who comes to Higgins because she wishes to rise in society from selling flowers on the street to working in a proper flower shop. She impresses Higgins by the sheer percentage of her earnings that she is willing to spend on this plan, and it is that spirit that prompts him to make his wager with Colonel Pickering, aside from giving him the opportunity to show off. But Higgins takes Liza beyond the level she had hoped to attain, to a point at which she is unsure how she can support herself, although she ultimately manages to adapt and find an independence she had never imagined possible. She achieves this final transformation, however, without the aid of Higgins. Her father, by contrast, contrary to his ambition, gains great wealth but feels destroyed as an individual.

In *Golden Boy*, boxing manager Tom Moody is looking for a successful fighter so he can afford to divorce his wife, marry his girlfriend Lorna, and revitalize his career. Joe Bonaparte, who breaks the hand of Moody's current fighter while sparring, seems to fulfill that role. Joe desires wealth and success and has the ability to get it, but initially holds back. Moody and Joe discover that the problem lies in Joe's real passion: music. He pulls his punches to save his hands. His father has long dreamed that Joe would become a concert violinist, though he will not force him to make this choice. Joe falls for Moody's girlfriend, Lorna, and she for him, although she does not know how to let Moody down. Joe commits to fighting to win Lorna, but, ironically, that makes her go back to Moody. In his last fight before his crack at the title, Joe kills his opponent, which brings him to his senses. He realizes that he can no longer fight, but his hands are now too ruined to return to music, so he drives away with Lorna, who is delighted to see the old Joe back, to start a new life of anonymity, but happiness. As his manager and family celebrate his victory in the ring, they receive news that the pair just died in a car accident.

Golden Boy is a study of ambition, with its pitfalls and rewards. Besides the "golden boy" Joe Bonaparte, who has such an array of talents that he could be successful in fields as diverse as music and boxing, the rest of the characters all display different aspects of ambition. Tom Moody, mobster Eddie, and Siggie (Joe's brother-in-law) each feed off the talent or hard work of others to get ahead. Out of purely selfish motives, Moody bullies Joe into committing everything to boxing, knowing that he could become rich as Joe's manager and not from any regard for Joe. Indeed, as he realizes the growing affection between Joe and Lorna, he actively grows to hate the boxer. Eddie coerces Moody to let him buy into Joe for the profits, and helps get him hooked on the good life to keep him hungry for victory. Siggie's ambition is more modest, but no less pecuniary. He had wanted his father-in-law to buy him and Joe a taxicab out of his hard-earned savings, so they could go into business for themselves, working a split shift to double their money. But Joe's father refuses, knowing Joe is capable of much better.

Not all the characters are out for themselves. Lorna has a far more generous nature. She encourages Moody to have faith and keeps his spirits up when they flag. Despite her love for Joe, Lorna refuses to let Moody down out of respect for what he has done for her in the past. And there is also Joe's brother, Frank, whose ambitions are more socially oriented. A union organizer, he gets beaten up like Joe, but in pursuit of something in which he sincerely believes—supporting a workers' strike. As he explains, "I don't get autos and custom-made suits. But I get what Joe don't" (318). Frank fights to feel that he is part of something bigger than himself and to feel that what he does makes a difference. In many ways this is all Joe wanted all along, which we see in his admiration of his brother, but he allowed his ambition to get out of hand.

Mr. Bonaparte has worked hard all his life and wants to see his youngest child happy above all else. He knows Joe has ambition and wants to do something of which he can be proud, and he is willing to support Joe's boxing efforts if they will really make him happy. He bought his son a $1,200 violin for his twenty-first birthday, but quietly puts it away rather than use it to persuade Joe to pursue a musical career at the expense of boxing success, even while he is repulsed by the violence of the boxing. Early on he insists, "What ever you got ina your nature to do isa not foolish" (250), and he is right. Joe's true nature was to play music all along, as we see in the tender look on his face when he holds a violin, and as he confesses to Lorna. He explains that he feels defined by music, but he cannot see how to translate that into the fame and fortune he craves: "You can't get even with people by playing the fiddle" (264). He sells out for what he sees as a more certain path to riches, for which he pays dearly, with his life.

Joe played the violin for ten years, and won countless competitions and a scholarship to the Erickson Institute. But, he complains, "I don't like myself, past, present and future. Do you know there are men who have wonderful things from life? Do you think they're better than me? Do you think I like this feeling of no possessions?" (252). He wants to travel and change his life, and, backed by his fight team's insistence that "the fist is mightier than the fiddle" (257), sees boxing rather than music as the means to this end. He has always felt ostracized by mainstream society because of his name, his intelligence, and his violin, but fighting allows him to be popular, especially once he decides to no longer pull his punches to save his hands. His initial self-doubt, and later arrogance, ensure that the audience never loses sight that this is a bad choice. Speaking about Joe to his father, Lorna suggests, "You could build a city with his ambition to be somebody" (295). But his father points out the destructive potential of such ambition, suggesting that it is more likely that the city will be burned down, which turns out to be a sad, but true, prophecy.

The Great White Hope opens with the media-named Great White Hope, Frank Brady, a white boxer and heavyweight champion, being persuaded to come out of retirement to fight African American boxer, Jack Jefferson, to prevent him from taking the title. Jack is keen to excel in the white man's world, openly taunting his opposition with his ability and the white establishment with his white lover, Ellie Bachman. Easily beating Brady, he returns in triumph to Chicago where Ellie's mother tries to get her daughter away from him, but Ellie refuses to leave. The establishment plots to bring him down using Ellie. He is arrested on charges of transporting her across state lines for immoral purposes. He escapes to Europe to avoid jail, but is unable to find regular income there: in England they will not allow him to fight, in France they are appalled at his brutality against Klossowski, in Germany they mock his race. His degradation culminates in Hungary, with him playing Uncle Tom in a disastrous performance of *Uncle Tom's Cabin*. Having found a new Great White Hope in the Kid, Jack has been offered a reduced sentence if he will return and throw the fight. He initially refuses, saying he will only fight to win, but after the deaths of his mother and Ellie, the latter by suicide after he brutally rejects her, he agrees, and after a vicious fight, allows the Kid to become the new champion.

If Brady does not fight Jack, and he is reluctant to take him on because he is now retired though primarily because of Jack's color, then Jack can claim the championship belt, used as an icon denoting superiority throughout the play. This is why Cap'n Dan, a former heavyweight champion, and others, insist that Brady fight "to teach a loudmouth nigger" (18) a lesson. They honestly believe that when Jack beats Brady, "it's the biggest calamity to hit this country" (36). The federal agent, Dixon, who is devoted to helping bring Jack down, is determined that "We cannot allow the image of this man to go on impressing and exciting these people" (82). Although the threat of Black Power is more endemic to the time when the play was written rather than when it was set, white America's irrational fear of a race they had for so long subjugated underscores the whole play.

For the fight against Brady, the white establishment, in control throughout the play, insists on using Cap'n Dan as the referee, and having the prize money an unfair split of 80/20, expecting Brady to take the larger share. The fight is set for July 4th, to make it seem like a political contest for American independence (implying that only whites are truly American), and placed in Reno, a predominantly white city, to restrict the number of African Americans who can attend to support Jack. Jack accepts these conditions because he so badly wants to be the champion. He needs to prove himself against the white establishment, even when, or because, they have all the power, money, and political and media clout. By winning the heavyweight title, even if only for a short time, he does best them, which is why they are so determined to bring him down, by any means available. The charges they bring against him are bogus, based as they are on the statutes to catch prostitutes, not real couples, although few accept an interracial relationship.

Jack's pride—as fierce as his ability—is instrumental in his downfall, since it makes him a greater target. His mother tells us, "Tried to learn him like you gotta learn a cullud boy, dassn't, dassn't, dassn't, that ain't for you! Roll right off him" (59). Jack smiles as he fights to show how easy he finds it, taunting his opponents, even letting them hit him, just to further display his confidence. Ironically, in being forced by financial necessity to play Uncle Tom, he accepts a role he has spent his life avoiding. Alongside his pride, Jack also has great talent, integrity, and energy, all of which the establishment eventually grinds out of him. Jack does not want to be an African American hero; he fights for himself, to satisfy his own sense of self and ambition. Although many African Americans support him and take pride in his victories, he tells them to find pride in themselves and their own actions, not his.

There are also many African Americans who dislike Jack as intensely as whites do, seeing his cocky manner as reflecting badly on the African American community, and his affair with Ellie only feeding the stereotype of the black man who lusts after white women. Given his lascivious reputation, they are reluctant for him to be seen as an icon of their community, for he can only do them a public disservice with such an negative image: "For a Negro today, the opportunity to earn a dollar in a factory should appear to be worth infinitely more than the opportunity of spending that dollar in the emulation of Mr. Jack Jefferson" (45). Others, such as Scipio, who preach separatism, go further, suggesting that Jack has become a white puppet who lives by white standards in a white world, and should be ridiculed for this rather than lionized.

The forced entry of the officers into their Wisconsin hideaway represents the continuous intrusion of the establishment into Jack and Ellie's lives. They are no longer allowed any privacy, because of Jack's fame and the controversial reality of their interracial relationship. The reporter, Smitty, is forever following them, trying to break them up, or dig up some dirt he can publish to discredit them. Jack's love for Ellie may seem ambiguous: does he use her, as he uses his fighting, to challenge and provoke those in power? He turns on her viciously toward the end, which leads to her suicide, but he pays his penance by agreeing to throw the fight. He turns on her largely out of embarrassment at the level to which he has brought her, where he must sell off his boxing gloves to raise cash and cannot make love to her. She has challenged him by declaring that he is no longer his own man: the establishment has eliminated every option except those they offer him in their efforts to reclaim the belt. She may be right, but it is a truth he cannot accept, which is why he drives her away.

Jack is ahead of his time in his rebellion against the white establishment. He resists roles placed on him by whites and African Americans, and although forced to play certain stereotypical roles, he does so with a bombast that satirizes them and makes them his own. Yet they are still used against him, for his challenge to a white-dominated society cannot be allowed to succeed. We are prepared for his tragic downfall by various visual motifs, such as the repeated crowd scenes where initial support turns to antagonism. Public opinion is ever unpredictable, but when it is virtually owned by the opposition, Jack stands little chance of a fair hearing. For beating Jack at the close, and defeating not only the man but the challenge for which he stood, the Kid is carried aloft with the belt of victory, resembling *"the lifelike wooden saints in Catholic processions"* (133).

Pygmalion opens with Henry Higgins, a professional phonetician who helps people change the way they speak so they can pass in high society, impressing a crowd with his ability to locate where individuals come from by their accents. He boasts how he could teach a cockney flower girl to speak like a duchess. The next day that flower girl, Liza Doolittle, comes to his residence to pay for speech lessons so she can get a job as a clerk in a flower shop. Colonel Pickering, Higgins's friend and colleague, wagers Higgins that he cannot pass Liza off as a duchess at the Ambassador's garden party, and the housekeeper takes her out to clean her up. Liza's father, Alfred Doolittle, arrives to extort money from Higgins, and although Higgins is a match for his manipulation, Doolittle makes off with five pounds, impressing Higgins with his audacity.

Training goes well, and Higgins takes Liza to visit his mother as a test. While there, they have unexpected visitors, the Eynsford Hills, including Freddy, who falls for Liza. They are fooled by her appearance and demeanor, as are the people at the garden party. While Higgins and Pickering celebrate, Liza gets angry, realizing they do not care about her future, and runs off to Higgins's mother. The next day they go to find her, meeting Doolittle, who complains that his life has been ruined because Higgins told an eccentric millionaire about him, and the millionaire has given Doolittle a regular income. Higgins asks Liza to return, and she refuses, declaring her intention to become a teacher of phonetics, possibly marry Freddy, and leave Higgins for good. Higgins feels sure she will return.

Although many performed versions of this play, including the popular musical adaption it spawned, *My Fair Lady* (1956), all depict Liza and Higgins united by the close, Shaw himself insisted that they do not get together. He wrote an afterword in which he denounces sentimental interpretations of his play, and explains that Higgins must remain an inveterate bachelor, while Liza marries the penniless Freddy, and, after financial difficulties, opens a flower shop with funds provided by Pickering.

The fact is, Higgins is too self-involved to be a suitable husband for anyone. His reshaping of Liza, as he corrects her accent and grammar, dresses her in beautiful clothes, and moves her into polite society, is simply a power game, by which he displays the power inherent in class status, money, and gender. Because he is upper class, wealthy, and male, Higgins believes he has complete control over Liza, which is why he cannot accept her rebellion at the close. It is a power he wields without conscience, as he refuses to even consider Liza's position and how what he does may affect her life. His housekeeper, mother, and even Pickering, ask him what will happen to Liza after his experiment is through, and each is cast off with a flippant answer because Higgins cannot understand why this would be a concern. Even Pickering, another privileged male, although more sympathetic, does not really understand the effects of their "game," and is bemused by Liza's response after the garden party.

Liza realizes that her previous life as a flower girl has been destroyed, and runs to Mrs. Higgins in confusion. She does not have the class or wealth to back up her new voice and appearance, so could never truly thrive in Higgins's world. She can only marry Freddy because he is penniless. However, she reaches a new understanding, realizing she can become independent by teaching what she has been taught. Thus, her whole vision of herself changes, and this is a more profound transformation than sprucing up her accent and putting on a pretty dress. With this comes the strength that allows her to become entirely independent of Higgins, resist any romance with him, and firmly leave at the close. Liza ends up changed both internally and externally, unlike Higgins, who remains totally static.

Liza's father is less lucky than she. An interesting subversion, as the man whose ambition is to be utterly unambitious but who is compelled into becoming the opposite of what he wishes to be, he is a man content with poverty and life as a garbage collector. He extorts only enough money for a drunken spree, refusing more when it is offered because he does not want to be tempted to save and thus take the first step toward middle-class respectability and its inherent responsibilities. Higgins thoughtlessly sends a joking letter to an American millionaire, who subsequently bequeaths Doolittle a yearly allowance if he will lecture on the morality he abhors. He feels compelled to accept the stipend, and his life is no longer impoverished, but neither is it as free and simple as it once was. Forced to become middle class, he must now embrace restrictive middle-class morality and marry his wife.

FURTHER SUGGESTED READING

Berst, Charles A. Pygmalion: *Shaw's Play with Myth and Cinderella.* New York: Twayne, 1995.

Brenman-Gibson, Margaret. *Clifford Odets: American Playwright 1906–1940.* New York: Atheneum, 1982.

Guare, John. *The House of Blue Leaves.* New York: Viking, 1972.

Moldoveanu, Mihnea, and Nitin Nohria. *Master Passions: Emotions, Narrative, and the Development of Culture.* Cambridge, MA: MIT Press, 2002.

Odets, Clifford. *Golden Boy.* In *Six Plays of Clifford Odets.* New York: Random House, 1939: 231–321.

Reynolds, Jean. Pygmalion's *Wordplay.* Gainsville: University Press of Florida, 1999.

Sackler, Howard. *The Great White Hope.* London: Faber and Faber, 1971.

Shaffer, Peter. *Amadeus.* New York: Samuel French, 1993.

Shaw, George Bernard. *Pygmalion.* New York: Dodd, Mead, 1930.

Turner, Ralph H. *The Social Context of Ambition.* San Francisco: Chandler, 1964.

Weales, Gerald. *Clifford Odets, Playwright.* New York: Pegasus, 1971.

American Indian Experience

Indians by Arthur Kopit (1968)
According to Coyote by John Kauffman (1986)
Body Indian by Hanay Geiogamah (1972)

The figure of the American Indian is possibly the most stereotyped in American history. The stereotypes range from the early settlers' descriptions of American Indians as childlike savages engaged in hedonistic lifestyles to exotic images of natural figures free of civilization, the numerous sensationalist dramatizations on stage and in film of the "seductive squaw" enamored of white men, the "Noble Savage" with his primitive leanings and awe of white superiority, and the sadistic "Savage Redskin." These images have been accepted into popular American culture, supporting the myth of the Wild West, despite their insulting inaccuracies. The small body of dramas that honestly reflect the American Indian past and present have a major imperative to expose these stereotypes for what they are. Passing over dramas like the popular John August Stone's *Metamora* (1940), which merely fed these stereotypes, this chapter considers plays that challenge limited images of the American Indian experience.

The American government has historically vacillated between two opposing policies toward American Indians: maintenance and abandonment. In the first they isolate Indians on reservations, keeping them apart from mainstream society; in the second they try to enforce assimilation. It was not until 1924 that American Indians were legally allowed to hold dual citizenship of both the United States and the tribe to which they laid claim, even while many of these tribes continued to be stripped of their sovereignty into the 1960s. Provoked by loss of identity, reduced government support, and abject poverty, American Indians staged sometimes-militant protests, from the late 1960s onward, over land acquisition and the economic strengthening of many tribes as gambling became a viable source of revenue. It is this social background that informs the plays in this chapter.

One reason for the paucity of realistic (as opposed to sensationalistic) American Indian drama is the small number of American Indian playwrights. Although performance has always been a central part of American Indian culture, it has not been in the form of scripted dramas in the linear Western mode demanded by most theatergoers. It is only in the closing decades of the twentieth century that we have witnessed the rise of American Indian playwrights, some working in linear forms, but others incorporating the more circular patterns of Indian ritual in their work.

Arthur Kopit's *Indians* offers a historical narrative of how badly American Indians have been treated in their native country. Building his story around the exploits of Buffalo Bill gives Kopit's play a focal point through which to tell its tale of broken treaties, degradation, and humiliation. The action of the play has Buffalo Bill relive his life in an effort to understand how he deviated so far from his original intentions. Past events from how the West was won are reenacted, and it becomes clear that the legend of the Western hero taming a savage land is a fraud; the West was conquered mostly by stupidity and greed, which have been mythologized to try to justify what was done. Buffalo Bill's "Wild West Show" becomes emblematic of this deceit.

According to Coyote by John Kauffman is written in dramatic style, but as a monologue to preserve the sense of the storyteller's art so dominant among American Indians. Not concerned with the history of white treatment of American Indians through the past centuries, Kauffman tells a tale grounded in American Indian culture, a creation myth surrounding the ancient trickster character of Coyote.

Hanay Geiogamah was the first published American Indian playwright, and the first to examine the contemporary American Indian experience, including the problem of alcoholism. His *Body Indian* shows the condition of American Indians in today's society. Although white-influenced government has a mostly negative impact on these people's lives, Geiogamah's focus is on the American Indians he presents on the stage. Geiogamah is concerned about the ways in which American Indian communities often obstruct their own advancement by becoming too self-involved and lacking in concern for the "body Indian." The tale of Bobby Lee is a parable of both social and spiritual dimensions.

Indians explores the relationship between our cultural images of Buffalo Bill, American Indians, and the "Wild West." Through stories told by John Grass, Sitting Bull, and Chief Joseph, we learn much about what happened to American Indians during the later part of the nineteenth century, and it is a history of governmental restrictions, betrayal, and broken promises. The artifacts in the opening scene indicate that this was a period fraught with death and violence; however, we discover that the death and violence have been largely directed at the Indians rather than caused by them. Buffalo Bill rides onstage performing his "Wild West Show," but Kopit ensures that we see the undercurrents surrounding this image. Buffalo Bill's egotism and desire for fame have compromised his values. Although he respects American Indians and their culture, he has become increasingly instrumental in their devaluation and destruction throughout America.

To maintain popularity, Buffalo Bill kept changing his show. What had begun as an effort to convey an accurate portrayal of American Indian life, to give audiences a better understanding of this native culture, gradually became an inaccurate, sensation-seeking spectacle. The influence of the writer, Buntline, is insidious, as he mythologizes Buffalo Bill into a symbol of a Wild West that he thinks people want to believe, and has Buffalo Bill play the swaggering role he creates. Kopit illustrates how little whites understand tribal ways, and how they reduce a multifaceted culture to simple, insulting stereotypes. Buffalo Bill's "Show" has been instrumental in this, exhibiting a caged Geronimo, who is made to describe acts of rape and murder against whites, or Buffalo Bill's stories about defeating fifty drunken Indians on his own. Such fabrications inspire ignorant hatred of American Indians to the point where men get the bloodlust to kill as indiscriminately as Duke kills Spotted Tail.

At Buffalo Bill's Presidential performance—a sensationalistic play filled with evil Indians who get slaughtered, and the character of Uncas declaring white superiority and insisting that Indians deserve death—he no longer even employs Indians to allow the tribe to gain some revenue, but casts non-Indians in their place. Even fellow showman Wild Bill Hickok becomes sickened by such inaccurate melodrama, and acts out by behaving as the Indians have been unfairly accused of doing, indiscriminately killing Buntline and attacking the "virgin maiden"(who ironically turns out to be fairly willing). However, the audience ignores the satire and equally applauds both displays of violence. They were never interested in being educated as Buffalo Bill had originally intended, but simply entertained.

Sitting Bull is desperate to bring food, clothing, and hope to his people, and though he initially saw Buffalo Bill as an ally, he accuses him of selling out. One example is how Buffalo Bill kept shooting buffalo for his "exhibitions" and helped to virtually eradicate this crucial tribal food source. While Buffalo Bill brings senators to see the poor conditions of Indians on the reservation, taking partial responsibility for what has happened to them, the whole exercise becomes futile. The senators alternately make excuses and feign innocence, or exhibit outright disdain for the state of the Indians. Neither side understands the other; each argues from a different premise, and with different sets of values. The Indians want to live as Indians, the whites think they want to live as whites, and it becomes increasingly obvious that their meeting will solve nothing; the government representatives view Sitting Bull as a nuisance rather than an equal. Soon after, Sitting Bull and his people are wiped out by government forces at the Wounded Knee Massacre.

In the play's finale, Buffalo Bill talks to the spirit of Sitting Bull, who excuses him, suggesting that what the whites did to the American Indians would have happened with or without Buffalo Bill's intervention. Buffalo Bill declares his

continued support of his country's Indian policy, but his speech only exposes
the terrible way in which Indians were treated—a series of forced removals,
diseases, destruction, and greed. Indian spirits rise to speak about their deaths
in counterpoint to Buffalo Bill's attempt to justify what whites did as Manifest
Destiny, further underlining the unfairness of the way American Indians were
treated. Buffalo Bill finally admits his guilt, even as he continues to perform
his show, illustrating his inability to change, despite full knowledge of what
damage he causes.

John Kauffman wrote, directed and performed *According to Coyote,* having
created it out of stories told to him by his Nez Percé grandparents and other
tribal members. Intended as children's theater, the play is complex enough to
be performed for any age. In a series of short episodes, Coyote takes us through
the creation of the world initially populated by an Ancient People shaped like
animals, to the point where they are divided into their human tribes. Coyote
assists humanity with important gifts of fire and tribal identity, but remains
an animal at the close of the play.

To emphasize the American Indian origin of these stories, the play's staging
draws on traditional motifs of the Plains Indians. A circular floorcloth in red
and blue with a symbolic representation of the coyote at the center is center
stage. Encircling this are animal footprints and human handprints, encircled in
turn by symbols for mountains and fire. Though Coyote begins in contemporary dress, he adds makeup and Plains Indian clothing as the scenes progress,
while authentic American Indian rhythms and sounds punctuate each episode.
In the first story Kauffman weaves together biblical, scientific, and Nez Percé
creation stories to show the equal validity of each, thus building credence by
association for the American Indian version.

Storytelling is key to the American Indian culture, which considers myths
as tribal treasures in which the telling demands many rules and restrictions.
Entertaining characters and events often mask the moral core of the story, and
According to Coyote belongs to this tradition. The figure of the trickster appears in the mythologies of many cultures, but is particularly prevalent in
American Indian culture, where he is depicted as an invincible scoundrel who
continually bounces back from disaster. His resilience in the face of adversity
emphasizes human possibility as much as it suggests the likelihood of divine
intervention, and makes him an apt metaphor for American Indian survival as
a whole. Coyote is such a trickster, whose failings and limitations often result
in his demise, but who matures through his experiences to become a heroic
figure by the play's close. Yet Coyote remains an ambiguous hero, a mix of
the benefactor and the wastrel.

As wastrel, we see Coyote tricked, chased, and pitched down, usually through
his own arrogance, irresponsibility, or sheer foolishness. He teaches lessons in
humility, sensibility, and manners by negative example in a series of episodes.
He takes back the blanket he had given to the rock as a gift, then insults the

Nighthawks who initially save him from the rock's vengeance, so he gets crushed by a rock in punishment. Aiming to get the best name at the naming ceremony, he oversleeps, arrives late, and must remain Coyote. Dancing off with a star with which he has irrationally fallen in love, he drops back to earth to form Crater Lake. Diverted from his plan to eat Rabbit, he dreams about the better meal suggested by the rabbit, when he should be paying attention to Rabbit's plot, and he gets burned to death. Finally, he fails to follow the Death Spirit's directions and loses his wife. But despite these all too-human flaws, he is also an immortal who can be brought back to life after each failure, who gives fire to mankind and creates the tribes.

Coyote's role as benefactor becomes evident when the Creator names him chief of the New People and commissions him to teach them how to live. Soon after, Coyote steals fire from the Skookums at the top of the mountain and, with unusual forethought, manages to relay it along to Wood, who can absorb it and prevent it from being recaptured. He then teaches people how to draw out the wood's fire by using two sticks. Killing the Monster of Kamiah is equally ingenious, as he allows the monster to eat him, then cuts its heart out from the inside, and his creative force is again underlined as he designates tribes related to the monster's body parts.

In the play's final scene Coyote is allowed to climb to Spirit Heaven, but the rope he climbs is cut by people he has tricked in the past and he falls to earth, becoming the coyote animal we know today. On the surface his immortality appears lost, and yet it continues in the stories we still tell of trickster figures, be they in the storytelling of American Indians or in the cartoon figure of Wile E. Coyote.

Body Indian instantly dispenses with romanticized images of American Indians in its opening scene, set in an enclosed, dingy apartment with two drunken couples lying there asleep. Bobby Lee enters, also drunk, and on crutches because of losing a leg from a train accident after passing out on the tracks. He struggles into his Uncle Howard's apartment, on one final binge, in search of emotional support for his plan to enter alcohol rehabilitation. What he receives at the hands of his friends and relatives is unrelentingly harsh, as they steal money from him each time he passes out, even pawning his artificial leg. Bobby sees what they have done to him as he wakes to find his money and leg vanished, and is forced to relive the horror of losing his leg.

Geiogamah writes for an American Indian audience, presenting what he sees as realistic American Indians—free of European-American stereotypes—who struggle for dignity, identity, and hope in a hostile contemporary society. Geiogamah's concern that these characters be played realistically is conveyed by his notes on accent and pronunciation to ensure authenticity of speech. Unconcerned with historical caricatures of American Indians or the blame that must be assigned to whites in their treatment of this cultural group, he looks at American Indians in the present. When images of past injustices appear in his work, they are only there to emphasize the nature of cause and effect, and how such events impact on the present. Geiogamah depicts Indian life with a brutal honesty, with all of its problems, not as a call to arms but as a call to intro- spection. He wants American Indians to think about their actions and consider what can be done to sustain a culture he insists is worth saving. *Body Indian* is concerned with the way American Indians mistreat each other, rather than any external prejudice they face.

Friendly on Bobby's entrance, once he passes out, his relatives turn menacing as they roll him for cash on a pretext of needing more wine. They do not even stick together in their treatment of Bobby but attack in subgroups, accusing each other of hiding their findings. Even when *delirium tremens* sets in and they do need more wine, no one will admit to having cash to pay for it, which is why they take Bobby's leg. While Geiogamah tempers his message with humor, his desire for American Indians to help themselves by treating each other better comes through as an urgent one if the American Indian is to survive.

Bobby's character is indicated by his decision to pay $400 for his alcohol detox treatment, when he could get it for free; this marks him as a man of dignity and nobility, despite his current condition. He does not want to be dependent—on alcohol or government handouts—and is trying to help himself with his own money gained from leasing an allotment of land he owns. Sadly, his friends and relatives are too wrapped up in their own needs to offer any support; indeed, they actively work against him by stealing his money. This is a troubled group and Geiogamah does not blame white society for their weak- ness. He suggests that by their failure to work together, their automatic as- sumptions of the worst, and the way they give in so readily they have brought much of this misery on themselves. Instead of supporting Bobby, they under- mine his efforts to be self-sufficient, and by this they undermine their own community. Bobby's final cry can be seen as a frustrated acknowledgment of his own foolishness for trusting such weak people, people too fearful of getting close and too concerned with their own superficial needs, but it is a cry that should never have been allowed to happen.

On the surface this seems to be a play about the terrible effects of alcoholism and the stress of living in an uncaring society, but it is more than that. Geio- gamah explores the way all people, but, in his view, particularly American Indians, tend to abuse, degrade, and hurt each other and themselves in their efforts to survive. This is endemic to American Indian groups not just because their struggle is so drastic, but because they are so bound together. The com- munity we see in Howard's apartment may be flawed, but it is a tight-knit community nonetheless, where all are related to some degree and they provide testament to the vitality of the "body Indian."

The action of each scene is similar, but not repetitive. In every one we hear them talk, see them drink, Bobby passes out, and the others steal from him. However, each scene focuses on a different aspect of these people's lives. While the first scene establishes relationships and the pattern for later scenes, the next two scenes focus on the plight of the men and then on the women. The fourth scene offers the perspective of the younger generation, and the final scene shows the outcome. We learn that the men mostly drink to escape the indignity of their lives, and the women, whose representation appears a little more positive by their ability to at least sympathize with each other, live lives filled with drudgery and poverty. In an unusual twist, the younger generation in this play offers little hope, as they display the same problems we see in the older characters—no money, a lack of hope, and a sense of moral dislocation, as they engage in shallow and meaningless pursuits. Young and old alike take advantage of poor Bobby.

While Bobby is the only one on literal crutches, the other characters all use alcohol as a crutch; they are constantly in search of the next drink to ensure that they do not sober up enough to look too closely at their condition. Drinking for these people has become a kind of ritual, sadly replacing former rituals which were far less self-destructive. Unable to find jobs, they spend what little money they get from the government on alcohol. Money is a major issue here and, though they joke about it, we see that their poverty is not temporary but a permanent condition, one that wears away at their very souls and lies at the heart of their desperation. Yet their moments of song and dance indicate a desire for happiness, and the fact that they remain a living culture, despite their poverty, offers hope for the future, in spite of the play's disturbing conclusion.

FURTHER SUGGESTED READING

Auerbach, Doris. *Sam Shepard, Arthur Kopit, and the Off Broadway Theater.* Boston: Twayne, 1982.

Geiogamah, Hanay. *New American Drama: Three Plays.* Norman: University of Oklahoma Press, 1980.

Geiogamah, Hanay, and Jaye T. Darby, Eds. *Stories of Our Way: An Anthology of American Indian Plays.* Los Angeles: UCLA American Indian Studies Center, 1999.

Green, Donald E., and Thomas V. Tonnesen, Eds. *American Indians: Social Justice and Public Policy.* Madison, WI: Institute on Race and Ethnicity, 1991.

Kauffman, John. *According to Coyote.* In *Playwrights of Color.* Eds. Meg Swanson and Robin Murray. Yarmouth, ME: Intercultural Press, 1999: 579–87.

Kopit, Arthur. *Indians.* New York: Hill and Wang, 1969.

Stedman, Raymond William. *Shadows of the Indian: Stereotypes in American Culture.* Norman: University of Oklahoma Press, 1982.

Stone, John August. *Metamora and Other Plays.* Bloomington: Indiana University Press, 1940.

Asian American Experience

The Wash by Philip Kan Gotanda (1987)
F.O.B. by David Henry Hwang (1980)
Kimchee and Chitlins by Elizabeth Wong (1994)

Asian American theater is far more viable and active in America than one would think based on Broadway or its publication record, though we are beginning to see more Asian American plays in print. There have been numerous self-produced Asian American dramas, performed as monologues or based in the community rather than performed in mainstream theaters. The Asian American experience is as varied as the nationalities that make up this group, with immigrants hailing from Japan, China, Korea, Vietnam, Singapore, Taiwan, the Philippines, and the South Pacific islands. It is impossible to represent them all in this brief chapter, but it should be acknowledged that each group has its own distinct culture.

The relatively limited period in which people of Asian ethnicity have lived in America and had the luxury of artistic expression beyond survival or evading prejudice has resulted in Asian American playwrights of predominantly Japanese, Chinese, and Korean origins, and this chapter considers plays based on these three ethnic groups. What they have in common is that while each playwright looks at the Asian American experience from a different angle, they collectively expose stereotypes, broaden our perspective of Asian American identity, and encourage people to adopt a greater ethnic understanding and tolerance.

Philip Kan Gotanda's *The Wash* depicts constraints affecting Japanese Americans through the problematic relationship of an older couple. Gotanda makes no effort to explain what may seem unfamiliar motivations for his characters, leaving audiences to work them out for themselves. The text is peppered with Japanese American references and Japanese words and phrases that remain untranslated on the stage; this gives the dialogue authenticity but it also makes parts of the play less accessible to non–Japanese American audiences. Instead of pandering to the majority, Gotanda forces them to understand his culture on its own terms.

David Henry Hwang's *F.O.B.* looks at differing attitudes toward ethnicity expressed by two young Chinese Americans and a new immigrant, "Fresh-off-the-Boat." Hwang's blend of Chinese and American mythology, behavior, and speech allows him to accurately convey the beliefs and struggles of Chinese Americans in America. Giving voice to a group rarely depicted fairly (if at all) in mainstream literature, he challenges stereotypes and offers in their place far more complex characters who deserve more attention.

In *Kimchee and Chitlins,* Elizabeth Wong looks at a Korean American–run general store that comes into conflict with Harlem locals. Through their story, she depicts many concerns that go beyond the Asian American experience and can be applied to all American ethnicities: problems of interracial discord too often culminating in violence, the demeaning use of stereotypes, the media's white bias that marginalizes all ethnicity, and the loss of cultural heritage in those who assimilate. Her answer to most of these troubles is to call for heightened awareness of cultural differences among people of all ethnic groups to defuse the ignorance that lies at the root of the discord. She calls for people to reach out across that cultural divide and bridge the gap to strengthen the whole multicultural community.

The Wash focuses on male-female relationships, but through the lens of Japanese American attitudes and culture. After forty-two years of marriage, Masi Motsumoto leaves her husband, Nobu, to expand her horizons, regain her self-esteem, and pursue a relationship with a more suitable partner. Nobu stoically continues in his same routines, refusing to accept that his wife has left him. Culturally restricted from doing anything to fix his marriage, and without the strength to make the "grand gesture" of suicide on realizing that she has definitely gone, he is left devastated and alone.

Nobu and Masi break up partly because he is too stubborn to ask her to return, but also because they should never have been together in the first place. Masi never loved Nobu, and in all their years together never found the happiness she discovers with Sadao Nakasato. In the Japanese culture depicted in the play, a woman is expected to live for her husband and children and not give a thought to her own needs and desires. Living in America, with its cultural ideal of self-reliance and one of the highest divorce rates in the world, certainly clashes with such beliefs. Masi's Japanese background tells her to stand by her family, so she has withstood years of unhappy marriage before going against her upbringing and leaving her husband. The fact that she continues to care for him—doing his laundry (the "wash" of the title) and preparing his food—even while living in a separate apartment, testifies to the difficulty she has in making a clean break.

Masi and Nobu have a connection she finds it hard to ignore, but it reveals itself to be little more than habit, especially from her perspective. With the love of Sadao, however, Masi gains the courage to leave her husband's laundry behind and her burdensome responsibilities to the past. Sadao is an enlightened Japanese American male who can cry in public and feel no shame, contribute to the household chores, compliment his woman, include her in all aspects of life, and allow her far greater freedom—all impossibilities for Nobu, who has a very traditional attitude toward women.

While Masi is prepared to move on with her life, Nobu lives in the past. He hates change; when he eats at Kiyoko's restaurant, he always sits in the same seat and eats the same meal. Nobu is nostalgic for the way life used to be—as indicated by the old lullaby he sings—but other people's lives move on and Nobu is left behind. His kite is a symbol of a freedom he is unable to grasp— the possibilities of America he feels are unavailable to him because of his Japanese heritage. At the close of act 1, scene 9, Nobu imagines that his kite soars high, showing his longing for the greater freedom he felt as a child, but the weight of his own life and the traditions he feels he must live by keep him and his kite on the ground. He gives the kite to his grandson, Timothy, as a sign of acceptance; Timothy, whose allegiance to his cultural background is weaker, may be freer to fly it.

Nobu is attracted to Kiyoko, but just as he never flies his kite, he never allows himself to consummate this relationship. He is unable to believe that his wife has permanently left him—this is partly why he never asks Masi to return. It is not his ego that causes him to think so but a culturally induced disbelief that a wife can behave independently. He accepts her visits to bring him food and do his laundry as natural, because he still sees it as her duty. Nobu is a narrow traditionalist—from insisting that his kite be built a specific way to rejecting his daughter and her child because she married an African American. He loves his wife and children, but his pride prevents him from expressing that love, and he cannot accept their behaving independently of him.

Curley Sakata, Kiyoko's cook, provides an interesting contrast to Nobu. Like Nobu, he has a firm sense of his own identity but without being so restricted. His outlook on life is more open-minded, and he mocks Nobu when he sees him. It is partly his Hawaiian upbringing, but Curley takes life as it comes and enjoys it. He drinks beer, despite Kiyoko's complaints, because he likes to drink. He has none of the terrible self-control that leads Nobu to bottle up his emotions. But Nobu is disgusted with men like Curley, seeing them as brash and undignified, and could never behave in that way.

Nobu and Masi's children are third-generation Japanese Americans, and we see in them a clear dilution of Japanese ways and a stronger embrace of mainstream American culture; their names, Marsha and Judy, reflect this. Both are concerned for their parents, but do not exhibit the traditional Japanese sense of duty. Of the two, Judy is more rebellious: long before she suggested that her mother leave her father and she herself married an African American without parental consent.

Despite Nobu's self-centered behavior, Gotanda ensures that we still feel sympathy for him because he is a victim of his culture rather than a real tyrant. We are shown his tender side when he is with Kiyoko and when he sings his lullaby. Even Masi has to admit that he has always been very loving and good with children, and we witness this when he finally meets his grandson. Despite all this, however, Nobu sadly ends up alone, and it seems to be a fate he cannot avoid given his cultural background and his inability to adapt to changing circumstances.

In *F.O.B.* three young people with different degrees of connection to China form a relationship triangle twisted by gender and ethnicity. All three lie, creating and evading truths, as they move around each other in an uncomfortable dance of courtship. Steve, the new Chinese immigrant, vies with second-generation Chinese American Dale for the attention of Grace, a first-generation Chinese American who resents the patriarchal background of both Chinese and American cultures to which the men subscribe, alternately leading them on then slapping them down, and finally settling on Steve as having more promise. But the real conflict here lies in their differing outlooks on life.

Steve, the newcomer, takes on the persona of Gwan Gung, a Chinese deity, to build up his self-esteem. He is distressed to discover how little people in America care or even recall this figure, but what relevance does such a violent, mythic god have in modern America? While he need not abandon his Chinese roots to advance in American society, too strong an adherence to older Chinese ways may impede his progress. Steve's background remains uncertain: is he the son of a wealthy Hong Kong businessman come to get an M.B.A. to help out the family business, or an impoverished immigrant from mainland China escaping the hardships of his homeland? Because he is meant to represent all immigrants, he can be both and everything in between, and he conveys the concerns of anyone coming to American shores from another culture. One thing he insists on is the deceptiveness of the American promise, and the lies of the white Americans who pretend to offer so much, yet in reality give so little. However, it is a promise in which Dale still believes.

Steve has a pride that insists he need not hide his origins, nor does he feel limited by them; he wishes to be himself and mocks Dale's efforts to conform. Steve sees himself primarily as a Chinese man in America, whereas, in his efforts to advance in American society, Dale has behaved subserviently and tried to eradicate every aspect of his Chinese heritage. Rightly recognizing that whites remain a privileged race in America, Dale desperately tries to fit in by becoming white, only he cannot escape his skin color, which will forever betray him. For all his talk about mixing with people who drive Porsches, it becomes evident that he has not been accepted by this group and is alone. He has also estranged himself from his family, calling them "yellow ghosts" (32). Sadly, it is he who is the ghost, since he has no identity, having given up his heritage in an effort to embrace another that refuses to even see him. Having worked hard not to be Chinese, he ends up being no one. The equality he seeks is a sham; Steve sees this from the start and refuses to play the assimilation game.

Arrogantly, Dale prejudges Steve, determined to see him as a Chinese bumpkin to justify having set aside his own heritage. What lies beneath his arrogance is self-loathing at his own inability to be white. He hates Steve because he sees Steve as representative of everything he has spent his life trying *not* to be in terms of speech, behavior, and appearance. Steve switches between playing the role Dale has assigned to him and defying his every expectation; he switches from perfect English to broken English, but then suggests that they dine at a French restaurant rather than a Chinese eatery. In this way Steve toys with the stereotype that Dale is determined to believe. Dale voices this stereotype in the Prologue and reiterates it in the coda to show that he has refused to learn anything from meeting Steve. Steve contradicts Dale's whole description of what a new immigrant is like, for he is neither ugly, stupid, clumsy, nor clannish.

Having come to America as a child, Grace recalls how she was shunned by American-born Chinese Americans because of her poor English. Unlike Dale, she is less resolved to become totally American and refuses to view the Chinese as a backward race. She speaks to Steve as the woman warrior Fa Mu Lan, but out of nostalgia rather than pride. Her description of Fa Mu Lan as a "ghost" indicates her belief that she has lost her Chinese heritage as a result of living in America, and her tale of how Fa Mu Lan returns home to a slaughtered family indicates the lack of connection she feels toward her Chinese relatives.

Though Grace feels disenfranchised in terms of ethnicity, America has empowered her as a woman, and she will not allow either man to dominate her. Caught between the extremes of Dale and Steve, she declares that it is hard for her to be either Chinese or American in America, and feels excluded from both worlds. As the three play out their mock Chinese opera, Grace displays an uncertainty toward either culture, since both threaten her as a woman. When she mimes killing Steve as Gwan Gung, she is killing those elements of Chinese culture she sees as demeaning to women. When she finally chooses to go with Steve at the close, we can see this as a decision to recommit to her heritage, although she does this on her own terms by forcing Steve to give up his role as Gwan Gung and become a fellow human being with whom she can be an equal.

Assigned to cover a Harlem clash between blacks and a Korean American–run store, television news reporter Suzie Seeto, the protagonist of *Kimchee and Chitlins,* is tricked by a jealous colleague into broadcasting a biased story. Suzie's brief report results in hate calls and an escalation of the conflict, as each side strives to be heard. Suzie decides to follow the story past the day or so of coverage usually given to such events by the media to discover what sparked this unrest. Rather than support her quest for truth, her boss suspends her, but she continues to investigate the social tensions underlying the clash until she reaches a life-changing understanding. Witnessing four black youths attack a Vietnamese boy whom they take to be Korean, she recalls her own distress at being confused with another Asian girl at school. This allows her to recognize two truths: first, although prejudice and discrimination demean and belittle, people do not take time to look closely at anyone outside their own cultural group; and, second, she has been hiding from the fact that she is "yellow." Where this knowledge will take her is an open question, as she remains suspended and unsure of her future, but at least it will be a more honest future.

There remain conflicting reports over what occurred to make the community boycott the Korean American store and protest outside with signs. Suzie tries to discover what happened to Matilda Duvet while shopping at the store. The Reverend Carter says the Koreans attacked Matilda and have been insulting blacks since the store opened. The Koreans say Matilda fainted after getting violently upset over a mispricing, and insist they have been courteous to everyone. Matilda is too busy worrying about relatives back in Haiti to even recall what happened. Grocer Mak has his business ruined and the ultimate blame can be leveled at nothing specific, just a general atmosphere of mistrust and easy hatred, exacerbated by the unfulfilled dreams of both sides. This is the story Suzie finally wants to tell, but her white boss, Mark Thompson, does not see it as newsworthy.

Suzie is Asian American, but speaks only English, and according to Mark has "nothing exotic, nothing Asian about her" (416). But Mark's view of Asian culture is blinkered by stereotypes, so it is hardly surprising that he patently ignores events showing anything more complex. Suzie is rankled that people might think she got her job through affirmative action rather than by merit; she also feels unhappy that because of her ethnicity she is always picked to report on race issues. She longs to be promoted to anchor and escape her ethnicity, but by the close of the play she has done neither.

On arriving at the scene of the protest, she gets footage of the outspoken Reverend Carter calling the storeowner a "Korean monkey" (404), suggesting that he go back to Korea. Suzie is shocked to hear such undisguised racial slurs and attitudes, seeing them as anachronistic in the supposedly enlightened 1990s, but that is only because she has been leading a sheltered life. The deeper she probes into this neighborhood, the more she realizes that the hatreds and prejudices so deftly exposed in the 1960s have not evaporated; they have just changed direction or gone underground, ready to resurface at the slightest provocation.

The Reverend Carter admits to being prejudiced and a bigot, but declares, "A black man in America can never be a racist. To be a racist, you have to have power" (431). He does not even have the power to force the media to pay attention to him as he tries to use the boycott to bring some more pressing concerns of the black American community into the spotlight. The Asian American community is no less marginalized. Ignored by the dominant white society, these subcultures are left to bicker with one another, their hatreds fed by ignorance of each other's cultures. The Koreans are guilty of stereotyping the blacks in their community just as they themselves are stereotyped by blacks and others in the neighborhood. Both ethnic groups are wary of each other, but it is largely because they cannot see past the stereotypes. Wong's use of black American and Korean choruses, who constantly disagree as they comment on the action and forever harp on their differences rather than commonalities, deftly presents these warring subcultures.

People like Nurse Ruth Betty see Mak as insulting because he does not touch her hand when taking money or look her in the eye, but his behavior is dictated by what is proper in Korean culture where his actions would be viewed as highly respectful. Both sides make fun of the broken English of the other rather than try to listen to what they are saying. It becomes obvious that these ethnic groups have more in common than they realize or allow themselves to recognize. Neither can get a bank loan to start a business; both are overworked, underpaid, often mocked or mistreated; and all are undervalued by America as a whole. A telling moment occurs when we learn that Ruth Betty, Suzie, and Soomi have all fantasized about changing their appearance to look more like women of the dominant culture, and, more importantly, less like women in their own.

The reactions to these events by Willie and Soomi, the storeowner's nephew and niece, indicate the extreme responses people have in their quest for a solution to troubling social problems. While Willie gets a gun and threatens violence, Soomi offers to nonviolently counterprotest by singing songs and displaying a sign stating "Yellow is Beautiful"—an ironic echo of the black American slogan of the 1960s. Neither approach seems workable, so both Willie and Soomi try to act more American and assimilate into the larger culture. Wong suggests that none of these responses are valid, and offers another option. Mak and Barber Brown, fellow businessmen, have a friendly relationship, but they are not true friends and have not invited each other into their homes. That kind of close, personal interaction, in the end, is what Wong suggests is necessary if the community is to go beyond mistrust and become unified.

The title refers to foods that are prized by each culture as part of their heritage and identity; the possibility of connection is raised by the potential friendship between Brown and Mak. Mak gives Brown some kimchee to help cure his sinus problem, but Brown finds that the kimchee alone just makes him sneeze. However, he discovers that if he mixes the kimchee with his chitlins, he has a tasty meal that clears his sinuses. The symbolism in this is obvious: if each side can overcome its deeply held prejudices and join hands with the other, together they can create a stronger, more effective community. But when Brown offers the true hand of friendship by inviting Mak into his home for dinner at the close, Suzie points out that such an idealistic ending has only been invented, leaving it for those watching to make it a reality.

FURTHER SUGGESTED READING

Chin, Frank. *The Chickencoop Chinaman and the Year of the Dragon.* Seattle: University of Washington Press, 1981.

Espiritu, Yen Le. *Asian American Panethnicity: Bridging Institutions and Identities.* Philadelphia: Temple University Press, 1992.

Gotanda, Philip Kan. *Fish Head Soup and Other Plays.* Seattle: University of Washington Press, 1995.

Hwang, David Henry. *F.O.B. and Other Plays.* New York: Penguin, 1990.

———. "Philip Kan Gotanda." *BOMB* 62 (Winter 1998): 20–26.

Lee, Josephine. *Performing Asian America: Race and Ethnicity on the Contemporary Stage.* Philadelphia: Temple University Press, 1997.

Ng, Franklin, Ed. *Asian American Family Life and Community.* New York: Garland, 1998.

Street, Douglas. *David Henry Hwang.* Boise, Idaho: Boise State University Press, 1989.

Wong, Elizabeth. *Kimchee and Chitlins.* In *But Still, Like Air, I'll Rise: New Asian American Plays.* Ed. Velina Hasu Houston. Philadelphia: Temple University Press, 1997: 395–450.

Yamanchi, Wakako. *12–1-A.* In *Playwrights of Color.* Eds. Meg Swanson and Robin Murray. Yarmouth, ME: Intercultural Press, 1999: 231–60.

Betrayal and Guilt

A View From the Bridge by Arthur Miller (1956)
Buried Child by Sam Shepard (1978)
The Little Foxes by Lillian Hellman (1966)

Central to the plays in this chapter are themes of betrayal and guilt, and the inevitably related issues of blame and responsibility. Miller and Shepard see the American tendency toward denial as self-destructive, and suggest that it is better for people to accept their guilt in order for life to go on. Eddie Carbone dies rather than accept his guilt in *A View from the Bridge*. It is possible that the characters in *Buried Child* face theirs and move toward a more hopeful future. However, there are also those who refuse to accept guilt and continue their betrayals, as in Lillian Hellman's *The Little Foxes*. Such is the venal amorality of the modern world, Hellman suggests, that this behavior goes unpunished, and possibly is even sanctioned.

Guilt and responsibility are concerns that Miller addresses in nearly every play he has written, but they are central to *A View from the Bridge*. Miller often presents us with ambivalent characters who cannot be easily categorized as heroes or villains, such as Eddie Carbone. They make mistakes, but they do not do so maliciously, and they often feel guilty for what they have done. But Miller wants us to realize that guilt is not the answer, because, as a passive reaction, guilt is destructive, as opposed to the active reaction of accepting responsibility. To passively accept guilt leads to complacency or even paralysis, but if we actively transform guilt into an acceptance of responsibility for our actions, Miller believes that we will be able to transcend it.

The working title for the script of Arthur Miller's *A View from the Bridge* was *An Italian Tragedy*. The Italian community in Red Hook was a close-knit group; the law of the land did not concern them as much as their own codes of honor and respectability did. This was a society in which blood was thicker than water and to betray a family member, as Eddie does, was the ultimate sin. The play was written at the height of the Red Scare, when the House Un-

American Activities Committee (HUAC) hearings were whipping up anticommunist fervor, and friends were being coerced to inform on friends. When Miller was brought before the committee in 1956, he refused to give them any names. Using Eddie Carbone as his example, Miller shows that informing may have the law on its side, but it is morally indefensible and a dreadful betrayal of those against whom you inform.

In Sam Shepard's *Buried Child*, the fragmentation of character and speech we witness signals the psychological fragmentation these family members experienced, having been raised in such an abusive home. Expressionistic exaggerations of character, event, and behavior result in an almost gothic sense of horror, although the set is intentionally realistic by contrast. The play transcends its naturalistic setting to become a mythic exploration of family guilt and betrayal, conveyed by a complex web of symbols. Although Shepard rewrote this play for a 1995 revival, this chapter refers to the original 1978 production, for it is that version that is most commonly available.

Lillian Hellman's *The Little Foxes* is unusual in that its central characters are predominantly horrendously selfish people. By their endless machinations and by their tenacity and quick thinking, perhaps even a grudging respect, they engage our interest, but they do not elicit our sympathy because they are hopelessly amoral. They go largely unpunished for their crimes, which are both moral and criminal. We watch as the expected bonds of affection between siblings, spouses, parents, and their children are continually broken and ignored, as the Hubbards connive and betray one another in their quest for wealth and power. Since they end up potentially richer than they began, we see that Hellman offers no satisfying moral conclusion, but a vision of materialistic ruthlessness that is set to sweep the nation.

In Arthur Miller's *A View from the Bridge*, Eddie and Beatrice Carbone house two illegal Italian immigrants, Marco and Rodolpho. Related to Beatrice, they have come to America to find work. Eddie has an unacknowledged attraction to his wife's niece, Catherine, who also lives with them, and when she and Rodolpho start to date, Eddie betrays both immigrants to the authorities. Trying to preserve his reputation, Eddie denies what he has done and fights Marco, resulting in Eddie's death.

Eddie Carbone has a guilty secret; he wants to sleep with his niece. To get what he wants, he willingly puts others at risk: he tells the Immigration Bureau about Marco and Rodolpho so they will be deported back to Italy. That will prevent Rodolpho from taking Catherine from Eddie. Because Eddie refuses to accept responsibility for his actions, his guilt drives him toward his own destruction, and he pays with his life. He does not break any criminal laws, as the lawyer Alfieri is quick to point out, but there are moral laws that need to be upheld as well.

A moral responsibility toward others and the self lies at the core of Miller's plays: to neglect either personal or social responsibility is self-destructive. But a moral responsibility can only be fully recognized by those who have an understanding of their own identities—as individuals and members of a society. Eddie recognizes the responsibilities he has for others, but goes against them anyway in a misguided belief about what his responsibilities are toward Catherine. By going against all he had previously believed, Eddie loses his sense of self, shown by his demanding his name from Marco, insisting that Marco has slandered his reputation by declaring that Eddie is the informer. This pits him against Marco, who, we know from the chair lifting scene at the close of act one, is far stronger than Eddie. By fighting Marco, Eddie is causing his own death by refusing to accept responsibility for what he has done.

Eddie dies still insisting that he has done nothing wrong, even though his desires for his niece and his betrayal of his wife's cousins are apparent to all. Blinkered like a horse, he refuses to see things from any other perspective than that of his own innocence. Such a refusal is not enough to save him, although it may make him more sympathetic as a character. He intends to do good, but everything goes sadly wrong because he cannot handle his own emotions. When you betray all that you believe in, you betray yourself, which is what Eddie does. He knows that informing is wrong, and he knows that his love for Catherine is wrong, yet he cannot help himself. He tells Alfieri, when trying to imply that Rodolpho is too effeminate, that even a mouse can break a hold if it really wants to, yet at the play's close he cannot break the hold Marco has on his knife arm. This suggests that Eddie wanted to die, rather than face the consequences of his betrayals.

From Catherine's early years, Eddie has been overprotective of his wife's niece; because he can never have her, he wants to ensure that no one else gets a chance. He would like her to remain a beautiful, innocent Madonna, pure and untouched, but he cannot prevent her emergence into womanhood. His shyness with Catherine turns into petulant resentment as his guilt grows, though he never consciously admits to his feelings for her. The only time the truth comes close to emerging is when he is drunk and kisses her. He casts doubts on Rodolpho's manhood to try to make himself feel more secure, and he tries to convince others that Rodolpho is a homosexual so that he can convince himself, but all he has is very circumstantial evidence. He offers Catherine more freedom toward the end, but by then it is too late.

Eddie's friends and neighbors act as a barometer of local opinion. They begin as close friends of his, admiring him for helping out his wife's relatives. They even side with him against Rodolpho, although they have a growing respect for Marco. However, they turn completely against Eddie as soon as they learn about his betrayal. Eddie is fated to die, partly because of who he is and partly because of the world in which he lives. There is a sense that he is inevitably rushing toward his doom, and that there is little that can be done to save him: given the same situation, he would make the same mistakes and the result, therefore, seems preordained.

But failure, in Miller's eyes, should not be blamed on an indefinable hostile fate or social system, but on individuals who refuse to accept their responsibilities and honor their connection to fellow human beings. Miller sincerely believes that humankind has free will, and it is the choices people make in their lives that determine their direction. It is easier to blame others, but the fault often lies in ourselves. It is the flaws in Eddie's character that ensure his defeat, rather than any divine authority. Individuals are responsible for their own fate: they determine their destiny by the quality of the choices they make throughout their lives. Eddie chooses to act on his baser impulses, trying to keep Catherine away from other men and informing on his wife's cousins. The deeper motivation for his actions is his lust for Catherine, an emotion he does not choose, but could choose to better control.

On more than one occasion, Eddie's eyes are described as being "like tunnels" to convey the sense of inevitability in his destructive behavior. Also, the phone booth from which Eddie calls the authorities begins to glow as Eddie feels the temptation to make the call; this contributes to the sense of fate underlying the play. As Eddie approaches the phone, Alfieri disappears into the darkness and the phone lights up to place Eddie in the ill-fated spotlight that kills him, but it is a spotlight he freely chooses to enter. The sense that Eddie is the author of his own fate is finally underscored by the irony that he dies by his own treachery, on his own knife.

In *Buried Child*, Dodge and his wife, Halie, live in the same house but are apart. He sits immobile on the sofa for much of the play, while Halie is either offstage or reminiscing about a son who died, called Ansel. Their eldest son, Tilden, brings in produce from outside and another son, Bradley, cuts their father's hair while he sleeps. Tilden's son, Vince, whom Dodge has made his heir, arrives with his girlfriend, Shelley, and takes possession of the family homestead, chasing off Bradley and taking Dodge's place after his death. At the close Tilden walks on carrying the corpse of the child Dodge had drowned and buried years previously, as Halie, offstage, comments on the wonderful crops outside.

Shepard depicts three generations in the lives of a grotesque family. Their bizarre behavior and outwardly exaggerated defects symbolize inner psychological defects and archetypal generational conflicts that have shaped these characters' lives. On a mundane level, the plot relates how the family farm passes from one generation to the next and goes through cycles of decay and regeneration. But on the mythic level, the play tells a family story of guilt and betrayal, in which the older generations have abdicated their responsibility, and handed down an inheritance of emotional sterility that the younger generation needs to recognize, understand, and transcend.

This family constantly argues over minor things to avoid having to face the big issues, including their own failures and complicities. The number of times characters cover themselves or each other with blankets, coats, or corn husks symbolizes the extent to which all are complicit in hiding from the truth and each other. This is a family so buried in guilt that they have lost the power to communicate, even on a daily basis. Halie's infidelity (past and present) and Dodge's drinking have greatly contributed to the breakdown of this family, and they bear the brunt of the guilt. Dodge is evidently worn out from the start, a picture of ill health, showing how the effects of guilt wear a person down until there is hardly anything left. His impotence (and eventual death) are signaled by his prone position on the sofa, and his burial under Tilden's corn husks.

Unwilling to move on, Dodge tries to deny the possibility of new growth, even as Tilden covers him with the corn he has picked. Dodge's drinking is a classic reaction to guilt, as a person attempts to obliterate the memory of past deeds with alcohol. What Dodge has done—drowned his wife's illegitimate child—we do not learn until near the close of the play. It is implied, though never with certainty, that the child is the result of an incestuous relationship between his youngest son, Ansel (now dead), and his wife, Halie, although it is also possible that the father was Tilden. There is also uncertainty about whether Ansel ever existed: he may be a figment of Halie's imagination to help her deal with the death of the child that Dodge buried.

Halie's emotional estrangement from her family is shown both by what she says and by the fact that she frequently speaks from offstage, creating as great a distance from her family as she can. Her black garb at the start suggests mourning, and she talks at length about her dead son Ansel, but it is more than him for whom she mourns: she mourns for her whole family. Her change to yellow clothing and the armful of yellow roses she carries in the final act contribute to the possibility of hope as the burden of death seems to have lightened, but Halie is drunk, and still ends the play offstage as she began, so any progress remains ambiguous.

Dodge's oldest son, Tilden, displays no affection for his parents or for his own son, Vince, but his care for the land has rejuvenated the farmland. It is also he who embraces the body of the buried child, by which action he acknowledges the family crime, allowing them to move on. Bradley, Dodge's next son, tries to dominate his father by cutting Dodge's hair, but is displaced in turn by Tilden's son, Vince, who throws away Bradley's false leg (indicative of Bradley's own impotence) and takes Dodge's place on the sofa. Dodge has willed Vince all his property, disinheriting his own sons in favor of a grandson he hardly knows. One assumes this can only be an decision based on spite. The inheritance Dodge leaves his sons is shown in their inability to feel appropriate emotional responses—thus both intimidate and steal from their father and symbolically molest Shelley—Tilden by stroking her fur coat and Bradley by sticking his fingers in her mouth.

Vince left this "home" at sixteen, and this is his first time back in six years. Dodge and Tilden pretend not to recognize Vince, and Dodge swiftly becomes argumentative and abusive to the visitors. When Vince departs to buy his grandfather more whiskey, thoughtlessly leaving his girlfriend without protection, Shelley is manipulated by Tilden, Dodge, and Bradley, who play out a competitive game of confession and hostility toward each other and her. But Shelley survives, even showing an ability to care as she tries to understand their strange behavior, and slowly draws out the truth. When Vince returns, drunk, he pays his family back by refusing to recognize them, and his brutal behavior becomes an echo of theirs. It is uncertain if this family can escape this cycle of violence.

Tilden's earlier entrances with crops reflect on his final entrance with the corpse of the buried child: all connect to suggest fertility and progress. Darkness and rain are replaced by bright sun, the rain creating new growth and suggesting that death can be replaced by new life. The "sun," which brought out the crops, is echoed by the "son" in Tilden's arms. If the buried child has been the source of the family curse, then its exhumation may signify the end of that curse, and an expiation of the sins of the previous generation. The dead son, which the family has avoided and denied, has been brought to light and faced, and the murderer, Dodge, has died, which allows the living son, Vince, to take charge with a clean slate. However, there remains the danger that Vince will not take the chance his father offers, and may instead fall into the ways of his grandfather, as he assumes Dodge's posture at the close and seems about to lose his partner, Shelly, who has declared her intention to leave.

The Little Foxes relates the trickery and betrayals of the materialistic Hubbard family, as they strive to finance the construction of a lucrative cotton mill in their hometown, which will further betray the township but make them a fortune. Brothers Ben and Oscar have made their contribution, but, to her annoyance, sister Regina's ailing husband, Horace Giddens, refuses to invest in the scheme. Not wanting to risk an outside investor who may demand a controlling share, Oscar persuades his son, Leo, a bank employee, to take $88,000 worth of bonds from Horace's safe-deposit box to use as collateral, intending to have them returned before the theft is discovered. Horace finds his bonds gone but instead of pressing charges, he plans to keep quiet to make his wife suffer from knowing their money financed the deal, but she cannot touch the profits. She reveals her contempt for her husband, refuses to fetch his heart medicine, and watches as he collapses, soon to die. Subverting her husband's plan, she blackmails her brothers into a 75 percent share of their profits, but her daughter, Alexandra, leaves in disgust, refusing to watch her family's predatory behavior.

The ruthless Hubbard siblings break both moral and criminal laws in their ruthless quest for ever more money. Not content with cheating and gouging the townsfolk on interest charges, they strive to exploit them even further with insulting wages and heavy-handed management. The new mill will bring prosperity to no one but the Hubbards, which can be seen as a betrayal of the town, but what shocks us even more is their capacity to betray one another.

From the start, we should see that there is little trust between brothers and sister; even as they scheme together, they are constantly vying for the upper hand and checking on one another. Yet they trust even less anyone outside the family.

Regina begins the trickery by using the unavailability of her husband—pretending that Horace is holding off investing as he wants a larger share of the profits—to persuade her brothers to increase her share. The truth is, she has heard nothing from her husband. But her brothers are no less conniving, so we hardly sympathize with the way she treats them. For a while it looks as if they might have the upper hand as they "borrow" her husband's bonds and cut her out of the deal entirely, but they underestimate her opportunistic ingenuity and her capacity for betrayal. Deliberately hastening Horace's death and threatening her brothers with legal action over the theft of the bonds, she forces them to give her the lion's share. In some ways it is hard not to admire the way she turns the tables and rectifies her father's sexist decision to leave his money to his sons alone.

It is unsurprising that Regina is so hard, given her family background. Her declaration that there are not enough people in the state who have not been cheated by her brothers to make up a jury tells us all we need to know about their business practices. The eldest, Ben, who is unmarried, keeps Oscar under his thumb by promising to leave his wealth to Leo. Ben reacts expediently and without conscience to every change in circumstance, swiftly stripping away part of his brother's share to keep Regina satisfied and pressing for the cousins Leo and Alexandra to marry to keep the money in the family. Ben suspects foul play in his brother-in-law's speedy demise, but has no evidence to support his suspicions, though we can be sure he will not settle for being bested by his sister and will betray her the first chance he gets.

Oscar is even worse; betraying his responsibility as a parent, he encourages his own son's thievery. He married Birdie for her family's plantation and abuses her mentally and physically. She is continuously belittled and berated; we even see him slap her when she interferes with his plans. Having long since turned to drink, Birdie confesses that in twenty-two years of marriage she has not had a single happy day. She is from the old, defeated Southern aristocracy, and the Hubbards belong to a new Southern order, having risen from trade, and they never let Birdie forget this.

Regina's marriage is no less of a sham. She married Horace out of desperation and has long been unhappy with him, even lying about a medical condition so that she will no longer have to sleep with him. When first we see her, she is flirting with the married Chicago businessman who will become their business partner. The only satisfaction she gets from her own marriage is the control she thinks she exerts. Careless of her husband's heart condition, she tricks him into returning home from the hospital, not so she might tend him as a loving wife but so she might better cajole him for money. When Horace tries to ruin her financial opportunity, she viciously turns on him. She calmly watches as he struggles to rise from his wheelchair and climb the stairs to retrieve his life-saving medicine, which may not be murder in any legal sense but is by every moral code. It is also certainly a betrayal of the marriage vows.

Horace is no saint. He has gone along with his in-laws for many years, lending them money from his bank for their business practices; he has had mistresses to make up for his wife's withdrawal of affection; but his illness has caused him to reassess his life. Tired of his grasping, argumentative in-laws, and declaring himself content with what he has, Horace refuses to invest in the greedy scheme, wishing to die with a clean conscience. He still loves his wife, but realizes that she has no love for him and only holds him in contempt. It is less a betrayal than a justified form of revenge when he tries to arrange it so that his bonds are used for the deal in a way that ensures that she will gain no benefit from it. He tries to hurt her where he knows it will actually do some damage—financially. Because of his earlier than anticipated death, his plan fails, but he does manage to gain one victory over his wife—by convincing his daughter that she must leave the family immediately before she too becomes corrupt.

The younger generation offers little hope in the play. Leo is evidently as cruel and corrupt as his father; his own mother detests him. Alexandra may leave, but this is a slight moral victory as the family will continue with their exploitative plans regardless of what she does. As Ben suggests, there are people like them all over the country and they will always come out on top because they are so ruthless, holding nothing sacred in the pursuit of business, prepared to betray anyone for their own advancement—even spouse, sibling, or child.

FURTHER SUGGESTED READING

Abbotson, Susan C. W. *Student Companion to Arthur Miller.* Westport, CT: Greenwood, 2000.

Carnes, Patrick J. *The Betrayal Bond: Breaking Free of Exploitive Relationships.* Deerfield Beach, FL: Health Communications, 1997.

Griffin, Alice, and Geraldine Thorsten. *Understanding Lillian Hellman.* Columbia: University of South Carolina Press, 1999.

Hellman, Lillian. *The Little Foxes.* New York: Viking, 1966.

Lederer, Katherine. *Lillian Hellman.* Boston: Twayne, 1979.

Miller, Arthur. *After The Fall.* New York: Viking, 1964.

———. A View from the Bridge *and* All My Sons. Harmondsworth, U.K.: Penguin, 1961.

Piers, Gerhart, and Milton B. Singer. *Shame and Guilt: A Psychoanalytic and a Cultural Study.* New York: Norton, 1971.

Pinter, Harold. *Betrayal.* New York: Grove, 1978.

Roudané, Matthew. *The Cambridge Companion to Sam Shepard.* New York: Cambridge University Press, 2002.

Shepard, Sam. *Buried Child.* New York: Urizen, 1979.

Wilcox, Leonard. Ed. *Rereading Shepard.* New York: St. Martin's Press, 1993.

Courtship

Cyrano de Bergerac by Edmond Rostand (1897)
The Heiress by Goetz and Goetz (1948)
Love Letters by A. R. Gurney (1988)

An exploration of the way courtships are considered in modern drama reveals a predominance of failed relationships, usually due to a misunderstanding or lack of seriousness on the side of one (or both) of the participants. It is interesting to note that whether set in the seventeenth, nineteenth, or twentieth century, there are classic things all romantic partners do to try to attract their love, from flattery and teasing to offers of concern and protection, to sincere protestations of affection and admiration in person or by writing. All three plays considered in this chapter end without the couple getting together, but the process by which they come to this varies as much as do the individual lovers themselves.

Against a contemporary French theatrical movement toward naturalism, Edmond Rostand chose to be purposefully artificial and whimsical. His plays shunned the concept of the "well-made play," celebrating the romantic and the sentimental. His play, *Cyrano de Bergerac,* written in open verse, is based on a real person who had lived in seventeenth-century France. It initially seems like a classic tale of unrequited love, but becomes more complex: Roxane loves Cyrano all along, but does not realize it until it is too late.

Cyrano has all the prerequisites of the perfect lover: he is generous, entertaining, intelligent, and courageous, yet he cannot bring himself to court the woman he loves, convinced that she would be repulsed by his enormous nose. Roxane has all the same qualities that he has, plus beauty besides, but falls for the handsome soldier, Christian. Yet it is Cyrano all along who courts her, for Christian uses Cyrano's words, voice, and feelings to win her heart. However, because of Christian's untimely death, Cyrano cannot reveal this ruse, and the pair only discover their mutual love as Cyrano is dying. Yet the humor in the play, predominantly resting on the larger-than-life wit and exploits of Cyrano, overrides the sadness of its characters' lives, allowing Cyrano to die content with a life well lived.

Set in nineteenth-century New York, *The Heiress,* an adaptation by Ruth and Augustus Goetz of Henry's James's novel, *Washington Square,* shows a far darker view of the way people play at relationships. What has all the markings of a romantic courtship with compliments, flowers, and poetry, followed by the promise of an elopement in the dead of night, turns ugly as we are forced to recognize the suitor's true motives and the impact these have on an innocent young girl's life. Catherine Sloper is psychologically abused by a father who constantly belittles her, as well as by the love of her life, who jilts her when he realizes that he cannot gain her full inheritance by marrying her without her father's consent. She does, however, exact her revenge, which shows us the growing strength of women as the century progressed.

A. R. Gurney's *Love Letters* is a more recent tale of a wealthy middle-class boy and girl who have known each other since second grade, yet somehow never quite fulfill the love they hold for one another. Both unhappily marry other people and, although they have a brief affair, it comes too late and fizzles out as Andy opts for a safer domestic life and chooses to drop Melissa, leading her to suicide. Their story is told exclusively through a series of letters and cards they have sent one another over the years, from formal responses to invitations or holiday greetings, to heartfelt missives exploring their relationship to each other, their families, and the rest of the world. The two actors sit together on stage for the entire performance, but do not physically interact. They read single lines or whole messages, and create a dialogue out of the words they have each written the other over the years.

Cyrano de Bergerac begins with Christian and Roxane falling for each other's looks, while the title character displays his greater worth in an exhibition of intellect and brawn. He confesses that he loves Roxane but can never hope to win her because of his appearance. Invoking an old friendship, for they are cousins, Roxane asks Cyrano to protect Christian and to encourage him to woo her. Since Christian is tongue-tied in love and Roxane desires elegantly expressed sentiments, Cyrano provides the words for Christian to win her. On learning that Roxane has married Christian, the Comte de Guiche, who also desires her, immediately sends Christian and Cyrano to war in revenge, later placing them in the heart of the conflict. While they are away, Cyrano risks his life every day to write to Roxane in Christian's name, which draws Roxane to the battle site to tell Christian that she now loves his soul more than his looks. Before Christian and Cyrano can tell her the truth so she can choose between them, Christian is killed, so Cyrano remains silent. Roxane enters a convent and fifteen years later Cyrano, mortally injured, arrives to keep his weekly visit; as he dies, Roxane recognizes her true love.

The play proposes the idealistic belief that talent and wit can compensate for unattractiveness and allow a man to triumph over a more attractive rival to win the beautiful woman. Cyrano is a poetic creation rather than a realistic figure: he displays a dashing persona, despite his physical ugliness, alongside an attractive sense of freedom and independence. Despite its surface sentimentality and the idealism of its conceit, the play is very modern in the tongue-in-cheek nature of Cyrano's romantic extravagance. He slides easily between grandiose sentiment and utter self-deprecation, and, despite his considerable abilities, never takes himself entirely seriously.

Like any well-born woman of her time, Roxane has led a sheltered life. Yet, she has sufficient intellect and spirit to want to choose a husband for herself rather than settle for an arranged marriage with someone like Valvert, and the boldness to instigate her relationship of choice as she enlists Cyrano's aid. In her innocence she chooses the handsome Christian, despite his unfashionable dress, over the more worthy Cyrano. She admires her cousin, but overlooks him as a suitor. We see the shallowness of her choice early on: she swiftly dismisses Christian when he attempts to speak to her without the aid of Cyrano, and then equally swiftly agrees to marriage as soon as Cyrano gives him prettier words to speak. But she has been manipulated by both men to this end and, from her point of view, has responded to an earnest and heartfelt courtship.

Yet Roxane grows in stature and understanding. She courageously comes through enemy lines to bring food and inspiration to the man who wrote her the letters, who has now won her soul. She asks Christian's pardon, "For being young and vain and superficial,/ And loving you for merely being handsome" (159), and displays a new maturity. When she finally discovers who had actually written those letters, she rebukes Cyrano for his years of silence, earnestly sad that they have lost their opportunity to be husband and wife. But Cyrano assures her that he has been content enough with their years of friendship, which if anything have been purer than any sexual relationship.

Despite his inarticulate awkwardness and his desire to take advantage of Roxane's willingness to kiss, Christian is no villain. Indeed, as Cyrano insists with his dying breath, Christian also truly loved Roxane. Christian's love for Roxane is initially as shallow as hers for him, based on looks alone, but it is not diminished by his discovery of her intellect and spirit. His decency is indicated by his attempt to speak directly and his decision at the battleground to tell her the truth and release her for Cyrano if she would prefer to be his wife. His personal courage is no less than Cyrano's, as he too defends Ligniere and challenges Cyrano to win the respect of his regiment. He is as loath to have Roxane marry him for his looks alone as Roxane is to marry someone without wit and charm: "I want her to love me as I am!—/ Crude, unpolished, unpoetic me!/ As I am or not at all!" (163). But his unfashionable dress and pedantic speech, juxtaposed against the elegance and wit of Cyrano, indicate his unsuitability for Roxane, which is reinforced by his incredulous reaction upon learning that Cyrano has repeatedly risked his life to send Roxane letters from the front. Christian may love Roxane, but Cyrano loves her more.

Even the villain of the play, de Guiche, is not without redemption. His desire for Roxane is as genuine as that of Cyrano and Christian, and although seemingly foppish, he shows courage, too, and wins the grudging respect of his men when he stays to defend Roxane. But he is vindictive, offering a good foil to the generosity of Cyrano, who would rather allow Roxane to go to Christian and be happy than try to win her for himself. Cyrano's generosity comes through repeatedly; for instance, before Christian dies, Cyrano tells him that Roxane had chosen Christian rather than Cyrano when asked whom she truly loved, while in reality the question had never been posed.

Cyrano's behavior is often outlandish and extravagant, as in his refusal to let Montfleury take the stage and handing over to the theater all of his money in recompense, or in his composition of an extempore ballad while dueling with Valvert. But Cyrano can also be timid and insecure, as when he doubts his own ability to ever be loved. In public he poetically celebrates the largeness of his nose, but in private he berates his "monstrous countenance" (39). "There's nothing Sir, I wouldn't dare" (26), he exclaims, but it is not entirely true. He would prefer to face one hundred men alone than to speak his heart to a single woman. These extremes make him lovable rather than insufferable, allowing us to admire the skilled poet as we sympathize with the frustrated lover. It is the depth of his love that initially wins over Roxane, who hears it in his speech, but has been misguided as to the speaker. It is his complexity and depth as a lover that wins her soul: she reads it in his letters and it binds her to him for life.

In *The Heiress*, Dr. Austin Sloper cannot forgive his daughter Catherine for the fact that her birth caused the death of his beloved wife. Since she is painfully shy and rather plain, Sloper despairs of finding her a suitable husband. Catherine tries to please her father, but he constantly finds fault, which only accentuates her awkwardness. Her cousin Maria is engaged to Arthur Townsend, to everyone's approval, for although Arthur is boring, he has good prospects. His cousin, Morris Townsend, is far more personable and, to her surprise and delight, sets his cap at Catherine. Her father is convinced that Morris is only after her money and forbids her to marry him. The couple agree to a six-month separation, and Sloper takes Catherine to Europe. On her return, Catherine determines to elope with Morris, but on learning that she has partly disinherited herself, he fails to come at the appointed time, leaving town instead. Devastated by this betrayal, Catherine becomes as cold and ruthless as Morris and her father. She calmly accepts her father's news of terminal illness and teases him about the possibility that she may marry Morris after his death. Two years later, after Sloper has died, Morris returns and hopes for a second chance. Catherine leads him on, but when he joyfully comes to the house to collect her, she refuses to answer the door.

Sloper expects his daughter to marry, and invites his widowed sister, Mrs. Penniman, to live with them to help make Catherine more marriageable. Catherine is kind and intelligent, even capable of wit, but her father's continual slights and blatant disapproval make her tongue-tied, clumsy, and even more shy. He sees her as "an entirely mediocre and defenseless creature with not a shred of poise" (19), and insists that her large inheritance is the only reason a man would be enticed to marry her. Yet when someone is attracted by that inheritance alone, Sloper does all he can to prevent the marriage—not because he wants Catherine's husband to love her, but rather because he insists that his son-in-law be more respectable than Morris. Mrs. Penniman is noticeably less choosy, encouraging the match even when it becomes clear that she knows what kind of character Morris is. She leaves them alone together and pushes each to pursue the relationship.

Catherine wants to marry, but to someone she can love and who will love her. Morris is initially so attentive and pleasant to Catherine that the audience may be fooled along with Catherine that he truly has personal regard for her beyond her thirty thousand dollars a year. Set beside the pedantic banker, Arthur, the cousin seems a far more interesting match. From the start, Morris gently flirts with Catherine, complimenting her looks and anticipating her needs; he buys her flowers, pays frequent visits, and behaves as if he is passionately in love with her. Like any good nineteenth-century suitor, he writes her poetry, tells her he cannot sleep because of her, and thinks of her constantly. He even pretends that he sometimes feels awkward and shy to make Catherine feel less self-conscious, and defends her against her father's criticisms.

But Morris's self-assurance and tendency to show off should rouse our suspicions—he is too slick. In addition, we learn that he has no money and lives off his widowed sister, which makes him a profligate in the eyes of his contemporary society. We could interpret Morris's reticence to push for marriage against Sloper's consent as concern for his future wife's relationship with her father, but by the second act he makes his true motives clear. We witness him appreciatively looking over the house and its furnishings as Mrs. Penniman invites him to sample the doctor's food, drink, and cigars while Sloper and Catherine are away in Europe. He confesses to Mrs. Penniman that the mere ten thousand dollars a year that Catherine has all her own, without her father's portion, is simply not enough to keep him as he would like.

Sloper is antagonistic to Morris throughout, trying to embarrass him in front of Catherine; but Catherine does not care. She is only concerned that he love her, and she has convinced herself that this is true. Though a little bemused by Morris's passion, she cannot help but respond to it, unaccustomed as she is to being loved. She candidly tells Morris that she loves him, and agrees to marry him, even if it means going against her father's wishes. Her innocence is emphasized by her belief that her father will be fair with Morris when he comes to ask for her hand in marriage. But Sloper does all he can to discredit her suitor. He tries to coerce Mrs. Montgomery, Morris's sister, to inform against him. She valiantly resists, defending her brother: "I can only suppose that Morris is more mature in his feelings than I had thought. This time he has not sought out superficial charms, but has considered the gentle character beneath" (40). And we wish that she were right, but it is evident that even she knows her brother is fortune-hunting. She compassionately warns Sloper not to reveal Morris's true motive to Catherine for "it would break her heart!" (41). The fact that Morris decides not to elope with Catherine immediately, even when she is willing, further proves that his interest is in the inheritance alone. He sees the plan to take Catherine to Europe as an opportunity for Sloper to become accustomed to the match, rather than offering any fear that Catherine might forget him or fall out of love.

In desperation, as he knows no other way of preventing the match after the European trip evidently fails, Sloper tells Catherine that Morris must be after her money because she is neither beautiful nor clever. Crushed by her father's cruel candor, Catherine jumps at the opportunity to elope with Morris. Yet Morris cannot agree without the chance that Sloper can be placated, and since Catherine makes it clear they will never receive anything from her father, it is little surprise to the audience that Morris never keeps their appointment. Her revenge in the final scene perfectly mirrors this earlier betrayal. In the two-year interim, she has become dignified and attractive, to such a degree that Morris finds her personally admirable beyond her wealth. Just as he had avoided an embrace when leaving Catherine, she now does the same to him, though he, as she had been, is too excited at the prospect of their marriage to notice. "Yes, I can be cruel," Catherine tells her aunt, as she turns the tables on Morris. "I have been taught by masters!" (89). It is clear that Catherine's innocent heart has been so hardened by her experiences that she will never allow herself to love anyone again.

Love Letters gives us extracts from notes and letters that the fictitious Andrew Ladd III and Melissa Gardner have written to each other since they were children. As children they tease, cajole, and begin to share their dreams and desires. She will only be his Valentine as long as she does not have to kiss him. As they mature, they begin to consider a sexual relationship, but since they are sent to different private schools and summer camps, and are rarely home at the same time, they never get the chance. When Andy invites Melissa to attend his school dance, she goes off with someone else, telling him that he felt too much like a brother, yet his resulting fling with Gretchen upsets her. They try again at college, but he feels too pressured to perform. And so it goes, through his Navy service and relationship with a Japanese woman, his marriage, children, and election to political office, and her two marriages, children, artistic highs and lows, and several breakdowns. They have a brief affair but, fearful of his political standing, and unsure of the wisdom of a relationship with such a volatile woman, Andy ends it, and a few months later Melissa kills herself. The final letter is one Andy wrote to Mrs. Gardner after the funeral, assessing his relationship with Melissa.

The two are very different characters. Andy is the more staid of the two. Coming from a stable family background may be part of this, but he is the type who likes to do what is expected of him, never shake the boat, and keep things orderly. Melissa, on the other hand, is free-spirited and rebellious, making Andy seem like a prude by comparison, but she is also far less secure. She has a disastrous family background, with a mother who drinks and repeatedly divorces and remarries, a father whom she has written out of her life, and a stepfather who tries to molest her. It is unsurprising that she turns out emotionally unstable with bouts of alcoholism and depression. To underscore their characters, she becomes an artist, and he, first a lawyer, then a successful politician.

People often write in letters things they can never say out loud and use their writing to extend their world by forging a connection with another person. Andy offers this as a reason why he enjoyed exchanging letters with Melissa: he was able to live vicariously through her, and have a more exciting life. Yet writing is also problematic because of the slippery nature of words, which in letter form can be as concealing as they are revealing, and the letter can become a way of avoiding connection. As Gurney points out, "Writing is what brings Andy and Melissa together, but it is also what keeps them apart" (viii). Andy is the one who prefers that they write rather than talk on the phone, and it is he who puts an end to the possibility of their physical relationship, choosing to end their affair and stay with his wife. He insists that they keep writing, since he needs his connection to Melissa, but he uses the letters to control her and keep her at a safe distance. Understanding this, she feels she has nothing left for which to live, and her suicide comes as little surprise.

What may be more surprising is Andy's final declaration of love in the letter he writes to her mother after the funeral. It seems like his only moment of real honesty, something he has only just discovered and admitted to himself. Prior to this, his letters have mostly been evasions designed to keep Melissa attached but not too close. At one point, after their failed attempt to get together at college, Melissa exclaims, "I know you more from your LETTERS than I do in person" (28), and suggests that they stop writing if they really want to get closer. But he insists that they continue to write because, "I love writing to you . . . I feel like a true lover when I'm writing to you" (29). But what he gives her is mostly fake, his own creation, and not the real Andy Ladd. Andy rarely commits to paper his deepest feelings, or anything personally honest; hence his silence when he's in Japan, and his refusal to write about what happened there.

While Andy's declaration that he thought he gave Melissa a sense of balance is met by a mocking look, she thanks him for admitting, "I don't think I've ever loved anyone the way I loved her, and I know I never will again. She was at the heart of my life, and already I miss her desperately" (55). After all his evasions and compromises, he finally speaks from the heart and acknowledges what he has lost though his own timidity. The way Gurney has their sentences blur together during the brief period of their earlier affair conveys the excitement of that time, and the suggestion that these two, at that moment, were able to speak with one voice, contrary to the numerous disagreements and criticisms that had gone before. However, Andy selfishly chooses career and comfort over this excitement, and only discovers now, after her death, how much poorer his future life will be as a result of this sacrifice.

FURTHER SUGGESTED READING

Amoia, Alba della Fazia. *Edmond Rostand*. Boston: Twayne, 1978.

Bell, Ian F. A. *Washington Square*. New York: Twayne, 1993.

Cate, Rodney M., and Sally A. Lloyd. *Courtship*. Newbury Park, CA: Sage, 1992.

Chweh, Crystal R., Ed. *Readings on* Cyrano de Bergerac. San Diego: Greenhaven, 2001.

Goetz, Ruth, and Augustus Goetz. *The Heiress*. New York: DPS, 1948.

Gurney, A. R. *Love Letters*. New York: Plume, 1990.

Inge, William. *Bus Stop*. New York: DPS, 1956.

Murstein, Bernard I. *Paths to Marriage*. Beverly Hills: Sage, 1986.

Rostand, Edmond. *Cyrano de Bergerac*. Trans. Charles Marowitz. Lyme, NH: Smith and Kraus, 1995.

Wilde, Oscar. *The Importance of Being Earnest*. London: Nick Hern, 1995.

Death

Riders to the Sea by John M. Synge (1904)
Bury the Dead by Irwin Shaw (1936)
'night Mother by Marsha Norman (1983)

The appearance of death, attitudes toward it, and its impact on those left behind are common themes in modern drama, as in all literature. While some playwrights seek placatory justification for their characters' deaths, others portray them as a senseless waste. We see a consideration of both perspectives in J. M. Synge's *Riders to the Sea*, with its Biblical references and the tragic death of a woman's husband and six sons. While Synge ensures that we understand that these men were needlessly lost through poverty, we also see a mother comforted by her faith.

The contraction of religious belief among many during the past century has affected attitudes toward death. Because of a wavering belief in the afterlife and the suspicion that death may not be part of some greater plan, it has become harder to view death as reward or salvation; instead, it is seen more as a needless loss. Because of the countless deaths caused by war during this period, from two world wars to more recent conflicts, including those in Korea, Vietnam, and the Persian Gulf, it is unsurprising that a number of modern plays consider the plight of the soldier killed in conflict, encompassing the feelings of those killed, the reactions of officers, relatives, and friends, as well as possible rationales for such slaughter. A prime example of this is Irwin Shaw's *Bury the Dead*, which takes place during the "second year of the war that is to begin tomorrow night" (5). It takes as its premise the refusal of the slain to be buried, through which Shaw explores social perceptions of death, most particularly at times of war, from the side of both the living and the dead.

Not everyone clings to life so tenaciously. There is also the issue of suicide, the person who decides to take his or her own life, a topic that is explored in sympathetic detail in Marsha Norman's *'night Mother*. A number of modern plays, such as Brian Clark's *Whose Life is It Anyway?* (1978), deal with people who are terminally ill or approaching death through aging, and the focus in most of these plays is on how the living communicate with the dying, and on how to die. In 'night Mother the decision to die has been made before the play begins. Whether or not Jessie will commit suicide is not the issue; more to the point is why, and we are shown how the mother reacts to her daughter's drastic decision.

Set on Aran, an impoverished island off Ireland, Riders to the Sea begins with two sisters, Cathleen and Nora, hiding evidence of their brother Michael's drowning. They decide that it is better for their mother, Maurya, not to know for sure that he has been drowned because her hope for his return partly sustains her. Bartley, Maurya's last remaining son, prepares to transport two horses across to the mainland for sale. Full of superstition, the women worry, and their fears come true. As Bartley rides to the sea on his red mare, Maurya has a vision of his ghostly brother riding behind him on the other, grey pony, and soon after we hear that the grey has knocked Bartley into the sea to his death.

Our focus is not on the multiple deaths, but on how the living are affected by them and how they cope with their seemingly endless mourning. Synge engages our sympathy for the women as they vainly wait for the men of their family to return. They have their faith tested by a never-ending stream of misfortune. Bartley reportedly told his sister that for his mother's sake he cannot die: "Almighty God won't leave her destitute . . . with no son living" (176), even though he knows there is a strong chance he won't survive. It turns out that God does just this; yet Maurya's faith is sufficient to sustain her. Making the best of events, she finds comfort in the belief that all of her male children are now together, and she has no more sons left to grieve, so she can finally relax. As she stoically declares, "No man at all can be living forever, and we must be satisfied" (189).

Her stoicism is born of her faith, and religious references run throughout the play. The title reflects passages from Exodus (15:1)— "The horse and his rider hath He thrown into the sea"—and Revelations (6:1–8)—"And I looked and beheld a pale horse: and his name that sat on it was Death." These combine to convey the fated nature of Bartley's end. Besides these biblical allusions, there are further echoes in the way the three women sprinkle holy water on Michael's clothing, reminiscent of the three women anointing the body of Jesus on Easter morning, and indicative of the resurrected vision Maurya has just had of Michael.

However, this Christian belief is blended with pagan superstition. Beliefs that the dead often cause the death of a loved one out of loneliness, and that they dislike people using their former possessions, condemn Bartley on two counts. He dies as company for his brother or as punishment for wearing his brother's shirt. It is also significant that Maurya cannot give Bartley her bless-ing while holding Michael's stick. The point is that in such a community the dead are viewed as having power beyond their demise, perhaps because they so outnumber the living.

Despite the high tide, extreme wind, and persuasions of the local priest enlisted by Maurya to keep him home, Bartley insists on making this trip. But it is the family's extreme poverty that forces him to go and not any death wish: they desperately need the money he can obtain from the sale. Their poverty is emphasized by the squabble Bartley has with his sister over using a piece of rope to make a halter for the horse: even such a small item has extreme value in this impoverished household. As the last surviving male, Bartley feels compelled to provide for his family.

With no source of income available on the island, the men of Aran are forced to face the hostile and dangerous waters that surround them to prove their manhood, and the women cannot stop them. Never seeing Michael, but just the remnants of his clothing, is a powerful symbol of the depths to which a man can be reduced by the elements: a pile of worthless rags. To illustrate mankind's continual and often tragic struggle against nature, Maurya loses six children and her husband all to the sea. The white boards that have been set aside to create a coffin for Michael when his drowned body is found are now to be used for Bartley, once the family can afford the nails—the play ending with another indication of the extreme poverty of these people's lives.

What should be a place of safe haven, a loving family, is turned upside down by death, as Maurya's speech indicates on taking Michael's walking stick: "In the big world the old people do be leaving things after them for their sons and children, but in this place it is the young men do be leaving things behind for them that do be old" (181). What hope for the future is left for these people as their young men disappear? A culture cannot be sustained by the women and elderly alone. There is a sense of dreadful waste verging on apocalypse as we watch a community become decimated by poverty and pointless death, and the women forced to struggle on alone, despite any comfort given to them by their faith.

Bury the Dead exposes the randomness of death, as it questions the validity of wars, and forces us to acknowledge the humanity within a pile of corpses. In the middle of a battlefield, a burial detail complain while digging a grave for their fallen comrades, but they do not perceive those they bury as human with any rights to individuality, as the collective grave indicates. A priest and rabbi arrive to pray for them, but the dead stand up and refuse to be buried, wanting to maintain their connection to the living world. Superior officers, priests, and the partners and relatives of the dead all unsuccessfully try to persuade them to lie down in their grave. One of their own generals tries to shoot them down, but they just walk away. Devastated by his failure, he is forced to watch as the living soldiers join the dead in a walkout on the institution of war. Shaw has pointed out a simple solution to war: if people refuse to fight, then a war cannot occur.

From the play's start we are made aware of the soldiers' reluctance to kill, as the First Soldier declares, referring to the enemy, "I get a lot more pleasure killin' rats then killin' them" (7). These are not professional soldiers, but men drafted for the war, taken away from their regular lives, and death scares them. The examining doctor's descriptions of how each of the dead men died is a litany of the terrible things that happen to soldiers in the course of a conflict. These living soldiers are initially uncomfortable with their dead fellows-at-arms, but the openness of their fallen comrades gradually wins them over; they exchange cigarettes, sing, and finally combine forces against the real enemy—the war itself.

Shaw's play raises serious questions about how we view the dead, especially in time of war. Initially it seems that the sergeant is the only one who has any respect for the bodies they are burying, but what he really respects is the way they died, in action. No one wants to recognize the individuality of the deceased, preferring to cover them up as soon as possible with a swift burial so they do not have to think about them, and the church seems complicit in this aim. As the First General declares, "War can be fought and won only when the dead are buried and forgotten" (28). By this, Shaw points out that if people were forced to face the reality of death brought about by such conflicts, they would be less eager to engage in war. The Generals realize that men who refuse to be buried cannot be conveniently forgotten, and this could destroy the morale of those continuing to fight.

The Generals tell the dead that it is their patriotic duty to be buried, but the corpses ignore them; it was patriotism that got them killed in the first place and they want no part of it. The First General declares, "We're a civilized race, we bury our dead" (21), but fails to see the irony in such words—for what truly civilized race so lightly creates so many corpses to be buried? The phrase "bury our dead" begins to take on unpleasant connotations beyond the concept of literal burial. Death is something with which most of us are uncomfortable, so we bury any connection to it as quickly as possible. We use euphemisms, such as "passed on" or "laid to rest," to avoid even talking about death, and insist on heavenly rewards to alleviate our fears about the possible end that death might mean. These dead refuse to accept the notion that "There is peace in the grave" (25), or the religious dogma that people are better off dead so they can enter heaven. They resent having lost their lives for "twenty-five yards of bloody muck" (23), and have decided to make sure others do not make the same mistake.

The Captain challenges the Generals to talk to the corpses directly rather than remain at their usual distance from the men they so casually order into battle. He tries to force them to confront the humanity of the fodder they have been using to prosecute this war, but the Generals resist to the end. But for all his sympathy, the Captain has little more understanding of the needs of the dead than the Generals do. He listens to their complaints, but then imposes his beliefs on them. He insists that the world is an awful place in which they have no rights and "the only sure things are death and despair" (24), so they are better off dead and free of it. The dead disagree, asserting their intention to reclaim the earth for themselves, for they are no longer going to allow themselves to be told what to do by others.

Since superior officers, philosophy, and religion fail to persuade the dead to lie down, various relatives are brought in to try. This achieves exactly what the army had been avoiding—it allows the corpses to become individualized, for when they talk to their nearest living connections we learn something about each of their lives. By humanizing the dead in this way, Shaw prevents us from making death so tidy. A silent corpse may seem devoid of humanity, but when it talks back we are forced to recognize the life that has been lost forever. They are given names, backgrounds, and individual reasons why they do not want to be buried. We also witness individual people's responses to the death of a loved one, which are more personal than those of commanding officers, and further bring these corpses "to life." Webster's wife is the only one who does not ask her husband to lie down; she complains he has taken so long to stand up for himself. For Shaw, her concern applies to all people called up to serve their country in a war in which they cannot personally believe.

In 'night Mother we listen as Jessie Cates prepares her Mama to accept her impending demise. Norman refuses to sentimentalize the play's issues; this is no easy death because of terminal illness but a conscious ending of a life. Jessie is a middle-aged epileptic who, since her divorce, has been living with her mother. She has recently come to a realization of how unhappy her life is. Her decision to commit suicide reflects a need to take control of her life—the loss of control being symbolized, to some extent, by her epilepsy. We are not witnessing a debate so much as an explanation; Mama cannot make Jessie change her mind. Jessie's attempt to rationalize her decision is not for herself, but for her mother. Her effort results in a moment of connection and, possibly, understanding, between the two characters.

When Mama conjures up the accepted clichés by which we tend to regard suicide—suicidal people are overly upset, retarded, deranged, abnormal—we realize that Norman subverts such responses because Jessie is presented as none of the above. Jessie is calm, intelligent, rational, and essentially ordinary. This makes her suicide all the more shocking because its impulse resonates in many of our lives: we can no longer separate ourselves from those who commit suicide as if they have no connection to our "normal lives."

The bedroom door is the focal point of the set so we never lose sight of Jessie's aim—to go into that room and kill herself. The door is a point of both "threat and promise" (3), which encompasses the extreme possibilities of Jessie's act. We are not allowed to expect a dramatic turnaround or rescue, and never doubt that Jessie will successfully commit suicide. The play shows why she has come to this decision and how her mother reacts. Though Jessie tells her mother about her plan to commit suicide in advance, this is neither a cry for help nor an indication that she wishes to be stopped; it is not a spur-of-the-moment decision. Jessie has waited until she feels well before going through with her suicide plans, and her desire to kill herself cannot be attributed to her illness, but goes deeper.

Norman establishes familiarity with a realistic set, colloquial speech, and the mundane activities Jessie performs. This is stripped away as Jessie announces her decision to kill herself, and the two characters struggle for control. Jessie has the advantage of surprise, but Mama rallies and tries to bring reason, threats, bribes, and diversions to bear, even suggesting that Jessie may foul up and end up as a vegetable. What she has not grasped is that Jessie already feels like a vegetable. When Mama tries to take responsibility for the suicide onto herself, Jessie objects: "It doesn't have anything to do with you!" (72), and she is right. Mama finally sees this and acknowledges Jessie's autonomy, allowing her to claim ownership of herself.

Jessie's decisive, competent actions contrast with her appearance, which is "vaguely unsteady" (2). Her paleness suggests the paucity of her life spirit. Jessie's control is only psychological, and she is forever threatened by a physical betrayal. For this reason alone, her current sense of determination and control offers her something she cannot afford to ignore. It gives her an energy and a "sense of purpose" (2) she has lacked all her life. Always a loner, people, including her own family, tend to avoid contact with her, for Jessie makes them uncomfortable. She never leaves the house; Jessie and her mother even have their groceries delivered. Her mother is a stranger to Jessie, despite the familiarity of living together in a regular routine. Jessie's life has become little more than a series of lists and schedules. The house is filled with Mama's clutter rather than a joint mess, for Jessie's presence has left no mark, indicating how little of Jessie actually remains.

Given the person Jessie has become, she feels she has no future, so she may as well end it now rather than live on without hope. In doing so she takes charge. Tired of having other people rule her life, she wants control for herself. She has logically eliminated every reason she might have had for remaining alive: "I'm just not having a very good time and I don't have any reason to think it'll get anything but worse. I'm tired. I'm hurt. I'm sad. I feel used" (28). Jessie's belief and action are not meant to be an answer for others; this is merely what Jessie believes is true for herself. All she has left that is her own is her life, and she declares her right to say "no" to it. She embraces death as her only remaining choice.

Yet Norman still allows us to sympathize with Mama as a survivor with her guilt as she mourns the loss of her daughter. Part of the play's strength comes from Norman allowing us to sympathize with both Jessie and Mama. Both are given an opportunity to confess and unburden themselves of various failures and jealousies. Mother and daughter finally manage not only authentic communication, but intimacy. Such a moment gives Mama something to live for. Her life, in many ways, has been as empty as Jessie's, yet she chooses to live—

just as rationally as Jessie chooses to die. As she tells us: "I don't know what I'm here for, but then I don't think about it" (49).

FURTHER SUGGESTED READING

Brown, Linda Ginter. *Marsha Norman: A Casebook.* New York: Garland, 1996.

Clark, Brian. *Whose Life is it Anyway?* New York: Dodd, Mead, 1978.

Giles, James Richard. *Irwin Shaw.* Boston: Twayne Publishers, 1983.

Hawkins, Anne Hunsaker, James O. Ballard, and Theodore Blaisdell, Eds. *Time to Go: Three Plays on Death and Dying.* Philadelphia: University of Pennsylvania Press, 1995.

Kastenbaum, Robert. *Death, Society, and Human Experience.* New York: Merrill, 1991.

Kiely, David M. *John Millington Synge: A Biography.* Dublin: Gill & Macmillan, 1994.

King, Mary C. *The Drama of J. M. Synge.* Syracuse, NY: Syracuse University Press, 1985.

Moller, David Wendell. *Confronting Death: Values, Institutions, and Human Mortality.* New York: Oxford University Press, 1996.

Norman, Marsha. *'Night Mother.* New York: Hill and Wang, 1983.

Shaw, Irwin. *Bury the Dead.* New York: DPS, 1936.

Shnayerson, Michael. *Irwin Shaw: A Biography.* New York: Putnam, 1989.

Synge, J. M. *Riders to the Sea.* In *Five Great Modern Irish Plays.* Ed. George Jean Nathan. New York: Random House, 1941: 173–89.

Treadwell, Sophie. *Machinal.* London: Nick Hern, 1993.

Decisions and Life Choices

The Price by Arthur Miller (1968)
Krapp's Last Tape by Samuel Beckett (1958)
The Cherry Orchard by Anton Chekhov (1904)

As the twentieth century progressed, it seemed that people were being offered more and more choices regarding the way they lived their lives. Be it in relationships, education, religion, or job opportunities, choices had become almost a way of life, and the resulting decisions could affect each and every life.

Modern drama responded to a growing concern with making the right choice by depicting characters like the Franz brothers in Arthur Miller's play *The Price* who each make definite choices that affect their outcomes. Although they make those choices willingly, and neither has fared badly in life, each reaches a point where he needs to question if he chose wisely. As Victor complains, "You've got to make decisions before you know what's involved, but you're stuck with the results anyway" (47). The play considers the way all too many of us live our lives, caught between illusion and reality, fearful of facing the truth, and resentful of the lives of others, ever wondering if the price we paid for what we have was worth it.

In *Krapp's Last Tape* by Samuel Beckett we meet a character who clearly made all the wrong choices and comes to an understanding of this as we witness him assessing his life one final time. Although the play is less overtly comic than many absurdist works, it remains true to the essential tenets of absurdist drama that Beckett helped to pioneer. The aim of Theater of the Absurd is not to depict lives as ridiculous, as much as devoid of purpose and without recognizable meaning, and that succinctly describes the life of Krapp, whose excremental name is certainly intentional.

Anton Chekhov, on the other hand, is famous for his ability to realistically portray those who avoid choice and decisions and live their lives in a kind of suspended animation because they do not have the courage to break free of the familiar and their routines. *The Cherry Orchard* depicts a group of characters who mostly seem utterly unable to act decisively, even when such action appears both feasible and possible. Chekhov called the play a comedy, but the play's first director, Constantine Stanislavsky, considered it a tragic expression of Russian life, and the text hovers between the two. Written while Chekhov was dying of tuberculosis, which may account for its preoccupation with weariness and the futility of human behavior, it was his final play.

The Price introduces us to the Franz brothers, Victor and Walter, who meet after a long estrangement while selling off their deceased father's belongings. Having sacrificed a scientific career to become a New York cop and look after his father, Victor is uncertain that he made the right choices. His brother Walter, who broke away from the family, became a surgeon, but we discover that he is no more satisfied with his life. The two brothers meet, argue, and part, and it seems to be the semiretired furniture dealer, Gregory Solomon, waiting for them to agree on a price for the furniture, who understands how life works.

Victor Franz is an archetypal underachiever; a good son and husband, who sacrificed his ambition to ensure the security of his family. His brother, Walter, is an archetypal overachiever; a successful, wealthy surgeon and entrepreneur. While Victor is initially awed by the attic and its contents (which represent their family past), Walter is merely amused—offering a sense of how each brother perceives his family ties. Walter likes to live firmly in the here and now, erasing the past almost from memory, which is why he is so uninterested in what happens to his family's belongings. But Victor has tremendous nostalgia, trying, through objects like his father's old records, to recreate the time when his family was still together. The two brothers take opposing views on everything and, from their polarized positions, have become unnecessarily embittered and jealous of one another.

As products of the same background, the brothers illustrate the extreme possibilities within every person's life, only restricted or freed by the choices that each of us makes. Walter suggests that, because of past decisions, they both feel they have only lived half a life. But both appear to have got what they wanted from life—Victor, love, and Walter, fame and fortune—and for this each paid "the price." For Victor, the price was the sacrifice of fame and fortune, and for Walter, the sacrifice of love. Although it seems that together they make a whole, both have made a difference by their separate lives, but neither gains complete satisfaction from this, each wanting, in some part, the other's life. All their talk does is show them that what they thought they had achieved may not have been so real after all, which leads them to further resentment and dissatisfaction. Solomon is right in his suggestion that it is sometimes better not to talk too much, but just to accept life at face value and enjoy what you have.

Miller does not want us to choose one brother over the other but to sympathize with both for what they have lost, and admire each one for what he has achieved. Sadly, they are unable to bury their resentment of each other to do this. Each is equally ignorant of the costs the other has faced; Walter cannot understand why Victor gave up college to look after their father, assuming that Victor quit so he could live a "real life" (82). Similarly, Victor knows nothing about Walter's breakdown and divorce caused by the intense pressure of his lifestyle, and assumes that he lives a life of ease. Both are proud of their careers when challenged, but that nagging jealousy of what each perceives the other to have won will not allow them to get past their anger and shame.

Walter and Victor each remember the past differently, coloring it with their own individual interpretations. Walter insists there was no love in their family, to justify having left it, while Victor insists that love was there to justify having stayed. Victor rejects Walter's attempts to make amends because he cannot accept Walter's view of what happened, just as Walter cannot accept Victor's rationale because it would make him look the villain. In reality, Walter lost his wife and children because that was the price he had to pay for the professional success he craved, just as Victor lost his science career because family meant more to him. Both made the decisions they made willingly, and for all their dissatisfaction, would probably make the same choices again if given a second chance.

Victor's wife, Esther, also voices dissatisfaction with how her life has turned out, and drinks too much to ease her frustration. She is desperate for a more glamorous life free of money worries. But like her husband, she, too, made choices that have led to this point; it is partly to satisfy her needs that Victor remained on the force for so long. Despite their struggle for money, Victor and Esther have a happy marriage on which they can look back fondly and laugh, which is more than Walter can do.

Their father had given up because he believed in the system and could not cope with failure when that system broke down during the Depression. Losing both his wife and most of his fortune almost simultaneously was too much for him to bear. As Victor explains, "Some men just don't bounce" (45). He burdened Victor with his remaining life, pretending destitution to avoid being alone. Walter sees this as despicable, but Victor sees it as truly pitiable.

Solomon, the wise figure his namesake suggests, witnesses the brothers' struggle but refuses to takes sides, knowing the struggle is pointless. This is a character who understands the ironies of life, and, after three wives and a daughter who committed suicide, he knows what he is talking about. His philosophy is to accept whatever happens and not get stuck trying to change or even understand the past. As he explains, if his dead daughter came back to life, "what would I say to her?" (113). Despite his eighty-nine years, he exudes life and humor, and the play ends with his laughter, which is, finally, the only effective response to catastrophe, a response the Franz family should keep in mind.

Krapp's Last Tape introduces us to Krapp, who at the age of twenty-four began recording a tape every year on his birthday, reviewing a previous year before making the new tape. Now turning sixty-nine, he begins by listening to a tape he made thirty years previously, at which time he had just listened to a tape from about ten years before. Thus, the audience receives a picture of Krapp's life and development from his twenties to the end of his sixties. We learn what decisions have affected this man's life to reduce him to his current poverty and shabbiness.

At thirty-nine, Krapp had seen himself "at the . . . crest of the wave" (14), and his decision to reject love and life seemed an amazing insight, but at sixty-nine he considers this moment the start of his downfall. He fast-forwards the tape at the point when his younger self is about to announce his revelation, for it is an insight in which the sixty-nine-year-old has lost interest. Instead, Krapp is looking for the description of an encounter with the girl he decided back then to abandon. The final image he relates is of the pair of them getting stuck in the weeds while out boating, and all around them life goes on. This turns out to have been the moment when his whole life became stuck, and he ceased to move for good.

The importance of setting the play in the future is manifold. There is a practical element, in that when this play was written the tape recorder was a new invention and Beckett needed to set the play in the future at a time when it was realistic for Krapp to have been making tapes for forty-six years. But it also helps to underline Krapp's relation to us all and ensure that he is not relegated to the past where he can be deemed irrelevant to our current lives. Furthermore, it carries the suggestion that the play might only offer a possible future, which may be changed before we travel too far on the path Krapp has chosen.

Krapp begins the play as a clown figure with his purple nose, white face, and baggy, ill-fitting clothes, performing a "routine" with his banana peel. We are soon forced to see the direct contrast between this comic appearance and his tragic inner life. The potential humor of the opening is quickly deflated as we learn of the alienation toward which this man's ego has forced him—a life of waste and loss. Every one of Krapp's felt experiences has been of loss—of his father, mother, lovers, and, finally, of himself. Krapp at sixty-nine is a picture of humanity reduced to nothingness, as he has stripped himself of all connection to others, which is what makes us human after all, in his quest for something that simply cannot be known.

Krapp's evidently restricted senses of sight and hearing are indicative of the restricted life he has forced himself to lead. His shabby, ridiculous, outer appearance has become a mere reflection of his impoverished, shabby, and ridiculous inner life, now that he has wasted his potential. As we learn more about him, we begin to see his long and barren life filled with meager pleasures— alcohol, bananas, occasional sex, and an obsession with words—which are his only distractions in the dark hole he now inhabits. Set apart from work, love, family, religion, and companionship, Krapp's few remaining pleasures have become meaningless even to him.

Krapp has exchanged a "real" life of feeling for a "reel" life of mechanization. Since the earlier Krapp is only on tape, rather than a figure on the stage, he is dehumanized. We see how Krapp's misguided impulses have created a flawed human being who has become like his tape recordings: prone to repetition and eventual silence. His behavior is mechanistic and his body a faulty machine beyond repair, highlighted by his lifetime problem with constipation. Krapp talks back to his machine, but he cannot really communicate; it is, after all, only a machine. His reactions and responses cannot affect the other speaker; all he can do is to switch himself on or off. His taped voice, likewise, cannot communicate with him as it is only a mechanical voice from the past, and no longer exists. His rituals are the only remaining way he has of announcing his existence. By the end of the play, however, he has lost both the desire and capacity for even these empty rituals, and so must cease to exist.

There is a distinct contrast between the strong and pompous voice of Krapp at thirty-nine and the cracked tones and halting diction of Krapp at sixty-nine. His voice, just like his life, has dried up. When he begins to record the tape for his sixty-ninth birthday, Krapp cannot complete it for he runs out of words. Instead, he returns to his "farewell to love" (13) and becomes lost in regret. He describes his thirty-nine-year-old self as a "stupid bastard" (24) and denigrates him as he recognizes the major mistakes he has made. He never should have chosen to ignore the larger world and concentrate on himself in the way he did. In retrospect, he can find no justification for his choice to withdraw from the larger world, because that choice has led him to achieve nothing and to reach nothing but a dead end. His great book only sold seventeen copies.

Krapp has come to the end of his recording project because he has nothing left to record. His life no longer has any point, and he has reduced it to such a state. At thirty-nine he believed he was making the right decision to rid himself of all "distractions" and could not see how he would ever regret such a decision—at sixty-nine, we see that regret. The past thirty years have been a total waste, for those distractions he has rid himself of were his life and he has lost them for good. There truly is nothing left to say as the tape runs on in silence. We are left, finally, with a stark and unpromising image of Krapp, isolated in an encroaching darkness, bleakly registering his lonely failure by complete silence.

At the start of *The Cherry Orchard*, Madam Ranyevskaia returns, impoverished, to her Russian estate. Unable to raise sufficient funds to pay off the mortgage, the estate is sold at auction to local businessman Lopakhin, who intends to build holiday villas on the property, an idea he had suggested the family try, but which they had refused. Unable to sacrifice the cherry orchard, which reminds them of their childhood and the family's former glory, Ranyevskaia and her brother Gayev lose the whole estate.

Frustrated by their refusal to accept reality or act on their predicament, Lopakhin declares, "I've never met such feckless, unbusiness-like, queer people

as you are" (358). Although Lopakhin's idea may seem like an excellent solution to the family dilemma, in the way it destroys the cherry orchard—the
play ends with the sounds of an ax chopping down the trees—it implies a
destructive rather than a constructive impulse. Lopakhin frequently recalls his
lowly origins, and the decimation of the estate seems, in part, as a way to exact
revenge on the estate to which his father and grandfather were bound as serfs.
This is despite Lopakhin's apparent gratitude toward the family for aid they
have given him in the past. Chekhov's personal opinion of villas was that they
were venues of tedium and futility, in which nothing of note was ever achieved.
Lopakhin is a member of the new bourgeois order rising in Russia, part of the
growing revolutionary ferment in the country that had been increasing over
the past twenty years and would culminate in the Russian Revolution of 1917.
However, Lopakhin's failure to propose to Varia marks him as another inde-
cisive character, despite his business acumen. He is unable to find meaning in
anything deeper than materialistic acquisition.

Ranyevskaia and Gayev are representatives of the old Russian aristocracy,
prone to decadence and irresponsibility, unable to preserve itself. The nursery
in which we begin and end highlights their childish irresponsibility and romantic illusions, which make them so ineffective. Ranyevskaia has been abroad
for five years, avoiding memories of her young son's death. While in France
she lived with a lover who disappeared when her money ran out. Her daughter
Ania discovered her living in poverty and has brought her home. Ranyevskaia
is kind-spirited but undignified and immoral by the standards of her time. She
largely survives by refusing to recognize her impoverishment, lending money
she cannot afford to Pishchik, who is similarly in debt, and spending irrespon-
sibly. Prone to emotional outbursts, she continuously reacts, but rarely acts,
incapable of even running her own estate. At the close, she plans to return to
her lover using the money sent by a relative to try to buy back the estate.

Just as Ranyevskaia hides from her responsibilities in her love affairs, Gayev
resorts to billiards to escape from his incompetency at life. During the three
months over which the play takes place, he is unable to raise sufficient funds
to even pay off the interest on the mortgage. Like their neighbor, Pishchik, he
tries to stay optimistic, but his luck seems far worse. Pishchik is saved by
various resources discovered on his property, but the once-profitable cherries
from the orchard can no longer be sold since no one recalls the popular recipe
once used to dry them for the market, so Gayev cannot save the estate. He
takes a job at the local bank, but Lopakhin insists that it will not be for long,
since Gayev is too lazy to work.

Varia and Ania, Ranyevskaia's daughters, are the next generation. More
focused than their elders, Varia plans to join a convent, since Lopakhin is evidently incapable of commitment, but one wonders if this will really suit her
spirit. Ania plans to elope with perpetual student Trofimov, whose optimism
about a better future would be more convincing if he himself could complete

his degree or stay in one place. Like so many of Chekhov's characters, Trofimov likes to glorify the concept of hard work without actually doing any himself. Ania is initially upset at losing the family estate, but her youthful optimism leads her to look for a new and better life elsewhere. However, the vagueness of her plan provides little real hope that this will be accomplished, especially attached to a man who refuses to fully commit by declaring them to be "above falling in love" (367).

The servant class seems no more decisive. Dooniyasha is torn between the accident-prone Yepihodov, who has proposed marriage, and her unreciprocated admiration for Yasha, who toys with her affections as he waits for an opportunity to return to Paris with Ranyevskaia. Yepihodov declares that he cannot decide whether "to live or to shoot myself" (355), but like everyone else, he does nothing. Gayev's ancient manservant, Feers, who sees freedom as a misfortune and desires a return to feudal days, is as decrepit as the system he praises, and provides no better solution. Perpetually worried about the family's health, ironically and pointedly he is left ill and alone at the close, as the family to whom he has given his life leaves, having forgotten to take him to the hospital.

Trofimov sums up everyone's problem, "We just philosophize and complain of depression, or drink vodka" (368), and he is as guilty of this as the rest. All of them prefer to talk rather than act. Yet at the play's end there is an air of hope. This is perhaps not so much for that better future Ania vaguely describes, as relief over not having been forced to make any firm decisions. The play began with an arrival and ends with a departure, with little in between that was substantially altered or completed beyond the estate changing ownership; relationships and futures remain incomplete as no one has the strength to make the necessary commitment. It is unsurprising that the last person we see is Feers, drained of strength, lying down on the stage, a fitting metaphor for the entire cast.

FURTHER SUGGESTED READING

Beckett, Samuel. *Krapp's Last Tape*. New York: Grove, 1960.

Chekhov, Anton. *The Cherry Orchard*. In *Plays*. Hammersmith, U.K.: Penguin, 1951: 331–98.

Elder, Lonnie, III. *Ceremonies in Dark Old Men*. New York: Farrar, Straus and Giroux, 1969.

Gilman, Richard. *Chekhov's Plays*. New Haven: Yale University Press, 1995.

Griffin, Alice. *Understanding Arthur Miller*. Columbia: University of South Carolina Press, 1996.

Knowlson, James. *Samuel Beckett,* Krapp's Last Tape: *A Theatre Workbook*. London: Brutus, 1980.

Miller, Arthur. *The Price*. New York: Viking, 1968.

Otten, Terry. *The Temptation of Innocence in the Dramas of Arthur Miller*. Columbia: University of Missouri Press, 2002.

Peace, Richard. *Chekhov: A Study of the Four Major Plays.* New Haven: Yale University Press, 1983.

Smith, Joseph H., Ed. *The World of Samuel Beckett.* Baltimore: John Hopkins University Press, 1991.

Williams, Tennessee. *Sweet Bird of Youth, A Streetcar Named Desire, The Glass Menagerie.* Harmondsworth, U.K.: Penguin, 1962.

Growing Up

Member of the Wedding by Carson McCullers (1950)
Brighton Beach Memoirs by Neil Simon (1982)
The Glass Menagerie by Tennessee Williams (1945)

Adolescent concerns regarding burgeoning feelings of sexuality, responsibility, and social connection have been the subject of many modern dramas. The children we witness growing up in these plays are as varied as the problems they face. But wherever they reside, all are teenagers facing typical adolescent concerns regarding their place in society and their relationship to others. In many plays, writers draw on their own experience growing up, making the drama as much confession as a representation of the joys, dilemmas, and difficulties children face as they turn into adults. Modern dramatists are largely in agreement that adolescence is a period of profound change, and one that needs sympathetic treatment, and, to this end, many representations of adolescence on the stage have been depicted, predominantly, from the child's point of view.

Carson McCullers's *Member of the Wedding* was first published as a novel in 1946, but she adapted it into a play four years later at the suggestion of Tennessee Williams, who saw its dramatic possibilities. Though McCullers only wrote one more play, her contribution to drama is important in the way in which she went against traditional dramatic structures of the time in *Member of the Wedding*. By constructing a play that consists mostly of dialogue with very little action, she helped to expand the boundaries of theatrical possibility. The play portrays the development of twelve-year-old Frankie Addams from childhood into teenage adolescence.

Brighton Beach Memoirs by Neil Simon is the first of a semi-autobiographical trilogy about fourteen-year-old Eugene Jerome (Neil Simon) and his upbringing in Depression-era Brooklyn. We witness Eugene discover puberty and the complicated interrelationship between family members that ensures the continued survival of all. Eugene, like Simon, is a keen observer of life, so the action unfolds through his eyes as he comments on what occurs like a teenage Greek Chorus figure.

The Glass Menagerie, by Tennessee Williams, is strongly autobiographical, informed by the adolescent behavior and concerns of the young Thomas "Tennessee" Williams, and his relationship to his mother and his sister Rose. With its portrayal of a family abandoned by the father and a mother who devastates the lives of her children in her efforts to maintain control, we see depicted many of the difficulties faced by adolescents. These difficulties are often caused as much by the failings of their parents as by their own fledgling personalities.

Member of the Wedding follows the development of twelve-year-old Frankie Addams, who grows tired of playing with the young children and wants to become a part of the adult world she sees around her. Her childish plot to join her brother on his honeymoon and be accepted by this adult world is easily defeated, so she runs away in disappointment. Realizing that this, too, is an inappropriate response, she returns home after she cools down and stops trying to accelerate her growth. By the play's end she has grown past her reliance on the motherly Berenice, been accepted by the older children, and is beginning to show an interest in boys.

McCullers saw *Member of the Wedding* as an "inward" drama, in which the movement is propelled by internal conflict rather than external action—that conflict being the development of its protagonist, Frankie Addams. To convey this sense of internal drama, McCullers locates the main actions of the drama offstage—the wedding, Frankie's attempt to go with the newlyweds, and the deaths of young John Henry and Berenice's foster brother, Honey. These events are just reported to the audience. This directs the audience's attention to the emotional effects of these events themselves. We witness Frankie Addams's feelings as she feels trapped between childhood and adulthood and yearns for acceptance in adult society, while still needing the comfort of her childhood world.

Frankie feels isolated and caught between two worlds, those of children and adults, uncomfortable and awkward in each as she plays out the angst of most adolescents regarding her interest in the opposite gender, her fears of being accepted by society, and her annoyance at being treated as a young child. She wants to become a member of the older girls' clubhouse, and is crushed when a contemporary of hers, Mary Littlejohn, has been accepted, but she has not. She is forced to watch and listen from inside the kitchen as the girls cross her yard on the way to their clubhouse and sing their songs.

It is within this kitchen that she seems to be kept as a child, having to play with her seven-year-old cousin, John Henry West. The hot summer kitchen emphasizes her frustration with this childish world she longs to escape. Her restlessness in playing with such young children, and her dissatisfaction with the doll her older brother, Jarvis, has brought her, show her impatience with childhood. She aspires to be an adult like Janice, her brother's fiancée, and resolves to change her name to Jasmine to sound more like her and to accompany her brother and his new wife on their wedding trip. Her desire to be grown up is undercut by her childish expectations about what it will mean to be adult. She has the temper and lack of proper understanding of a child, so it is little wonder that the adults continue to exclude her. The inappropriate outfit she obtains for the wedding further underlines her unpreparedness for the adult world, as does her running away when they refuse to allow her to depart with the newly married couple.

Yet Frankie is twelve, and has a strong desire to embrace adulthood. Her vision of herself as growing from an "I" person into a "me" person, indicates an innate understanding between the self-absorption of childhood, and the more socially demanding world of adulthood, even though she still thinks of boys like Barney MacKean as "nasty." Her fear that she may become a freak because of her height reflects her concern with social norms, as well as her worries about her impending puberty. With her mother dead and her father and older brother emotionally distant and unable to understand the needs of a young girl, it is left to the family's motherly cook, Berenice, to help Frankie through this troubled time, which Berenice does by patiently listening and by offering calm advice.

Berenice comforts Frankie when she needs to be comforted, taking her on her knee as a mother would. So it is significant that by the close of the play Berenice decides not to go with Frankie and her father into their new house; this indicates that Frankie has sufficiently outgrown her need for a mother by this point. We are prepared for Frankie's growth in the final act, by our knowledge that the sheet formerly hung in the arbor as a curtain for Frankie's plays is gone, indicating her changing interests and abandonment of childish games. This is further underlined by Frankie's altered reaction to Barney MacKean, whom she now views as a "Greek god." She has also been accepted by the older girl crowd and no longer feels so isolated. The death of her young cousin could act as an additional symbol of the death of the childhood she has now left behind. Frankie's growth is finally a natural one, reliant on the processes of time that she had unsuccessfully tried to accelerate.

Brighton Beach Memoirs introduces the Jerome family, who are financially struggling to survive during the Depression years. The family's head, Jack Jerome, works at two jobs to support his own family and that of his widowed sister-in-law, Blanche. His eldest son, Stanley, who is eighteen, tries to help, while the younger son, Eugene, only fourteen, takes us through the resulting ups and downs of their endeavors and the changing pressures and relationships between family members, up to news of more relatives likely to join them as Jews begin to flee fascist Europe. Through it all, Eugene explores the world of adult responses and fears that he soon must join.

At turns comic and serious, many of the play's more humorous moments deal with Eugene's burgeoning sexuality as he blackmails his brother into de-

scribing what their cousin Nora looked like when he caught her coming out of
the shower, and the two discuss girls and masturbation. In act two, Stanley
gives his brother a postcard of a nude woman, provoking Eugene to declare to
his journal that his sexual interest is now at a peak. Simon suggests that the
onset of puberty is a time of joy and wonder, and certainly not a shameful
stage of life, as it has been depicted in more Puritanical times.

At fourteen, Eugene still possesses the innocence and idealism of youth,
reflected in the era of comparative innocence in which he was raised, before
the horrors of World War II arrived on the scene. Life was difficult, but not
impossible, and Eugene's optimism and faith in the strength of his parents
serve to make this an uplifting portrayal of a young man growing into manhood. Eugene learns by watching his family about the difficulties and challenges adulthood will bring, and because his family resolve their problems
through compromise, what he learns is predominantly positive.

Although Eugene is the central character, he is only in the initial stages of
growth. Actually on the verge of adulthood are Eugene's brother Stanley, and
their cousin Nora. At eighteen, Stanley already works to add to his family's
income, but finds himself under the threat of being fired unless he writes a
letter of apology for defending a black colleague insulted by his boss. Once
Stanley has explained his principled reasons for having been fired, he continues
to show adult resolve by deciding to apologize as asked to keep the job his
family needs. However, it is not always so easy to make the right decision, and
Stanley is still prone to immature responses, even though he is throughout
motivated by his regard for his family's welfare.

After his father has a heart attack from overwork, Stanley tries to increase
their income by gambling, and loses an entire week's wages. Shamed by his
mistake, he runs away to join the army, but after a day realizes that he needs
to return home. His impulse in this circumstance is a measure of his growth—
he returns home not because he wants to remain a little boy but because he is
ready to fully accept the burdens of adult responsibility and knows his family
needs him with them.

Nora, two years younger than Stanley, has a less secure relationship with
her immediate family, possibly because her father recently died and her mother
suffers from uncertainty. For much of the play Nora and her mother, Blanche,
are at odds, as Nora strives to become independent and her mother worries
about her growing away from her. Nora is given the opportunity to audition
for a professional dance role in a Broadway musical, but Blanche and Jack insist
that she stay in school until she graduates. Nora childishly resents what she
sees as her chance at fame slipping away, refusing to view the larger picture
the adults see. This leads her to treat her mother meanly, until the pair finally
sit down and talk through their mutual fears and needs, and come to a better
understanding and realization of the extent of their love for each other.

The world of adulthood is not shown as an attractive one, but full of
burdensome responsibility, which weighs heavily on Jack, his wife Kate, and

Blanche. Jack shows this strain by his heart attack, and Kate and Blanche in their sisterly dispute as they violently argue and lash out at each other. Kate feels overwhelmed by having to assume Jack's leadership responsibilities while he is sick, and Blanche both grieves for her husband and feels uncomfortable having to rely on her sister's family. Harsh words are exchanged, but finally, like sensible adults, they resolve their dispute, working out a plan by which Blanche can become more independent. In Simon's subsequent plays in this trilogy, we see Jerome grow up into a sensible and responsible figure, which is unsurprising given the flexible and supportive family in which he was raised.

The Glass Menagerie is narrated by Tom Wingfield, who explains why he ran away to sea, leaving his painfully shy, disabled sister, Laura, and domineering mother, Amanda, to fend for themselves. He relates the failed attempts by him and his mother to draw Laura out by sending her to college and by bringing to supper one of Tom's workmates, Jim, who already has a girlfriend, but who momentarily brings Laura out of her shell.

The play is a memory play, and all we are shown is related through the lens of Tom's guilty memory, after he has abandoned his family in search of adventure. Williams's staging captures this emotionally driven mood, as he autobiographically recreates much of his own childhood, with dim lighting, recurring musical themes, and screen images. We watch Tom replay his early life as he recalls the formative moments of his past. Williams too had lived in poverty without a father, dominated by a strong mother, wasting his talents working in a shoe factory, and feeling guilt over his neglect of a shy sister (who had been given a lobotomy in the absence of his protection).

Tom and Laura's father left when they were young, and their mother seems trapped in memories of her youth, as if she has retreated to the past to avoid the impoverished unpleasantness of living in the present and the sad fact that her husband left her. Her efforts to maintain the fantasy she has created of the South and her idealized childhood seem increasingly detrimental to the development of her children. Amanda is even willing to sacrifice her daughter's potential happiness by co-opting Jim, as if he were one of her own suitors, to boost her spirits. She is also as unforgiving of her children as she is of the husband who left, and voices constant disappointment at all they do. It is little wonder that neither exhibits much self-esteem.

As a mother, Amanda is in danger of seeming like a monster. She relies on young Tom as the family provider and so refuses to grant him any freedom to pursue his own dreams, even though she knows he is unhappy. She dominates by maternal privilege, treating him as a small child, for to allow him to see himself as an adult might lead to rebellion. But growth cannot be halted, and as he grows into an adult—ironically, sooner rather than later, given the responsibilities she places on him—Tom tries to rebel, although Amanda quells such moments of rebellion by reminding him of his responsibility to Laura. She forces her illusions on both her children and manipulates them to create her own ideal environment. Through dramatic posturing she ensures their guilt, and uses that to force them into doing what she wants.

Laura hides behind her difference from her mother in a world created for her by her records and glass animals. Her records are old and evoke a euphoric past where she can be happy. Through her glass creatures she creates a safe, innocent world where she is in charge, in contrast to the scary, confusing world she glimpses outside her room—an exaggeration that reveals how many children feel at times. Neither the outside world nor her own mother can accept Laura's extreme sensitivity, but she does not reject the world so much as it rejects her. The only place she has left is her fantasy world. Her home life has been whittled away as her father leaves and then Tom. Outside of her fantasy world she is utterly dependent, so much so that she must even ask her mother what it is she should be wishing for on the moon.

Before leaving, Tom felt trapped in a routine job that was crushing his sensitive spirit and desire to be a writer, but could not quit out of responsibility toward his family. Amanda constantly took pains to remind him of this responsibility to keep him there. At work Tom is as isolated as Laura is at home, and at home Tom feels as though he has been nailed up inside a coffin and cannot breathe. He desperately wants to escape, but Tom cannot leave home as cleanly as his father did, and his only escape, initially, is into dreams of adventure stimulated by the movies. Tom is aware that the movies are not real, but he tells himself they might be because he can see no other form of escape. What he wants is to live someone else's life, as is the case with so many adolescents, because he has no idea what to do with his own.

When Tom does leave it is only a physical escape, as his family continue to psychologically torment him. After his initial sense of freedom, disillusionment sets in and turns to guilt as his imagination transforms innocent and unconnected items into cruel reminders of his poor sister, and Tom becomes trapped by his own remorse—unable to return, but also unable to progress. His feelings of guilt for Laura are greater than Amanda's because he sees Laura's difficulties, whereas Amanda ignores them to avoid such guilt.

Laura is as easily broken as her glass animals, which make up the menagerie of the play's title; her mother's attempts to relive her youth through Laura completely desiccate Laura's last shreds of self-confidence. Amanda continuously expects too much of Laura, especially when she refuses to acknowledge her daughter's limitations. Yet Williams insists that there is "much to admire in Amanda" and we should include love and pity in our judgment of her (228). She is admirable in her endurance, for her life has not been easy: abandoned by a husband and left to raise two children on her own.

Amanda's use of "we" and "us" rather than "you" when talking of Laura, denotes the bond she has forged for her daughter's future—she intends to hold onto Laura for life. But we need not see anything sinister in that, because this ensures Laura's safety as she has no one else. Amanda has been a failure all her life and tries to make up for this by organizing everyone around her and forcing them to be successes. What goes wrong with this plan is her limited imagination; she cannot accept the roads of life her children would choose, and tries to manipulate then onto roads of her own choosing, as do many parents. But, in this case, these are roads that are entirely unsuitable. Laura's job as a secretary and Tom's in the shoe factory are both entirely antagonistic to their natures. Each escapes their mother's plan, but have nowhere else to go, so remain in a kind of "Peter Pan" stasis, unable to fully develop into adults and take on proper social responsibility.

FURTHER SUGGESTED READING

Blos, Peter. *The Adolescent Passage: Developmental Issues.* New York: International University Press, 1979.

Bogasian, Eric. *SubUrbia.* New York: TCG, 1995.

Carr, Virginia Spencer. *Understanding Carson McCullers.* Columbia: University of South Carolina Press, 1989.

Johnson, Robert K. *Neil Simon.* Boston: Twayne, 1983.

Karpel, Mark. *Family Evaluation.* New York: Garner, 1983.

Leverich, Lyle. *Tom: The Unknown Tennessee Williams.* New York: Crown, 1995.

McCullers, Carson. *Member of the Wedding: A Play.* New York: New Directions 1951.

McDowell, Margaret B. *Carson McCullers.* Boston: Twayne, 1980.

McGovern, Edythe M. *Neil Simon: A Critical Study.* New York: Ungar, 1979.

Parker, R. B. *The Glass Menagerie: A Collection of Critical Essays.* Englewood Cliffs, NJ: Prentice Hall, 1983.

Presley, Delma E. The Glass Menagerie: *An American Memory.* Boston: Twayne, 1990.

Simon, Neil. *Brighton Beach Memoirs.* New York: Random House, 1984.

Swados, Elizabeth. *Runaways.* New York: Bantam, 1979.

Williams, Tennessee. *Sweet Bird of Youth, A Streetcar Named Desire, The Glass Menagerie.* Harmondsworth, U.K.: Penguin, 1962.

The Heritage of Slavery

The Piano Lesson by August Wilson (1987)
Slaveship by Imamu Amiri Baraka (1967)
Mulatto by Langston Hughes (1935)

The Drama of King Shotaway (1823), by William Henry Brown, is reputedly the first play known to have been written by an African American, and it was about a slave uprising on the island of St. Vincent. The American history of slavery has had a profound effect on everyone to some degree, but it is those Americans descended from slaves who, understandably, feel it the most. Modern drama has not been shy in provoking African Americans to recognize the nature of their whole history in America as being heavily impacted by the heritage of slavery, mostly with the double view of ensuring that others recognize the institution for the inhumanity and horror that it was, as well as encouraging those with slavery in their past to claim this experience as part of their cultural identity.

The lesson of the piano in August Wilson's *The Piano Lesson* is rooted in the heritage of slavery. Slavery, to Wilson, is a key historical period in the African American sensibility and should not be ignored or forgotten. The African American response to their experience of disinheritance, colonization, and oppression exhibits an incredible resilience of spirit in the very fact that they survived. Just as Jews celebrate their emancipation as a race from Egypt every year at Passover, Wilson believes African Americans should have a similar celebration to remind them of this part of their history. He sees too many African Americans running away from the history of slavery, and insists that it must be squarely faced.

Despite layers of symbolism and a ghostly manifestation, Wilson's play is largely realistic, drawing in its audience with detailed characterizations and gentle humor. Imamu Amiri Baraka's *Slaveship*, by contrast, is a revolutionary drama that is far more confrontational, though it offers many of the same lessons as Wilson's does. The major difference lies in Baraka's anger and violence, which has produced a fiercely uncompromising play, purposefully written and designed to upset white audiences and unite African Americans to demand better treatment. *Slaveship* shows white audiences the source of the rage many African Americans feel at the way they have historically been treated. With little plot and hardly any discursive dialogue, Baraka creates a mood to convey the horrors and repercussions of African American enslavement through a series of symbolic actions and tableaux. The play is a highly ritualized account of the history of African Americans, told in order to provoke a rebellion among living African Americans, who, Baraka believes, still need to cast off the psychic yoke of slavery and claim both heritage and rights from a white society that continues to restrict and enslave its ethnic groups.

Mulatto, by Langston Hughes, is an earlier piece that deals with another aspect of slavery through its exploration of the problems caused by miscegenation. Many white slave owners, to improve their workforce or out of sheer physical desire, slept with female slaves and fathered numerous children. The practice often continued past emancipation, since many former slaves had no means of escaping the plantations that offered them their only source of income. The offspring from these relationships were considered as much slaves or servants as their mothers, but were set apart as "mulattos" and found themselves caught between the world of whites and African Americans, accepted by neither one. *Mulatto* was Langston Hughes's first full-length play. Remarkably, it ran for a year on Broadway and went on to tour, despite only sporadic interest during the 1930s in African American drama. In form, it is a typical melodrama of the period, but its impact is increased by its forthright approach to what would have been an inflammatory contemporary issue.

The Piano Lesson centers on the Charles family and the wrangling between siblings Berniece and Boy Willie over a piano that represents the family's history of enslavement. As the play opens, Boy Willie comes up from the South with his friend, Lymon, to sell a truckload of watermelons and with hopes of selling the family piano to raise funds for a land purchase back home. His sister Berniece, who has moved North to escape the past, will not allow him to sell the piano. The house is haunted by the ghost of Sutter, whose family had owned Berniece and Boy Willie's ancestors in the days of slavery. In order to exorcise this ghost, a decision must be made about the piano, and what evolves is a compromise between the siblings in which the family's history takes precedence.

Berniece and her two uncles, Doaker and Wining Boy, all gain greater self-worth and renew their spirits by reconnecting with their historical and cultural heritage. Being African American to Wilson has little to do with the color of one's skin: it is more a state of mind and a way of viewing the world. He sees too many African Americans as ready to accept negative white assessments of their culture, and insists that they need to define that culture for themselves. Integral to that definition is an embrace and understanding of their own history in America. The catalyst for their learning is the central conflict between Boy Willie and Berniece over the piano, which represents an argument over whether to honor their slave ancestors or put the family's past enslavement behind them.

Boy Willie's desire to sell the piano can be viewed as a desire to be free of the past, but this desire is also his way of honoring his ancestors and building on their heritage. For him, selling the piano is not a denial of the past, but a validation. Berniece, on the other hand, wants to keep the piano, but refuses to pass on its full legacy to her daughter, or accept it into her own life, which does no honor to her family ancestors. Berniece ignores her family legacy, teaching her daughter, Maretha, white community values rather than those values by which her African American family have lived and died.

The opening description of the Charles house tells us that something is wrong because of its "lack of warmth and vigor" (xvii). The people who inhabit this house are not living fully and exist in a kind of deathly stasis. Boy Willie comes to wake the house up, literally and metaphorically. His hollering and bombast will force them to reengage with the world and the past from which they have set themselves apart. Though in his thirties, Boy Willie retains all the vitality and enthusiasm his youthful name implies.

Frustrated by his willingness to work and the lack of opportunity he has been given to do so, Boy Willie's determination to own land stems from a need to ensure that he has work for the future that will benefit him and not whites. He will not settle for the exploitative sharecropping into which his father had been forced. The play's epigraph makes clear Boy Willie's dream and plan for the future: "Gin my cotton/Sell my seed/Buy my baby/Everything she need" (ix). The lyric underlines the importance of tilling your own land. Owning Sutter's land will give him a firmer economic and social footing.

The piano symbolizes the Charles's history of slavery and freedom, and this is something they need to own. Owning the piano strengthens the family; allowing someone else to own it will weaken them all. Boy Charles, Boy Willie's father, knew this, which was the reason he stole the piano in the first place: "Say it was the story of our whole family and as long as Sutter had it . . . he had us. Say we were still in slavery" (45). For Boy Willie to sell the piano to the whites to gain his land acts as a metaphor for assimilation and all its dangers. To play the piano is to claim and possess it, and everything for which it stands: the blood and suffering of the Charles family as well as their strength and spirit.

The piano was first claimed by Boy Willie's great-grandfather, who, in defiance of its white owners, carved his entire family history into the wood. That claim was reaffirmed when Boy Willie's father and uncles stole it from the Sutters. They did this, significantly, on Independence Day, making the act a strong statement of the family's complete independence from the Sutters. Boy Willie takes this claim one step further by trying to claim the original family property from Sutter's heirs. But Boy Willie must learn that it is neither wise nor necessary to sell off any part of your heritage, and it is better to progress by other means.

Sutter represents the role of whites in African American history. His great weight conveys the opulence and greed of a man who has fed off the labor of African Americans for years. But Sutter has fallen, quite literally, as he tumbled down the well. Sutter's time is passing; he is dead, and although his ghostly presence objects, he cannot cover up the decline of his family's control. His brother lives up North and is willing to sell his Southern heritage to "the enemy," in the form of Boy Willie. One of his sons has moved North and the other is an idiot, thus indicating the decline of white power in the South.

The rise of the ghosts of Yellow Dog shows the contrasting growth in power of African Americans in the area. The demise of Sutter and other whites points to an African American ability to wreak vengeance and acts as a warning to whites to behave better in the future. All this should make the way easier for African Americans to take control of their lives in the South, if only they can build the motivation to do so, as Boy Willie intends. Boy Willie's family history has been one of resistance to white control, and it is unsurprising that he chooses the same path.

The repetition of names in the Charles family indicates a strong connection to past generations, but it is a connection Berniece denies. She does not want her peaceful but empty life disrupted by her brother's noise and energy. She resists the life Boy Willie brings into her household, making him unwelcome and devaluing and denigrating all he does. She sees his independence as troublesome: "He don't want to do nothing unless he do it his way" (77). Such independent behavior in an African American is sure to create trouble in the white community, and Berniece prefers the easier road of capitulation.

Berniece is fearful of her heritage and of her own color, and she transmits this self-effacing fear to her own daughter, Maretha, encouraging her to conform to white expectations, teaching her to be quiet and unassuming, greasing down her hair to make her look more like a white girl. She conveys no inkling to the girl of her true African American heritage, refusing to pass on the family history and any trait she associates with African American life. Boy Willie sees her treatment of Maretha as stripping her of a valid identity. He believes that Maretha needs to be given a sense of her family in order to be able to build a pride in herself. This will allow Maretha to become a viable and valuable member of the African American community. Rather than view his color as limiting, Boy Willie sees it as liberating. He uses his family history as a source of strength and pride, unlike Berniece who sees that same past only as a source of shame and anguish.

However, despite his strength, Boy Willie cannot win the battle against the ghost alone—he needs the help of his sister and the support of his family. A lesson the piano teaches them is that they must be united before they can turn their former bondage into a full sense of freedom. The piano leads brother and sister to join together against their real enemy, Sutter, rather than fight each other. Berniece creates a song that draws on her past and her heritage to chase off the ghost. Her playing releases the piano's spirits, as it acknowledges and embraces their presence; they rally to strengthen both her and Boy Willie, and the ghost is defeated. Since Berniece has rediscovered how to use the piano, Boy Willie is content to leave it with her as he heads back South. The play closes triumphantly with Berniece singing "Thank you" in celebration of her reconnection to her past, her family, and, through these, a stronger and more fulfilling life in the present.

Slaveship offers a selected history of slavery and its repercussions, beginning with the roundup of men, women, and children in Africa to be brought to America for sale. We witness the indignities and horrors of their sea voyage, their sale on the auction block, and life on the plantations where they mostly worked. The Reverend Turner tries to lead a revolution, but the whites are given advance warning from Tom, another slave, and the Reverend is hanged and the rebellion squashed. Baraka takes us through what he sees as a misguided embrace of white religion, up to the violence of a black nationalist uprising that leads to the beheading of the integrationist African American Preacher and restores to a people long deprived of such, a sense of community.

Slaveship tries to provoke its audience to action, to embrace Baraka's vision of the African American as warrior rather than subservient underdog. Baraka believes that by showing African Americans their African origins and the indignities their ancestors survived during the Middle Passage and subsequent slavery, he may help them to rediscover a pride in their race and view the future with more dignity and purpose. White audiences are purposefully alienated—the first section of the play is mostly shrill, and predominantly in Yoruba—to allow them to better understand the alienation Africans felt being forcibly taken away from all they knew and transported to a foreign land.

Baraka intends for the play to arouse the maximum disgust in those who watch it. He creates an environment that includes the audience, eliminating any sense of separation between stage and audience. To involve the audience, actors crawl around in chains, howling, beneath the banked seating, run through the aisles, and toss a dead baby to an audience member. The seating encircles a re-creation of the steerage of a slave ship, with cramped living conditions, with a three-foot ceiling, no lighting, and slaves chained to the floor. We are not *told* what happened as much as visually *shown* the horrendous, claustrophobic conditions these people faced, which is a far more visceral and troubling experience. We watch as these people are dehumanized, stripped of their language and their freedom, separated from partners, friends, and children, and cramped into a stinking living space many would declare unfit for animals. Baraka even includes a pregnant woman, who is forced to give birth in such squalid surroundings.

Conditions are brutal, underscored by continual moans and cries, and demonstrated by various beatings, the torture and rape of Iyalosa, the force-feeding with funnels of those who refuse to eat, and the callous way the sailors mock their "cargo." The voices of Captain and sailors are tape recordings, to emphasize the dehumanization that occurs to those who dehumanize others. Those aboard, referred to as "black gold" by the Captain (190), have been taken away from everything familiar: land, people, heritage, even sunlight and fresh air. It is little wonder that as they struggle to survive, some become reduced to less than human behavior, with Dademi strangling herself and her child in despair, and Lalu, a former tribal leader, sexually attacking young Imani. At the slave sale we see them further treated like animals, one woman having her breasts exposed to make the sale, and the auctioneer calling the women "heifers" (205).

Yet a spirit and a tribal identity prevail, though grounded in revenge, as evidenced by the early resistance of men like Akoowa and Akano, who cannot break free but pray to black gods for weapons to fight the "Devils. White beasts. Shit eaters" (195). Most of the slaves resist when brought aboard the ship, and later the men break through the wall that divides them from their womenfolk and restore some of the unity they have lost. After chanting in Yoruba, they seem strengthened by hearing their own language, even in a song of sorrow. On the plantations, under the guidance of Reverend Turner, a rebellion is attempted, which is brutally quashed by the whites, who learn about it in advance from a fellow slave, Tom. By turning slave against slave, the whites rule all the more easily by fracturing the slaves' sense of community.

On arriving at American shores two contrary identities emerge—the resistant warrior character who has been evolving on the voyage and is sworn to resist whites; and the caricatured "Southern coon," an Uncle Tom figure who bows and scrapes to appease the oppressor and ingratiate himself. Tom's self-deprecating, broken English, filled with compliments for the "bosses" and declarations of how happy he is with his condition while he sings and dances, is repulsive: "Yassa, boss, yassa massa Tim, yassa, boss I'se as happy as a brand new monkey" (200). Tom's routine is alternated with a warrior dance and a women's dance celebrating African roots. While Tom is a mask many African Americans wore to survive, it is one that destroys any sense of self and creates self-hatred. Through the warrior figure, Baraka declares the possibility for African Americans to recognize their life force and potential for power, and become heroes rather than clowns.

Baraka is as concerned with how whites have pressured African Americans to quietly accept their own enslavement as he is with the injustices of slavery itself. Slavery is both disturbing and ironic, taking place in a land supposedly built on liberty and freedom. Baraka insists that the exploitation and betrayals have not ended, largely because whites still refuse to accept culpability for what was done, which is one reason he omits any references to emancipation. One of the institutions he sees as attempting to restrict African Americans is the Christian church, so Tom becomes the foolish Preacher, mouthing gibberish and scratching his rear end, while persuading his parishioners to integrate and forget their African history.

In response to the Preacher's insistence on nonviolence, Akano issues a battle cry and leads the enslaved in a song of rebellion and self-identification: "When we gonna rise up. . . . When we gonna lift our heads and voices/ Show the world who we really are" (210). Atowoda further boosts their spirits by claiming that their African ancestry makes them descended from "The first man to walk this star" (210), while Iyalosa performs a Yoruban ritual. As the Preacher vainly cries for help from a white Jesus, he is killed by this inspirited group, indicating a victory over a religion that has sought to contain their justified rage. A Black Power banner is raised, which the cast salute, as they ask the audience to dance with them as the head of Preacher/Tom is tossed to a Yoruban chant. Thus Baraka displays the potential power that comes with an African American tribal identity and solidarity—the power to cast aside forever the yoke of slavery.

Mulatto is set in the South in the post–World War I era. Black housekeeper, Cora, has lived with white plantation owner, Colonel Thomas Norwood, for years, bearing him several children. Cora persuades the Colonel to educate their "mulatto" children so they might get good jobs up North, but he refuses to acknowledge them as his legitimate offspring. When Bert, their youngest child, was seven, the Colonel severely beat him for calling him "Papa" in front of whites. Bert has grown up angry and rebellious, refusing to accept his identity as a black man, seeing himself as white. Cora worries that Bert's behavior will ruin their relatively comfortable situation, and the Colonel worries about how changing racial attitudes in the North might affect his plantation. He finds Bert's attitude offensive to a point where he threatens to kill him. Bert and his father try unsuccessfully to connect, end up fighting, and Bert kills the Colonel. Trying to escape, Bert is cut off by a mob and returns to the house where, to the mob's annoyance, he shoots himself rather than be caught.

The play comes out of the dilemma Hughes expressed in an early poem "Cross," which illustrates the mulatto's inner conflicts regarding "being neither white nor black." The injustices suffered by Bert and Cora, and, indeed, all blacks in the rural South, are forcefully presented, but with Bert and Cora's development the play goes beyond mere thesis drama. It is Bert's stubborn pride (ironically inherited from his father) that brings about his downfall and death, more than his unhappy, untenable situation. He keeps insisting that people see and treat him as white, but this is simply not possible in such a society, as well as being an unfortunate negation of his entire African American heritage. Cora knows this, which is why she is so anxious to get her children educated, even at the cost of virtually prostituting herself, so they might be able to go North and live freer lives. In contrast to Bert, Cora shows patience and dignity as she waits for her son to realize the totality of his tragic situation.

However, Hughes also allows us to sympathize with the Colonel, who does struggle against his own prejudices. He wants his children to be educated and is proud of their success, but does not want blacks in general to be successful.

He cannot let go of what he sees as the perfect dream of Southern plantation life, when blacks knew their place and big money could be made by exploiting this subservient population. But his time as a privileged plantation owner is passing, as African Americans are gradually throwing off the psychological detritus of slavery and becoming too independent to work under the terrible conditions or for the poor pay he offers.

Although Bert looks nearly white, neither his father nor the town can see him as anything but black, so they cannot acknowledge the kinship Bert desires. Bert is almost lynched just for complaining to the white, female post office clerk about a damaged parcel. Bert is caught in a dilemma: he cannot be white but he does not want to be black, so he ends up hating both—and hating himself. Bert's suicide indicates a new understanding, and can be seen as a final act of courage and self-determination. Cora provides the voice of reason; she understands the necessary compromises of life for blacks in the South and sees the future belonging to mixed children like hers, and her words of hope continue to ring, despite the tragedy enacted through her son.

FURTHER SUGGESTED READING

Baraka, Imamu Amiri. *Slaveship*. In *The Great American Life Show*. Eds. John Lahr and Jonathan Price. New York: Bantam, 1974: 188–213.

Benston, Kimberly W. *Baraka: The Renegade and the Mask*. New Haven: Yale University Press, 1976.

Boucicault, Dion. *Octoroon*. In *Plays*. Ed. Peter Thomson. New York: Cambridge University Press, 1984.

Brown, Lloyd. *Amiri Baraka*. Boston: Twayne, 1980.

Brown, William Wells. *The Escape, or, A Leap for Freedom*. Knoxville: University of Tennessee Press, 2001.

Conniff, Michael L., and Thomas J. Davis. *Africans in the Americas*. New York: St. Martin's Press, 1994.

Hughes, Langston. *Five Plays*. Bloomington: Indiana University Press, 1963.

Meltzer, Milton. *Langston Hughes: A Biography*. New York: Crowell, 1968.

Miller, R. Baxter. *The Art and Imagination of Langston Hughes*. Lexington, KY: University Press of Kentucky, 1989.

Shannon, G. Sandra. *The Dramatic Vision of August Wilson*. Washington, DC: Howard University Press, 1995.

Thompson, Vincent Bakpetu. *The Making of the African Diaspora in the Americas, 1441–1900*. New York: Longman, 1987.

Wilson, August. *Joe Turner's Come and Gone*. New York: Plume, 1988.

———. *The Piano Lesson*. New York: Plume, 1990.

Wolfe, Peter. *August Wilson*. New York: Twayne, 1999.

Historical Heritage

Abe Lincoln in Illinois by Robert E. Sherwood (1938)
The American Clock by Arthur Miller (1980)
The Lion in Winter by James Goldman (1966)

There has often been a tendency in the modern world to dismiss the past, as Henry Ford did with his statement that "History is bunk," and pretend that it has no influence on the present. Most modern dramatists insist that the past cannot be so readily ignored. Major historical events, beliefs, and people reverberate through the ages, and it is dangerous to deny this. To understand the relation between action and consequence or cause and effect, it helps to establish what the past entails and how it affects the present. When modern dramatists write about historical times and people, their aim is often to show the ways in which history impacts the present. Many dramatists consider the central importance of the past as being its ability to help us define who we are in the present. Arthur Miller has written about the past as "merely a dimmer present, for everything we are is at every moment alive in us" (*Timebends* 131).

Of the three plays in this chapter, two deal with particular periods in American history, and the other takes place during the reign of Henry II of England in the twelfth century. Robert E. Sherwood's *Abe Lincoln in Illinois* concentrates on the life, influence, and decisions of a single historical figure, while Arthur Miller's *The American Clock* takes a broader stance, considering the wide-ranging impact of a whole period, that of the Wall Street Crash of 1929 and the Great Depression that followed. Although the events of James Goldman's *The Lion in Winter* take place so many centuries earlier, it becomes evident that throughout history the burdens on leaders and political figures remain constant, and the complex and often devious ways of the politician have changed little over the years. Notably, these plays resonate with the contemporary society for which they were written and continue to have relevance in current times.

Written as the storm clouds of World War II were gathering, *Abe Lincoln in Illinois* directly addresses America's reluctance to join in the European conflict by asking us to witness the parallel in Lincoln's initial pacifism and gradual realization that, despite his reluctance, he must get involved in a civil war to save American democracy. Sherwood uses dramatic license to depart, at times, from recorded fact, and includes imaginary characters to provide a more cohesive drama. However, he also includes sixty pages of notes citing sources on which he based the play.

In a series of brief scenes, Sherwood takes us from Lincoln's early days in New Salem, Illinois, in the 1830s, through major events in his personal life in Springfield and his burgeoning political career, to his election as president in 1861. So it covers the making of a president rather than the presidency itself, although Sherwood includes some foreshadowing of how the presidency will run. We are offered insight into the person Lincoln was, both public and private, and the tensions that continually lay beneath his open manner. We are shown Lincoln's background and beliefs, so we may better understand what he did and said. We are shown the internal and external influences that combine to color Lincoln's decisions and political direction. Thus we see the process by which a man of peace can willingly lead a nation into war.

With forty-six named characters, plus extras, *The American Clock* is an ambitious play. It is best viewed as a mural in which one can see individuals at close range, but when one stands back the larger society with its pattern of interconnections becomes visible. In the play, Miller tries to balance epic elements with intimate psychological portraits to give a picture of a society and the individuals who make up that society. The play uses the horrors of the 1930s to illustrate how America survived in the past, in order to teach us how to survive in the similarly threatening 1980s.

Miller's Jewish Baum family face difficulties, but survive by striking a balance between their own needs and those of others. Moe's dignified strength, Rose's vitality and ability to live with contradiction, and Lee's discovery of the importance of humanity as he discards limiting ideologies all point toward a positive future. The play ends, significantly, with a sense of optimism, even if all the problems the characters face have not been fully resolved. It leaves us with a sense of hope despite the evidence of continuing difficulties, because we have been shown that however bad the world becomes, humanity's capacity for love, faith, and connection cannot ever be fully crushed.

The Lion in Winter deals with the political and personal wrangling of Henry II in his futile attempt to keep his kingdom together after his death. The reason for his failure, Goldman suggests, is the inability to love or trust that runs through his family. These same failings lie behind many of the worse moments in human history. Goldman tries to stick to known historical facts in his presentation, although he admits to simplifying some of the political maneuvering and conflating time to move events along at a more dramatically acceptable pace. Because there was no law of primogeniture in Henry's time, a single son rarely took over his father's throne, so Henry fears that, like Shakespeare's King Lear, he will be forced to divide the lands he has spent a lifetime uniting.

Abe Lincoln in Illinois dramatizes Abraham Lincoln's life from the time of his romance with Ann Rutledge until he leaves Springfield to become president. In 1831, Lincoln is twenty-two, arriving in New Salem, Illinois, where he helps clerk the local elections. The schoolteacher befriends him, extends his education, and advises him to move somewhere bigger. But fearful of large towns, Lincoln becomes postmaster and stays. He is well-liked and is selected to run for State Assembly as a conservative Whig. He agrees to run for political office to increase his standing, so that he might propose to Ann with whom he is deeply in love. He does nothing in the Assembly once elected, and, when Ann dies before they ever have the opportunity to marry, he moves to Springfield to open a law practice and dally with political office. Mary Todd decides he has prospects and determines to marry him. Fearful of her ambition, he jilts her on their wedding day. Two years later, he meets an old friend, Seth, who motivates him to take a stance on slavery, an issue he has been dodging. Returning to Mary, he marries her and enters the political arena in earnest. Unsuccessful during his elected term in Congress, he takes an unpopular stance against the Mexican War and loses his seat. He follows this with a run for the U.S. Senate, displaying his growth as a polished and convincing speaker. His relationship with Mary sours, even as he is nominated for president and wins the election. The play closes as he heads to Washington to take office.

Lincoln comes from poor beginnings, a family of impoverished backwoodsmen, and he rises from these humble origins to the presidency of the United States. He is depicted as a man prone to depression and doubt, but capable of forceful idealism once roused. His friend, Josh, suggests he has the capacity to be a "great philosopher" or a "great fool" (56). His open and honest manner draws all to befriend him, even the Salem delinquents, who respect him and follow his instruction. We see his nurturing side as he assists Ann, later nursing her on her deathbed, and helps Seth's little boy. Although he is selected to run for public office because those in power believe they can manipulate him, he proves fiercely independent and principled once elected. However, the support of his friends remains important, because he lacks faith in his own abilities and needs their assurances, at times, to continue.

Lincoln's desire to improve his position is evident from his decision to become literate and leave the backwoods to join New Salem society. Here he is educated in politics by the men who befriend him. His love for Ann, Sherwood suggests, is what catapults him into public office, as he tries to gain respectability to become a fitting husband. When she dies, it sets him back substantially, and it is five years before he runs again for public office. Mary Todd's ambition may encourage him to pursue the presidency, but their relationship is far less satisfactory. It may allow him to rise politically, but at the cost of any private happiness.

While studying with the schoolteacher, Lincoln declares that if he had to choose between politics and teaching, he would select the latter. Once sitting in the State Assembly he says nothing and loses his seat. He later runs for the position of Elector rather than Member of Congress because he is uncomfortable with having to vote on any possible outbreak of war. Fearful of abolitionists, seeing them as warmongers, and refusing to speak at their rallies, Lincoln nevertheless disapproves of slavery, but refuses to get involved in the debate, feeling that slavery is upheld by the Constitution, since slaves are property. "I am opposed to slavery," he tells us. "But I'm even more opposed to war" (75).

However, once he commits himself, we see a different story. Sherwood patches together parts of Lincoln's more famous speeches to convey his evolving convictions. Lincoln loses his seat in Congress because he is too outspoken, specifically by coming out against the Mexican War. In debates against Stephen Douglas for the Senate and then for the presidential nomination, he wins by a landslide, despite calling for an end to slavery and reluctantly promoting the need for civil war to achieve this. Against the gusto of Douglas's speech, he sounds calm but sincere, as he reveals the hypocrisy behind Douglas's stance and refutes all his negative assertions. Using anecdote and humor to convey his points, Lincoln speaks without notes, as if directly from the heart, and swiftly wins his audience. Drawing on the Declaration of Independence, he declares that slavery is unconstitutional, and the Dred Scott decision (which tried to assert African American inequality), wrong.

What causes Lincoln's change of mind is a hypothetical creation of the playwright, though based on known beliefs of Lincoln. The earlier Lincoln is shown to be a man of doubt, indecision, and even indifference, but in 1842 a change takes place and his character evolves into a figure of passionate conviction and decisive action. Sherwood allows Lincoln to meet with Seth, an old friend heading West with his freedman, Gobey, in the hopes of establishing a free society. Sickened by the concept of slavery, Seth declares that he would rather start a new country than belong to one that would support such an institution. Feeling that America would lose more by the loss of such citizens as Seth than she could from restricting slavery, Lincoln determines he must block any expansion of slavery to the West, a belief that develops into a declaration that slavery is evil and must be abolished entirely. His patriotic prayer over Seth's sickly child is effectively a prayer for the survival of the United States through troubled times ahead, a prayer in hindsight we know was answered, but at the time would have been provoked by genuine fear.

The American Clock tells the story of America in the 1930s through the conflated stories of a vast array of characters. We meet businessmen like Jesse Livermore and William Durant who lose everything, and more successful entrepreneurs like Arthur A. Robertson and Theodore K. Quinn. We learn the plight of farmers like Henry Taylor, young intellectuals like Joe and Edie, and an assortment of people from all walks of life. At the center, Miller places the

Baum family, who are partly autobiographical. Through the Baums he explores, even more deeply, the concerns and demands of such a time. The father, Moe, loses a prosperous business but keeps on going, even as his wife, Rose, begins to fall apart under the strain. Their son Lee goes from childhood to adulthood as he travels through the nation, and finally comes to terms with the demands of living in America.

Despite hardships, Miller sees the Depression as a positive period in American history, when the morally corrupt old order disintegrated, leaving the ground cleared for new structures. The main difficulty came in the uncertainty as to what these new structures should be. In the play, Miller illustrates how neither socialism nor fascism offered ideal social systems, as each is too extreme and ultimately flawed. While the former privileges the community, the later privileges the individual; what is really needed is a balance between the two. People in the 1930s struggled to understand this balance. By the 1980s, Miller saw America as needing to relearn this lesson in order to combat a mounting spiritual malaise.

In presenting his mural, Miller allows no scene breaks and presents us with a fluid montage of constant action. The characters often address the audience directly, as if to include them as part of the throng. He creates a collage of the American people, and begins the play by presenting two quintessentially American pastimes—jazz and baseball—with the band playing "Million Dollar Baby" to emphasize the 1920s American obsession with wealth. Miller also blends together people's speech to create a single voice—the voice of America. Speech flows between the cast, with one character completing the sentence of another, to suggest a community of one mind, connected by outlook, similar values and beliefs, and desire.

The play is also unified by joint narrators Arthur Robertson and Lee Baum. Lee, youthful and initially naive, attempts to make sense of events as they unfold. Robertson, older and wiser, has an intuitive understanding of events even before they occur. Together they analyze how America survived the calamitous Depression and what future lessons can be taken from her survival. Both are involved in the action, not as outside commentators but as participants, which gives their words a greater credibility. Through these narrators Miller wonders why it was that the Depression did not destroy America. The answer he offers is not the more generally accepted one that Roosevelt saved the country, but that it was the American capacity for belief in the possibility of a better future.

Robertson's opening Biblical image of the country kneeling before a golden calf evokes a prophecy of doom. We all know what happened to those original misguided idolaters; they paid a harsh price for their faith in wealth. These people, too, will suffer, as the Wall Street Crash is imminent, and will spark a sequence of events resulting in the Great Depression, the most widespread disaster faced by the American people since the Civil War. Even the shoeblack, Clarence, puts all his savings into the almighty stock market. He refuses to accept that he could lose in this venture, despite Robertson's kindly advice for him to cash in his shares. When the market crashes, as we know it will, Clarence is left with less than $50.

Even after the Crash we see people who refuse to face the truth. Some financiers, like Randolph Morgan, commit suicide; others, like Jesse Livermore, initially comfort themselves with empty optimism over the possibility that someone like John D. Rockefeller will save the day. Livermore so believes in economic prosperity that when he finally comes to recognize his own ruin, he loses all faith and is unable to continue living. William Durant has a clearer vision, looking his own ruin in the face. He knows that suicide is no answer, recognizes the illusion of the wealth he had garnered, and will not fall prey to it again. Durant may have lost General Motors, but we later learn that he survives and lands on his feet by running a bowling alley in Ohio.

It was not just the city people who suffered. Due to weather conditions as punishing as the stock market, the products of the farmers failed as much as the dealings of the city financiers. Miller shows the Taylors's farm being put up for compulsory auction by its bank creditors. The neighbors, threatened by similar treatment, rally around their fellow farmer. By a show of physical force, the only power they retain without having any money themselves, they enforce a sale of Taylor's property for $1, and return it to him. It will be a momentary victory, for he has no money to run a farm whether he owns it or not, and he will soon be forced out onto the road to make a living.

The Depression allowed America to start anew, to go back to her beginnings where everyone was a stranger and needed to forge new connections. Miller shows how people survive by random acts of kindness, often performed by people who do not even know the recipient: Brewster helping Taylor, Callaghan helping Banks, the Baums helping Taylor. Such acts of kindness are positive signs of connections being forged, even though many remain out only for themselves. As a recipient of such kindness, Taylor, for his part, is neither lazy nor expectant. He is prepared to work for his food and does not expect a handout; he is uncomfortable asking the Baums for even that much. His lack of greed is evident when he only drinks half of the glass of water they give him.

The Baums feel sorry for Taylor, but cannot be fully responsible for him; he must accept responsibility for his own condition. Moe explains: "Life is tough, what're you going to do?" (142). Lee, idealistically, does not accept this as a valid response, and is unhappy with what he sees as his father's refusal to take responsibility for Taylor. Grandpa's reaction, however, is worse. He insists that people are not connected and you should only "worry about yourself" (143), as he does. Miller makes it clear that we should not believe Grandpa. Earlier on, we were shown how wrong his views are when he insists that Hitler can only stay in power for six months at most. We have also just witnessed his unrealistic response to Taylor's plight, suggesting the man should simply borrow money to buy his farm back. Grandpa is living in fierce denial of the changing times and what he says is not credible. Moe's philosophy is a lot less selfish and preserves a necessary balance; he helps a little, but not to a point where he damages his own prospects.

Miller uses the three main Baum characters to illustrate the major different reactions he perceived people had to the Depression: Moe responds practically, Lee ideologically, and Rose emotionally. In combination, the three offer a comprehensive picture of the overwhelming impact of the Depression on the American psyche and disposition. Apart, they allow us to explore personalized aspects of the larger social changes that occurred during this period. Wealthy enough at the start to have a chauffeur, they, like so many others, overinvest in stocks. We watch as the clock runs out on their prosperity. The whole family is initially distracted by acquisition. Their Grandpa has become a nuisance who has to be shunted back and forth between the sisters rather than embraced as an emblem of the family's connection. They waste their time in petty jealousies and quarrels. Rose is jealous of her mother-in-law; Moe enjoys nastily teasing his sister-in-law. Moe is so busy that he scarcely has time for his own son (unaware of how old he is or when he had his last haircut). They will learn, through the trials of the Depression, how to become a closer and more fulfilled family unit.

Lee's final identification of Rose with America as a whole rests on her ability to accept contradictory beliefs. This is indicative of the binary nature of the American psyche. Rose can simultaneously support concepts of capitalism and freedom, socialism and elitism, humanitarianism and racism, for at the heart of these beliefs lie her essential optimism and belief in life. It is these that allow Rose, and the rest of America, to survive and continue to function. Rose sings out at the close of the play, refusing to give in. Although a little wistful at first, everyone joins in her rendition of "Life's Just a Bowl of Cherries." The country has been saved, not just by the onset of war, as Robertson suggests, but also, as Quinn adds, by a reaffirmation of belief in itself, only partly engendered by President Roosevelt. Quinn leads the final chorus with his soft-shoe dance, as everybody sings together, including, hopefully, the audience, providing a prime picture of America the brave, prepared to sing and dance with life in the face of every disaster.

The Lion in Winter begins with Henry II, an agile fifty, with his young mistress Alais Capet, sister to Philip, the King of France. Though having won his position through subterfuge and battle, recent years of peace have led Henry to desire a peaceful succession, which will maintain what he has built, rather than see it torn apart. Unfortunately, his three remaining sons, Richard, Geoffrey, and John, are each determined to get the most power for themselves, and they cajole, betray one another, and lie as they jockey for position. While Henry favors giving John his kingdom, his estranged wife, Eleanor of Aquitaine, prefers her chances with Richard, over whom she has more control. Philip insists that Alais be married to one of Henry's sons, as agreed to in a past treaty, but Henry desires her for himself. The sons keep changing alliances, even joining with the foreigner Philip when they feel it might give them an upper hand; they are clearly willing to murder each other to get the crown. In disgust, Henry imprisons all three, and plans to marry Alais and have more sons. However, realizing the futility of this, as he cannot protect those sons once dead, he frees his existing offspring and decides the only solution is to live forever.

Goldman intends this partly as a political farce. We watch the convoluted plotting of the Plantagenets and Capets as they vie for power. Characters listen behind doors, keep switching sides, and comically misread each other's actions. Though set in 1183, the political intrigue, backbiting, and lack of truth or honesty displayed could quite easily belong in modern times. Goldman reinforces this by using anachronistic speech, putting modern idioms into the mouths of his twelfth-century characters.

Henry is the lion of the title, and the winter is both the time in which the play is set and Henry's approaching old age. As a Count, at eighteen, Henry had met Eleanor, then Queen of France, and swept her off her feet, persuading her to annul her marriage to the king of France and wed him, thus bringing with her great wealth and Aquitaine, a large province within France. By twenty, Henry was King of England, with extensive lands in France, which he further extended through battle and treaty. In hindsight, we know that, after his death, Richard became king but abandoned his responsibilities to go on the Crusades, leaving his brother John in charge. John's weakness led to the Magna Carta, in which he signed over many of his powers and took the first steps toward a constitutional monarchy, which contrasts with the supreme sway Henry held. Henry ultimately realizes that he cannot control things after his death, which is why he frees his sons and effectively gives up his quest to preserve his kingdom intact.

Richard Lionheart is the soldier, Geoffrey the supposed brains, and John the best looking. Though collectively they reflect their father, individually they are inadequate. Richard has had a compromising homosexual relationship with Philip, which Philip only pursued in hopes of upsetting Henry. He is also easily manipulated by Philip and his mother, Eleanor, having none of the strength of his father. Geoffrey, despite his intelligence, consistently misreads the situation and his constantly changing allegiances ensure that no one trusts him. He also struggles against an inferiority complex as the consistently overlooked child. At sixteen, John is a petulant, self-absorbed youth, willing to betray anyone, including his father, for his shot at power. But he is too stupid to even maintain the secrecy of his trickery, such as when he lets Eleanor know about his pact with Philip, thus giving her ammunition to revitalize her contest with Henry.

Had Philip been Henry's heir, Henry's hope to keep his kingdom intact may have come to fruition, because Philip is far stronger than any of Henry's sons. Only seventeen, and King of France for the past three years, Philip proves to be a worthy political adversary to Henry. He is far more aware of the demands of the political game than Henry's sons are. He displays strength by refusing to allow Henry to patronize him, and instantly sees through the subterfuge when Henry pretends to accede to Eleanor and give Richard the crown and Alais. Philip knows he need only bide his time to exact revenge for the lands and reputation his father lost to Henry, as none of Henry's sons will be able to control him as Henry has done.

Henry's relationship with Eleanor is as problematic as the relationship he has with his sons. At times each professes love for the other, but they also categorically deny it. Their actions speak little of love. Both understand how politics works, know each other's strengths and weaknesses, and, one suspects, keep each other close only to know their enemy the better. As potential equals in political subterfuge, they use each other and their children to play the game. It is a game of which Henry grows tired, but which Eleanor refuses to stop. They vie for ascendancy over the other, and end up in a stalemate. Eleanor returns to her house arrest, but she contentedly remains a thorn in her husband's side.

Henry's choice of John for heir and husband to Alais is most likely because he sees him as the most malleable, but that would also make him the least likely to stay on the throne once his father was gone. Henry knows he needs to find a way to satisfy the other two so that they would leave John alone, but they all want the same thing. Henry understands that his family hate him, but he intends to get what he wants by being the "master bastard" (8). That his children are so weak and untrustworthy should not surprise us, given the upbringing they have received. Richard points out how they grew up watching the constant fighting between their parents. All three sons feel distanced from their parents, never having felt truly loved nor able to trust either one; so it follows they too are incapable of love or loyalty.

Every member of this family is willing to betray and even kill each other, if necessary. Ironically, it is Henry, the "master bastard," who finally displays compassion, by letting his sons live, despite knowing that they can only wreck his accomplishment. It is Eleanor who highlights the play's humanitarian message when she declares, "Oh, my piglets, we're the origins of war. Not history's forces nor the times nor justice nor the lack of it nor causes nor religions nor ideas nor kinds of government nor any other thing. We are the killers; we breed war. We carry it, like syphilis, inside" (56). These people are all intrinsically rotten, for whatever reason, living without love, trust, or compassion. While people still exist without such qualities, Goldman suggests, war will always be inevitable.

FURTHER SUGGESTED READING

Abbotson, Susan C. W. *Student Companion to Arthur Miller.* Westport, CT: Greenwood, 2000.

Bertman, Stephen. *Cultural Amnesia: America's Future and the Crisis of Memory.* Westport, CT: Praeger, 2000.

Bigsby, Christopher. *The Cambridge Companion to Arthur Miller.* Cambridge: Cambridge University Press, 1997.

Brecht, Bertold. *Galileo.* Trans. Charles Laughton. New York: Grove, 1966.

Goldman, James. *The Lion in Winter.* New York: Random House, 1966.

Lawrence, Jerome, and Robert E. Lee. *The Night Thoreau Spent in Jail.* New York: Hill & Wang, 1970.

Meserve, Walter J. *Robert E. Sherwood: Reluctant Moralist.* New York: Pegasus, 1970.

Miller, Arthur. The American Clock *and* The Archbishop's Ceiling. New York: Grove, 1989.

————. *Timebends: A Life.* New York: Grove, 1987.

Schroeder, Patricia R. *The Presence of the Past in Modern American Drama.* Cranbury, NJ: Associated University Press, 1989.

Sherwood, Robert E. *Abe Lincoln in Illinois.* New York: Scribner's, 1947.

Shuman, R. Baird. *Robert E. Sherwood.* New York: Twayne, 1964.

The Holocaust

Playing for Time by Arthur Miller (1981)
The Diary of Anne Frank by Frances Goodrich and
   Albert Hackett (1955)
The Deputy by Rolf Hochhuth (1963)

The horrors of what happened to the European Jews under the control of the
Nazi regime in the 1930s–1940s were so intense that it was not until the 1960s
that most writers were able to approach the topic, and this delay was even more
evident among playwrights. The immediacy of drama made portrayals of the
Holocaust on stage particularly disturbing, and, some felt, inappropriate. Many
felt that anything less than the reality of what went on in the extermination
camps actually occurring on stage, which would be impossible for any actors
to perform, would only lessen the impact of what had occurred and would be
an insult to those who died. However, an increasing number of dramas have
attempted to speak to those horrific events, exploring them from every angle,
some to bear witness and ensure we have an historical record of what happened,
others in an attempt to understand how people could so brutally murder their
fellow human beings in such numbers.

Some dramas explore the stories of those who survived, such as Arthur
Miller's *Playing for Time;* others those who perished, such as Frances Goodrich
and Albert Hackett's dramatization of *The Diary of Anne Frank.* Some consider
those whom they saw as responsible, and the few who worked against them,
as in Rolf Hochhuth's *The Deputy.* Whatever their focus, these dramas are
universally disturbing in their portrayals of people's inhumanity to one another. All the plays in this chapter are based on real people and real events,
which makes the stories they tell all the more disturbing on one level, but on
another, inspirational, in the hope offered by those who resisted.

Written by wife-and-husband team, Goodrich and Hackett, *The Diary of
Anne Frank* is based on the original diary written by Anne Frank, who died at
the age of fifteen in Bergen-Belsen during March 1945. It covers just over two

years of her life, when she lived in an attic above a factory in Amsterdam with her own and another family. It ends when they are discovered and taken away by the Gestapo. Although many of the lines are direct quotes from Anne's diary, the play offers a more objective version of events, which is less centered on Anne, and allows us to better see the stories behind all the characters involved.

Playing for Time is an adaptation of the memoirs of Auschwitz survivor, Fania Fenelon. Not intended to be an accurate historical record, Miller uses the event of the Holocaust to reflect on issues he saw plaguing American society in the 1980s, with its increasing tendency toward alienation, violence, and social irresponsibility. For Miller, Auschwitz is a powerful symbol of contemporary life, with its accustomed violence, lack of communication and social responsibility, and dehumanization of feelings. Miller wanted the play to warn us to remain vigilant against evil, and to inspire audiences that such evil can be overcome if people will allow themselves to care for one another and connect. He uses Fania's story as a lesson in how to survive and maintain a sense of humanity in the face of the worst possible dehumanizing force.

Written in free verse, *The Deputy* is a lengthy play, which takes over six hours if performed in its entirety. The text includes a sixty-five-page appendix that documents many of the events and people being dramatized. Although based on real people and events, Hochhuth alters some details and characters for dramatic effect. Pointing out that it is impossible to realistically convey the atrocities of the Holocaust on a stage, Hochhuth nevertheless includes some harrowing scenes that have forced many to see the Holocaust with new eyes. Woven throughout the action are lengthy discussions of the intricate policies and religious and national politics behind the various alliances and events of World War II, mostly highlighting the intrinsic immorality of the conflict, which Hochhuth sees based on secular concern rather than moral imperative.

This controversial play suggests that Pope Pius XII, Christ's deputy on earth, whose role should be to take on the suffering of others, failed to voice a fundamental Christian principle by not publicly condemning Hitler's program; this resulted in the extermination of 6 million Jews. Hochhuth insists that such failure to speak out against evil makes those who stay silent complicit in the deed itself. His play explores why people chose to resist or participate in this atrocity, or, like the Pope, remain neutral. In contrast to the Pope's inaction, we follow the exploits of Father Riccardo Fontana and Kurt Gerstein—one an Italian Jesuit priest, the other a Protestant German SS officer—both men who risk their lives to save Jews and so take on the burden Hochhuth feels the Pope should have accepted.

Playing for Time depicts Fania Fenelon's experiences at Auschwitz during World War II. Nazi officials want a prisoner orchestra and Fania, with her musical background, is swiftly recruited, along with Marianne, a girl whom Fania met on the train that brought them to the extermination camp. Their usefulness saves the musicians from heavy work and being put to death. The orchestra is made up of Jewish prisoners and non-Jewish Poles. All struggle to maintain the Nazis' interest in their music, living at the whim of evil men like Dr. Mengele, and most survive to see their camp liberated.

The arrival at the camp is a study in dehumanization. Conditions in the boxcar that brought them were bad enough, but now the Nazis attempt to strip away all dignity and identity. These people are literally stripped of everything that allows them to feel human: their luggage, their clothes, even their hair, and then they are tattooed with numbers. These are the "lucky ones" who are not taken straight away to be killed and "cooked" in the crematorium. The contrast between the way the Kapos brutally strike the prisoners and the care with which they handle their belongings is indicative of the way in which *things* have become more valuable than people. But although treated as worthless, it does not mean they are; it is a definition they must struggle against to maintain their spirits and survive.

To survive is the primary aim in the camps, but Miller wants us to realize that there are different ways to survive, and some routes may lead to a more profoundly disturbing spiritual death, as happens to young Marianne, than the most unpleasant literal death. Survival comes at a cost, but there are certain prices a person should not pay, for to survive without retaining a basic humanity is hardly survival at all. Fania's survival is both realistic, given the fallibility of human nature, and uplifting, in that she refuses to let go of her basic humanity. We see her vacillate between assertions of independence and obsequiousness; sometimes she makes demands, other times she simply goes along, but she maintains a defiantly humanistic core throughout.

Key to survival in this camp are the notion of identity and the ability to maintain one's humanity in the face of dehumanizing Nazism. The orchestra women maintain an identity as musicians that buoys their spirits, and they have a strengthened sense of community, which allows them to be more human and humane. When Fania is brought to audition, they greet her with kindness; Elzvieta (a Polish Catholic) wipes her face and Etalina (a Jew) gives her bread. The orchestra plays loudly as much to announce their existence as to protect Liesle (drowning her out because she cannot play the piece). The music has become an outlet for pain and desire, as well as their means of survival; quite literally they are "playing for time."

Miller has been criticized for his depiction of Nazis as possessing human qualities, from a love of good music to Mandel's infatuation with the boy who came in on the transports, and her evident distress when she is forced to let him go to the gas chamber. Mandel will one moment take a woman's child and viciously beat her with a riding crop, and the next display a genuine concern for Fania's well-being; but such contradictions are essential to her depiction. Miller recognizes that to imply that the Nazis are not human because of their inhumane agenda is to lessen the impact of the lesson of the Holocaust that he so keenly wishes to convey. The fact is, Nazis were human beings, and they could at times display humane reactions—they were not complete monsters, even when they behaved monstrously.

It is clear that Marianne will have trouble surviving. She has led a sheltered, protected life up until now: "I was in school or at home all my life" (8). Though twenty years old, she acts far younger, and her reactions are childish. She clings to Fania for support, drawing sustenance from her, literally and spiritually, to the point where she starts to drain Fania's strength. Unable to face even single corpses, as in the boxcar, and later in their bunk, it is not surprising that she remains protectively ignorant of the more massive slaughter taking place. She capitulates to her captors, body and soul, becoming a prostitute and losing every ounce of self-respect. She has no conscience, and so her behavior creates in her no feelings of guilt. She refuses to recognize any responsibilities in her drive to continue living, not even any responsibility to her own self and to her own dignity. Thus, she becomes a mere husk of a human being.

Fania realizes early on that if she is to survive, she must both hold on to a sense of self and have a goal for the future toward which she can strive. Initially, she makes a mistake regarding her sense of self. She denies her Jewishness and insists on her identity as a French woman: "I'm not Jew-shit. I'm French" (15). In this she denies an important aspect of herself that she will need to recognize to survive; it will help provide her with pride, moral values, and a sense of companionship with the other Jews. Luckily she comes to see this before it is too late, and we witness her claim her Jewishness. Her main goal, "to try to remember everything" (17), is highly effective, and further feeds her capacity to survive.

Fania's sense of commitment to others allows her to think beyond herself as she tries to survive. In the boxcar she had reached out to others, and we also learn that she has been a longtime member of the French Resistance. Fania does not turn away from the dead, as Marianne does, but she also does not want to be associated with them at first. On finding both the corpse in the boxcar and another in the bunk, she calls out to have them dealt with by someone else. In each case her cries are in vain, indicative of the fact that she must learn to deal with the dead herself—this is part of her responsibility as a survivor, which she finally accepts. Fania forces herself to continuously look out the window and take on extra duties so she will see everything that happens. She wishes to be a faithful recorder and firsthand witness to what went on in this place. This play is testament to her victory.

The Diary of Anne Frank begins with Anne's father, Otto Frank—the only family member to survive the extermination camps—finding his daughter's diary on a brief visit to their former hideaway in an attic above a warehouse in Amsterdam, before leaving the country. As he reads it, the voice of Anne takes over, and the events of the Frank family's attempt to escape the Holocaust are acted out before us, from their initial arrival at the attic to their eventual discovery and deportation to the camps. The Franks generously share their quarters with the self-absorbed Van Daan family and Jan Dussel, an elderly local dentist. We watch as this disparate group of Jews squabble and compromise, fall out and bond, and somehow continue to hope, even as they are captured by the Gestapo.

What many people first get from this account is a tremendous sense of loss. Anne herself is an intelligent young girl, if somewhat willful. She is full of life and curiosity, and might have had a bright future were it not for Hitler's determination to exterminate the Jews. Indeed, we are drawn to sympathize with all these people who have given up their former lives, and suffered for over two years the privations of living in cramped conditions with little food, privacy, or distraction, unable to go outside or freely move around during work hours, fearful at every moment of discovery. Just as we feel we have got to know them, we learn that all but Anne's father died at the hands of the Nazis.

These people are not perfect; they have their periods of selfishness as well as selflessness. It is this that makes them all the more human. The mundane details of their day-to-day existence also contribute to this perception. Their will to survive belies the popular myth that Jews did little to save themselves, just as the erstwhile assistance they received from Mr. Kraler and Miep Gies shows that there were those whose morality prevented them from going along with Hitler's program, despite the risk to their own lives. The pressure under which Kraler lives because of this is indicated by his stay in hospital for ulcers. Kraler speaks of hundreds of Jews throughout Holland being hidden by the local inhabitants, and these helpers do not see themselves as heroic, but act out of compassion and distaste at how the Nazis behave.

The play offers a primer on the treatment of European Jews at that period, as Anne relates what has happened leading up to their going into hiding. The Frank family are German born, but moved to Holland to escape persecution in their native land. When the Nazis take over Holland, Otto Frank is forced to sell his business, and all the Jews are made to wear yellow stars at all times. In addition to this, they are no longer allowed to attend schools; ride on bikes, streetcars, or in private cars; or attend such public venues as the cinema. By 1942 the family were fully aware of their fate if caught, which is why they decided to go into hiding, in hopes that they might stay hidden until the Germans were defeated. We later learn from Dussel, when he joins them two months into their stay, that the Nazis are rounding up all the Jews, searching houses and taking anyone they find. Children arrive home to find their parents gone. No one with any Jewish blood is spared, regardless of their degree of religious observance or affinity toward Judaism.

When we first see Otto, his movements are weak and uncertain, and he appears ill and aged before his time. This is what life at Auschwitz has done to him. Only three years previously, he had looked "much younger" and "his movements are brisk, his manner confident" (10). It is predominantly Otto's strength, democratic leaderships skills, vision, and goodness of heart that keep this group going. As he tells his daughter when he gives her the diary, "Always remember this, Anneke. There are no walls, there are no bolts, no locks that anyone can put on your mind" (26). Although they are physically trapped in a small attic, they are never spiritually trapped. Thus, while incarcerated, they all continue to hope for the future, educating the children, and allowing a relationship to develop between Anne and Peter Van Daan.

The inescapability of their fate, and the spirit with which they face it, are indicated in a brief scene when Peter persuades Anne to remove her yellow star, since they never intend to go outside. When Anne removes her star, she points out that the cloth underneath still shows the form of the star, just as they cannot escape being Jewish. But Anne also refuses to throw away the star, as it is the Star of David, and by keeping it she claims her right to be Jewish. We see Anne's spirit continue to blaze, despite her frequent nightmares about being taken by the Nazis, as she thoughtfully creates gifts for the entire group to cheer them up on the first night of Hanukkah.

Their discovery is a case of bad luck rather than carelessness. A thief comes at night to steal a radio from the warehouse beneath their hideaway, and Peter falls while trying to extinguish a telltale light. Despite our prior knowledge that these people will die, we are drawn in to hope as we hear of the Allied invasion, and Miep brings joyful news about the success of D-Day. But the thief is caught and betrays them to the authorities. Even as the Germans are losing the war, they take these people off to their deaths.

One of the most quoted lines of the play comes from Anne, as she tries to inspire Peter and give their suffering a universal relevance: "I still believe, in spite of everything, that people are really good at heart" (168), and she insists that the world is just going through an ugly phase, as she had done in her relationship with her mother. This belief inspires Otto at the close to avoid bitterness and insist on looking for that good in people. However, some critics complain that the line is taken out of context, used by the playwrights to give the play a more uplifting and less political close. The actual diary written by Anne, as opposed to this theatrical adaptation, also revealed Anne's bitterness toward an indifferent Christian world, frank discussion of her budding sexuality, her sister's Zionism, and her mother's deep faith, and such omissions do tend to reduce complex ethical issues to easy platitudes about love and forgiveness.

The Deputy begins in 1942 and takes us from the Papal Legation in Berlin, via Rome, to Auschwitz. Protestant Kurt Gerstein works as an SS Officer to collect firsthand evidence of what the Nazis are doing, in order to help expose them, and his reports motivate Father Riccardo Fontana to try to persuade the Pope to speak out against these atrocities. Against a background of political maneuvering and mounting abuse against even Jews who have been baptized, the Pope stands firm in his decision to stay neutral and say nothing to condemn Hitler's program. Riccardo decides to join the transports in solidarity with the

Jews and is mortally wounded attempting to kill the evil Doctor, a sadist in charge of selection for the gas chambers and medical experiments at Auschwitz, where Gerstein is also apprehended while trying to help a prisoner escape.

Gerstein is a heroic figure, willingly endangering himself and his family by his involvement. Aware that this involvement may label him as a killer, because he works from within the SS as one of their officers, he explains, "That I can never shed this uniform is my part-payment of the debt of guilt that burdens all of us" (268). He commits acts of sabotage against the slaughter, tries to motivate outside forces to complain, and persuades other officers to delay in order to buy more time. He also hides a Jewish friend, Jacobson, in his apartment, later convincing Riccardo to give him his cassock and passport to facilitate an escape. His brave efforts to free Riccardo and then Jacobson from Auschwitz toward the close culminate in his arrest and probable death.

Gerstein's time in a concentration camp as a political prisoner has bolstered his sympathy for the victims of the Holocaust, but he is at heart morally opposed to the Final Solution, and feels no ambivalence about his duty: "A man who sets up factories which serve no purpose but to kill his fellowmen with gas—this man must be betrayed, must be destroyed" (77). Still a patriot, he dismisses Hitler as a criminal who is destroying German honor with his behavior, and, wrongly or rightly, believes many Germans are unaware of what is happening or too fearful for their own safety to intervene.

The Catholic Church's refusal to defend the Jews in any way at first seems based on the fact that Jews were not their congregants, but this becomes less credible as events proceed. We learn of the Church helping Germans to round up Jews, and they even allow the Nazis to take baptized Jews without complaint. The Germans have tested the waters by requesting a huge ransom for the Italian Jews, to which the Pope offered to contribute, an action that only confirmed the belief of the Nazis that they could do whatever they liked to Jews and the church would not speak out against them. The Pope's offer is a moral sop, and he knows as well as the Nazis that it is an empty offer, for they will not really give up any Jews in return for a ransom. "If the Pope kept his mouth shut then, after such a fantastic demand—why not now?" (185), officer Salzer surmises, continuing to send Jews to their deaths, after he has crudely insulted and threatened them for good measure. A letter of protest from a Bishop, which was actually sent without the Pope's knowledge, confirms German suspicions that the Pope has given them a clear go-ahead; they assume that the Pope has had an underling write this letter merely to salve his conscience.

Some Catholics have made attempts to thwart the Germans, giving Jews refuge in monasteries, but this is only a small number of those under threat and mostly Jews who have been baptized and thereby renounced their Jewishness. As the Germans round up families of Jews, like the Luccanis, from under the Pope's own windows, Riccardo feels that the Pope must be forced to speak out, but the Pope is more worried about a Russian threat to his Church should he speak out against Hitler, who is holding the Russians back. Riccardo plans to go with the arrested Jews to show solidarity, embracing the role as deputy, to sacrifice himself to atone for what he sees as the guilt of the Church. He wears a Jewish star to try to provoke the Pope. However, though angry, the Pope backs away from his challenge, and, like Pontius Pilate, literally washes his hands of the whole business, insisting on his own blamelessness.

The Pope is depicted as a cold man, more worried about Jesuit investments and Church manuscripts than human lives. He describes the deportation of the Jews from Rome as "extremely bad behavior" (198), but no more. When trusted counsels, like Riccardo's father, Count Fontana, make their indignation felt at his inhumane inaction, he drafts a document that is so vague and grandiose in its verbiage, refusing even to name the Jews, that it is clearly meaningless; he then returns to the financial issues that most concern him. Ironically, throughout, we are led to believe that the Germans would have taken seriously any open dissension from the papacy, but none was ever given.

As diplomats, serving the politics of office rather than human conscience, Church officials embody the true banality of evil, which is manifest through acts of omission as much as acts of commission. Concern for their own survival makes them wary of defending the Jews. Thus Gerstein's attempts to inform them about what happens to Jews in the extermination camps fall on deaf ears, despite his insistence: "That blood guilt, Excellency, falls upon us all if we keep silent"(27). Hochhuth portrays numerous Nazis as equally banal, despite their more active complicity. Adolf Eichman, in charge of transporting Jews to the camps, is portrayed as a bureaucrat, hosting a bowling party where he calmly discusses the need for more efficient killing techniques, as if he were discussing an industrial production line rather than human beings. Other guests expound upon the Nazi view that the extermination of Jews is a scientific and social necessity. When the Luccani family are taken, the men who arrest them are disturbingly ordinary: a German sergeant who follows orders, and two loutish Italian fascists out to get whatever they can.

The Germans are not portrayed as outlandish figures of evil, with the exception of the Doctor, based on Josef Mengele. His evident relish at the outrages he commits and his utter disdain for humanity allow Hochhuth to compare him to the Devil. His attempts to destroy Riccardo's faith—mocking him for his weakening resolve to die, telling him how meaningless his death will be amid such casual slaughter, and sending him to work in the crematorium—add to this image. But Hochhuth does not allow him victory; although Riccardo dies, he does so in an act of defiance against this devil and becomes a tragic hero. Though Christianity may have failed in the person and institution of the papacy, the active faith of both Riccardo and Gerstein saves us from dismissing Christianity as dead. Yet Riccardo's victory is muted by the play's final announcement about the ineffectiveness of the Papal announcement, and the declaration that "the gas chambers continued to work for a full year more" (285).

FURTHER SUGGESTED READING

Bentley, Eric, Ed. *The Storm Over* The Deputy. New York: Grove, 1964.

Bigsby, Christopher, Ed. *Cambridge Companion to Arthur Miller.* Cambridge: Cambridge University Press, 1997.

Davidowitz, Lucy. *The War Against the Jews.* New York: Behrman House, 1976.

Des Pres, Terence. *The Survivor: An Anatomy of Life in the Death Camps.* New York: Oxford University Press, 1976.

Goodrich, Frances, and Albert Hackett. *The Diary of Anne Frank.* New York: Random House, 1956.

Hochhuth, Rolf. *The Deputy.* Trans. Richard and Clara Winston. New York: Grove, 1963.

Miller, Arthur. *Incident at Vichy.* New York: Viking, 1965.

———. "Our Guilt For the World's Evil." *New York Times Magazine* (January 3, 1965): 10–11, 48.

———. *Playing for Time.* Woodstock, IL: Dramatic Publishing, 1985.

Sherman, Martin. *Bent.* New York: Avon, 1979.

Skloot, Robert, Ed. *The Theatre of the Holocaust.* Madison: University of Wisconsin Press, 1982.

Ward, Margaret. *Rolf Hochhuth.* Boston: Twayne, 1977.

Wyman, David S. *The Abandonment of the Jews: America and the Holocaust 1941–1945.* New York: Pantheon, 1984.

Illness and Disability

The Elephant Man by Bernard Pomerance (1979)
The Good Woman of Setzuan by Bertolt Brecht (1943)
Angels in America by Tony Kushner (1990/1991)

Society's perception of what constitutes illness and disability, along with its treatments of such, have changed throughout the last century. While medical professionals have developed a better understanding of and treatments for both mental and physical illness, many areas of fear and ignorance remain. Many plays written on these themes are attempts to humanize the stories of those afflicted and to promote a better understanding of what afflicts them in order to encourage the general public not to demonize or exploit these people; these plays strive to make us understand the difficulties and pressures they face each day. Other modern dramatists have chosen to use illness as a metaphor for whatever they see as wrong with modern society. Some approach the theme of illness from both perspectives.

Bernard Pomerance's *The Elephant Man* is based on the true life story of a nineteenth-century figure, John Merrick, who was known as "the Elephant Man" because of massive deformities caused by his condition. Seeking to direct the audience's attention to the intellectual and sensitive individual afflicted with these deformities, rather than his illness, Pomerance suggests that the actor playing Merrick use only minimal differences in movement and speech to portray him, and have his deforming growths displayed only through descriptive language and some slide-show images, rather than by makeup or costume. Pomerance guides us to look beyond surfaces, to recognize Merrick for the kind and sensitive soul he was, and, by extension, to see the metaphorical illness existing within many whose outer appearance belies their inner corruption.

Bertolt Brecht was a propounder of "Epic theater," a kind of intellectual agit-prop, which attempts to provoke audiences toward social action. He saw realism as disconcerting, with its tendency to support the status quo in its efforts to present true life. Epic theater intentionally alienates its audience, by emphasizing its own artifice. This demands that people reexamine what they had previously perceived as reality, employing rational thought rather than unreliable feelings. He expects audiences to recognize the sad state of society once they have been freed from social restraints, and hopes they will then initiate change. Although the title character of Brecht's *Good Woman of Setzuan* is in some sense schizophrenic, in that she behaves as two totally separate people, the play is not an exploration of the consequences of mental illness. Brecht uses the suggestion of this illness as a metaphor for his view on how morality fares in the modern world—in his opinion, not very well. The action centers on the desire of Shen Te to be good, and the impossibility of acting in a moral fashion in modern society, given the way in which it operates.

Brecht uses songs and poems to focus attention on specific philosophical issues, such as when Shen Te sings "The Song of the Defenselessness of the Gods and the Good People," in which she questions why evil exists and why gods, if they are truly powerful, seem incapable of preventing it. The song asks the audience to consider that evil is not an outside force, but one of human origin, the same as goodness, and, therefore, it is up to humans to stem it. Characters in the play frequently speak directly to the audience, sometimes to confront them with social and political messages, but also to tell them what misfortunes to expect, to encourage audiences to go beyond just watching to see what happens, but to consider why and how bad things happen, which would make people better able to stop them from happening in the future.

Tony Kushner's two-part epic, *Angels in America,* is made up of two plays that span a period of five months during the mid-1980s, in which he both sympathetically chronicles the spread of the AIDS epidemic during the Reagan years and uses the illness as a metaphor for much of what he believes is wrong with American society. Together the plays relate a vast, sprawling saga comprising eight acts, broken into fifty-six scenes and an epilogue. Kushner mixes fantasy and reality, comedy and anguish, dirty politics and spiritual mysticism, personal dramas and world history, to create a dazzling work full of ingenuity and provocative ideas. The action takes place around New York City and in a heaven that resembles San Francisco after the 1906 earthquake—suggesting an outlook that stretches across America, across a century, and even beyond the bounds of life itself.

Kushner considers illness both in actual terms, as AIDS infects a nation, and in metaphorical terms, as he depicts the sad state into which society has generally fallen. While the motion of the first play, *Millennium Approaches,* tends toward destruction and breakdown as people grow further apart through ignorance, misunderstanding, fear, or just plain self-absorption, the second play, *Perestroika,* indicates a reversal of this dynamic. More comic in presentation than the first play, *Perestroika* depicts characters coming to terms with their lives and one another, learning to forgive and move on. Issues are resolved, growth occurs, people learn to better cope with loss, and the life principle beats back death. Although AIDS still exists, and not everyone has his or her ideal life and/or partner, a sense of hope and potential love pervades the play. That hope largely rests on the human capacity for change and adaptation, which is highlighted in the play's epigraph.

The Elephant Man begins in 1884, in the London Hospital at which John Merrick will later find refuge, where we meet Dr. Frederick Treves being welcomed as the new lecturer in anatomy. Discovering Merrick in a storefront sideshow, Treves brings him to the hospital for examination. The public, outraged at the apparent exploitation of Merrick in the sideshow, close the operation, forcing him and his manager, Ross, to flee to Belgium. There, they are again restricted from setting up show, and Ross sends Merrick back to England in disgust. Attacked on his arrival, Merrick is brought back to Treves by the police. The hospital takes him in permanently, although the doctor has trouble employing anyone to tend him because his appearance is so frightful. Treves tries to give Merrick the more normal life he desires, introducing him to women and society, including the actress, Mrs. Kendal, whose compassion benefits Merrick more than the doctor's restrictive ministration. Ross tries to reclaim Merrick now that he is a social success, but Merrick refuses to work with him again. Treves guiltily wonders how far he has been complicit in a similar, though well-meaning form of exploitation. On completing the church model he has been building, Merrick dies in his sleep, and we learn of his obituary.

Placed in a workhouse when he was only three by a mother who could not look at him, Merrick has developed a huge head with massive growths front and back that deform his mouth, obliterate his nose, and almost cover one eye. His condition is not elephantiasis, as his nickname suggests, but rather stems from a fungal growth that also smells terrible unless he bathes frequently. His limbs, except for one delicate hand and arm, are also deformed, and he is lame from a hip disease he contracted as a boy, and must use a cane to walk. The workhouse made him scrub floors and he was routinely beaten until Ross took him away, but only to use him as a sideshow display.

In his pitch Ross declares, "To live with his physical hideousness, incapacitating deformities and unremitting pain is trial enough, but to be exposed to the cruelly lacerating expressions of horror and disgust by all who behold him—is even more difficult to bear" (3). But Ross is the one exposing him to such ridicule. He abuses Merrick, calling him a "bloody donkey" (4), and steals Merrick's share of their take, abandoning him when he fails to be profitable. When he tries to get Merrick back, he clearly views him as property rather than a person. Merrick may be deformed on the outside, but, in his inner life he is as beautiful as the church he builds, unlike many around him whose outer appearances disguise inner ugliness. But as Merrick knows, like Romeo, people refuse to look beneath the surface and judge by outer appearances alone. Ross, we learn, is full of internal sickness, indicative of the truly degenerate character he is—just as the smooth-talking surface of Lord John, one of the society people to whom Treves introduces Merrick through the assistance of actress Mrs. Kendal, hides a profligate who squanders other people's money. Later, Treves shares his vision of the entire upper class as inwardly deformed by privilege and wealth into ruthless, dissipated, and ignorant people—everything that Merrick is not.

Because of his grotesque appearance and inability to speak clearly, Merrick is seen as less than human by most people he meets. The police regard him as an imbecile and ignore his requests for justice, not taking the trouble to decipher his speech. He is mocked, patronized, and treated as if he had done something wicked to bring this illness on himself, yet he takes all in stride, and never complains. He amazes the Bishop with his religious knowledge and outlook, believing firmly that he will be saved by Christ, and does not resent his afflictions. Merrick generously forgives Ross for stealing his money and abusing him. He displays genuine sympathy for others, such as the "Pinheads," and Porter, who gets fired for sneaking in to gawk at Merrick. By contrast, supposed humanitarians like Treves seem incapable of feeling, yet Treves advises Merrick to be less sympathetic if he wants to be like other people. However, Merrick knows Porter was treated too harshly, and refuses to be so limited in his mercy and understanding, refusing to accept the rules by which Treves lives, which finally leads Treves to question those rules himself.

Social reaction toward Merrick is indicative of an ambivalent attitude toward disease, from which many people shy away. They do not see the act of putting Merrick on display as indecent, but Merrick himself as indecent in his outward appearance. Their outrage at his being on display is meant to save him, yet it leads to him being beaten and having his only means of support taken away. Later the public sends in sufficient donations to the hospital to support him for life, but this is the same public who nearly dismembered him on his return from Brussels. Treves points out that Merrick's callers use him as a mirror to reflect back their obsessions, and do not actually see him at all, but Treves is as guilty of this as the rest. His intentions may have been more honorable than Ross's, but they turn out to be little less exploitative, as Treves uses Merrick to advance his own career.

Treves comes to recognize Merrick's humanity, and sees the man of intelligence, sensitivity, and imagination beneath the deformity, although it is not until after he analyzes his revealing response on seeing Mrs. Kendal naked in front of Merrick. Treves had brought in Mrs. Kendal, thinking that an actress would better be able to mask her horror and allow Merrick to meet a woman socially for the first time. Her question about Merrick's penis, and the fact it looks normal, indicates that she sees something in Merrick that Treves still resists knowing, that he truly is normal in many ways and has the same desires as other men. She tries to alleviate his acute loneliness, becoming his friend, introducing him to high society, and showing him her naked body. Treves's admonition to Merrick at this point, "Are you not ashamed? Do you know what you are? Don't you know what is forbidden?" (42), shows that for all he has told himself and Merrick, he does not see Merrick as normal and he becomes ashamed of his own calling as a doctor.

Treves begins to question the strict rules by which he lives and limits his compassion. He recognizes that his need to assert authority has often superseded any seeming acts of charity he has performed. He realizes that he needs to see his patients as real human beings rather than case studies, and begins to have nightmares in which he guiltily imagines a vengeful Merrick. But Merrick has nothing but words of gratitude for what little Treves has done for him. Merrick's meticulous construction of the church model, which he began when taking up residence at the hospital, acts as a metaphor for the way in which Merrick reconstructs himself in the eyes of both society and himself. He recreates himself in order to become better accepted by a society that remains blind to his true worth to the end, judging him finally by his deformity, as indicated by the hospital director's obituary. Merrick's one desire had been to be normal, a desire that finally kills him, but that he feels was worth the cost. By sleeping in a "normal" position, he essentially commits suicide, as the weight of his head crushes his windpipe. We are left to ponder if that was a fair price for such a noble soul to have to pay.

In *The Good Woman of Setzuan,* the gods seek a good person to try to end the poverty and drought that plague the province. Since the prostitute, Shen Te, offers them shelter after they have been turned away by all the wealthy people, they reward her for her goodness with one thousand silver dollars. Rejecting her former profession and opening a tobacco shop, Shen Te attempts to do the good works the gods expect of her, only to discover that to survive she must create an alternative and more ruthless self, her cousin Shui Ta, to protect her interests. Throughout the play she alternates between these two roles, getting into constant trouble as people take advantage of Shen Te, then having to bring in Shui Ta to sort things out. Shen Te falls in love with Yang Sun, giving him money that she needs, only to discover that he is using her and refuses to marry her without more money. Still loving Yang Sun, she turns down offers by the wealthy barber, Shu Fu, finds that she is pregnant, and becomes Shui Ta for an extended period to launch a successful tobacco factory to provide for her future child. Unable to find Shen Te, Shui Ta is arrested for her murder. The gods come to serve as judges, Shen Te confesses what she has done, and the gods depart, delighted that she is still alive, but without offering any solution to her dilemma. This task is left to the audience in the epilogue that follows.

Brecht's suggestion that people must become akin to being schizophrenic in order to ensure their survival suggests an illness in society itself. It is impossible to escape the evils of the modern world without becoming psychotic. In the modern world, Brecht insists that there is no chance to maintain a positive value structure without you or it being destroyed. The evil of society is evident from the start, which is why the gods had such a hard time finding anyone to offer them shelter. In Setzuan, all the residents are selfishly out for themselves, regardless of the harm they do to others. The area's drought is indicative of the paucity of goodness the province contains.

Shen Te is the epitome of goodness in a Christian sense, in her regard for others and her desire to assist others, even at a cost to herself. A gentle, motherly figure, she exudes love and compassion for all; she is willing to give everything she has to help others. But the Christian ethic, in its purest sense, which insists that a person give all and never take, proves impossible to uphold in a world of "give and take." To survive, which she must if she is to continue to do good, Shen Te finds that she must create the epitome of capitalism in Shui Ta. Each time he helps her surmount her problem and she thinks she can dispense with him, her difficulties mount. First she is in danger of losing a night's business, then her shop, then the shop of someone else, and, finally the future of her child. Each time the solution comes down to cold-hearted business tactics rather than compassion or fair play.

Shui Ta's pragmatism is not attractive, but it is acceptable given the way the world operates. Shen Te recognizes the terrible practicality of her alter ego, even as they stand opposed on nearly every point. He works the system, making friends with the local police, getting rid of those leeching off Shen Te without giving anything in return, cheating others who would cheat her if they could, and making better deals with a tough business approach that does not allow itself to be swayed by compassion. In Shui Ta's tobacco factory, even the duplicitous Yang Sun can rise, by being equally ruthless and brutal. But Shen Te's pseudoschizophrenia is self-destructive in that it will not allow her to act naturally, even while it is the only way for her to survive. Indeed, it nearly destroys her, and the locals may be right in thinking her murdered, as she weeps in her back room for sorrow at what Shui Ta is forced to do, while she is hardly ever seen.

Because of her love for Yang Sun, who is worthless and uncaring in return, Shen Te destroys the old couple who lend her money and then need it repaid when the man falls ill. This allows us to question even her goodness, and wonder how much the gods might be to blame by sullying her with money in the first place. They forced her to become part of a capitalist system in which she must constantly struggle to keep her head above water, frequently resorting to the nefarious practices of her alter ego, and at times having to sacrifice others to stay afloat herself. Brecht wishes us to recognize that when the good are so easily destroyed in this manner, we have come to accommodate evil within the social system, and the humanitarian response should be to seek better justice in the world and make crucial changes.

The gods begin the play looking well-fed and decently dressed, especially in comparison to the residents of Setzuan, but they become more haggard and ragged as the play proceeds, as their contact with human beings wears them down. They are only too eager to leave at the close and return to the shelter of heaven. They are truly incapable of helping with human problems, indicating that it is useless to look to any gods for help, and problems need to be solved by the people who cause them. The gods' unhelpful resolution insists that to live is to suffer, and they expect Shen Te to accept this and carry on. Brecht would ask that the world be changed so Shen Te can be offered a better option. By this he questions the rightness of Christian principle, being a determined believer in Marxism, which considers Christianity the "opium of the masses," and unsuitable as a workable social system.

Angels in America, Part One: Millennium Approaches begins at the funeral of Louis Ironson's grandmother, and the scent of death increases as Prior Walter tells his lover, Louis, he has AIDS. Unscrupulous Jewish Republican lawyer Roy Cohn tries to recruit Joe Pitt, a young, Mormon law clerk, to join the Justice Department so he can use his influence. Louis tries to support Prior, but finds it too intense, and guiltily walks out. Joe asks his agoraphobic wife, Harper, about Roy's offer, and she refuses to move to Washington. When Joe sees Louis crying, he comforts him, leading to the discovery that he is a repressed homosexual. Roy learns he has AIDS, but since the accompanying label of "homosexual" will weaken his political influence, he refuses to be called homosexual, even though he sleeps with men; instead, he announces that he has liver cancer. Harper tells Joe to take the job and she will leave him, but he wants to hold their marriage together, even against Roy's advice, and decides his conscience cannot allow him to take Roy's job. Drunk, he phones his mother, Hannah, to confess his homosexuality. She leaves Utah, coming to New York. Prior, who has been in and out of the hospital, hears voices and is visited by ancestors who prepare him for the coming of the angel. As Roy's condition worsens, the ghost of Ethel Rosenberg, whose execution he facilitated, sits watching. Louis and Joe meet and decide to have sex, as the Angel appears to Prior.

In *Part Two: Perestroika*, the Angel tells Prior to insist that people stop changing. Prior decides he cannot do this, and wrestles the Angel to get into heaven to return the book of prophecy. Louis and Joe spend time together, and while Joe says he loves Louis, Louis cannot condone Joe's manipulative legal practices and connection to Roy Cohn. Both try to rekindle their original partnerships, but Prior and Harper reject them, having moved on and become independent. Roy gets AZT, but dies in agony with Ethel Rosenberg watching. Although intensely disliked by all around him, they show him grudging respect, and even Ethel assists in saying Kaddish over his body. Hannah rescues Harper, and looks after her until Harper realizes the pointlessness of life with Joe, and discovers a new outlook. Hannah also helps Prior return to the hospital, face his angel, and reject his mission. The epilogue, set four years later, shows us Prior still alive, intending to hold on to life as long as possible.

The constant overlap and shifting dynamic of the plays' characters echo Harper's vision of the dead souls networking to protect the earth, only these are predominantly living souls whose changing interrelations, although often messy, also indicate human mutability. Kushner reinforces his emblem of human connection with split-focus scenes, in which different events play out concurrently, with sufficient common ground to suggest simultaneity. Connection is further emphasized by the way disparate characters appear in each other's dreams and visions, and how everyone becomes linked by various relationships. The characters' fears, desires, losses, and achievements frequently echo each other, indicating how similar human beings are regardless of gender, race, age, or sexual preference, to which end, Kushner would suggest, people should have no difficulty eventually uniting. The true illness in society is not AIDS, as much as people's selfishness, which makes them incapable of forgiving and embracing others.

The plays teach us much about the process of AIDS and how it affects people physically and psychologically. Both Prior and Roy have AIDS, and while Roy dies in incredible pain, Prior remains alive after nearly five years and is determined to keep going. We see the stress under which Prior's partner is placed, wondering if he has the disease and whether he has the strength to stand by his lover. We also see the fears of abandonment and readjustment of self-image Prior must face, alongside the ups and downs of the effects of the disease as Prior and Roy switch between home and hospital. We learn of the potential breakthrough with AZT medications, but how they are kept for the privileged few. The epigraph to *Millennium Approaches* suggests that when we live in unpleasant times, pain becomes our means of knowing we are still alive and should be accepted, and this doubles as an apt metaphor for living with AIDS.

Prior tells the story of an ancestor in a leaking boat who randomly drowned passengers to stay afloat, seeing it as a metaphor for modern life, particularly living with AIDS. Everyone is in such a boat, "waiting, terrified, while implacable, unsmiling men irresistibly strong, seize . . . maybe the person next to you, maybe you, and with no warning at all, with time only for a quick intake of air, you are pitched into freezing, turbulent water and salt and darkness to drown" (*Millennium*, 42). The modern world has become filled with people like the Reagan family, whom Louis describes as having no connection or love between them, as everyone avoids such responsibilities. Roy insists that this is the only way to be—you can either be nice or effective—and it is better to live alone so one can be more ruthless. But such isolation exacts a cost on the soul.

Prior is openly homosexual, whereas Roy refuses to be so labeled for he sees that as announcing oneself as a loser. Roy buys his way with stolen money and threats into the best drug programs, but they do him little good. Although we may admire his spirit and vitality, as do many other characters, his basic selfishness tells us he is rotten within, full of the selfish values Kushner wants to expose, and deserves to die, unlike Prior, who is told by Harper that, "Deep inside you, there's a part of you . . . entirely free of disease" (*Millennium*, 34). But Roy is at least unlike Joe, who sees homosexuality as sinful, and ruins his own and Harper's life by trying to repress it. Joe admits he married Harper because she seemed so messed up that next to her he was bound to look good—

hardly a solid basis for any relationship. Although Joe rejects Roy's job, he accepts his philosophy, which is why Louis eventually rejects him as poisoned. The play's central image is that of the Angel—perfect, but dangerous—for perfection implies stasis, and the Angel's disgust with change and evolution makes her the enemy of humankind and a symbol of the death principle opposed to that of life. To survive, society must embrace progress and change because that is what life is all about, just as the AIDS community needs to resist the Angel's call to nostalgia and passivity if it wishes to survive. Roy is a man of action who demands, and therefore receives, power; by contrast, Louis, despite his political liberalism, seems ineffectual, by which Kushner prepares us for the truth that change is never easy. The struggle between principles of life and death is found throughout the play, and in a sense it is the struggle itself that denotes life, supported by Kushner's close association of life with sex. Harper, despite the apocalyptic fears against which she constantly struggles, still desires life, indicated by her desire to become pregnant. Prior, though living with AIDS, refuses to be diminished by it, and though sick, desires life, because all life is sacred, regardless of the quality of that life. The play ends with his words of hope: "This disease will be the end of many of us, but not nearly all, and the dead will be commemorated and will struggle on with the living" (*Perestroika*, 146).

FURTHER SUGGESTED READING

Brecht, Bertolt. *The Good Woman of Setzuan.* New York: Grove, 1965.

Dingwall, Robert. *Aspects of Illness.* New York: St. Martin's Press, 1976.

Edson, Margaret. *Wit.* New York: Faber, 1999.

Fisher, James. *The Theater of Tony Kushner: Living Past Hope.* New York: Routledge, 2001.

Frank, Arthur W. *At the Will of the Body: Reflections on Illness.* Boston: Houghton Mifflin, 1991.

Geis, Deborah R., and Steven F. Kruger. *Approaching the Millennium: Essays on* Angels in America. Ann Arbor: University of Michigan Press, 1997.

Graham, Peter W., and Fritz H. Oehlschlaeger. *Articulating the Elephant Man: Joseph Merrick and His Interpreters.* Baltimore: Johns Hopkins University Press, 1992.

Gray, Alasdair. *Working Legs: A Two-act Play for Disabled Performers.* Glasgow: Dog and Bone, 1997.

Kleber, Pia. *Exceptions and Rules: Brecht, Planchon, and* The Good Person of Szechwan. New York: Lang, 1987.

Kramer, Larry. *The Normal Heart.* New York: NAL, 1985.

Kushner, Tony. *Angels in America.* New York: TCG, 1992.

Pomerance, Bernard. *The Elephant Man.* New York: Grove, 1979.

Sontag, Susan. *Illness as Metaphor.* New York: Farrar, Straus & Giroux, 1978.

Speirs, Ronald. *Bertolt Brecht.* New York: St. Martin's Press, 1987.

International Cultural Communities

M. Butterfly by David Henry Hwang (1988)
"MASTER HAROLD" . . . *and the boys* by Athol Fugard (1982)
I Will Marry When I Want by Ngugi wa Thiong'o (1977)

As the last century progressed, it almost seemed as if the world were shrinking as globalization created a single international community bound together by increased telecommunications, the Internet, and a global economy. Yet, there remains a tendency to overlook important differences in culture that influence how people behave and react. Obviously, there is a great wide world beyond the United States and Britain, whose playwrights tend to be better known in the West, and this chapter can only touch on a small selection of plays that inform us of this. In an effort to be as diverse as possible, the three plays selected focus on people from China, France, South Africa, and Kenya, and each deals in part with the idea of the damage caused when differing cultures clash, to give a sense of how important a role culture plays in the lives of everyone.

The idea for *M. Butterfly*, a play that explores misconceptions between Eastern and Western cultures, came to David Henry Hwang when he read a newspaper story about a French diplomat, Bouriscot. Bouriscot had led a twenty-year affair with a Mr. Shi, whom he had believed to be a woman, during which time he passed secret information to the Chinese at his lover's request. The story indicated Bouriscot's evident lack of knowledge of the East, citing his assertion that Chinese women were very modest and shy with their lovers. Hwang knew this to be untrue, but recognized in it the Western colonial dream that stereotypes Asian women (if not all "good" natives) as submissive and respectful. Bouriscot had fallen in love with a stereotype, not a real person, and Shi must have consciously used this stereotype to trick him. Hwang adapts this story into a play, renaming the participants Gallimard and Song Liling.

The "M" of the title stands for Monsieur. The Puccini opera *Madame Butterfly*, in which an American naval officer, Pinkerton, buys Butterfly as a wife, gets her pregnant, and then deserts her, after which she commits suicide, is a Western creation. It is firm evidence of the pervasive influence of the stereotype Hwang saw in the Bouriscot episode, and he decided to deconstruct this opera through the lens of Bouriscot's experience and explore the cultural aspects of his betrayal. The play is not intended to be anti-West in the way the West stereotypes the East, since Hwang understands that the East also stereotypes Westerners. He is also not particularly interested in how Song sexually fooled Gallimard, nor in suggesting that Gallimard might be a closet homosexual. For most of the play, the audience is as seduced as Gallimard by this false image of acquiescent femininity, assisted, no doubt, by the exotic costumes in which we first see Song garbed. Hwang's intent behind the play is to ask both East and West to set aside damaging and limiting cultural, sexual, and racial misconceptions, and seek the truer equality he believes better reflects reality.

"*MASTER HAROLD*" . . . *and the boys* by Athol Fugard, also deals with cultural collision, but within the same society—that between blacks and whites in a South Africa divided by the bigotry of apartheid. The play is partly autobiographical, and examines some of the author's personal experience as a white South African. He expands the shame he felt after spitting on his boyhood friend, Sam, after a rare argument, into a metaphor for the shame of the entire South African nation and its troubling apartheid system. The white superiority on which apartheid rested is exposed as a sham, and Fugard suggests that through better education and communication it could be combated. At seventeen, Hally is an intelligent and sensitive individual, which makes the fact that he reverts to a racist stance all the more disturbing in its implication of the depths to which prejudice runs in South Africa. Under stress, his racist training sadly wins out over his humanitarian instincts.

Ngugi wa Thiong'o's *I Will Marry When I Want* offers an encapsulated history lesson on the Mau Mau rebellion against British rule in Kenya, which precipitated Kenya's independence, alongside the story of a simple family fooled by local business tycoons into losing what little they had gained from that rebellion. Although white oppression had supposedly been challenged by the Mau Mau, we soon realize that Kenya is still economically dependent on foreign money. The play also conveys the way African attitudes toward courtship, family relations, and business have been challenged by values alien to that culture. Ngugi's overt criticism of the economic policies of Kenyan leaders in the play led to it being banned in Kenya and Ngugi imprisoned for two years. Originally written in Gikuyu, a native Kenyan language, in 1982 the play was translated into English by Ngugi and fellow writer Ngugi wa Mirii.

In *M. Butterfly*, René Gallimard, a French diplomat previously on duty in China but now in jail, relates how he fell in love with Song Liling, a Chinese opera star. Not realizing that Song was a man, Gallimard embarked on a relationship in which he envisioned "her" as the beautiful and submissive title character from Puccini's *Madame Butterfly*, and himself in the role of the foreigner who seduces and abuses her. Song plays his game in order to get confidential information from him for her government, and feed him misinformation to give back to his. She pleasures him sexually, and even pretends to give him a son to bind him to her. After giving disastrous advice about Vietnam based on faulty information given by Song, Gallimard is returned to France and Song is punished by her own government for losing this valuable source of information, spending four years laboring on a farm. She is later sent to France to get more information, and for fifteen years Gallimard keeps her as his mistress, until their espionage, and Song's gender, are uncovered, and Gallimard is sent to jail as a laughing stock. On reflection, he realizes that he is closer to the character of Butterfly, betrayed by her lover, and, dressing in Song's kimono and wig, kills himself as the original Butterfly had done.

Even after knowing how he has been betrayed, Gallimard still longs for his Butterfly and the way things were, indicating that he has never truly seen Song, but only the fantasy of "her" he has created in his imagination. Neither strong nor good-looking, Gallimard has always felt inadequate with women. He loves *Madame Butterfly* because it tells the story of a brave and beautiful woman who will give everything to a mediocre man, like himself. Stuck in a passionless marriage, undertaken as a career move, he seeks sexual thrills elsewhere and Song fulfills his every desire. It is unsurprising that he refuses to look any deeper to see her for what she truly is. Like the women in pornography, Butterfly appears utterly compliant, holding herself as worthless, willing to be degraded, and allowing the man to completely dominate her.

Gallimard snobbishly insists that he is not like the crass American, Pinkerton, but his treatment of Song is only marginally better. He does all he can to torment and humiliate Song by ignoring her for weeks to see how desperate he can make her become and even conducting an affair he finds personally distasteful, solely because it upsets her. He enjoys the rush of power such deceits give him and the approbation he receives at work for having a foreign mistress. He feels himself superior because he is a Westerner and, although there is no evidence to support this belief, he refuses to accept that it could be otherwise. His own society supports his view, rewarding him with a promotion on witnessing his new aggressiveness, self-confidence, and apparent understanding of China. Yet, unlike Pinkerton, Gallimard does offer Song a real marriage, although she refuses, and later takes her in and provides for her back in France. Such actions allow him to be more sympathetic than his operatic prototype, though little less patronizing.

Despite playing the role of Butterfly to Gallimard's Pinkerton, Song is not entirely submissive at the start, and even warns Gallimard of his limited understanding of the Chinese. She is self-assured, mocking, often taking the lead, and politically astute. When Gallimard speaks about Butterfly's suicide as an act of beauty, Song quickly points out that if positions were reversed and this were a relationship in which a homecoming queen had been ditched by a Japanese businessman, no one would be calling her suicide beautiful, but rather an act of insanity. Yet Gallimard insists that She become his Butterfly and, to win his confidence, Song accepts the challenge. In his assumed cultural superiority and misunderstanding, Gallimard interprets her earlier actions as bold and outspoken on the surface to hide a shy and fearful heart. No wonder it is so easy to fool him into giving away state secrets just to show off and to trick him into believing that Asians really admire Westerners, want to be like them, and will always bow to what they see as a greater power, offering no resistance, when, in reality, the opposite is closer to truth.

Gallimard is utterly unaware of how Eastern society works. He allows Song to entertain him in her apartment, not realizing how scandalous that would seem to her society. On his return to France, he still holds this false image of China as more civilized, even while his wife points out how similar France and China are, as the French riot in the streets in Paris. This scene also comes shortly after we have just witnessed the inherently uncivilized treatment that Song's fellow citizens have put her through after Gallimard's departure. As Song explains as a witness at the reenactment of Gallimard's trial in Paris, Western men see themselves as masculine and powerful with their weapons, industry, and wealth. By contrast, they view the East as feminine and weak, full of poverty, and delicate, artistic sensibilities, just waiting to be dominated by the stronger West. Song suggests that, given this biased cultural background, Gallimard could not but view any Easterner as female, regardless of the individual's true gender.

China is not pictured as blameless or even the victim in this cultural impasse. Song may play the role of Butterfly, but it is one she knows to be false and it is she who takes on the role of the betrayer Pinkerton by the close, calling out "Butterfly" over Gallimard's corpse. She also tells us much about the negative aspects of Chinese society since the Revolution. China has become very restricted, with little room for freedom of expression or action. For all the talk of equality, men still dominate and people are generally kept oppressively cowed by authority. We see the uncomfortable contradictions within the new order as Chin instructs Song, insisting that Song not indulge in any homosexual practices, while also demanding that she play the role of concubine to Gallimard in exchange for state secrets. Later we see Song beaten and publicly humiliated, and forced to give up her craft as an opera singer to work at manual labor, despite all she has done for the cause with her spying, as the country becomes xenophobic and antagonistic to its own cultural past.

Set in South Africa in 1950, "MASTER HAROLD" . . . and the boys introduces us to Sam and Willie, two black men who work in the tearooms belonging to white, seventeen-year-old Harold's parents. Harold, called Hally to those close to him, is friendly with both men, and has shared his school lessons with Sam to have someone with whom he can talk on an intellectual level. He feels uncomfortable with his disabled, belligerent father, so Sam takes on a fatherly role and Willie that of an older brother. After work, Sam is helping Willie prepare for a dance contest and Hally arrives from school to do his homework. He and Sam talk, recalling a time when they flew a kite together, and comment on various political and social issues. All is friendly until, shortly after Hally has heard the troubling news that his father is on his way home, Sam crosses a line by chastising Hally for not showing his father enough respect. Hally takes out the fear and anger he feels toward his father on Sam, insisting that he call him "Master Harold," and tells a racist joke to belittle him. In response, Sam shows him his bare behind, at which point Hally spits in his face. The more mature of the two, Sam backs down and offers Hally another chance at friendship, but the boy is too ashamed and leaves. The play closes as Willie dances with Sam to distract him from Hally's behavior.

Hally's disabled father embodies the whole apartheid system, his debilitating illness a metaphor for the racism that held South Africa back for so many years. Yet he is afflicted by more than a bad leg: he is also a drunkard, prone to borderline psychotic ranting against blacks and insistent that Hally accept his racist outlook without question. His attitudes have emotionally influenced his son, even as Hally intellectually recognizes them to be false and prefers the more educated, nonprejudiced ideology of Sam. When frustrated by his father's limitations, the son behaves with the same prejudice, using Sam as a scapegoat to draw attention away from his own insecurities. This, Fugard suggests, is the central impulse behind apartheid: aside from the economic advantages of keeping blacks poor so they can be better exploited, it allows whites to cover up their own shortcomings by a pretense that they are superior just because they are white. Hally can either follow his parents' lead or try to right the wrong, but if he chooses the former he will end up as bitter and twisted as his father.

The confrontation between Sam and Hally is sparked by the conflict within Hally between the corrupt legacy of apartheid he has inherited from his birth father and the more humane education and moral guidance he has received from Sam, his preferred father figure. The conflict between the two begins verbally, but escalates to such outlandish gestures between them as spitting from Hally and Sam baring his buttocks. It becomes uncertain where they can go next. Sam's decision to eschew violence and attempt to renew their relationship is a positive one, but it is one for which Hally is evidently not yet ready, as Willie suggests by emphasizing Hally's youth.

The "boys" of the title, refers to the adult males, Sam and Willie, as they are disparagingly called by many whites. But Sam, especially, despite the evident limitations of his life (he works in a tearoom), has a composure and intellect that belie the white assessment of blacks as inferior. Although the seven-year friendship between Sam and Hally may seem incongruous, given their backgrounds (and the fact that the play dared to depict black and white actors on the same stage was considered revolutionary in South Africa), this is overshadowed by the delight both gain from their interplay. For the most part, these two display both affection and respect for each other. Sam is more aware of the fragility of their relationship than Hally, but he maintains a faith that it can survive, which is supported by his evident love for the boy.

Willie is less intellectual than Sam, but full of enthusiasm, and he is equally likable. He exhibits a physical exuberance to balance the mental exuberance of his friend. He treats Hally as one would a younger brother and Sam as an older brother, to whom he, too, looks for guidance and advice. When Sam, in his disappointment over Hally's behavior toward him, considers hitting the boy, it is Willie who breaks the tension by reminding Sam of Hally's youth. It is also Willie who tries to cheer Sam up after Hally has walked out. But Willie can be overbearing, as he has been with his submissive girlfriend Hilda, an ironic echo of the relationship between Hally's parents, showing how similar these racial groups really can be.

Two central metaphors used by Fugard are the kite and the dance (which will be picked up in Brian Friel's *Dancing at Lughnasa*). The kite represents the hope of racial cooperation. Sam designs, builds, and flies the kite, despite young Hally's doubts and embarrassment over the project. Its flight marks a positive moment for Hally, who expects to be "perpetually disappointed." Yet the young Hally misses the significance of the memory. Sam had made the kite to cheer up Hally after they had been to a bar to carry home his drunken father. The kite was meant to teach Hally to look up, rather than down in shame. But Sam now reveals something of which Hally had been unaware; the bench to which Sam had tied the kite was "Whites Only," and only Hally could sit on it. Sam insists Hally is now old enough to open his eyes, stand up, and walk away from such benches, and thereby discard any tolerance of racial prejudice.

Sam's engaging and subtle analysis of the dance contest for which Willie practices as a symbol of a harmonious world where no one "bumps" into anyone else, not only tells us that Sam is intelligent and perceptive, but also helps Hally to realize that black South African culture is not as primitive or empty as he has been told. For Sam, the dance represents the possibility of integration, just as he, the expert dancer, has integrated white education with black know-how. Yet Hally refuses to learn to dance. Our only hope is that this is a result of his evident immaturity, indicated by his frequent inability to see the implications behind what is said and done, and not a sign of an irredeemable adherence to racist ideology.

I Will Marry When I Want tells the story of a poor Kenyan laborer, Kiguunda, his wife, Wangeci, and their teenage daughter, Gathoni. Initially content with his small plot of land, Kiguunda naively mortgages his land to pay for a ceremony to consecrate his own marriage in the Christian church to please his prospective in-laws, believing that John Muhuuni, the son of local magnate, Ahab Kioi wa Kanora, intends to marry his daughter. Meanwhile, Muhunni impregnates Gathoni and casts her off. Gathoni's parents try to coerce Kioi into offering restitution, but Kioi is rescued by his wife, Jezebel, and Kiguunda's family loses their land to the bank. It appears that the whole thing was an elaborate and ruthless plot by Kioi to gain Kiguunda's land for development. The play is largely concerned with the betrayal of the common people in Kenya by their postindependence leadership. The expectation was that, in the aftermath of colonial rule as Kenya declared her independence, the land would be restored to the Kenyan people. However, it seemed as if Kenyan independence only exacerbated the desire of a wealthy, Kenyan few to attract European investment, as they took land away from the indigenous population to build factories specializing in exported goods that offered little benefit to any but these wealthy few. This is what happens to Kiguunda as Kioi plans to build an insecticide factory on his land.

The wealth of men like Kioi depends on European connections; he acts as a figurehead for foreign industrial investments. His presence as director of banks and other companies provides a façade that such businesses are owned by Kenyans. His reward is a sizable chunk of the profits for very little risk or work. This betrayal of the Kenyan people by the ruling elite is further highlighted by Ngugi's negative association of Christian names with his villains, which he sees as running against African culture. Kioi's wife is called Jezebel, and like her biblical counterpart, she assists her husband in forcibly appropriating the land of another. While the Bible's Jezebel assists King Ahab in acquiring the vineyards of Naboth by having him stoned to death, the Jezebel in *I Will Marry When I Want* helps her husband, also named Ahab, to avoid recrimination by pulling a gun on Kiguunda when he threatens Kioi's life, and thereby allowing Kioi to keep the land out of which he has tricked Kiguunda. Her Western gun against Kiguunda's Mau Mau sword further emphasizes their differing allegiances, who is in control, and how they plan, through a superior technology, to stay in control.

Ngugi sees the conversion of African peoples to Christianity as another way the Western world has sought to dominate and subvert African culture. He depicts this cultural treason when he shows Kiguunda forced to take the name of Winston Smith and Wangeci that of Rosemary Magdalene on exchanging wedding vows in the Christian consecration of their marriage. This forcible change of identity illustrates just one way in which the roots of cultural imperialism remain to flourish in Kenya and detract from traditional Kenyan customs. Kiguunda and Wangeci become perverted by Western materialism in their social aspirations through the marriage of their daughter into wealth; this makes their loss of land a suitable punishment. At the play's start they had been happy with what little they had and had betrayed that contentment by striving for something more and, more importantly, something tainted by Western influence.

The fact that Gathoni defied her parents in traveling to Mombasa with Muhuuni is another way in which Western values have brought misfortune to this family. Traditionally, a daughter would do whatever her parents wished. Gathoni is as naive as her parents when it comes to dealing with the Kioi family. She believes Muhuuni when he says he will not marry a girl who has not conceived, so she gets pregnant, expecting him to then marry her. He casts her off in the same way his parents cast off her parents once they get what they want from them. In the same way, Ngugi sees the Mau Mau as having been betrayed by the postindependence Kenyan government.

Kiguunda becomes a drunk, a sad contrast to the proud landowner from the play's start, and Gathoni becomes a barmaid, but despite this regression the play ends on a determinedly hopeful note. The family's neighbor, Gicaamba, a former member of the Mau Mau revolutionary army, joins with Kiguunda and others in renewing their Mau Mau oaths to reclaim the land from foreign ownership, thus showing they have not yet been defeated, even if progress is slower than they had expected.

There have been references throughout the play to the oaths taken by Mau Mau not to betray one another to the British authorities or to sell land to the Europeans, and these serve to convey the nobility of the Mau Mau cause against the deceit and violence of the Homeguard, whose ascendancy to power is described as achieved through crooked means. The Homeguard was a quasi-military branch of the British police force made up of African loyalists who were supposed to restore calm after the disruptions of the Mau Mau attacks. What they did instead was help identify and detain Mau Mau members, which Ngugi views as the worst kind of treachery. The martyred Mau Mau leader, Dedan Kimaathi, is held in contrast to the Homeguard as a man of honor. Ngugi sees men like him as being the true progenitors of Kenya's freedom, and the rightful heirs to political leadership in Kenya.

FURTHER SUGGESTED READING

Fugard, Athol. "*MASTER HAROLD*" . . . *and the boys*. New York: Penguin, 1984.
Gikandi, Simon. *Ngugi wa Thiong'o*. New York: Cambridge University Press, 2000.
Hwang, David Henry. *M. Butterfly*. New York: NAL, 1988.
Killam, Gordon Douglas, Ed. *Critical Perspectives on Ngugi wa Thiong'o*. Washington, DC: Three Continents, 1984.
Lorca, Garcia Federico. *III Tragedies*. New York: New Directions, 1955.
Lynch, Daniel C. *After the Propaganda State: Media, Politics and 'Thought Work' in Reformed China*. Stanford: Stanford University Press, 1999.
Nazareth, Peter, Ed. *Critical Essays on Ngòugòi wa Thiong'o*. New York: Twayne, 2000.
Ngugi wa Thiong'o. *I Will Marry When I Want*. London: Heinemann, 1982.
Skloot, Robert. "Breaking the Butterfly: The Politics of David Henry Hwang." *Modern Drama* 33 (1990): 59–66.
Soyinka, Wole. *Madmen and Specialists*. New York: Hill and Wang, 1971.
Street, Douglas. *David Henry Hwang*. Boise, Idaho: Boise State University Press, 1989.

Ungar, Sanford J. *Africa: The People and Politics of an Emerging Continent.* New York: Simon & Schuster, 1985.

Walcott, Derek. *Dream on Monkey Mountain and Other Plays.* New York: Straus and Giroux, 1970.

Walder, Dennis. *Athol Fugard.* New York: Grove, 1985.

Wertheim, Albert. *The Dramatic Art of Athol Fugard.* Bloomington: Indiana University Press, 2000.

Issues of Sexuality

Equus by Peter Shaffer (1975)
A Streetcar Named Desire by Tennessee Williams (1947)
The Normal Heart Larry Kramer (1985)

Open displays or discussion of sexuality in modern drama swiftly escalated as the twentieth century progressed, beginning with a virtual silence about such matters to a point where talk about sex has become relatively commonplace and full frontal nudity hardly even shocking. In 1947, the "rape" of Blanche DuBois in *A Streetcar Named Desire* is only inferred, as it takes place offstage, but by 1975 we watch Alan Strang, in *Equus*, simulate an orgasm while naked onstage, and by the 1980s, playwrights were relatively free to openly discuss homosexuality. Some plays use sex as a means of titillation or to shock their audiences; others explore issues of sexuality with greater sensitivity, striving to expand our understanding and tolerance of both heterosexuality and homosexuality.

The period of burgeoning sexuality that comes with the onset of puberty often seems the most problematic, at times even traumatic. Moral expectations and an entrenched social prudery that has long made us squeamish in matters of sexuality make this a time of suppression as well as discovery. How young people learn to express (or repress) their sexuality and how they view that of others often stays with them into adulthood. Seventeen-year-old Alan Strang, the teenage protagonist of Peter Shaffer's *Equus*, presents an extreme case of adolescent sexuality gone awry through the skewered instruction he has received from his parents and his own desire for companionship and spiritual fulfillment. The psychiatrist brought in to examine Alan, after he has mutilated six horses, is both horrified and attracted to the strange sexual religion Alan creates for himself. Shaffer's play suggests an underlying relationship between sex and religion; both, when most satisfying, have roots in the spiritual and both can have unpleasant consequences, often leading to violence, when restricted.

But it is not just among adolescents that sexuality can cause problems. At the center of *A Streetcar Named Desire*, by Tennessee Williams, is Blanche DuBois, a grown woman, who initially survives but then destroys herself through a sexuality she cannot control. After a youthful marriage to a man whom she discovered to be gay on their wedding night and drove to suicide by her disgust, Blanche begins using sex as an escape from a guilty and stultifying life. Haunted by her passing youth, she preys on young boys until she is virtually chased from town after a scandal with a student from the school at which she taught. Blanche's perverse and tortured sexuality is balanced against the healthy sexuality of her sister, Stella. Stella's husband, Stanley, is attracted to both, but it is Stella who wins his allegiance as she delivers him a healthy child and Blanche is taken off to a mental hospital.

Although there are references to homosexuality in *A Streetcar Named Desire*, Larry Kramer's *The Normal Heart* is a more direct consideration of homosexual sexuality and the political and personal pressures on gay men in particular. Kramer sets his play in America during the nationwide spread of AIDS in the early 1980s, and recounts the striving of a small group of activists to try to bring the plight of the gay community, which was the worst hit, to public attention, and to encourage strategies within that community for its future survival. The play is both a historical account of the early days of AIDS and an examination of gay life in general and how those lives were impacted by this epidemic. Kramer designed *The Normal Heart* as a type of modern agit-prop, which is reflected not only in the characters' constant calls to action but also in the set design, with its white flat covered in written facts, figures, and names associated with AIDS. His central protagonist, Ned Weeks, is largely autobiographical, so Ned's declarations directly reflect Kramer's beliefs regarding both gayness and the ongoing AIDS crisis.

The events of *Equus* are related largely through a series of flashbacks by psychiatrist Martin Dysart, who has been trying to discover why a formerly quiet teen gouged out the eyes of a group of horses. Dysart relates his findings, that Alan, in response to his father's anger and his mother's religious teachings, formed a personal religion that helped him to deal with his growing sexual feelings, but that unwittingly led to this dreadful crime. It becomes clear that Dysart envies Alan's passion, even though it manifested itself so destructively, and feels disillusioned with the restrictive world of normalcy he inhabits by contrast.

Despite its combative setting inside a boxing ring, the opening images of a boy tenderly fondling the sculpted head of a horse, which appears to reciprocate his affection, seem at odds with the knowledge we are soon given that this same boy has recently stabbed out the eyes of six horses with a steel spike. The boxing ring setting warns us of the violence to come, but it is more the psychic torment of the boy than the physical pain of the blinded horses that undergirds the drama. This is a crime so heinous that most doctors view him as unworthy of help and want him locked up in jail. Dysart, however, finds himself emotionally drawn to the power of the passion that must have caused such behavior.

Dora Strang, Alan's mother, has devoted years to reading the Bible to her son and instilling in him the belief that sex must be "spiritual" or it is sinful and that God is always watching with eyes that are everywhere. Central to her belief is the idea of Christ, and the painful death he underwent, a scene of which she has placed on her son's bedroom wall. We will find that she is partly to blame for her son's unorthodox sexual development, but the authoritarian treatment by Frank Strang, Alan's father, is also responsible. Fiercely controlling, Frank forbids Alan to watch television and mocks his wife's religious beliefs to the point where he rips down her picture of Christ and, what will later become highly significant, replaces it with a picture of a horse. Frank blames Alan's religious upbringing for his crimes and accepts no personal responsibility. But Alan is largely led by his father's mockery of Christianity, and a home life of constant tension from which he needs an escape, to create a religion of his own.

Having had Christ's picture on his wall exchanged for that of a horse, it is unsurprising that the god of the twelve-year-old Alan's new religion takes the form of a horse. He calls it Equus, and just as his picture of Christ had been in chains, Equus must always wear a chain in his mouth for the "sins of the world." The riding stable where he works becomes a Temple, from which he takes horses late at night to ride naked and bareback until he reaches an orgasm, which makes him feel as if he is united with his god. Thus he merges sex and religion, and unites both spiritual and sexual longing in a fashion that satisfies his growing need for release, exacerbated by his unhappy home life with constantly bickering parents. Under hypnosis, Alan reenacts his bizarre ritual for Dysart, who feels stimulated by the resulting scene of freedom, unfettered by what he sees as stifling social restraints.

The blinding of the horses grows out of Alan's increased desire, as he grows older, to experience sex with a girl, and the accompanying guilt that God must be watching his attempt to commit such a sin. Jill Mason, another stable employee, persuades Alan to take her to a sex movie. To the embarrassment of both father and son, Frank attends the same show, which prompts Alan's association of guilt with sex. Following this, Jill tries to seduce Alan at the stable, but his fear of being watched by God (who in his religion appears as a horse) leads him to impotence. Angry at both her and the possibility that having seen his sinful behavior his God may now abandon him, he threatens Jill with a steel spike and, when she flees, turns on the watching horses in a state of panic and stops them from looking any longer.

Having uncovered Alan's secret, Dysart knows he can work with the boy and make him "normal," but there is a part of Dysart that does not want to do this. Alan's fervor and passion, although dangerous, are at least less predictable, more original and alive than the normalcy Dysart sees as restricting himself and others. Dysart's childless marriage is mutually convenient but without passion, and he sees Alan's ability to experience such ferocious passion as enviable. In archetypal terms, what Shaffer shows us is the difference between the Apollonian and Dionysian approaches to life. Dysart is the embodiment of the Apollonian, with his rational mind and controlled emotions, but balanced against this is the irrational, wild passion exhibited by Alan in his moment of orgiastic freedom riding across the open field. Shaffer asks us to question which is ultimately the more fulfilling.

A *Streetcar Named Desire* begins with the arrival of Stella's sister, Blanche DuBois, looking for shelter from the mess she has made of her life. Stella's husband, Stanley Kowalski, resents Blanche's intrusion, and when he sees her attempting to ensnare one of his friends, Mitch, breaks up the relationship and rapes Blanche when his wife is in the hospital delivering their child, which sends Blanche over the edge into madness.

The play illustrates many of Williams's concerns regarding sexuality, such as the consequences of nonconformity, and the seemingly inevitable destruction of sensitive or romantic souls by those who are insensitive or materialistic. Set in the Elysian Fields district of New Orleans—a run-down tenement section of town—the name becomes an ironic allusion to paradise. Instead, this play is full of sex and deadly violence, evoked by the steamy atmosphere of its New Orleans location, snatches of blues music, and streetcars named "Desire" and "Cemeteries."

The name of the family mansion Blanche has lost, Belle Reve, means "beautiful dream," and indicates the dream-life Blanche creates in trying to avoid the truth, the most awful part of that truth that she drove her gay husband to suicide by her disgust at his sexual preference. It is this past that forever threatens to overwhelm her, indicated by the continual intrusion of the "Varsouviana," which was playing at the ball during which her husband killed himself. Blanche lives in a fake world of sentimental illusion because reality would destroy her, and constantly bathes herself, as if she can wash away the taint of her guilt. Her white dress and name, meaning "white woods," indicates not innocence but a paucity of spirit. On the surface she seems vivacious and flirtatious, but this is a sham, for when her guard drops we see how frightened and drained of life she really is.

Blanche is fatally divided, caught between the desire to be a lady—young, beautiful, and concerned with old-fashioned Southern ways—and a bohemian—erring and excessive in her appetites. Chasing her lost youth, she intermittently chases young boys to the point where she must leave a scandalized town and start afresh. In New Orleans, Blanche hides her real age and shady past as she tries to attract a decent man to clean up her life. She nearly fools Stanley's colleague, Mitch, into believing her to be the lady she insists that she is. But her attraction to young men will continue to cause trouble: it led her into an unsuitable marriage and more recently lost her job, and she cannot resist flirting with the newspaper boy. We should realize that marriage to Mitch will not solve her problems and it is the inability to satisfy both sides of her nature that causes her downfall. Blanche seeks love, but her very delusional nature works against her ever finding this.

In opposition to the deathly whiteness of Blanche is her younger sister, Stella, who is healthy, pregnant, and full of life. Stella loves Blanche but, unlike her sister, has rejected her refined, Southern heritage in favor of a more brutal, low-class existence with Stanley, who offers her a life of the senses. Stanley provides her with all she needs, including an exciting, guilt-free sexual relationship. In comparison to Blanche, Stella seems open and sincere, but she is not naive and will only allow Blanche so much leeway; although she humors her sister to keep things smooth, she knows what Blanche has become and is largely unimpressed with her airs. At the close of the play she allows Blanche to be taken to the asylum because to acknowledge that her sister has been raped by her husband would ruin a marital relationship on which she depends, and, in this matter, she chooses ignorance over truth.

Stanley sees Blanche as a disruptive force in his household, as Stella picks up Blanche's snooty habits and grows critical of him. His response is to become increasingly belligerent toward Blanche. He has no time for illusions and insists on facing reality, which clearly puts him at odds with Blanche. Williams continually depicts him in animal terms—bringing home the meat, eating like a beast, pacing, howling—and points out Stanley's "animal joy in his being" (128). Being at heart an animal, Stanley likes to display his strength and control, and protects his territory with increasing violence, beginning with throwing the radio out the window. He attacks Blanche for losing Belle Reve and spoils Blanche's relationship with Mitch by telling him what he's found out about her—that she was a virtual prostitute at a hotel in Laurel and lost her teaching post because of an affair with a seventeen-year-old student. Stanley's final act of aggression is his "rape" of Blanche, although Williams wants us to view the rape ambiguously, suggesting that Blanche might have been seducing Stanley all along. Blanche's only defense against Stanley is to flirt with him, which she admits to Stella that she has been doing, but Stanley takes this flirting at face value and, being a man of action with little capacity for moral guilt, acts on it by reciprocating in the worst possible way.

Elysian Fields may be a kind of paradise for men like Stanley who embrace lives of the senses and are completely comfortable in their sexuality. He is self-assured and does what he wants. Always himself, he plays no games, having a lack of pretension and perception that Williams wants us to respect; Stanley sees through Blanche from the start. He has a permanency and strength about him that contrasts with Blanche's impermanence, fragility, and sexual uncertainty—Blanche wants to be a "lady" but feels continually tripped up by her sexual desire, which she feels society requires her to suppress. Blanche and Stanley each strive to win Stella to their side, but it is unsurprising that Stanley is the eventual victor. The world he offers Stella is full of color and genuine passion, a world from which Blanche is utterly alienated and which she can only fear. Stanley has no refinement, but he truly loves life and women. Stella is attracted to him as a female to a strong male. They fight and make up, just like their neighbors, Eunice and Steve, and these bouts of violence seem like nothing more than a spillover from the sheer passion of their existence and nothing about which to be truly alarmed.

The Normal Heart introduces us to Ned Weeks and various gay friends who begin to contract AIDS in the early 1980s. Although clearly an epidemic, the public is largely unaware and uninformed about it, preferring to remain in ignorance, seeing it as a gay disease about which they need not be concerned. The gay community's cautious efforts to cope with this crisis allow for little progress in raising funds or awareness for the cause. This frustrates Ned, who becomes ostracized from this community because of his outspokenness, even voted off the board of the organization he helped to found. Alongside the political action, we see Ned deal with his own insecurities as a gay man, fall in love with Felix, watch Felix die of AIDS, and build a better understanding with his heterosexual brother, Ben.

Ned faces obstacles that have been created by both the gay community and the larger society beyond. One issue is the way in which gayness is stigmatized by society to such an extent that many gays are forced to lead double lives, fearing to come out of the closet. Not only does this place jobs, lodgings, and social standing in jeopardy, but it may also estrange people from their own families and set them up as targets for hate crimes. Some, like Felix, feel pressured to marry women and have children just to appear "normal." Others, like Bruce, the vice president of a bank, keep their private lives well away from the workplace, as do numerous writers and television industry workers, who fear to publicize the cause of AIDS in case supporting it might unintentionally "out" them. But, Ned complains, if no one writes about what is happening, then the gay community will never get the support it needs to effectively combat the disease.

In an effort to lay low and not bring attention to themselves, the play implies that the majority of gays avoid politics, and those who get involved in it are sometimes so radical they tend to worsen the gay public image. Kramer insists that there is a poor public understanding of gays, and the fear of being stereotyped, and thereby limited, when labeled "gay" further encourages gays to stay hidden. Kramer suggests that society, as a whole, wants gays to remain in the closet, because it prefers not to acknowledge gayness or the occurrence of AIDS. This makes it difficult for them to get any major newspaper to even admit that AIDS is a problem.

The gay community is also antagonistic to the truth Ned tries to get them to face because their sexual behavior has become part of their political agenda and to change would seem like a defeat. Ned acknowledges the difficulty for gays to relate nonsexually, since sexual activity has become the way in which they socialize, and the freedom of such behavior becomes addictive. But as Mickey realizes, with AIDS on the loose he may have done more harm than good by campaigning so long for the "right to be free and make love whenever, wherever" (103). Ned insists that by allowing themselves to be defined purely by their sexuality, gays are unnecessarily limiting themselves: "The only way we'll have real pride is when we demand recognition of a culture that isn't just sexual" (114). He lists famous men who were reputedly gay, whom he feels need to be claimed and acknowledged as gay in order to improve social expectations of gayness. A better political agenda, Ned suggests, would be to fight for the right to get married, but this is something the public cannot accept when they refuse to recognize gay men as capable of love. To this end, throughout the play, Ned tries to educate his brother Ben about gayness.

Ben loves Ned but is uncomfortable with his sexuality, as evidenced by his reluctance to embrace him, his lying about the need to ask his law partners for permission to do *pro bono* work for a gay organization, and his refusal to be on Ned's honorary board. Ned angrily tells him: "One of these days I'll make you agree that over twenty million men and women are not all on this earth because of something requiring the services of a psychiatrist" (67–68). If he can make Ben see him as "normal," it is the first step to getting all of society to see this. Ned points out how similar he and Ben are, apart from their sexuality. He tries to get Ben to accept that gayness is not a matter of choice; people are born gay, not created, and so should not be viewed as abnormal. Ned understands that this needs to be accepted by the wider society if gays are ever to be treated as equals.

Kramer intentionally counters the dominant social expectation of gayness by having little effeminate speech or behavior and portraying many of his gay characters as "manly," pursuing the same careers and interests as most men. The media is unhelpful in such efforts, tending to skewer the public perception of gayness by depicting its extremist tendencies. Ned points out, "The single-minded determination of all you people to forever see us as sick helps keep us sick" (69). To view gayness as a sickness, he insists, implies that it can be cured, removing any need to accept it.

The central relationship of Ned and Felix allows the audience to witness a monogamous, committed couple, and the specific problems such couples face when they are gay. Both suffer from many of the same difficulties as heterosexual couples: being attracted to the wrong people, suffering from insecurities as they build a relationship, and being fearful of commitment. But they also have to face the fact that Felix may not be able to leave his insurance money to Ned as his next of kin, and they are not permitted to legally marry.

The play ends with a series of hopeful images despite the death of Felix. Ned and Felix undergo an unofficial marriage to declare their love and commitment, and Ned acknowledges advances in the gay community, citing the high attendance at a gay dance, in the same college room where he had earlier "wanted to kill myself because I thought I was the only gay man in the world" (123).

Finally, Ned and Ben kiss and embrace; through his brother's evident pain, Ben has seen his humanity and begins to treat him as an equal. As the play's title suggests, the heart of a gay man is normal: it has the same capacity for love and pain as that of any heterosexual.

FURTHER SUGGESTED READING

Adler, Thomas P. A Streetcar Named Desire: *The Moth and the Lantern.* Boston: Twayne, 1990.

Anderson, Robert. *Tea and Sympathy.* New York: Random House, 1953.

Gianakaris, C. J. *Peter Shaffer.* New York: St. Martin's Press, 1992.

Griffin, Alice. *Understanding Tennessee Williams.* Columbia: University of South Carolina Press, 1995.

Kramer, Larry. *The Normal Heart.* New York: NAL, 1985.

Kushner, Tony. *Angels in America.* New York: TCG, 1992.

MacMurraugh-Kavanagh, M. K. *Peter Shaffer: Theatre and Drama.* New York: St. Martin's Press, 1998.

Mahoney, E. R. *Human Sexuality.* New York: McGraw-Hill, 1983.

Mass, Lawrence D., Ed. *We Must Love One Another or Die: The Life and Legacies of Larry Kramer.* New York: St. Martin's Press, 1997.

Moran, Jeffrey P. *Teaching Sex: The Shaping of Adolescence in the 20th Century.* Cambridge: Harvard University Press, 2000.

Shaffer, Peter. *Equus.* New York: Avon Books, 1975.

Williams, Tennessee. *Sweet Bird of Youth, A Streetcar Named Desire, The Glass Menagerie.* Harmondsworth, U.K.: Penguin, 1962.

Jewish American Experience

Awake and Sing by Clifford Odets (1935)
The Tenth Man by Paddy Chayefsky (1959)
Broken Glass by Arthur Miller (1994)

The first half of the twentieth century was particularly marked by sporadic outbursts of American anti-Semitism, especially during periods of national stress, including both world wars, and the Great Depression. The pressure to assimilate versus the desire to maintain a familiar ethnicity, as with any immigrant group, has been constant, but perhaps more insidious with Jewish Americans whose appearance (all stereotypes aside) rarely distinguishes them from the majority. In these early years, in the effort to keep a low profile, few plays directly addressed the Jewish American experience, even though many were written out of that experience.

Issues of ethnicity were treated gingerly by dramatists until well into the 1960s. Ethnic issues, if addressed at all, were dealt with ambiguously to avoid censure or outright hostility. Despite a vibrant Yiddish theater, which catered to the tastes of immigrant Jews in a familiar language, there were few overt depictions of Jews on the mainstream stage. Although there was conspicuous involvement of Jewish Americans in mainstream theater during the entire twentieth century, from playwriting to production, only some of this involvement has resulted in plays that specifically address what it means to be Jewish in America, and the majority of these come from the latter half of the century. The plays chosen for this chapter offer a collective vision of the Jewish American experience, shaped by immigration, family life, the Depression, two world wars, and anti-Semitism. We learn about Jewish Americans at work, at home, and in the community, as they face changing gender roles and an increasingly secular world. Some of these depictions may feel stereotypical, but they are stereotypes grounded in essential truths, and they ultimately insist that the Jew in America has both dignity and complexity.

Clifford Odets's *Awake and Sing* is concerned with Jewish American family life in the Bronx during the Great Depression, and creates prototypical Jewish characters who have been much emulated, including the bewildered immigrant trying to understand an alien culture, the discontented first-generation youth seeking fame and fortune, and the feisty, though at times insensitive, Jewish mother. These characters display little in the way of religious observance but offer insight into the secular Jewish outlook and lifestyle. The realism of Odets's endeavor is made all the more telling by his use of authentic immigrant speech patterns, which earned him the title of "the poet of the Jewish middle class." Earlier drafts of the play contained far more Yiddish expressions, which were cut or translated into English to make the play easier for non-Jews to understand; what remains is an accurate and accessible portrayal of the Yiddishized English of many American Jews. The play's title comes from Isaiah 26:19, "Awake and sing, ye that dwell in dust," which represents a call to arms for American youth caught in the despairing grasp of the Depression.

Known as the Clifford Odets of the 1950s, Paddy Chayefsky's earlier plays were similarly set in the Bronx and filled with lower middle-class ethnic characters. However, *The Tenth Man* is more concerned with religious and urban issues than family life. Through its close relation to S. Anski's Yiddish classic, *The Dybbuk* (1914), *The Tenth Man* depicts the social adjustments that have to be made by Jews descended from those who lived in hermetic Eastern European shetls who now reside in contemporary, largely secular Long Island. Chayefsky reveals not only the differences between these two worlds, but also an important commonality: the same tenets of love and faith that supported and sustained the old Jewish world can continue to help Jews survive in the new.

Both Anski's *The Dybbuk* and Chayefsky's *The Tenth Man* deal with issues surrounding the exorcism of a troublesome spirit that inhabits the soul of a living person, but in very different settings and to very different ends. While Anski's play depicts ten Hasidim in an East European shtetl synagogue, Chayefsky's is set in a storefront synagogue in Mineola, Long Island, with a disparate collection of congregants. The story is no longer focused on two young lovers pitted against the community, but on a variety of conflicts that affect Jewish American people as they attempt to survive in an open, secular society. The characters in *The Tenth Man* represent a cross-section of American Jewry, and, through them, Chayefsky explores the implications of Judaism and Jewishness in mid-century America. Where Odets brought his audience into a Jewish home, Chayefsky introduces them to an Orthodox synagogue.

Broken Glass, by Arthur Miller, directly considers the issue of anti-Semitism among Americans and Jews in the 1930s, as news of the Nazi treatment of Jews in Europe filters through. Through the lens of a troubled marriage, we witness different reactions to events, including denial, resignation, and ignorance, all of which are shown to be tantamount to complicity. Sylvia's physical paralysis represents the moral paralysis of many Americans in the face of the Holocaust and anti-Semitism in general: horrified by the reality of what was happening, it became far easier to pretend that nothing was happening at all.

Set during the Depression, the start of *Awake and Sing* sees Ralph Berger discontented with life, his domineering mother, Bessie, and the restrictions of living in a crowded family home. Bessie scrabbles to keep the family together in lean years, with her daughter, Hennie, getting pregnant out of wedlock. Hennie is pressured to marry naive and shy Sam Feinschreiber, a recent immigrant, to give the child a father, but she has no love for him and is deeply unhappy. She prefers the company of embittered war veteran Moe Axelrod, although neither would admit to this. Ralph wants to marry Blanche, but both families try to prevent this, wanting their children to marry someone wealthier. Ralph's grandfather, Jacob, tries to bolster Ralph's spirits with advice, then commits suicide, hoping the life insurance money will help Ralph make a better life. The family considers cheating Ralph out of the money, although Moe blackmails them to tell the truth. Ralph decides to let Bessie have the money and make his own way, revitalized by his grandfather's sacrifice, while Hennie runs off with Moe, leaving husband and child behind.

The Depression largely motivates the characters, as Odets explores how financial insecurity affects a family and what compromises it forces upon them. The threat of destitution and eviction is very real, and Bessie's fears are grounded in fact. Poverty is endemic, and although all share what they have as a matter of course, the youngsters, especially, dream of a future life less impoverished. These people had nothing with which to start, and so cannot understand the rich who jump off buildings because they have lost everything. Jacob may make the same leap, but out of hope rather than despair and the ardent desire to help his grandson. The past may be one of struggle, but all look to the future with hope.

The only two characters in the play who have sufficient funds are Uncle Morty and Moe Axelrod; neither one a positive figure. Morty is a businessman who avoids personal relationships and is spiritually dry, while Moe is a petty crook and physically limited, having lost a leg during Army service, which gained him a pension but left him bitter. Through such characters, Odets implies that the security of a regular income is not necessarily the answer, and it may be worthwhile, for the sake of personal fulfillment, to take a risk and embrace life's insecurities without fear, as Ralph and Hennie do by the play's end.

Bessie's domination of Ralph, and her insistence on having the insurance money, are not for personal gain but to try to hold the whole family together—not an easy task with the weak husband she chose. Her family is largely made up of idealists who dream, and it is up to her, the realist, to make sure they eat and have a roof over their heads. She sympathizes with her son's escapist desires, but feels grounded by the reality of being head of the household and restricts Ralph because she fears what would happen to the rest of the family without his financial contributions. She acts purely out of expediency: just as she tries to prevent Ralph's marriage, she pressures Hennie into hers—both actions are designed to protect the good of the whole. She honestly believes that the insurance money should belong to them all. Bessie will deny herself a hearty meal in order to put food on the table for the rest of the household. Like her father, she is, for all her complaints, a willing martyr.

Bessie's daughter has a similar strength of will, and rails against the restrictions of motherhood and her marriage to Sam, which her mother enforced to preserve the family's respectability. Her independent spirit got her pregnant in the first place, and her relationship with Moe is based on sexual tension and may have no future, but it is at least full of passion and offers something more promising than the dull life she faces with the mouselike Sam. Even though Hennie leaves behind her baby, Odets wants us to accept her decision to go away with Moe as a positive move toward a better future. Marrying Sam had been a bad move, and unfair to them both. Sam is a good father, and her baby will be well tended by him and his in-laws.

Ralph gives most of his wages to Bessie, and lives on a daybed in the front room. When he was younger, he had dreamed of travel and making his mark in the world, but life is grinding him down and he begins to feel overwhelmed. The pressure to be successful becomes crushing in an era when hard work no longer guarantees any reward: this confirms that the socialist, Jacob, is right to critique the American success ethic as potentially destructive. Resenting his mother's restrictions, Ralph considers life with Blanche, but her family are no more eager than his for them to marry, since neither has any prospects. She eventually agrees to be sent away and he accepts that decision, realizing that he needs to establish himself before embarking on marriage. Jacob, who feels close kinship to his grandson, confesses his own wasted his life of study without action, and advises Ralph not to restrict himself too early by marriage, and not to talk but to do. Further encouraged to action by his grandfather's ultimate sacrifice, Ralph decides to get what he wants without financially hurting his family, by his own endeavors.

Despite the continual poverty and uncertainty of all their futures, the play ends on a positive note, as Moe and Hennie run away together and Ralph exudes energy in his newfound sense of direction. Although not unique to the Jewish American experience, the concentration on family, the work ethic, the pursuit of knowledge and socialistic tendencies, and persevering against great odds do combine to create a realistic picture of secular Jewish American life in the 1930s.

In *The Tenth Man*, we find the synagogue's sexton having trouble gathering a *minyan* (the set number of ten Jewish men needed for any public act of religious observance) for the morning service. He goes out to pull in strangers off the street. Foreman arrives with his schizophrenic granddaughter, who is destined for institutionalization, but whom Foreman believes to be possessed by the dybbuk (troubled soul) of a woman he had sexually wronged as a youth. His old friends help, advising him which Rabbi should perform an exorcism. He spends the remainder of the day vainly trying to get the right train to meet the recommended Rabbi. Meanwhile, the sexton brings in Arthur Landau, a troubled individual who agrees to make up their quorum. Arthur and the girl connect, and he tries to get the others to take her home and get her medical attention. She declares that she loves him and accuses him of having his ability to love restricted by a dybbuk when he denies his evident reciprocal affection. In fear for the girl's life, they get the Cabalist, who has just undergone a transforming religious experience, to perform the exorcism. The ceremony fails to alter the girl, but exorcises something from Arthur, leaving him ready to embrace life and take responsibility for the girl.

Through the play, Chayefsky offers the gentile audience detailed descriptions of the rituals surrounding Jewish religious observance, from the putting on of the *tefillin* (phylacteries) and *tallit* (prayer shawl), through the ways in which Jewish people pray, and examples of Jewish services from the everyday morning service with the Torah reading to the more rare and exotic ceremony of exorcism. The language may be anglicized, rather than using the Hebrew vernacular, but the form and content remain, and the entire play takes place inside an orthodox synagogue. We see a great contrast between the Cabalist, with his simple faith and devotion, and the synagogue's current Rabbi, only there two months, who is convinced that the only way to keep his congregation thriving is to cut down on the preaching and emphasize secular activities, with Youth Groups, a Young Married People's Club, Dramatic Society, Little League, bazaars, raffles, and bingo. The Cabalist insists on maintaining God and his Word at the center of his life, and appears so much the happier and more capable. He mocks Arthur's disbelief in everything as essentially limiting, since life is so complex and unknowable that to be appreciated it must be taken on faith.

The three elderly Jews, Schlissel, Zitorsky, and Alper, who, like the Cabalist, virtually inhabit the synagogue, are positive stereotypes of the Jew with a lust for life, consideration of others, and constant disputation about everything from choosing the best cemetery or Rabbi to the best train routes, the proper ways to recognize and exorcise a dybbuk, and the state of modern Jewry. Their chatter frames the play, emphasizing their kindly influence. Eager to help Foreman to fill out their day, they find the prospect of a dybbuk exciting, and assist in covering up the kidnapping of the girl to the father and police. When the Cabalist announces his vision of forgiveness, they celebrate with him, dancing and drinking, keen to live life to the fullest. Schlissel, as a professed communist, declares himself as disbelieving in God and dybbuks, but his actions belie his words, as he takes part in both the morning service and the exorcism. Faith for such men is automatic, almost like a gut response to the alien world beyond their synagogue. It is a faith that sustains them, and that Arthur has notably lost, which is why he is in the sad state in which we find him.

Arthur, a lawyer whose loss of faith caused him to turn to alcohol and adultery to escape the sham he felt his life had become, has broken up his family and brought himself to the brink of suicide. The girl whom Arthur meets at the synagogue describes him as a mystic in search of the meaning of life, and through his love of her he is able to assert the truth of such a claim and reject the negativity of disbelief. He may not fully embrace God by the close, but he does profess the need to love, and as Alper points out, they are pretty much the same thing. That is not to say these men will find such faith easy. The sexton's daily chore to find the ten men necessary for a *minyan* is representative of each character's struggle to find sufficient meaning to get through the day. The Rabbi is faced with trying to lead a spiritual community of men mostly absorbed by worldlier demands, and Chayefsky's solution—to insist on a restoration of faith and love—may work, but is idealistic. The coldness outside the synagogue suggests a hostile outer world, and when the men go out into this cold they usually get frustrated and lost, and find others unhelpful. This is balanced against the warmth of the community within the synagogue, most notably that among the older men, as they rally to assist one another, encourage the relationship between the girl and Arthur, and celebrate with the Cabalist with a joy that becomes infectious. But that hostile outer world, and the sexton's continual struggle to make up a minyan of the faithful, still remain. The girl's schizophrenia, which also remains, is indicative of the split personality of many Jewish Americans, caught between the old and new, the Jewish and the American, the religious and the secular. To preserve a working balance between the two continues to be a constant challenge.

Broken Glass tells the story of Sylvia and Phillip Gellburg, who after years of marriage realize they hardly know each other at all. Obsessed with work and his own desire to assimilate, Phillip has little time for his wife until she demands his attention by falling prey to a mysterious paralysis after seeing the events of Kristallnacht in the newspaper. Up until now Sylvia has been a quiet, self-deprecating Jewish housewife, but she needs to express her buried fears and longings to become a whole woman. Dr. Harry Hyman diagnoses the case as psychiatric, but his treatment is affected by his own lack of honesty. Against a background of mounting anti-Semitism, this couple approach a more open understanding with each other, and in an ambiguous finale, Gellburg has a heart attack while Sylvia regains the use of her legs.

Gellburg's problem is far more complicated than Hyman's assessment of him as a self-hating Jew. Declaring himself and his son to be the first or only Jews to do things, he seems not embarrassed but proud of his Jewishness. But is he proud of his achievements *as* a Jew or *despite* his Jewishness? This question remains deliberately ambiguous. Partly due to his recognition and fear of American anti-Semitism, Gellburg has severed his connection with other Jews, yet his own Jewishness is unavoidable: he has a Jewish wife, he speaks Yiddish, he is prone to Jewish folk beliefs, and his achievements mean more, either way, because he is Jewish. But Gellburg is so self-involved that he has no place for a community in his life. Even though he has striven to be accepted, he cannot feel comfortable in the anti-Semitic American community, nor is he happy in the Jewish community for which he feels such antipathy. What is worse, Gellburg has no place in the larger community of humankind; he has no sense of himself any more and has lost touch with his humanity. He no longer knows who he is or who he would like to become.

The blackness of Gellburg's dress and the paleness of his complexion emphasize the emptiness inside the man. He can be seen as being in mourning for his own life, and it is a life he himself is largely responsible for stifling. Internally, Gellburg is a mass of contradictions he finds hard to control. He has lost the ability to connect and communicate his true feelings to Sylvia; although he loves his wife, he cannot tell her so. His heart attack pushes him to reevaluate his life and recognize that he needs to change if he is to fix his relationship with Sylvia and his community. He finally determines to be a better husband and a better Jew—if it is not too late.

Sylvia, in direct contrast to her husband, feels closely connected to others. But as a "good Jewish wife" she has lived her life so long for others that she has lost connection with her own selfhood. As she exclaims: "I'm here for my mother's sake, and Jerome's sake, and everybody's sake except mine" (44). But Sylvia has settled and accommodated herself to a point that ultimately became untenable even for her self-effacing spirit, and this manifests itself in her objections to the Nazis' treatment of Jews in Europe. When Sylvia rises for the first time in the play, she is driven to do so by her fear that no one will do anything about the suffering in Germany; it also marks an important turning point in her relationship with Gellburg. She may have allowed herself to be a victim, like so many of the Jews in Europe; but now she fights back, and it is increasingly Sylvia who gives the orders.

In contrast to the pinched, repressed Gellburg, Hyman seems full of life—a romantic hero who even rides a horse. But Hyman informs us that doctors are often "defective," so we should look for his defect. Hyman has a reductive level of response to everything; it precludes any necessity for deep commitment and leads to an easier (if somewhat shallow) life. When problems loom, be it his wife's displeasure at his evidently roving eye or Nazi oppression, he creates an illusion to protect himself and prevent him from having to address the problem. But even his disengagement is less insidious than the open anti-Semitism of Stanton Case, Gellburg's ruthless boss. Case is stereotyped as the WASP anti-Semite, but this is a not-so-subtle inversion of the more usually stereotyped minority, such as the Jew. He passes his time at the yachting club while Gellburg does his dirty work, then discards the Jew swiftly after his usefulness is over. His presence illustrates unpleasant aspects of American anti-Semitism in the 1930s, based in groundless suspicions and overt racism.

Although the people in *Broken Glass* are Jewish, Miller wants them to be considered universals; a man like Gellburg may have problems as a Jew, but they stem from his problems as a human being. The essential nature of Gellburg's dilemma, resting on uncertainties regarding his own nature and worth, is faced by Americans from various backgrounds. To discover who he would like to be, Gellburg must put his Jewish heritage into perspective; he must learn to balance his ethnicity with his self-identification as an American citizen. In this way he can come to accept a positive self-image that combines individual and social needs. To strive for a kind of dual identity, which allows for both an individual and a social self, is the best road to contentment. The attainment of this kind of self-identification becomes a worthwhile lesson in self-liking, tolerance, and understanding.

FURTHER SUGGESTED READING

Abbotson, Susan C. W. *Student Companion to Arthur Miller.* Westport, CT: Greenwood, 2000.

Baitz, John Robin. *The Substance of Fire & The Film Society.* Garden City, NY: Fireside Theater, 1991.

Bigsby, Christopher, Ed. *The Cambridge Companion to Arthur Miller.* New York: Cambridge University Press, 1997.

Brenman-Gibson, Margaret. *Clifford Odets: American Playwright 1906–1940.* New York: Atheneum, 1982.

Chayefsky, Paddy. *The Tenth Man.* New York: Random House, 1960.

Clum, John M. *Paddy Chayefsky.* Boston: Twayne, 1976.

Considine, Shaun. *Mad As Hell: The Life and Work of Paddy Chayefsky.* New York: Random House, 1994.

Harap, Louis. *Dramatic Encounters.* New York: Greenwood, 1987.

Hoffman, Aaron. *Welcome Stranger.* New York: Samuel French, 1926.

Miller, Arthur. *Broken Glass.* New York: Penguin, 1994.

———. *Timebends: A Life.* New York: Grove, 1987.

Odets, Clifford. *Awake and Sing.* In *Six Plays of Clifford Odets.* New York: Random House, 1939: 33–101.

Pinsker, Sanford, and Jack Fischel. *Jewish American History and Culture.* New York: Garland, 1991.

Sachar, Howard M. *A History of the Jews in America.* New York: Knopf, 1991.

Uhry, Alfred. *The Last Night at Ballyhoo.* New York: TCG, 1997.

Weales, Gerald. *Clifford Odets, Playwright.* New York: Pegasus, 1971.

Latin American Experience

Zoot Suit by Luis Valdez (1978)
The Savior by Carlos Morton (1986)
The Cuban-Swimmer by Milcha Sanchez-Scott (1984)

Spanish and, later, French influence on Latin American theater restricted its autonomous development well into the twentieth century, but by the 1940s we see emerging a largely experimental theater that can be labeled "Latin American." Prior to the universal recognition of writers like Luis Borges, Carlos Fuentes, and Julio Cortázar in the 1960s, which seems to have popularized Latin American literature, any Latin American writings were hard to find. Even still, the amount of published Latin American drama in the United States hardly reflects the wealth that exists. Many Latin American playwrights, who live and work in Central and South American nations, write only in Spanish, and are largely unpublished. Even the work of Latin American playwrights in the United States was mostly in Spanish until the 1970s, when they began to switch to English, partly because so many Latin Americans had assimilated to the point where they spoke only English.

One of the few early mainstream representations of Latin Americans with which people would be familiar was the Puerto Rican gang in *West Side Story* (1957). Although the hot-headed, musically inclined underclass depicted there may seem like stereotypes in an age of heightened racial awareness, they are at least sympathetic stereotypes, and their presence in America, away from the poverty of their homeland in search of a better life, is a familiar Latin American story. But the musical's exploration of the Latin American experience is minimal at best. The plays discussed in this chapter have been published (and performed) in English, and are fully focused on Latin American experiences.

The onset of Latin American playwriting within the United States, as with most ethnic theater, began with playwrights mostly addressing audiences of their own ethnicity, concentrating on domestic situations, and often writing in a realistic style. However, since the 1980s, ethnic playwrights in general have become bolder in their attacks on white mainstream interpretations of American history and culture, grappling with aspects of American pop culture that threaten their identity and illuminating particular ethnic concerns and eclectic influences. Many of these later plays are more experimental in nature and are aimed at a wider audience. Luis Valdez's *Zoot Suit* bridges these two styles, with its domestic scenes balanced against the more expressionistic representation of Henry Reyna's horrendous experience with the American legal system.

Luis Valdez is the leading light of Chicano (Mexican American) theater, and is best known for the documentary play *Zoot Suit*. The first Chicano play to appear on Broadway, *Zoot Suit* places Mexican Americans into an American historical context as U.S. citizens. His characters are cross-cultural in everything they do and say, from dancing swing and mambo, to speaking a mix of English, Spanish, and "hip." Despite debts to Brecht and the Living Newspaper theater of the 1930s, the play incorporates traditional elements of Mexican theater, including aspects of the political *acto*, with its exposure of social ills; the mythic *mito*, with references to Aztec mythology; and the ballad style *corrido*, with dance and a musical narrative. In the 1940s, Chicano renegades purposefully stood out in their zoot suits, insisting that they not be ignored, and the play relates the aesthetic behind this as well as the resulting problems. The play's narrator, El Pachuco, a spiritual alter ego of its central protagonist, Henry Reyna, offers a powerful commentary on the difficulties of being Chicano in a racist American society.

Carlos Morton's *The Savior* deals with more recent events in El Salvador, a nation heavily influenced by American investment and interests. More serious than Morton's usual lighter-hearted comedies, the play shows the life, death, and metaphoric resurrection of Archbishop Oscar Romero, assassinated as a result of his uncompromising demands for justice for the nation's poor. Morton researched his topic for five years prior to writing, and interviewed many who had known Romero. What he discovered was a figure whose passionate struggle, belief in nonviolence, and ultimate self-sacrifice for his people made him Christ-like. Morton relates events with many intentional parallels to the Christ story: characters represent Simon Zealot and Judas Iscariot, events are reminiscent of the scene of temptation by the Devil and the Last Supper, and, at times, Romero speaks the words of Jesus. Although the play depicts a contemporary Latin American society, with its political, social, and religious dilemmas, the generic names of many characters indicate that the problems of El Salvador exist in other places around the world, universalizing its message regarding the power of nonviolence and faith.

As with so many of America's rising minority playwrights, Milcha Sanchez-Scott refuses to assimilate and compromise her ethnic identity, to which end, in her short play, *The Cuban-Swimmer*, she creates a dialogue peppered with Spanish words and phrases that an audience must try to follow as best they can. She centers our attention on yet another troubled Latin group, in this case the Cubans. Eduardo and Aída Suarez, Margarita's parents, are refugees from Fidel Castro's government, leaving everything behind in Cuba when they take the dangerous boat ride to America, where they can better prosper. The central religious metaphor of resurrection is a common one among Latin American playwrights, many of whom grew up in the Catholic faith, but Sanchez-Scott complicates her image with her feminist agenda.

Zoot Suit is narrated by Pachuco, who sets the scene and offers commentary throughout. Beginning at a typical barrio dance, two gangs face off before being violently attacked by the police, who arrest almost the entire 38th Street gang. The gang, and its leader, Henry Reyna, are indicted for the murder of the son of a Chicano rancher. While police and a character called Press—who represents all of the Los Angeles news reporters—talk about a "Mexican crime wave" and gang wars, it becomes apparent that these are largely fantasies born of wartime hysteria and media hype to increase circulation. As Henry and Pachuco talk in jail, we witness flashbacks, mostly involving Henry's home life, which humanizes the "criminals." A story of racism, mistaken identity, and defeated hope evolves. The police beat the suspects, the court case is a mockery, with Press leading the prosecution, and, although patently innocent, everyone gets sentenced to life. After a lengthy appeal, a series of riots, and the tireless efforts of a committee formed by various activists, they are finally released.

Valdez is known as a champion of Chicano rights, both politically and artistically, and most of his plays display a concern for social justice. In his writing he depicts the spiritual fused with the political, seeing them as inextricably combined. For him, myth is the spiritual basis of everyday reality; thus ritual plays an important part in the lives of his characters. It helps them affirm their identity and offers a refuge from the discrimination they routinely encounter. Thus Pachuco at times appears as an Aztec god or a *nahval* helping spirit to suggest the possibility of both dignity and nobility in times of stress. The central pressure on the Chicanos, as with other immigrant groups, is between assimilation and preservation of their culture. Viewed as foreigners in their own country, many become frustrated by the arrogant rejection they constantly receive from Anglo society, while the slums in which many are forced to live breed crime and anger from which it is hard to escape.

Based on historical fact, *Zoot Suit* relates the story of the 1942 Sleepy Lagoon Murder Trial and the resulting riots. But it is told with sympathy and understanding for the Mexican Americans involved, rather than from the establishment viewpoint. By closely focusing on Henry and his family, the Chicano stereotype is exposed as false; they are shown to be complex human beings. The sensation-seeking inaccuracies reported by the white press to increase their circulation, represented by the allegorical figure called Press, become evident, just as we also understand the pervasive reach of that press in the way Valdez uses newspapers throughout the set and properties. Valdez is revealing previously ignored truths about police brutality toward Chicanos, and a racist wartime paranoia, which, Pachuco insists, are not just problems of the past.

Pachuco, dressed in a zoot suit, embodies the macho *pachuco* stereotype— *pachuco* being Chicano slang for a young man—and he creates himself before our eyes. He represents a lifestyle and embodies a life force. He also illustrates Henry's inner attitude of defiance against an unfair system, as well as bolstering Henry's spirit and inspiring him to "hang tough" in jail. The suit is a means of commanding respect in its ostentation; rather than submissively staying in their place, the zoot suiters insist on recognition, even if it only provokes antagonism. If Chicanos cannot become part of mainstream culture, then they will create a sustaining subculture of their own. But Henry is not always in agreement with his alter ego. Henry refuses to give up hope that he may one day beat the system, a hope that Pachuco denies, but one that Valdez appears to validate.

Valdez seeks to transform the ways Chicanos see themselves as well as how they are seen by others, and the play depicts Henry's search for an identity and a sense of reality with which he can live. Press tries to impose a false identity on all Chicanos, with his talk of "MEXICAN BABY GANGSTERS" and "ZOOT SUITED GOONS" (38), but these headlines are as false as his summation as prosecutor in the trial of Henry and his friends: "Set these pachucos free, and you shall unleash the forces of anarchy and destruction in our society" (62). It is against such lies and depictions that Henry must fight to simply be viewed as human. At the close Henry hears that the police are falsely arresting his friend and is caught between violence and love: he chooses love, embracing his father, immersing himself in the family bond, wherein he can find a positive identity for himself as a caring and respectful son and brother, rather than allowing himself to become the figure of violence society seems to demand.

Throughout, the police behavior is racist and overtly violent: they see Chicanos as inherently crooked, and think nothing of beating them to exact a confession. They indiscriminately pick up everyone from the dance, just as they arrest Chicanos for stealing cars in which they have every right to be. Henry's initial reaction to the police is panic, not out of guilt but out of a justified fear that they will frame him for something. When Lieutenant Edwards tries to trick Henry into confessing to a crime, he suggests, "You know why you're here," and Henry's reply, "Yeah. I'm a Mexican" (31) is essentially true. Sergeant Smith openly refers to them as greasers and animals, describing their dress as monkey suits.

The way the court treats Henry and his friends is disgraceful and a mockery of the law. They are not allowed to bathe, cut their hair, or wear new clothes, so they will look disrespectable. The judge's behavior is stunningly unconstitutional. He has defendants stand whenever their names are spoken by any member of the court (an act conveying a sense of self-incrimination), declaring they cannot be told apart. He will not allow defendants to sit with their counsel, overrides all of their lawyer's objections (and threatens him with contempt for the mere act of objecting), while allowing the prosecution to make statements that contradict the witness' testimony. After Henry's girlfriend testifies to the truth of what happened, he places her in custody for a year. In his summation, George, Henry's lawyer, suggests that if the court finds them guilty of murder, they will murder the spirit of racial justice in America and this is just what they do. The boys are treated no better in the prison system.

The ranchers had attacked the 38th Street Gang, mistakenly believing them to be another hostile gang with whom they had had trouble earlier that evening. José Williams is killed by an unknown assailant, whose identity is never revealed. But we that know Henry is innocent; he had even tried to stop the fighting and his gang had just defended themselves. Time and again we see Henry led toward violence from which he repeatedly tries to withdraw, but each time the pressure becomes stronger. However, as George points out, the desire for a just society will not be satisfied through violence, but through law: "What matters is our system of justice. I believe it works, however slowly the wheels may grind" (42), and he stays with the case until they win. Henry seems to understands George's message on his eventual release: "We won this one, because we learned to fight a new way" (88).

Rather than the violent thug created by the Press, Henry is a hard worker, was considering joining the Navy to serve his country, loves his family and girlfriend, and stops more fights than he starts. Whether Henry will choose Della, his barrio girlfriend, or Alice, the Jewish advocate who helped him through his legal battle, is left up in the air, but they represent two different life choices. Circumstances and race remain in danger of propelling him, however reluctantly, into a life of crime, so there is the possibility he might die as a criminal. However, the play ends with a choice of endings for Henry's story, illustrating that there are options available for most Chicanos: a life of crime and early death from drugs, enlistment in the military and heroic death in battle, or a peaceful family life with wife and children.

The Savior begins six days after the assassination of Archbishop Romero, when a series of flashbacks relate the preceding three years since he took office. Initially thought to be an innocuous candidate for the head of the Catholic Church in El Salvador, Romero proves to have more strength and concern for the exploited poor of the country than either the government or the papacy had expected or planned. Equating Romero's religious teachings, social conscience, and refusal to bow to a ruling government that is clearly corrupt to communism, the ruling class turns against him, even as the people increasingly offer him their support. Killed by the Death Squad in a grotesque parody of the death of Christ, he enters through the audience at the play's end, "very much alive" (103), symbolizing his resurrection in the hearts and minds of the people—and the audience. As commentator, Celestina explains that Romero's death is "not the end, but the beginning" (57).

American interest and involvement in El Salvador is indicated by the presence of an American Reporter and Ambassador. Within the biblical parallel,
they take the place of the Roman onlookers and facilitators of Christ's crucifixion. The Reporter's patronizing commentary on the twisted evasions of the
President indicate that she knows both the truth of what is happening in El
Salvador and the extent of U.S. influence, which has turned the nation's leaders
into American puppets. The official currency is the *colon*, "But dollars will do
quite nicely" (65). She interviews Major D'Abussion, who describes Romero
and his Church as a bunch of hypocrites and complains that communists are
overtaking the country. He threatens that if funds are not sent to finance a
military government, America will lose out on South American oil and have
swarms of illegal immigrants trying to enter the country. Instead of correcting
his lies, the Reporter shows herself to be the hypocrite, by promising to print
everything that she has been told.

The Ambassador, like Pontius Pilate, offers Romero a chance to retract his
claims and take an easier way out, but Romero refuses. On being turned down,
the Ambassador washes his hands of the whole affair and leaves the Archbishop
to the corrupt ruling body of his own people, who destroy him just as the
Pharisees destroyed Jesus. But the Ambassador is more than an observer in El
Salvador; he has the power to offer Romero a safe escape, and the President is
driven out and replaced by a military junta under his direction and with American funds. Although he calls for the appearance of democratic rule and a reduction of military influence in the government, he is not really concerned
whether or not either is actually achieved, threatening to withdraw financial
aid and to bring in American troops should the poor be seen to be getting the
upper hand. Romero suggests that he send seeds and tractors rather than arms,
but the archbishop's pleas are ignored: America is as fearful of communism as
is Oligarchy, an allegorical character who represents the ruling authority in El
Salvador, and as unable to differentiate between communism and true socialism.

Throughout the 1970s, El Salvador suffered from a civil war in which many
died from the conflict but also from their long-standing poverty and starvation.
Morton depicts the deaths not only as physical, but also as spiritual and intellectual, because so many participants willfully blinded themselves to the exploitation and sad state of the peasantry and to the honest attempts by the
Church to alleviate these conditions. To represent the deadness both inside and
surrounding the cast, many are played by *Calaveras*, a pre-Columbian, Meso-
American skeleton figure of death.

The play educates its audience about life in rural Latin America, where half
the people live on less than $10 a month, and more than that are illiterate. In
El Salvador, the peasantry own little land: the majority of property is owned
and exploited by the richest few (often backed by foreign investment). Much
of what little land the peasantry had was flooded when a dam was built to assist
the rich landowners; this provoked the initial unrest. Romero calls for social
reform, as his priests create and run cooperatives, medical clinics, and farm-

workers' unions, but he is accused of undermining the country. While he preaches biblical teachings that offer hope to a people under constant threat of violence and starvation, his words are deemed subversive and dangerous by those in power.

When the Fathers initially discussed Romero's appointment, they were unimpressed, seeing him as a religious idealist, too displaced from social reality. They fear that he will reduce what little they do to help the nation's poor. Seemingly strengthened by each conflict, Romero wins over all but the most staid of the clergy to his point of view as he shows himself to be both honest and hardworking. His belief in the possibility of a nonviolent, peaceful solution never waivers, not in the face of atrocities exacted by the government Death Squads and rebels alike, nor when his own priests call for a more active response, nor after the slaying of his fellow clergy. His call remains for forgiveness and faith rather than vengeance. When one of the Fathers, Barrera, declares that he is sick of turning the other cheek, Romero insists that to do so "is the showing of great moral force that leaves the assailant overcome and humiliated" (77). The intermittent episodes, in which a peasant girl, Campesina, counters the assaults of a soldier on her loyalty and her person with nothing but her faith, seem to prove Romero right.

While the government continuously tries to blame the Church for the unrest, Romero points his finger at the real culprits: the greed of an uncaring ruling class and the lack of any impartial judicial system. He insists that the conflict is not between the government and the Church but between the government and the people, and he takes the side of the people. He refuses to be intimidated by the government or the papacy, when asked to back down, and his conversations with the President as he demands justice are polite but firm. He is neither swayed nor distracted by the President's evasions and bribes. His words of hope, nonviolence, and justice in the face of their opposites continue to resonate, even as his spirit lives on at the play's close, indicating the profound role religion plays in the Latin American ethos.

The Cuban-Swimmer was partly inspired by the concept of the Stations of the Cross, and, like *The Savior*, exhibits a strong religious influence and knowledge. When asked to do something practical, the Suárez family responds by falling to their knees to pray. Margarita Suárez is placed in the role of Christ. Where Christ trips and falls carrying the wooden cross on which he is to be crucified, ultimately rising in the Ascension, Margarita tires and sinks down in the water as she swims, ultimately rising at the close to win the race. At this point she is described as walking on the water, just as Christ once walked on the Sea of Galilee, further reinforcing their connection. In this we see Sanchez-Scott's desire to present Latin Americans in a highly positive light as well as her commitment to feminism in her creation of a female Christ.

There is a clear irony in making Margarita, with her Cuban blood, a long distance swimmer. Having been conceived on the boat coming over, Margarita is the pride of her family's achievement and testament to the fact that they made the right choice. Her younger brother, Simon, seems on the surface very Americanized, with his swearing, posing, baseball cap, and sunglasses, but no members of this family are reluctant to see themselves as Cubans; in fact, they display a fierce patriotism toward their island home despite living in Miami. Their boat is called "The Havana," Aída is an ex-Miss Cuba, and they partly want Margarita to win the race for Cuban pride (apart from it being good advertising for her father's business).

Mel Munson and May Beth White, two of the race's commentators and representatives of the mainstream, white, American culture, behave condescendingly toward the Suárez family, and symbolically and literally keep themselves above them in a circling helicopter. We never see them, but only hear their voices. The lack of personal connection makes it easier to feel antagonism toward them. They issue the usual banalities we hear from most commentators, trying to dramatize the event with hyperbole, and being more concerned with their own image than with any of the contestants. They do not expect Margarita to even finish the race, let alone win. Their shallowness is underlined by their clear preference for the mother's good looks over the daughter's strength and courage, as they try to get a closer glimpse at Aída. They have little regard for Margarita, scare her by flying in so close, and upset the whole family by their insensitive commentary. Such is the attitude of many majorities toward minority groups.

As Margarita swims into the oil slick, her family are faced with the dilemma of whether to help her, and ensure a disqualification that would kill their dream, or leave her to struggle. This is a similar dilemma faced by Christ's followers as they watched him carry his cross. To help would put them at risk, but to allow him to struggle on was as good as killing him themselves. Just as Christ received water to help keep him going, so too is Margarita offered a drink. The family choose to leave her struggling, though they shout their encouragement. However, by scene 4, the family become so busy in building Margarita up that they begin to neglect her. She has already become more of a symbol than a person to them, which makes her feel very much alone.

When the weather worsens, Margarita finally grinds to a halt in despair. She feels the guilt of failure, and imagines that the fish are biting her in punishment. Her father still urges her to continue, though the resolve of the rest of her family has weakened. At this point she poses as if on a cross, sacrificing herself to her father's dreams, and struggles on. She sinks into the sea as if dying, echoing the words of Christ on the cross, "Father forgive me," feeling that same momentary panic of abandonment. She disappears in the midst of prayer, showing that her belief remains firm. Her parents begin to blame themselves and are distraught, but then hear that their daughter has been seen nearing the finish line. She is described as walking on the water, in an echo of the resurrection, with the commentator declaring it to be a "miracle," which it is. In winning the race, Margarita wins for Cuba and her family the media attention they need to become recognized in the modern world.

FURTHER SUGGESTED READING

Antush, John, Ed. *Recent Puerto Rican Theater.* Houston: Arte Publico, 1991.

Boswell, Thomas D., and James R. Curtis. *The Cuban-American Experience.* Totowa, NJ: Rowman and Allanheld, 1983.

Elam, Harry J., Jr. *Taking it to the Streets: The Social Protest Theater of Luis Valdez and Amiri Baraka.* Ann Arbor: University of Michigan Press, 1997.

Fornes, Maria Irene. *Plays.* New York: PAJ, 1986.

Gonzalez S., Silvia. *The Migrant Farmworker's Son.* In *Multicultural Theater II.* Ed. Roger Ellis. Colorado Springs: Meriwether, 1998: 47–98.

Huerta, Jorge. *Chicano Drama: Performance, Society and Myth.* New York: Cambridge University Press, 2000.

Laurents, Arthur, Leonard Bernstein, and Stephen Sondheim. *West Side Story.* New York: Random House, 1957.

Machado, Eduardo. *The Floating Island Plays.* New York: TCG, 1984.

Morton, Carlos. *Johnny Tenorio and Other Plays.* Houston: Arte Publico, 1992.

Osborn, Elizabeth M., Ed. *On New Ground: Contemporary Hispanic-American Plays.* New York: TCG, 1987.

Sanchez-Scott, Milcha. *The Cuban-Swimmer.* In *Literature and Its Writers.* Eds. Ann Charters and Samuel Charters. New York: Bedford, 2001: 1882–95.

Valdez, Luis. *The Zoot Suit and Other Plays.* Houston: Arte Publico, 1992.

Law and Justice

Inherit the Wind by Jerome Lawrence and Robert E. Lee (1955)
The Crucible by Arthur Miller (1953)
Twelve Angry Men by Reginald Rose (1956)

The vagaries of law have often been the subject of modern drama. Whether a play offers an analysis of a case from differing viewpoints, highlights ethical dilemmas created by clashes between moral and legal law, or explores the actual process of a case, legal dramas inevitably engage the audience's judgment, alongside that of the judge and jury, and provide excitement, even if they do not always end with justice being done. Law and justice are clearly not synonymous in the eyes of most playwrights, and yet the idea of law, when performed responsibly and compassionately, continues to inspire.

The lengthy tribunals of the House Committee on Un-American Activities, known as HUAC, during the 1950s, has also inspired many modern dramatists to explore both the moral and legal aspects of such "show trials," along with how they get started and how they affect the public. Two of the plays discussed here have connections to HUAC, which subpoenaed people to prove that they had no connection to communism. Those who were subpoenaed often lost their livelihoods as a result (regardless of guilt or innocence). Echoes of this period in American history resound in numerous other dramatic works.

Inherit the Wind, by Jerome Lawrence and Robert E. Lee, concentrates our attention on the lawyers and the way in which a case is handled in open court. The title is taken from Proverbs 11:29: "He that troubleth his own house/ Shall inherit the wind," indicating the playwrights' sympathy with the defendant. The play is based on a real trial that took place in the 1920s in Dayton, Tennessee, commonly known as the Scopes Monkey Trial, in which a schoolteacher was charged with introducing Darwin in the classroom against the wishes of the school board. A few lines have been taken from those original court transcripts, but the play does not seek to offer a true historical account. Instead, it tries to draw a connection between that earlier trial and the HUAC hearings to gain a clearer view of the philosophy and impetus behind those hearings, with their similar agenda to restrict free thought in a nation supposedly founded on such freedoms.

Arthur Miller's *The Crucible* tells the story behind the Salem witch trials of 1692, centering our attention on the repercussions these trials had on the Proctor family as well as making an analogous critical commentary on the actions of HUAC. The printed play contains extensive notes detailing the historical background of Salem society in the 1690s and detailed facts regarding the actual lives of the main characters involved. Miller wanted his critics to know that he had not made up these events, but that people really allowed such things to occur, although he does not intend the play to replace historical record, for it is a dramatization and not a retelling.

Miller initially resisted the idea of depicting the HUAC hearings in the form of an old-fashioned witch trial as too obvious. However, as the HUAC hearings grew more ritualistic and cruelly pointless, he could no longer resist, despite the obvious risks, for the parallels were far too apt to ignore. He saw how both sets of hearings had a definite structure behind them, designed to make people publicly confess. In both cases, the "judges" knew in advance all the information for which they asked. The main difference was that Salem's hearings had a greater legal force, as it was against the law in America to be a witch in the seventeenth century, but it was not against the law to be a communist in the twentieth century. Miller does not attempt a one-to-one analogy between his characters and those involved in HUAC because that would have made the play too tied to its time. The reason the play has remained so popular is that it offers more than a simple history lesson about either the original 1629 Salem witch trials or about HUAC—what Miller explores are the prevailing conditions that cause such events.

In *The Crucible*, Miller draws our attention to the process and the ways in which the law, when used for political and private ends, can destroy the lives of others. We never actually step inside the courtroom as the site of the play's action, but hear secondhand what goes on and see how it affects the lives of everyone in Salem. Miller is concerned with the tension people experience between conscience and their predilection toward selfishness, and the inevitable moral consequences of allowing the latter an upper hand. *The Crucible* exposes the extent to which many people use troubled times, such as those that gave rise to the witch trials, to pursue selfish ends. In contrast to these types, Miller elevates and celebrates people of individual conscience, such as the Nurses and the Proctors, who refuse to do this.

Originally a television play, though since adapted for the stage, Reginald Rose's *Twelve Angry Men* takes us into the minds of a jury who are serving on a first-degree murder trial. It allows us to follow the process by which they examine the evidence given during that trial to discover, by uncovering reasonable doubt, that they must acquit the defendant. Although the jurors are never named, each one is a distinct personality, and Rose gives us a grandstand view into how their personalities and prejudices affect their judgment of the case. We are also reminded of the heavy responsibility jurors face, and the need for them to respect this responsibility if they are to uphold America's potentially egalitarian judicial system.

Set in a generic small country township, *Inherit the Wind* relates the trial of Bert Cates, brought up on charges for attempting to teach his students about evolution. A relatively minor case becomes a media event because of the principles involved and the two big-name lawyers called in to prosecute and defend. The prosecutor, Matthew Brady, argues that creationism is the only explanation for the world and to deny this, as science does, is sinful. The defense attorney, Henry Drummond, turns the case into an argument about free speech. Both understand that this is a landmark case that will influence the education of future generations. The minister's daughter, Rachel, who loves Cates, pleads with him to apologize, but after hearing her own father damning Cates to hell and then turning on her for objecting, decides to support Cates in his quest for knowledge. Cates is found unanimously guilty by the court but it is a pyrrhic victory for the prosecution, because Cates is only given a minimal fine, will most likely win on appeal to the Supreme Court, and has brought sufficient national attention to the archaic law that he broke for it to be struck down. Brady dies of a heart attack soon after the verdict, a broken man whose popularity has clearly passed.

Beginning with the town's children, the playwrights want us to realize from the start how little harmed a boy like Howard has been by knowledge of evolution. Later, Drummond points out that knowledge of Darwin has not made Howard forget his ten commandments, just as there being no tractors or telephones in the Bible does not make him view them as sinful. But these old-fashioned townsfolk are mostly creationists, and it is the town itself that is on trial for backward thinking. These people are so staid that they are horrified by Drummond's bright-purple suspenders. The head of the religious community is Reverend Brown, whose belief in the literal word of the Bible leads him to damn his own daughter, showing how far such overzealousness can go.

Cates is partly a target because he has stopped attending church, put off by Brown's insistence that a young child who recently died would writhe in hellfire because he had not been baptized. Brady unfairly twists the evidence against Cates by interpreting his private musings to his girlfriend about the relationship of God and Man into a declaration that God does not exist. It is up to Drummond to try to prove that it is possible to believe in the Bible and science simultaneously, as one does not necessarily negate the other. At the close, Drummond significantly leaves with copies of both Darwin and the Bible in his briefcase, indicating his ability to do this.

Brady has come not to prosecute Cates so much as to defend the state statute against teaching evolution, and so defend "the Living Truth of the Scriptures" (25). He views this as a fight to maintain people's belief in the Bible and God.

So that we are in no doubt that this is a real battle, on.his arrival the townspeople confer on Brady the honorary title of Colonel in the State Militia. Brown
shows his support for Brady with a banner over the courthouse stating, "Read
Your Bible," and a prayer meeting on the courthouse lawn during the trial.
Drummond naturally objects that these are unfairly prejudicial, and they
should at least give equal time and publicity to Darwin, but the judge dismisses
this as preposterous. With the same apparent prejudice, the judge also accepts
Brady's objection that all of Drummond's scientific witnesses—there to prove
the reality of evolution—are "Irrelevant, immaterial, inadmissible" (101). But
the truth is, technically, he is right, for the state law does not allow such views
to be spoken, regardless of whether they are correct or false.

The trial itself is a direct contest between Brady and Drummond: both criticize everything the other says and does to try to find an opening, like two
prizefighters sparring. Both play to the crowd, have specific pre-formed outlooks, and are excellent public speakers. It becomes an issue of credibility: which
of these two is the jury more likely to believe, for the focus is now on the
lawyers rather than the defendant. Drummond respects Brady, but knows he
is living in the past, so is ruthless against him in court. After his death, he
defends him against the sarcastic journalist, Hornbeck, pointing out that Brady
had the same rights as Cates to believe whatever he wanted.

Drummond is a known agnostic, with a reputation for defending even the
knowingly guilty and freeing them by exposing inequities in the laws they
have broken. Brady warns, "He'll try to make us forget the lawbreaker and put
the law on trial" (36). What Drummond insists is that the trial be about "the
right to think" (88), thus setting personal liberty against the laws of the land.
As he points out during the trial, if God had not wanted humankind to think,
then He would not have given us the power to do so. Since he is not allowed
to bring Darwin into the court, in a masterly cross-examination Drummond
puts Brady and the Bible on trial. By pointing to some of the incredible occurrences and plain inconsistencies in the Bible, Drummond weakens the crea-
tionist argument and catches Brady in uncertainty.

Brady is overweight and this is partly what kills him in the end, but it is a
symbol of his overindulgence in everything, including his own opinion at the
expense of others. He is so wrapped up in his own importance that it is he who
finally proves the ridiculous limitations of the law Cates has broken by allowing
Drummond to trick him into telling the open court that he personally speaks
with God and then contradicting himself by declaring that "each man is a free
agent" (125), to which Drummond can ask, then why is Cates in jail?

Bert Cates has undeniably broken the law, which is why he must be found
guilty, but the law is shown to be unjust. Our sympathy for Cates is automatic;
he is not grandstanding or trying to cause trouble but is a very meek and
ordinary man, in both looks and intellect. The jailer does not even want to
keep him locked in his cell. Cates simply feels that it is ridiculous not to say
what he knows to be a scientific truth. Although he almost gives in to pressure,

with Drummond's support, he decides to see it through. Cates pays a price for his stance: he loses his job and lodgings, and his life will be hard. But as Drummond points out, Cates has made it easier for the next person to stand up for what he believes, so he has done justice a good turn. Cates is also rewarded by the love of Rachel, who leaves her father, reads Darwin, and intends to stick by him in the future.

The Crucible begins with the apparent bewitchment of the Reverend Parris's daughter. Pressured by Thomas Putnam and rumors of the local girls doing something elicit in the woods, Parris has called in Reverend Hale to look for witches. Salem soon fills with tension as the girls accuse numerous townspeople of witchery and the judges start hanging many of those accused. John Proctor tries to bring people to their senses, but Abigail Williams, one of the girls with whom Proctor had had an earlier affair, tries to free John for herself by accusing his wife Elizabeth of witchcraft, and then John himself when John turns against Abigail. His only way out is to confess to witchcraft, which in all good conscience he decides he cannot do.

Although the original John Proctor was a minor figure in the Salem witch trials, Miller's Proctor becomes the central protagonist of *The Crucible.* He faces the dilemma of the innocent person who must falsely confess to a crime in order to save his own life. He considers telling this lie because he feels guilty over an adulterous affair for which he has not been punished. In sleeping with Abigail he committed a sin against his own standards of decent conduct, and when Hale suggests that the town is being punished for some secret "abomination," Proctor takes this to heart. He realizes, too, that were it not for his former relationship with Abigail, his wife would not be in danger. When Elizabeth effectively absolves him of his guilt in their final meeting, confessing her own past coldness and declaring her faith in his judgment, Proctor can reject the temptation to lie and die with honor.

Proctor's refusal to go along with the confession indicates his awareness that he has a responsibility to himself and his community, and his conviction that he would rather hang than participate in the false judgment of either. Through Proctor and the others who die with him, Miller wishes to show the heroism of these victims in order to lead us to recognize and celebrate such personal integrity. It will come as no surprise that when called before HUAC three years later, Miller, just like his hero John Proctor, refused to name names and accepted the consequences of his refusal.

Reverend John Hale, who initiates the prosecution, begins the play a conceited figure, seeing himself as a superior intellect to these villagers, happily determined to uncover their evil spirits; but events conspire to make him reassess his thinking. Initially, he lets his fascination with devils and witchcraft overwhelm the evidence of his senses, and he allows this to continue past the point when he can stop what he has set in motion. His questioning comes too late, but it helps to expose the closed, logical system of the judges when one of their number turns so strongly against them.

Judge Hathorne is described as a "bitter, remorseless" man, and he is certainly more concerned with his own power than he is with uncovering the truth. His refusal to even listen to others makes him contemptible, but Deputy Governor Danforth is worse. Although he listens to counterarguments, it is not with an open mind, and when he finally hangs the condemned—even with full knowledge of their innocence—he tries to justify his action by declaring that it is for a higher good. As a result, we should recognize in him an evil force. Danforth has jailed and condemned so many on the word of the girls that he is loath to accept that he has been deceived, as it would badly undermine his authority. Miller sees him as the "rule bearer" who fixes boundaries for these proceedings that, in fear and ignorance, he refuses to allow to be crossed. The security he seeks comes at a high price, and he does more evil than he intends merely by refusing to go beyond the narrow boundaries he has set himself and others.

Thomas Putnam is an example of a sour man filled with grievances against others, mostly ones that have been created by his own imagination, sense of self-importance, or greed. Greedy and argumentative, Putnam manipulates truth and law to his own vindictive ends. His wife, Ann Putnam, is no less self-absorbed and vindictive, and, for a religious woman, ascribes far too much value to silly superstition. The Putnams are typical of the worst kind of Puritan, whose religion has become mere show and who live narrow, venal, and selfish lives that ultimately damage themselves as much as their community.

Martha Corey and Rebecca Nurse are ideal Puritans who live their faith, showing kindness and compassion to others and displaying a gentleness in their lives that is rightly respected. The fact that such women can be accused of witchcraft and condemned to die helps underline the ludicrousness of the proceedings. Francis Nurse, the opposite of Thomas Putnam, is a man who puts others before himself and lives a genuinely moral life. In the past, Francis has acted as the unofficial judge of town disputes and has been a voice of calm reason, but it is a voice that becomes lost in the hysteria of the moment.

Evidently still in love with Proctor despite his ending the affair (for which she blames his wife), Abigail Williams cleverly uses the town's superstitious leanings to her own advantage to claim greater respect in the community and to revenge herself upon Elizabeth, whom she sees as having "blackened" her name by having dismissed her from service in the Proctor household. A masterly manipulator and actress, Abigail solicits the complicity of many of the town's young girls in accusing numerous townspeople of witchcraft. The way she sacrifices former friends like Tituba to the court, without a shred of concern, suggests an amorality in her nature. She eventually turns on her beloved Proctor in an act of self-preservation, and when the possibility arises of the town turning against the court, she quickly flees, stealing the Reverend Parris's savings on the way, proving what a truly disreputable character she is.

Mercy Lewis, Susanna Walcott, Betty Parris, Ruth Putnam, and Mary Warren are among the young girls who follow Abigail's lead. All have led limited lives up to this point, bullied by employers, forced to be quiet and subservient. Abigail offers them a chance to be at the center of attention and treated as special. They are attracted to the power they see themselves holding over the townspeople as they offer the judges any names they like. Their deceit in these matters seems clear, partly based on Mary's initial confession and finally because they run away to avoid any repercussions when the villagers start to object.

Twelve Angry Men begins with the judge giving the jury instructions before they retire to deliberate in a murder trial, which carries an automatic death penalty. The judge reminds them that their decision must be unanimous or they will be declared a hung jury and the case will go to retrial. On retiring, the jury takes an initial vote on the case and finds that only one of their number, juror #8, is prepared to say not guilty. He explains that he does not necessarily believe the accused to be innocent but wants to talk further before sentencing a man to death. They consider the defendant's character and the various pieces of evidence presented by the prosecution throughout the trial. The defense lawyer, it seems, has done little to present the defendant's case and the witnesses, we discover, are less than reliable. Gradually the jury finds reasonable doubt in nearly every facet of the case against the defendant. One by one, the jurors change their minds until they return a unanimous vote of not guilty.

The jury room in which they deliberate is purposefully empty and without character to direct all of our attention to the jurors themselves. Each of the twelve men has a different background, ranging from blue-collar and white-collar workers to a successful stockbroker, an architect, and a retiree. They run in age from their twenties to their seventies; some taking their responsibility lightly, others more seriously. Their personalities are similarly varied, from the bombastic and opinionated to the shy and retiring, the disengaged to the vengeful, the thoughtful to the thoughtless. None of these men is perfect—even #8 has doubts that he is doing the right thing and is capable of losing his temper—although none are entirely unsympathetic. They reflect those people with whom we are most familiar, and Rose ensures that we understand just how ordinary and universal they are by conferring on them only numbers rather than names. These jurors aptly reflect a judicial system that states that people should be tried by a jury of their peers.

The case being tried is not a show trial but a run-of-the-mill murder case, in which a young ethnic teen, also unnamed and equally representative, has been charged with killing his father. The trial has been fairly lengthy and the jurors are mostly eager to get on with their lives, but, as #8 points out, they have a moral responsibility to properly consider all the evidence before condemning a fellow human being. He also insists that the case is too clean to be true, and that nothing in life is ever that straightforward. He feels that too many questions were left unasked, the defense having done a terrible job, and the witnesses were unconvincing. The judge has directed them to deliberate honestly and thoughtfully, but it takes #8 in the jury room to ensure that they do—unfortunately suggesting that not all trials by jury are such considered affairs.

Juror #8 is the most sympathetic of the twelve as he alone champions justice from the start, but he is soon joined by others, especially those who had been initially reticent about pushing their opinions. He stands firm and will not let the more belligerent jurors intimidate the less self-assured as they struggle to be heard, offering them gentle support, mostly through looks and gestures. Only #3 holds out against #8's calm reasoning, though even he grudgingly accepts defeat and allows his vote to be changed to not guilty, unable to stand alone as #8 had done.

During the judge's instructions, it is already evident that #8 will face the most opposition from #7 who fidgets, #10 who is preoccupied with his cold, and #3 who has already decided the defendant's guilt. These three are the most opinionated and the least caring. From the start, #10 mocks the others for even attempting to deliberate, #7 complains about wanting to get to a baseball game, and #3 reveals himself as racist and prejudiced against youths, as we later discover, because of his own poor relationship with his son. His scorn works against him by provoking others, from the elderly #9 to the young #5, to come out in support of #8, rather than be seen to side with such a blatant bigot. He even manages to offend the Foreman, who actually shares his racist views. The battle comes down to a contest between the compassion of #8 and the brutality of #3, and it is thankfully the former who wins out—this time.

Initially only #8 is open-minded enough to take a sympathetic view of the defendant, who has led a hard life: his mother died when he was nine, his father is an ex-con with a temper, and he has spent time in an orphanage. It would be odd if he were not angry and wild. This description humanizes the defendant for the others, and allows them to reconsider the evidence.

The case rests on the issue of "reasonable doubt," a legal standard that finds a person not guilty if there can be any reasonable doubt regarding the evidence presented. The jurors, guided by #8, collectively uncover such doubt by allowing themselves to question each piece of damaging evidence. The murder weapon was supposedly a one-of-a-kind knife that had been seen in the son's possession but that had no fingerprints on it, and the son declares that he had lost it. Juror #8 produces an identical knife he has found to show the falsity of the shopkeeper's claim to its uniqueness, and points out that if the boy had intended to murder his father with that knife, why would he have shown it to so many people beforehand? Juror #11 later adds that if it had been a crime of passion, as others suggest, then why was the knife clean of fingerprints, and if the boy had been guilty, why would he have returned home later?

Both of the eyewitnesses are similarly questioned, especially as it becomes evident that both cannot possibly be telling the truth. The man downstairs who heard the son yell, "I'm gonna kill you," heard the body fall, and saw the accused run down the stairs, would not have been able to do so if a train had been passing by, as the other witness stated. They determine that this elderly and lonely witness may have lied to gain some attention, and they realize that it would not have been physically possible for him to have seen what he said he saw. Then #8 goads #3 into declaring that he will kill him to show how little such a declaration really means. We discover that the other eyewitness from across the street wore glasses, and because she didn't have them on in bed, from where she saw the incident, she could definitely have been mistaken as to the identity of the murderer. As they uncover more and more that is wrong with the case, each juror is won over and begins to help #8 discover even more holes. Jurors #2 and #5 uncover the fact that the entry wound does not match how the boy would have stabbed his father if he had done it.

They also question the boy's motive once again. Juror #6, honest but unimaginative, points out that there was strong evidence that the father had hit his son, but, as #8 points out, he probably did this often, so why kill him for it this time? This could have been a case of the final straw, but, on reexamination, the boy's alibi that he was at the movies but cannot recall actors and titles becomes more credible as #8 questions #4 about movies he has recently seen, and finds he cannot answer fully either. They have also realized that the father was a disreputable character and could have been killed for a number of other reasons by someone else; he gambled, often got into fistfights, and treated women badly. Such flaws in the case provide all the reasonable doubt both jury and audience need, and the play ends with the solid feeling that justice has finally been done.

FURTHER SUGGESTED READING

Abbotson, Susan C. W. *Student Companion to Arthur Miller.* Westport, CT: Greenwood, 2000.

Bloom, Harold, Ed. The Crucible: *Modern Critical Interpretations.* New York: Chelsea House, 1999.

Johnson, Bruce E. *Lawrence and Lee's* Inherit the Wind: *A Critical Commentary.* New York: Monarch, 1979.

Katsh, M. Ethan, and William Rose. *Taking Sides: Clashing Views on Controversial Legal Issues.* 9th Ed. Guilford, CT: Dushkin/McGraw Hill, 2000.

Lawrence, Jerome, and Robert E. Lee. *Inherit the Wind.* New York: Random, 1955.

Miller, Arthur. *The Crucible.* New York: Viking, 1953.

Munyan, Russ, Ed. *Readings on* Twelve Angry Men. San Diego: Greenhaven, 2000.

Murphy, Brenda. *Congressional Theatre: Dramatizing McCarthyism on Stage, Film, and Television.* New York: Cambridge University Press, 1999.

Rattigan, Terence. *The Winslow Boy.* New York: DPS, 1946.

Reisman, W. Michael. *Law in Brief Encounters.* New Haven: Yale University Press, 1999.

Rose, Reginald. *Six Television Plays.* New York: Simon & Schuster, 1956.

Wouk, Herman. *The Caine Mutiny Court-Martial.* Garden City, NY: Doubleday, 1954.

The "Life-Lie"

The Wild Duck by Henrik Ibsen (1884)
The Iceman Cometh by Eugene O'Neill (1946)
All My Sons by Arthur Miller (1947)

In *The Quintessence of Ibsenism* (1891), George Bernard Shaw explains the principle of what Henrik Ibsen saw as the "life-lie" and its relation to reality and idealism. Ibsen and Shaw both believed that many of us find reality so unpleasant that we try to cover it up with a mask of idealism, creating an alternative, unreal "life" for ourselves that is essentially a "lie." They see this as dangerous, for the further we move away from reality, the more damage we cause to ourselves and others in our efforts to maintain that idealistic mask. They are both realists in that their plays tend to strip away the masks their characters create for themselves and force the audience to see the true nature of such characters. Eugene O'Neill and Arthur Miller bring a recognition of this tendency to hide from unpleasant truths into American drama. While some may carry on by living the lie, others are drawn to face reality with varying repercussions. For some, this awareness is productive, but for others, it is ultimately destructive.

Ibsen and O'Neill both question the nature of truth and ask if truth is indeed reflective of reality. They wonder if truth telling is always necessary or even wise, and consider if it may be better for some to continue to live the lie. It seems that there are some kind of deceits that can be condoned, especially if no one is being hurt in the process, although there are others that must always be condemned. Miller may appear more idealistic, for he comes down more heavily on the necessity of truth, whatever the cost.

In *The Wild Duck*, Henrik Ibsen attempts to create characters who are psychologically real and who convey the idea that truth is relative to the individual and his/her particular personality and emotional needs. In this he presages the naturalism of Anton Chekhov. Both the Werles and the Ekdals live lives full of deceit. Some of that is external but much is internal, and Gregers's attempts to bring in the light of truth only damage everyone that truth touches, although it is the child, Hedvig, who pays the heaviest price, with her life.

The Iceman Cometh by Eugene O'Neill takes place in a bar filled with people who are unable to face the truth, who insist on living "pipe dreams," which are O'Neill's version of Ibsen's "life-lie." O'Neill suggests that everyone lives with these types of dreams, and to try to live without them is inherently dangerous. The dreams may be unattainable, but they at least offer hope. The titular "iceman" represents truth and death, which for some becomes one and the same thing. Theodore Hickey jokes about his wife having an affair with the iceman, but it turns out to be he who is the adulterer, and, in a sense, the iceman. The truth is rarely pretty or satisfying, and it is wrong for Hickey to try to force his friends to face it. His attempt is not selflessly motivated, but is a means of justifying the murder he has committed. But murder is a crime for which he must pay, and his attempt at justification only confirms what a selfish person he has been all along. Hickey represents a false prophet, bringing spiritual death to his followers, and this is reflected in his name. Theodore means "gift of God," suggesting a likeness to Jesus, just as the "iceman cometh" echoes the biblical description of Christ as bridegroom in the phrase the "bridegroom cometh." Yet the name Hickey counters this, suggesting "hick man"— someone who is easily fooled and the victim of delusions.

The play was completed by 1939, though it was not produced until 1946, but O'Neill sets the play in 1912 to show that disillusionment with society was already rampant in America before both world wars. The full text approaches five hours in performance and has fairly static staging, as people rarely enter or leave; but the play's impact mounts as we grow to really know these people. O'Neill has characters pass out or fall asleep rather than exit, so as not to break the flow of conversation and to allow for smooth transitions within the various groupings of speaking characters. Some of this is done with humor, which underscores the camaraderie of the characters and the warmth they offer one another; as the "iceman" approaches, the atmosphere chills to tragedy.

Arthur Miller's All My Sons, with its tale of a family torn apart by secrets and lies, portrays many discordancies that arose within American families during the 1940s. World War II helped drive a wedge between many fathers and their children; in some cases this was a physical or psychological wedge, but in the case of the Kellers, the wedge is an ideological one. The task was to redefine the role of the father in light of the changes taking place in society; the inability to achieve this accelerated the complete breakdown of the family unit, which is just what happens in the Keller household. Men like Chris and Larry Keller who had gone to fight were changed by their experiences; deeply affected by the sacrifices they saw their comrades make, they developed a heightened sense of social responsibility. This leads Larry to kill himself in shame at what his father has done, and it prompts Chris to set himself impossibly idealistic standards by which to live. Shaken by the horrors of World War II, society recognized the need for change, but the soldiers who fought often held different views from those who stayed at home about how to initiate that change. What Miller shows is that both parties are living a lie of sorts.

The Wild Duck begins with a dinner party at Werle's home. Werle is estranged from his son, Gregers, and attempts to reconnect with him prior to remarrying. Gregers remains adamant in his dislike of his philandering father, blaming him for his mother's death, and becoming further incensed upon realizing from what his naïve old friend, Hjalmar Ekdal, tells him about what has been going on in his absence, that Werle has been taking cruel advantage of the Ekdals. Werle set up Hjalmar's father to take the fall for an illegal business deal and married off his pregnant mistress to an unwitting Hjalmar. The Ekdals are blissfully ignorant of both these realities, but Gregers understands what has truly been going on and determines to enlighten Hjalmar, disinheriting himself and becoming the Ekdals's lodger. Hjalmar leads a comfortable life, in which he emotionally bullies his family to make up for his ineffectiveness in the real world. It takes time for the truth to make an impact on him, but when it does, he turns on his daughter, Hedvig, whose response is to sacrifice herself out of love for her father.

The only truly selfless character in the play is Hedvig, who openly loves her thoughtless father. At Gregers's suggestion, Hedvig decides to kill her wild duck to prove her love and ends up shooting herself. Her life is fairly empty, and she strongly identifies with the duck as an individual who is being restricted in a dark world and whose background is a mystery. Hedvig is going blind, by which her world will be further reduced. It is this hereditary condition that makes Hjalmar understand her true parentage, for Werle suffers from the same condition.

Werle may appear to be a monster, with his lascivious nature and grasping ways, but he becomes more sympathetic than those he has offended. He tries to make amends, offering his son a partnership and Old Ekdal and Hedvig a regular income. His marriage to the widow, Mrs. Sörby, is based on truth, since each has told the other about their pasts. Werle's past disreputable behavior is somewhat ameliorated by the officious rectitude of both wife and son under which he had clearly suffered. He was also tricked into marriage, just as Hjalmar was, by the expectation, in his case, of a fortune that never materialized. Werle only wounds people, as he did the duck, from which they can recover, but Gregers and Hjalmar are killers.

Gregers's unrelenting condemnation of his father and his constant meddling make him the villain of the piece, even though he is motivated by good intentions and only wants to bring out the truth. The truth can evidently be destructive, and should be handled with greater circumspection. Gregers views Hjalmar as "an unsuspecting child . . . without the slightest idea that what he calls his home is built on a lie" (233). But that is all Hjalmar's home could ever be built upon, since Hjalmar is incapable of facing reality.

While Hjalmar initially seems like the victim, with the naive blindness by which he has been led, any sympathy is swiftly lost on witnessing how he treats his family. If the family had to rely on his efforts alone, they would be destitute. His wife Gina's careful household management and running of his photography business and the money Werle pays Old Ekdal for copying services allow them to lead a comfortable, though frugal, existence. Hjalmar loves to exaggerate the inequities of his position, but he lives his life as he wants, avoiding work by pretending to be developing some grand invention and playing hunter with his father in the attic, where they keep a variety of birds and rabbits.

After the early death of his mother, Hjalmar had been raised by two doting aunts to believe that he should be the center of attention and need do little for himself. So he lords it over his family to puff himself up and repeats the words of others to make himself sound witty and profound, but his mind is as shallow as his father's. Nevertheless, his daughter idolizes him even though he is a superficial man—all words without action, all show without substance. For all his professed love of his father, he pretends not to know him at Werle's house, and he treats his supposedly beloved daughter even more dismissively, forgetting the treats he had promised, ignoring her need for diversion, keeping her home from school supposedly to save her eyes, then letting her do his photographic finishing, which harms her eyes, so he can go out and play. His rejection of her near the close becomes all the more brutal by its evident insincerity; he is not hurt, but sees another chance to play the martyr.

Hjalmar's neighbor, Relling, tries to make Gregers see how pointlessly idealistic he is by suggesting how few marriages could happily exist without some deceit. In Relling's view, the world is a troubled place and the only treatment is "to keep up the make-believe of life" (293). Ideals, he asserts, are the true falsehoods, because they are so impractical. "If you take away make-believe from the average man, you take away his happiness as well" (294). Therefore, Relling plants the invention idea in Hjalmar's head to give his life apparent purpose, just as he allows Molvik to believe he is demonic to assuage his guilt over drinking. Mrs. Sörby has the same practical outlook as Relling, which is why she chooses to marry Werle over Relling, because Werle is wealthy and has no drinking problem. She insists that she and Werle tell the truth to each other before they commit to marriage and they do, which tells us that it is possible to live with the truth, but it is an unwise proposition for people like Gina and Hjalmar, for whom the truth can only be destructive.

Most of these people live a lie, but their lives are made more livable by that fact. Some avoid the truth by drinking, like Molvik and Gregers's mother; others construct elaborate fantasies, like Hjalmar and Hedvig, which allow them to live more contentedly. Most people are too cowardly to face reality head on; even Gregers stood quietly by while Ekdal was set up and does not try to reveal *that* truth. His mission to open Hjalmar's eyes is also selfishly motivated, to ease his own conscience and to boost his false image of Hjalmar, through whom he tries to live vicariously. Having never committed to life himself, always staying on the periphery, he is hypocritical to assume the right to tell others how to live.

Each sees the wild duck as representative of their own take on reality. For Ekdal it symbolizes his love of the freedom of the outdoors; for Gregers it represents the truth; and for Hedvig, her isolation and sense of restriction. While the attempted slaying of the duck reunites Hjalmar and Gina, it comes at a high price. Gregers tries to insist that Hedvig did not die in vain, but Relling will not allow him this comforting illusion. He disgustedly points out that Hjalmar could never truly grieve, since he loves no one but himself and will use Hedvig's death as another opportunity to wallow in "emotional fits of self-admiration and self-compassion" (305), a concept that appalls Gregers, but that he finally accepts as true.

In *The Iceman Cometh,* Harry Hope runs a boardinghouse full of the flotsam of society. In the attached saloon, residents sleep off the night before, while Larry chats with the barman and speaks of "pipe dreams." The characters variously wake up and reveal their individual dreams, as they wait for Hickey to show up and enliven them. Hickey arrives but seems different, and tries to persuade them to give up their dreams as he has. They initially resist, but when they do break down and try, each fails, making them more downhearted than before. Hickey tries to understand what went wrong, and in so doing reveals the fact he has just killed his wife. Inspired by his confession, Parritt confesses to Larry about informing on his own mother. As the police take Hickey away, and he claims a defense of insanity, the residents use this to persuade themselves that what he had them do has been invalidated and was not real. All make this assertion except for Larry, who can no longer be detached as he had hoped and condemns Parritt, leading him to commit suicide in contrition.

O'Neill's cast of characters does not represent all of society, but rather the rejects of society, those people who have once had meaningful lives but for various reasons (mostly rooted in disappointment or disillusionment) have lost touch with them, leaving them with nothing except their "pipe dreams." These dreams sustain them, as Larry explains: "To hell with the truth! As the history of the world proves, the truth has no bearing on anything. It's irrelevant and immaterial, as the lawyers say. The lie of a pipe dream is what gives life to the whole misbegotten mad lot of us, drunk or sober" (9–10). Larry denies that he maintains any dreams, insisting that he is the detached exception to the rule, but this desire for detachment is Larry's pipe dream, for he cannot help but be involved.

The landlord, Harry Hope, who runs the boardinghouse/saloon, helps keep his residents alive and will always give them a drink when he sees they need it, although his motivation is selfish: he wants them around to boost his own sense of self-importance. It is he who immediately picks up on the possibility of Hickey's insanity, which will allow them all to resurrect their sustaining

dreams. These people's whole lives are contained in this one building. No one
ever wants to leave, and the windows are so full of grime that no one can see
through them, which ensures their isolation from a society with which none
of them can cope. This is a decayed building containing decayed people, yet
they still have "Hope" to keep them going and their various "pipe dreams" to
get them through each day. They respect each other's dreams and uphold them,
for without them they truly will cease to exist, as we see when Hickey momentarily explodes them.

The run-down appearance of each of these characters shows the toughness
of the lives they have led. While some have always been fairly disreputable,
others have made their mark in the past, but have lost touch with those glory
days. What remains is a group of ex-professionals, and ex-practitioners of life.
Ed Mosher sold tickets at the circus, Pat McGloin was a cop on the take, Willie
Oban a lawyer whose father turned out to be a major criminal, Joe Mott an
African American gambler who wants to be white, Piet Wetjoen an ex-Boer
commander, Cecil Lewis an ex-British commander, Jimmy Cameron an ex-war
correspondent, Hugo Kalmar a worn-out political editor, Larry Slade a disenchanted anarchist, Hickey a loose-living salesman, and there are the grasping
bartenders Rocky and Chuck, who also act as pimps for the bored prostitutes
Pearl, Margie, and Cora. Most use alcohol to escape the past or obliterate the
present and any need for a future.

Larry is disillusioned, having realized that any sociopolitical movement must
fail because men are too selfish. He tries to take "a seat in the grandstand of
philosophical detachment" (11), where he drinks to remain detached. However,
he begins to realize that this cannot work since he likes people too much and
always has time for them. We see this through Don Parritt's remembrances
and Jimmy's declaration: "You pretend a bitter, cynic philosophy, but in your
heart you are the kindest man among us" (44). Larry suffers because he sees
people as collectively rotten but still loves them on an individual level.

It might seem that these people can go no further down than this empty
existence in the "No Chance Saloon," but Hickey proves that they have further
yet to fall. "Pipe dreams" allow these people to recreate either past or future,
even while living in a dire present, which at least gives them the strength to
keep living. These people are separated from the outside world of "greedy
madness" (29) by their dreams. Hickey at first seems out of place, but we
eventually discover that he is the worst off of them all. He has just killed his
wife, Evelyn, mostly because of his own guilt at continually disappointing her
with his drinking and philandering, and his need to be free. He has dreamed
this into an act of kindness, but, ironically, is made to see the truth in the end
that he hated her rather than loved her as he had imagined, because she constantly made him feel resentful, having expected too much of him.

Hickey has made a living off other people's dreams as a salesman, and it is
not his place to try to dispel anyone's dream. He tries to stop the saloon regulars
from drinking (which helps them dream), so that they might face their dreams

to explode them and get on with their lives, as he thinks he has done. It takes a while for him to realize that those dreams are their lives, and all they really have. In ignorance, he nearly destroys them by trying to "help." Facing truth threatens to pulls them all apart and take away even the comfort of these shallow friendships. But they are resilient, and once Hickey's power is deflated by his admission of insanity, they begin to build new dreams for themselves— such as Harry Hope pretending he nearly got run over by a car to make his life sound more interesting. However, for a while they sit like dead men during the period Hickey will not allow them to dream. At this juncture they cannot even get drunk anymore. In one way they all want to see each other fail, as it gives them tacit permission to fail as well without having to feel bad that they did. Essentially, these people are rather unpleasant, and it is only their dreams that make them acceptable, by keeping them from seeing the miserable failures that they all truly are.

Hickey and Parritt are very similar: both destroy others to help themselves, and both pay the price. Hickey has to die because he has no dream left by which to live. "He vas selling death to me, that crazy salesman" (249), Hugo declares, after Hickey has been taken away, and it was true. All end up back to normal, except for Larry. Parritt has killed himself, largely because of what Larry has said to him, and Larry realizes that he cannot remain detached, as he has hoped. Earlier he had jokingly commented that he was ready for death, but with the realization that he cannot avoid suffering as a result of witnessing the terrible things others do, he truly wishes for the release of death, and he ironically embraces what Hickey had sought—a life without illusions.

In *All My Sons* Joe and Kate Keller live a lie, pretending that Keller is innocent of shipping out faulty airplane parts to the Air Force and that their son Larry is alive. To keep this lie going, Kate tries to block their other son Chris's engagement to Larry's old girlfriend, Ann Deever, and the family pressure Ann's brother, George Deever, into silence when he discovers the truth. But the truth cannot be hidden, and we learn that Keller knowingly shipped those parts to keep his business alive and avoided punishment by placing the blame on Steve Deever. Also, Larry is dead, having crashed his plane in an act of suicide for shame at what his father has done. As the truth comes out, Chris disowns his father and drives Keller to commit suicide to avoid facing his guilt.

Joe Keller is a "man among men" because he has "made it" in this society, and that, to many, is cause for respect and admiration. His regard for his sons is undeniable and his belief in the sanctity of fatherhood is clear as he cries, "A father is a father" (136), and in this cry affirms his belief that blood should always be put before outside concerns. He tells Chris: "What the hell did I work for? That's only for you, Chris, the whole shooting match is for you!" (102), and is eager to include Chris in his business. This desire to bond with his son is, in a sense, what frees him from moral responsibility and allows him to ship those faulty parts with a clear conscience. But he is guilty of the "life-lie." For most of the play he avoids the truths he innately knows will destroy him, and when he finally does acknowledge them toward the close, he destroys himself rather than face the consequences.

Keller shows pride in the ability he has to pass on such a thriving business firm, and it worries him deeply that Chris may not accept his gift. He revels in his financial and, therefore, social superiority. Having faced the accusations against him boldly, his boldness won him the case. But he has been morally misled by the mores of an unsavory society; a society Chris comes to describe as "the land of the great big dogs" (167). Keller has been taught that it is the winner who continues to play the game and society can turn a blind eye to moral concerns as long as the production line keeps rolling—this is the essence of capitalism. It is what he tries to teach his son, but it is something his son does not want to hear. It is not until the end of the play that Keller sees what his sons saw all along: we have social responsibilities beyond the immediate family and to deny these is to live a lie. Keller cannot survive the rejection of his sons, and he literally ceases to exist once this occurs, as he commits suicide.

Keller's wife, Kate, is the real kingpin of this family. It is Kate whom they must all please, and it is Kate to whom everyone turns for advice and comfort. Yet Kate is a woman who ignores realities of which she disapproves, such as the likelihood of Larry's death, and Chris and Ann's relationship. She focuses instead on anything she can adapt to her version of reality. Kate feels the guilt of what her husband has done, and throughout the play she threatens to burst with the pressure of keeping his dark secrets. Her insistence that Larry is alive is intrinsic to her ability to continue supporting Keller.

Chris has been set up as a moral idealist by his friends and neighbors, which is a hard role to fulfill, especially as he begins to question his own complicity in his father's lie. Many others look to him to determine how they should behave—he inspires their neighbor Jim Bayliss to want to become a medical researcher, and the Deever children to believe in Keller's innocence and their own father's guilt. But Chris is unsure as to what he wants to do for himself.

Chris feels torn between keeping his father happy by staying in the family business and refusing to get caught up in the morally suspect world of commerce. Chris's character is summed up in his military epithet "Mother Mc-Keller." He is both "mother" and "killer"; he has a desire to protect and destroy almost simultaneously, and this conflict finally burns him out. Chris tries to take responsibility for his fellow man in opposition to his father's evident lack of responsibility, but, ironically, without the support of his father he finally crumbles and returns to the safe inertia of his mother's arms. Larry Keller's rebellion was better sustained, in that at least he died for something he believed.

Like Chris, Ann is cautious, which may be why she and Chris are so well suited. Also, like Chris, in her firm rejection of her father (and her later request that Chris reject his father), she seems to be a fierce idealist. However, because of Larry's letter she knew from the start about Keller's guilt, yet kept quiet until she saw no other alternative to getting what she wanted, which compromises her idealism. This is a compromise Chris will have to make if he is ever to be happy. Even though Ann will be marrying into the family that destroyed her father, she knows that the worst thing to be in life is alone, and she is desperate to hold onto Chris. It is uncertain by the end of the play if she will succeed in this or not, as Kate, who has been trying to keep them apart throughout the play, seems to have reclaimed her son and holds him tightly in her arms.

FURTHER SUGGESTED READING

Abbott, Anthony S. *The Vital Lie: Reality and Illusion in Modern Drama.* Tuscaloosa: University of Alabama Press, 1989.

Abbotson, Susan C. W. *Student Companion to Arthur Miller.* Westport, CT: Greenwood, 2000.

Barnes, J. A. *A Pack of Lies: Towards a Sociology of Lying.* New York: Cambridge University Press, 1994.

Bloom, Harold, Ed. *Arthur Miller's* All My Sons. New York: Chelsea House, 1988.

Bogard, Travis. *Contour in Time: The Plays of Eugene O'Neill.* New York: Oxford University Press, 1988.

Guare, John. *Six Degrees of Separation.* New York: Random House, 1990.

Ibsen, Henrik. *The Wild Duck.* In *Four Great Plays by Ibsen.* New York: Bantam, 1959: 217–305.

Lebowitz, Naomi. *Ibsen and the Great World.* Baton Rouge: Louisiana State University Press, 1990.

Manheim, Michael, Ed. *The Cambridge Companion to Eugene O'Neill.* New York: Cambridge University Press, 1998.

McFarlane, James, Ed. *The Cambridge Companion to Ibsen.* New York: Cambridge University Press, 1994.

Miller, Arthur. *A View from the Bridge and* All My Sons. Harmondsworth, U.K.: Penguin, 1961.

O'Neill, Eugene. *The Iceman Cometh.* New York: Vintage, 1957.

Sartre, Jean-Paul. *No Exit and Three Other Plays.* New York: Vintage International, 1989.

Magic and the Supernatural

Blithe Spirit by Noël Coward (1941)
An Inspector Calls by J. B. Priestley (1946)
Prelude to a Kiss by Craig Lucas (1990)

Modern drama has not been immune to people's perennial fascination with magic and the supernatural, and a tale with a ghost or a supernatural twist has often performed well at the box office. Not bound by the mundane rules of ordinary life, ghosts and magical occurrences suggest the possibilities and dangers of freedom, and give playwrights an easy conceit by which to explore how people live and the preferred balance between responsibility and freedom to which people should best adhere. Supernatural manifestations have been commonly represented in such plays as Noël Coward's comical ghost story *Blithe Spirit* or, more rarely, in the darker, more socially conscious *An Inspector Calls* by J. B. Priestley. Whether the ghosts are comical or threatening, they seem designed to produce the same end—the truer realization by the living as to how they should live their lives.

Coward's *Blithe Spirit* features seances, ghosts, and a variety of astral hocus pocus. For Coward, plot is not as important as creating an intriguing situation that offers the potential for plenty of witty dialogue by which the characters (and audience) relish that situation. *Blithe Spirit* does not expect its audience to believe in ghosts, merely to be entertained by them. Coward is an acute observer of the social scene around the mid–twentieth century in all of its foibles and absurdities. With gentle humor, *Blithe Spirit* efficiently exposes and satirizes its characters' obsession with surface over substance and their tendency to privilege talk over action. Luckily, they have the common sense of the medium Madame Arcarti, a character whose views would traditionally have been the least credible, to save the day and send the ghosts back where they belong.

An Inspector Calls takes itself a lot more seriously. It is the best known of a number of plays written by Priestley that utilize the concept of a time-slip in their plots. Through a kind of supernatural precognition, the Inspector's questioning of the Birlings and Gerald Croft foreshadows future events and suggests a beneficent, ghostly force willing to get involved on behalf of the Eva Smiths of this world and ensure, at least, that their deaths are not in vain. Although *An Inspector Calls* incorporates many of the common elements of a typical mystery play, with its suspense, unraveling of clues, and series of plot twists, it is a mystery play with a twist, as there is no murder or murderer in the usual sense and Inspector Goole is no ordinary detective, but a ghostly inquisitor who promotes social conscience and social responsibility.

There are also plays like *Prelude to a Kiss* by Craig Lucas, whose whole premise relies on a magical occurrence, in this case, the switching of bodies between a young bride on her wedding day and an old man preparing for death. The use of magic is never really explained beyond the suggestion that it occurred because both parties had wished it to, and the conceit is used again to teach people how to better live their lives, as well as providing much comic relief. Ironically, despite our lack of knowledge or belief in magic or the supernatural, it appears that modern dramatists mostly view them as simple contributory factors in our constant quest to improve the quality of life, rather than anything truly mysterious.

Prelude to a Kiss was first performed in 1988, but this chapter references the better-known revised version that was produced two years later, which cut and added various subsidiary characters. To assist the audience in taking the "imaginary leap required to make sense of the story" (xv), Lucas suggests that scenery be minimal, and lighting and sound used to create a sense of magical possibilities. The play's epigraphs from "The Frog Prince" and *Howard's End* prepare us for a tale of transformation, motivated by a fear of death, and the drama plays much like a classic, romantic fairy tale, only set in modern times, with a couple who swiftly fall in love, then face a major challenge that must be overcome for them to live happily ever after.

In *Blithe Spirit*, Charles and Ruth Condomine are both on their second marriage, each having been widowed in their mid-thirties. Expecting an entertaining fraud, they invite a local clairvoyant, Madame Arcarti, to a dinner party along with their friends, the Bradmans. But Arcarti is the real thing, and conjures up the spirit of Charles's first wife, Elvira, who then refuses to leave. Only Charles can see Elvira, which first makes Ruth believe him to be mad, until Charles gets Elvira to indicate her presence by moving something for Ruth to witness. Ruth asks Arcarti to get rid of Elvira, but when she is unable to do so, Arcarti suggests that the spirit remains because someone is drawing her, and it is most likely Charles who subconsciously wants her back. Elvira tries to kill Charles to bring him over to her spirit world, but murders Ruth by mistake. Arcarti tries again to dematerialize Elvira, but brings back Ruth instead. Looking in her crystal ball for clues, Arcarti suddenly realizes that it has been the maid, Edith, wishing for the return of the wives, rather than

Charles, which enables her to dismiss them both, leaving Charles to revel in his newfound freedom, to the angry chagrin of his deceased wives.

The play is filled with stage tricks, such as the floating bowl of flowers that proves Elvira's presence to Ruth, and the crashing china and falling fixtures when the ghostly wives object to Charles's declaration of independence. There are also such set devices as the séances that open and close the play, and which are filled with classic eerie sounds, trances, moving tables, crystal balls, and ghostly rapping. All of these contribute to the visual fun, making this a far more entertaining play to see than to read.

Coward subtitles the play "an improbable farce," and it is, since it asks its audience to both believe in ghosts and find them comedic, as they would living people in the automatism of their responses. Highly entertained, we willingly suspend our disbelief, knowing because of the insistence of the dinner guests both that ghosts cannot appear and that they must, and fairly soon. The butts of much of the humor are those characters who refuse to believe in Elvira's presence. The audience, like Charles, is kept in on the joke because Elvira is present on stage for them to see. Coward keeps this conceit entertaining by changing the circle of those in the know. Initially we may be as skeptical as the Condomines, but then we join Charles and Arcarti in understanding that Elvira exists, while Ruth's skepticism makes her appear foolish. Later Ruth learns the truth, and it is the Bradmans who become the dupes. Later on, Charles and his two ghostly wives appear to know more about the spirit world than even Arcarti does.

The fact that the medium, Arcarti, despite her outlandish garb and clairvoyance, is actually the most down-to-earth character we meet makes the supernatural world she endorses seem all the more credible. With her commonsense aphorisms, bicycle riding, and infectious enthusiasm, Arcarti seems far more in touch with the real world than her hosts, evidenced by her wide-ranging knowledge of village gossip. The Condomines's oversophistication and evident superficiality make them seem fake by contrast. It is natural that it should be Arcarti who solves the mystery by pointing the finger at Edith, as she is the only character sufficiently able to look beyond her own concerns to understand what is actually happening.

As a ghost, Elvira behaves exactly as she had when she was alive: she sulks, whines, manipulates, and plots. Thus we see little difference between a ghost and a living person other than the color of her dress; Elvira, and later, the ghost of Ruth, are dressed completely in gray. Elvira describes the afterlife as a continual cocktail party full of famous figures, where she can play chess with Genghis Khan and watch Merlin do magic tricks. Her jealousy of Ruth leads her to murder, but since the afterlife seems so benign and death itself not quite so final, Ruth's fatal accident becomes less of a concern. We know it is only a matter of time before she rejoins us on stage, which deflects the seriousness of what Elvira has done. Life on the "other side" is clearly not so different, so death automatically becomes less something to be feared than merely a temporary inconvenience.

The ghostly premise of the play is just an excuse for Coward to craft a fairly typical comedy of manners, based on domestic disagreement, with the unusual love triangle of a husband caught between two wives (one of whom is legally dead), who, quite literally, fight over him. Each wife displays a mix of attractive and unpleasant aspects of character to ensure that we do not privilege one over the other, and Coward turns the tables by having both turn on Charles at the close, when he mocks their spirits and declares his freedom. But at no point is the audience allowed to really engage with any of these superficial people, so their fate can never be more than simply amusing, as the playwright intends. In many ways, the real magic here is Coward's sparkling dialogue.

Set in the North Midlands of England in 1912, shortly before the launching of the *Titanic*, *An Inspector Calls* depicts the self-satisfied and self-centered Birling family at a dinner party to celebrate daughter Sheila's engagement to Gerald Croft. Inspector Goole enters to break up their complacency and implicate each of them in the suicide of Eva Smith. After he has left, they begin to realize that the Inspector is not who he claims to be, and there has been no recent death like the one he described. This alleviates the guilt of the older family members, until the police call to say that a dead girl has just been found, and a police inspector is on his way to question them.

The Inspector's name is the first clue to his supernatural potential, suggesting ghoulish or ghostly origins. The fact that he apparently knows details it is impossible for him to know and foretells a death that has not yet occurred confirm this. Ironically, although a name like Goole implies a specter of the dark, the Inspector is anything but, and it is the apparently innocent Birling family who turn out to be truly rotten and evil in their callous and inhumane treatment of others. The Inspector brings the light of truth, quite literally: Priestley has the set lighting brighten as he proceeds to reveal these people's collective prejudiced, selfish, and vindictive behavior. He acts as a sentinel of morality, a potentially angelic force brought to teach the Birlings: "We don't live alone. We are members of one body. We are responsible for each other." And he warns them, "And I tell you that the time will soon come when, if men will not learn that lesson, then they will be taught it in fire and anguish" (54), words that would resonate strongly with an audience fresh from the experience of World War II.

From the start, we are prepared for the Birlings' carefree bubble to burst because we, like the Inspector, have the knowledge of hindsight. Arthur Birling's extravagant praise for the unsinkable *Titanic* just a week before her disastrous voyage and his pompous insistence that Europe will continue in peace and prosperity shortly before the outbreak of World War I, both show how wrong he can be. As the Inspector begins to chip away at Birling's complacency, it is clear to the audience who is on the side of right. The Inspector's accusations are an attempt to shake each family member into accepting responsibility for such calamities as the *Titanic* and war as much as for the death of Eva Smith/ Daisy Renton. It soon becomes clear that his task will be easier to complete with the more impressionable younger people in the room, Sheila and Eric. These two alone, on discovering there was no suicide victim, continue to acknowledge that they still did the things of which they have been accused to someone, while the others instantly give up what little sense of guilt they had begun to feel.

What the supernatural force of Inspector Goole allows us to see is the potential destructiveness of those apparently insignificant slights people often give to those over whom they feel superior. As Sheila insists, whether or not Eva exists is immaterial, as they are all guilty of treating a fellow human being badly when they had the choice to behave better. Arthur Birling chose to dismiss her as a troublemaker when she was only asking for a fair wage. Sheila also had her fired, just because she had been in a bad mood and was offended by what may have been a smirk at her expense. Gerald's attentions may initially have been more chivalrous, but he nonetheless uses her no less than Eric does. Gerald dropped "Daisy" when he became bored with her, and Eric got her pregnant then stole money from his father's business to help her out. The fact that Eva refused such aid proves that she has a stronger moral character than he, despite her predicament, and makes Sybil Birling's sanctimonious refusal of aid from her charity group, because Eva will not name the father, intentionally ironic.

Eva Smith is so named to suggest that she is a generalized abstraction rather than a real person, and she represents the poor who are intrinsically dependent on the higher classes. The ways in which these people have hurt poor Eva all reflect on the Birlings's own moral limitations—what Priestley sees as the weaknesses of the wider modern society, whose members have lost their sense of social responsibility. Arthur Birling is far too materialistic; after all, he only wants Sheila to marry Gerald in hopes that he can merge their two family businesses and is not really concerned about his daughter's happiness. Sybil is a cold woman who cares more for appearances than for what is right. Even Gerald proves himself to be predominantly self-involved and reluctant to take any blame or responsibility for his behavior. The Birling children have both been spoiled and are evidently insecure, but with proper moral guidance they might be salvageable. It is here that Priestley offers a glimmer of hope in what, otherwise, would be a pretty glum tale.

Peter and Rita, in *Prelude to a Kiss,* are intelligent young professionals who meet, fall in love, and marry. On their wedding day, an old man crashes their celebration and kisses the bride, resulting in their souls exchanging bodies. While Rita, trapped in the Old Man's dying body, creeps off to assimilate what has happened, the Old Man, who is delighted to be in a young body, goes on the couple's honeymoon with Peter. Peter senses that this is not his Rita but is unable to absolutely prove it, and it seems so incredible that he can scarcely believe it himself. Fearful of exposure, "Rita" pretends to be suffering from abuse, leaves Peter, and returns to her parents, who, ironically, do not know her as well as her new husband does. Peter tracks down the Old Man, and discovers what has happened. Though Rita looks like the Old Man the couple live comfortably together until they trick "Rita" into coming over and get the souls to go back into their correct bodies.

As in the best fairy tales, the love of the central protagonists is tested to discover its strength. Peter has insisted after only ten weeks of dating that he will love Rita until she is old, and now he has to prove it, as he lives with her in the form of an old man. For six days they live together, and Peter tells us, "It was as if we'd been married forever, suddenly, without the sex" (78), and he is able to tenderly kiss the "Old Man" on the lips because their relationship is so natural. Because he had sensed the exchange immediately, and does not enjoy his honeymoon with the fake Rita, we realize that it is the soul of Rita to which he is attracted, not her outward appearance. His faith is rewarded when he gets his wife back in her original form.

Peter has all along been able to take chances, running away to Europe when he was sixteen, or chasing after Rita; but Rita has been far more reluctant to take risks. Rita's experience transforms her in more than appearance. As a young woman she had lived cautiously, not confident in the possibilities of life. "I was freaked from the moment I woke up" (89), she announces, and has lived her life in constant fear of what might happen next. Unable to sleep soundly, determined never to bring children into such an awful world, she diminishes her own life force by such negativity and insecurity.

Just as the Old Man had been jealous of the potential vitality of her youth, she had been jealous of his evident thirst for life and sense of desire, qualities she was too timid to embrace. "If I could just know what it's like for one second of one day to have lived all that time and be so alive, so sure of something, anything. Oh, please God, let me know what it is to have so little to lose" (89). Both had seen the other as being full of life and the desire to switch places had been mutual, which is why it does not initially work when the Old Man first tries to switch back. Rita's prayer is answered, and, as the Old Man, she has learned not to be so afraid of life but to enjoy it as it comes. The fact that Lucas has her frame her wish in the form of a prayer suggests the magic here has been created by a divine authority.

Prior to the switch, the Old Man had been having a bad time. His wife had recently died, and he had been moved in with his daughter; he had also discovered that he had lung cancer and less than a year to live. He had not intended the switch but put it down to an act of desperation, an example of the way he has always lived—leaping first, asking questions later, and taking full advantage of every opportunity that came along. His different outlook on life is immediately evident once he becomes Rita, as he leaps into this new life and talks constantly of the future. Rita, by contrast, had only ever talked about the past, too fearful to contemplate what the future might hold.

Yet, having enjoyed his new lease of life, the Old Man realizes that he is ready to give it up, as he longs for the comfort of what he had: a life already lived and full of happy memories. His easy acceptance of his impending death further allows Rita to displace her fears and relax. The play ends with the young couple reunited and determined never again to squander any opportunities. They call each other a "miracle" in the possibilities they now see in their future life together; possibilities that have been expanded by their steadfast love and comfort with who they are. Thus, Lucas seems to say, the true magic is love itself, and what it can achieve.

FURTHER SUGGESTED READING

Chase, Mary. *Harvey.* New York: DPS, 1953.

Coward, Noël. *Blithe Spirit.* London: Samuel French, 1968.

DeVitis, A. A., and Albert E. Kalson. *J. B. Priestley.* Boston: Twayne, 1980.

Enright, D. N., Ed. *The Oxford Book of the Supernatural.* New York: Oxford University Press, 1994.

Gray, Frances. *Noel Coward.* New York: St. Martin's Press, 1987.

Kaye, Marvin, Ed. *13 Plays of Ghosts and the Supernatural.* Garden City, NY: Doubleday, 1990.

Klein, Holger. *J. B. Priestley's Plays.* New York: St. Martin's Press, 1988.

Lahr, John. *Coward, the Playwright.* London: Methuen, 1982.

Lucas, Craig. *Prelude to a Kiss.* New York: Dutton, 1990.

McPherson, Conor. *The Weir.* London: Nick Hern, 1998.

O'Keefe, Daniel Lawrence. *Stolen Lightning: The Social Theory of Magic.* New York: Continuum, 1982.

Priestley, J. B. *An Inspector Calls.* New York: DPS, 1945.

Marriage

Barefoot in the Park by Neil Simon (1963)
Dinner with Friends by Donald Margulies (1998)
Who's Afraid of Virginia Woolf by Edward Albee (1962)

During the development of modern drama, attitudes toward marriage have greatly changed. From a commonly held belief that couples are bound together for life, with the wife as a lesser partner, societal attitudes have shifted to a recognition that men and women are equal and that divorce is socially acceptable. Modern dramatists have tended to stir controversy by being in the vanguard of public opinion. Henrik Ibsen's 1879 *A Doll's House* shocked audiences with its portrayal of a wife who leaves her husband, but by the more permissive 1960s it became common for plays to portray couples splitting apart with little public condemnation. Marriage remains a commitment many desire to make, but not one as binding as it once appeared. Modern dramatists have fully explored the changing nature of marriage by considering what it takes to make a marriage work in modern times as well as the effect of divorce on couples who stay together and those who part.

In Neil Simon's *Barefoot in the Park* we meet a newly married couple who work through their initial fears and jealousies to discover that they are committed to each other, bound by a love that faces and survives the commonest perils of married life, from in-laws to extramarital affairs. The newlyweds Paul and Corie Bratter come to accept that they are different types and that they need to forge a compromise that will allow them to live together. Simon has an optimistic belief in the goodness of human nature that makes his early plays, especially, very appealing, though somewhat sentimentally old-fashioned. His work valorizes strong family values, committed marriage, and respect for parents by presenting us with characters who generally abide by such values. We fully expect Paul and Corie to easily resolve their differences and live happily ever after.

Where *Barefoot in the Park* is about newlyweds and the problems they face at the start of a marriage, Donald Margulies's *Dinner with Friends* considers what happens to marriages after a dozen years have passed, when the couple appear settled, with a couple of children and all the resulting routines and responsibilities. Years ago, couples who reached this point would stay together, whatever their feelings for each other, for "the sake of the children," but Margulies questions such sacrifice. Such a life is not for everyone, and in its portrayal of two couples, one who accepts the routine and another who rejects it, we explore both the potential and the threat of divorce.

Contrasting nicely with the idealism in *Barefoot in the Park*, Edward Albee's *Who's Afraid of Virginia Woolf* introduces us to another kind of married couple, George and Martha, an older couple who seem trapped in an abusive and uncomfortable relationship with no divorce in sight. We are left with the impression that this couple needs each other, and may even love each other, despite their antagonism and bitterness, which belie the common myth of marriage as some kind of comfortable balm. Meanwhile, the much younger couple who visit them, Nick and Honey, although initially appearing comfortable together, turn out to be even less well-suited to each other, and we must wonder how long their marriage will last or if they will become another George and Martha. In the spirit of the absurdist movement, Albee wishes to strip away surface presumptions to reveal the true inadequacies, fears, and longings behind these people's relationships, yet he does it in an almost realistic style.

The play's title highlights Albee's concern with the way people use fictions in their lives and relationships with others to allay fears and hide from truths, as well as to suggest an element of danger. The "wolf" is finally revealed to be George, whose masculinity Martha has been calling into question by feminizing the phrase, yet he is not as toothless as we suppose. Despite his ineffectual appearance, he is the one who elicits people's confessions and largely directs the increasingly unpleasant "games." The play peels off layers until an agreed truth is revealed. Albee seems to suggest that by stripping away the fictions with which we live, in marriage as in life, and accepting who we really are, we may see more clearly what has gone wrong and be able to fix it, or at least be better able to live with it.

Barefoot in the Park opens with Corie and Paul Bratter beginning their married life in their new apartment. Corie sets up her widowed mother, Ethel Banks, with the bohemian Victor Velasco who lives in their building. While Corie and Velasco are impulsive types, Paul and Ethel are more conservative, and all must learn to make compromises to become more in tune with their chosen partners, as living closely with another always involves some concessions. After a seemingly disastrous double date, Ethel ends up in a relationship with Velasco, while Paul and Corie nearly part. In response to this threat they change personas, with Paul becoming the daredevil and Corie the worrier and stern voice of reason. But when Paul suddenly panics while trying to emulate

Velasco by walking along an outside ledge, Corie runs to his aid and the two come together with a better understanding of the nature of compromise.

The prospect of a new marriage is as challenging as the empty apartment they begin to inhabit. The apartment is an uncomfortable fit at first—six flights up, no working heating system, and a large hole in the skylight—but the couple eventually transforms this into a cozy home, filled with their collective bric-a-brac, and such will be the direction of their marriage. The marriage, like the apartment, begins with a clean slate on which they need to draw in the parameters of their joint relationship. Both need to make compromises to find a common meeting point where both can be content.

From the start, in her enthusiasm for the barren, decrepit apartment, we can see that Corie is different from her husband, who is exhausted from the six-flight climb and complains about the temperature and damage to the skylight. He is more practical and conservative than she is, approaching life with a caution Corie cannot understand. Corie gets annoyed at what she sees as Paul's inability to enjoy life and holds his refusal to walk barefoot with her in Washington Square Park as a symbol of his restrictive approach to life. When he defends his way of life, she asks for a divorce, deciding they must be unsuited to each other. Although she loves him, she refuses to accept that Paul approaches life differently than she does, and nearly sacrifices her own happiness to such narrow-mindedness. Her blithe declaration that they should divorce is comical, given its insubstantial basis, though it is enough to shake Paul out of his complacency.

Although initially Paul had refused to compromise, his fear of losing Corie gives him the strength to live a little more boldly. However, he must learn to set limits, since one should not change completely for another person. Indeed, Corie soon realizes that she does not really want him to change; she asks for her old Paul back. In many ways their attitudes balance each other, and the need to change is only slight and therefore possible. Neither approach to life is shown as better than the other (and by reversing gender with the older couple, Simon avoids stereotyping the woman as the impulsive romantic), and by the end we realize that a balance between the two is better than one extreme or the other. Just as a male and female might complement each other by their differences, so these two outlooks on life—the impulsive and the conservative—each temper the other to ensure that both have a chance at fulfillment. Both change, a little, to show that it is possible for anyone to change, however difficult this may be, and to better understand each other. The two end the play once more united, singing the song Corie had earlier sung, only this time together. Paul has recognized his limitations and Corie has agreed to accept these, and meet him halfway, evidenced by her helping him off that ledge.

The capacity for change and compromise is reinforced by the play's older couple, Ethel and Velasco. They also offer a mirror to the newlyweds in that Victor is the wilder partner and Ethel the more conservative "spoilsport." Ethel, like Paul, is not enthusiastic about the apartment, initially finds the excesses of Corie and Velasco disgusting, and clearly lives as limited a life of the senses as Paul. But we are shown her unhappiness with her empty life and her recognition that she needs to make changes to improve her existence. Corie advises her to plunge into life and find someone to love, which is presumably what she has done with Velasco. Ethel gets drunk and sleeps over at Velasco's, and is delighted at how well she has slept without her backboard.

Velasco shows us that Corie's attitude to life, for all its attractive vibrancy, contains its own limitations and dangers, which Corie needs to recognize. Velasco and Corie immediately hit it off as kindred spirits, but their excesses are inconsiderate toward others; they should try to meet their partners halfway rather than expecting total submission. Both Paul and Ethel get upset stomachs from the exotic cocktail food Velasco forces on them, and are numbed by their experience at the Albanian restaurant. Velasco is forced to acknowledge his own limitations, as he breaks his toe trying to carry Ethel up the stairs and realizes he must change his diet. He vows to curb his appetites out of self-concern, but his decision wins him Ethel, who agrees to share his plain food with him that evening. In many ways, it is by witnessing the ability of this older couple to change and adapt to each other that inspires Paul and Corie to do the same.

Dinner with Friends begins with Beth telling her friends, Gabe and Karen, over dinner, about her split from Tom, her husband of twelve years. Both couples, all in their forties, have two children, and have known each other for years. As we later learn, Tom and Beth were originally set up by Karen and Gabe shortly after their own wedding. Tom now has a new girlfriend with whom he feels far happier, Beth soon begins another, more satisfactory relationship, and the only ones who appear unhappy are Gabe and Karen, as both are forced to reevaluate their relationship to the divorced couple and to each other.

From the start, Karen and Gabe are presented as a very close couple; they have the same hobbies and interests, and even work together. It becomes evident that Beth and Tom have both held them in awe and resented their model relationship. Excited about a recent trip to Italy in the play's first scene, Gabe and Karen chatter on as Beth distractedly waits for a chance to tell them she has separated from Tom. As they complete each other's sentences and thoughts, compliment one another, and kiss, Karen and Gabe do seem to have the perfect marriage. Yet this, we learn, is only a surface impression, for as we dig deeper we uncover fears and concerns below that surface that threaten even such an apparently well-matched couple. These fears are brought to the surface as they witness their close friends' breakup, for even in this first scene we see moments of disagreement between Karen and Gabe and recognize that there are cracks in their contentment. As the play progresses, these moments grow more strident and noticeable. While Beth describes to Gabe and Karen the clues she had missed regarding Tom's growing unhappiness, it becomes evident that both the listeners recognize aspects of their own relationship, which makes both ner-vous.

Beth feels bitter toward her husband, who has moved on to a new relation-ship, but her amazement at the rage and hatred he has displayed toward her only feed the realization that theirs was not a close marriage. She would rather believe that her husband was mentally unstable than correct in his criticisms of her behavior. The fact of their original unsuitability is heightened in act two, as we go back to when they first met and learn that both had fallen into mar-riage from a boredom with single status and a desire to be married like their friends Karen and Gabe. Neither seemed particularly attracted to the other, with Beth mostly ignoring Tom and Tom viewing Beth as a pretentious, self-obsessed oddball. Tom, we see by the longing way he caresses Karen's hair, largely married Beth because he could not have Karen.

Although it is traditional to sympathize with the wife whose husband walks out, Margulies does not allow us to sympathize with Beth for long. First, we watch Beth become aroused by her ex-husband's anger during a fight and they sleep together, which tells us that this breakup has been liberating for them both. She also turns on her friend Karen, who has only tried to support her through the breakup, when Karen is not immediately excited by news of her new relationship. Beth has swiftly survived her initial shock and found herself another husband, a man with whom she had had an earlier affair and whose own marriage she is now splitting up.

Margulies also insists that we see Tom's side, for Tom was never really suited for marriage, seeing it as a claustrophobic trap that restricted his whole exis-tence. As he tells Gabe, his marriage to Beth was wrong, and he had only gone through with it "because it was expected of me, not because I had any real passion for it" (73). On asking for a divorce, he tells Beth that he has been miserable "for so long he doesn't even remember what it was like to be happy" (11). His twelve years of marriage have been years of growing resentment and dwindling sexual activity; this is not a mistake he is prepared to make again and he has no plans to marry his new girlfriend, Nancy.

Tom feels drawn to Nancy because she makes him feel good about himself and is sexually available, whereas Karen had become cold and constantly criti-cal. Having gained his freedom by withdrawing from his wife and children, he refuses counseling or a trial separation, as he knows they are useless, and does not wish to waste any more time on a patently unhappy marriage. Despite disapproving of his actions, it is evident that Gabe feels some sympathy for Tom, even though he conservatively asks Tom to reconsider for the sake of the children. Tom rejects such a request as old-fashioned and unnecessary in the modern world.

But Tom and Beth have never been a match in the way that Karen and Gabe evidently are. While the latter have an occasional disagreement, they are es-sentially on the same wavelength, whereas Beth and Tom are worlds apart. Beth and Tom tried to ignore their differences for twelve years, but Tom's rebellion brought both to their senses, and each will be happier in the future because of this. Both are enthusiastic about their new loves in a way we have never heard them speak about each other. Ironically, their breakup puts pressure on the previously contented relationship between Karen and Gabe, who had thought Tom and Karen to be just like them, for they had also ignored their differences. Because their fellow couple has broken up, they fear for their own future as a married couple. Gabe forgets that he originally believed that Tom should never have married Beth. However, the relationship between Gabe and Karen is open and sharing in a way Tom and Beth's never was, and this will help them survive, even though Margulies wants us to realize that even the most perfect couples have doubts.

At one point Karen relates how nervous she had been at their wedding. Both had felt the same pressure Tom and Beth had felt to get married, though more as a need for a formal commitment to each other, something greater than simply living together. Marrying had relieved the pressure, as Gabe explains: "It's strangely comforting: there's no way out now, you've gone and done it; may as well relax and enjoy yourself" (57). But that view turns out to be too simplistic, and both learn that they cannot afford to relax too much: marriages need constant attention to hold together. Tom may be right to suggest to Gabe that his own relationship is not immune to breaking up, and while he does speak out of anger, it is evident that he hits a nerve.

On hearing about the breakup, Gabe and Karen initially sided with their own personal friend—Gabe with Tom and Karen with Beth—and are annoyed at each other for doing this. However, both come to see that they no longer want to preserve their friendships because Beth and Tom have changed, and this defuses their antagonism. They are honest enough with each other to admit that both are scared and shaken by events, and feel insecure in their marriage. This leads them to play the game they had played when dating, in which Gabe pretends to scare Karen, a game that takes on a renewed significance, but that affirms their affection for one another and preparation to face life's problems together.

Who's Afraid of Virginia Woolf takes place one evening, when Martha invites Nick and Honey back to her home for drinks after an evening function at the college where both husbands teach, and where Martha's father is president. She and husband George have been quarreling all evening and continue to squabble in front of their guests, drawing them into their warfare by treating it as a seductive game. Martha tells Honey about her son, which provokes George to a new level of viciousness since he had asked her not to mention him. Each tells a sad history, she of a controlling father who annulled her first marriage, he of a boy who accidentally killed both parents, which we are meant to suspect is him. Their candor makes their guests uneasy, but they reply in kind. Nick relates how he married Honey because of a phantom pregnancy and because of his ambitious plans to get ahead. Honey reveals that she aborted past pregnancies, but is once again pregnant. Increasingly drunk, all flirt with one another and keep switching allegiances. While Honey passes out and George reads, Martha takes Nick aside to have unsuccessful sex. In revenge, George declares that their fictitious son is dead, the guests leave, and George comforts Martha.

We change our ideas about the characters as the play proceeds, and no one ends up the way they first appeared, proving that appearances do continually deceive and we should be wary of them. George begins as an apparently emasculated wimp but grows in stature, taking on more control, becoming, for a time, quite menacing. Martha starts out a loud-mouth drunk, but becomes more sympathetic as we learn about her problematic past with a domineering father who continues to control everything she and her husband do. Nick begins as the "All-American" boy, but our admiration of him is diminished when he talks about his intention of "ploughing" a few "pertinent wives" (71) to sleep his way to the top, and as we witness his callous treatment of his wife. Even Honey, who initially appears so sweet and innocent, turns out to be aborting her pregnancies without a qualm.

Although we see some echoes of George and Martha in the way Nick and Honey are heading, the characters also complement each other in terms of personality and desire. Both Martha and Honey are emasculating to a point, but while Martha is an alcoholic who desperately wants a child, Honey rarely drinks and has been refusing to have a child. Honey is also mostly warm, open, and friendly toward others, as opposed to her husband, who is grimly polite and coldly ambitious. While Nick married Honey for her father's money and because he thought she was pregnant, despite the fact Martha accuses George of marrying her for money and position, it becomes clear theirs was a match of passion. These differences suggest that character and desire have little impact on the way these people's marriages turn out. This may be because they all have one thing in common—a desire to avoid the truth.

George and Martha's relationship seems grounded in masochism. Each invites the other to attack, so each can have an excuse for revenge. By describing what they do as "games," they create a socially acceptable ritual of abuse, an abuse in which they revel to release their bitterness and self-loathing. Both feel they have wasted their lives, and blame the other. Some of their games are deeply personal habits with rigid rules; others they invent on the spur of the moment. All of their games are spiteful, intended to hurt. Yet, George and Martha end the play very much together, as George tries to calm his wife's fears and they present an image of an intimate couple who desperately need one another.

Their underlying passion is partly what fuels their games, which to some degree give them a thrill in their otherwise dull lives. On a number of occasions Martha asks George to kiss her, usually when delighted at some witticism he has made, and she insists to Nick, who cannot sexually satisfy her, that George is the only man who ever has. Although George pretends to be unconcerned when Martha leaves with Nick, his anger is displayed when he throws his book, and then revenges himself by announcing the death of their fictitious child in order to hurt Martha back. At the center of George and Martha's relationship seems to be the fact they have no children. Whether a child would really have helped their marriage remains debatable, but both claim a need for that child, and their dual commitment to the illusion of their invented child seems a means by which they have remained close.

Nick and Honey are the next generation, and George tries to warn Nick about where he could be heading, but Nick is contemptuous of his advice. Each generation, apparently, insists on making their own mistakes. With his kinship to the college president, George could help Nick in his career, which is the only reason Nick suffers his company. Nick is a careerist in the way everyone assumed George would be, but it turned out he was too principled to pursue. That Nick and Honey turn out to each be so self-obsessed and innately indifferent toward the other bodes ill for the future, and the horrors of the relationship between George and Martha become almost preferable; at least they are connected. Also, the way in which both generations are guilty of killing their children, be it literally or figuratively, offers little hope for the future.

The song of the title, which Martha sings to George, appears to be an attempt to belittle him, offering a slur on his masculinity and calling him weak and effeminate; it's not even the "Big Bad Wolf" but only "Virginia Woolf." But the play reverses this by having George sing it to Martha at the close. Now she admits that it is she who is afraid, but we can only guess at what; perhaps of the type of independent woman Virginia Woolf was but she could never hope to be? George has also failed in his inability to get his book published, which has been his sole attempt to break out and make something of his life. In the admission of their failures, all they have left is each other, and that is what they cling to, desperately, at the close of the play.

FURTHER SUGGESTED READING

Albee, Edward. *Who's Afraid of Virginia Woolf.* New York: Atheneum, 1962.
Bigsby, Christopher, Ed. *Edward Albee: A Collection of Critical Essays.* Englewood Cliffs, NJ: Prentice-Hall, 1975.
Bloom, J. Don. *Married Cooperators.* Brookfield, VT: Ashgate, 1997.
Bottoms, Stephen J. *Albee:* Who's Afraid of Virginia Woolf. Cambridge: Cambridge University Press, 2000.
Durang, Christopher. *The Marriage of Bette and Boo.* New York: Grove, 1987.
Johnson, Robert K. *Neil Simon.* Boston: Twayne, 1983.
Klimek, David. *Beneath Mate Selection and Marriage: The Unconscious Motives in Human Pairing.* New York: Reinhold, 1979.
Margulies, Donald. *Dinner with Friends.* New York: TCG, 2000.
McGovern, Edythe M. *Neil Simon: A Critical Study.* New York: Ungar, 1979.
Roudané, Matthew. Who's Afraid of Virginia Woolf: *Necessary Fictions, Terrifying Realities.* Boston: Twayne, 1990.
Simon, Neil. *Barefoot in the Park.* New York: Random House, 1964.
Strindberg, August. *Dance of Death.* Trans. Arvid Paulson. New York: Norton, 1976.

Parents and Children

The Effect of Gamma Rays on Man-in-the-Moon Marigolds
by Paul Zindel (1964)
A Voyage Round My Father by John Mortimer (1970)
The Migrant Farmworker's Son by Silvia Gonzalez S. (1991)

The ways in which parents influence their offspring have changed over the past century, as society has imposed different pressures on the average family, but the parent-child relationship remains problematic for many. Modern dramatists tend to concentrate on the more problematic and abusive parent-child relationships, possibly because these make for better drama. Oftentimes such dramatizations are semiautobiographical, written from the perspective of the now-grown son or daughter—purgations or celebrations of how the child fared growing up with such a mother or father. Equally often, in the act of writing, the "child" comes to a better understanding of the parents' behavior. Paul Zindel's *The Effect of Gamma Rays on Man-in-the-Moon Marigolds* and John Mortimer's *A Voyage Round My Father* are both examples of such plays.

The Effect of Gamma Rays on Man-in-the-Moon Marigolds has as its central character an embittered mother, Beatrice, whose unrealistic dreams have been shattered and who vents her frustration on her two daughters. The title concept suggests that even in harsh conditions, beautiful flowers can grow, and we see this in one daughter's unrelenting enthusiasm for science. Beatrice is based on Zindel's own mother. His parents had separated when he was young, and his domineering, abusive mother raised him and his sister, moving them around as she pursued a variety of failed schemes. After college, Zindel taught high school chemistry for ten years, evidencing his interest in the sciences, and Tillie is modeled, in part, on his own juvenile experiences.

A Voyage Round My Father is a memoir of growing up in a middle-class English home in the 1930s with a dictatorial, blind father. Differing from a play like Robert Anderson's *I Never Sang For My Father* (1968), in which the son is apparently haunted by his past and tells of his uncomfortable paternal relationship as an act of psychological purgation, Mortimer merely retells the past. The father-son relationship that it reveals may not have been close, but the son clearly loved and admired his father, and the play is intended as a tribute. Closely autobiographical, with few fictionalized details, this memory play presents a chronological series of episodes unified by a narrator who appears as both boy and man. Almost a personal essay in dramatic form, the events described all appear in Mortimer's later autobiography, *Clinging to the Wreckage* (1982). Although none of the main characters are named, being referred to as father, son, and mother, this is not to universalize them, as they are uniquely the Mortimers, but more to emphasize the familial bond that exists beneath the surface, despite the lack of emotion expended on its upkeep.

The rift between father and son in *The Migrant Farmworker's Son* by Silvia Gonzalez S. is not autobiographical, but is both culturally specific and universal in its rendition. On the one hand, it is fueled by a conflict between the immigrant father's Old Mexican values and the son's fascination with American pop culture and desire to assimilate—a conflict affecting many immigrant families. In such families it is often the children, who attend local schools, who adopt most quickly the language, dress codes, and musical tastes of the newer culture, and who desire to leave the old behind to better fit in. This causes an inevitable clash with parents who wish to maintain their ethnic values and culture. In this play, the spirit figure, Oliverio, shows the possibility of compromise between the two, just as the ghostly Blue Peasants remind the parents of the sadness of their past, and protect the new generation from repeating it. On the other hand, the rift between the father and son is a product of the father's own abusive upbringing, which has led him to become a physically abusive parent himself, and his deep-seated guilt over his daughter's death, which he has suppressed. By communicating his awareness of these "weaknesses" to his son, and both admitting that they love each other, the two manage to reaffirm their relationship, and try to be more respectful of each other in future.

In *The Effect of Gamma Rays on Man-in-the-Moon Marigolds* we enter the untidy home of Beatrice and her two daughters: science-minded Tillie, and her older sister, Ruth, who is prone to seizures. Beatrice seems like a monster, full of caustic self-pity, keeping Tillie home from school to clean the house, talking sweetly to Tillie's teacher on the phone, then denigrating him in front of his pupil once she has hung up, and patently favoring Ruth—sharing her cigarettes and makeup with her—as she continuously belittles Tillie. To add to the chaos is "Nanny," the latest in a series of frail, elderly people who live with them in a kind of assisted living home-care arrangement to help the family earn some income. When Tillie becomes a finalist in the school science fair, Beatrice initially refuses to let her daughter participate, but when Tillie begins to cry, her mother relents. In a turnaround, Beatrice gets excited about Tillie's opportunity to shine, assists her, and plans to attend the presentation. However, she and Ruth argue over which of them can go, since someone must stay home to look after Nanny. Ruth turns on her mother, telling her what people have been saying about her at school, and Beatrice stays home, missing Tillie's victory, but wreaking revenge on everyone she can. This sends Ruth into convulsions, but Tillie refuses to be touched by her home life and continues to dream of a better future.

As a mother, Beatrice leaves a lot to be desired. Despite her moments of caring and concern, such as when she tends to Ruth after her fits or rallies around Tillie and her science project, she is predominantly self-absorbed and abusive to both. Accusing them to their faces of being stones tied around her neck, she blames them for her lack of attainment. Her occasional attempts to clean seem to make things messier, and the clutter of the home reflects her cluttered mind, full of crazy schemes to become successful. Yet these schemes, however improbable, such as opening a tearoom in their home, are what keep her from despair. We learn that she was once very much like Tillie, but lost her idealism along the way.

Referred to at the school as "Betty the Loon," Beatrice has never received any support for her schemes. She still feels the loss of her father, now dead, and had married young to please him. But soon she was divorced with two children to raise on her own, and it is clear that her life has been a struggle, and now she feels utterly isolated. That she drinks, and takes out her frustrations on her own children is reprehensible, but she has no one else in her life. Next to Tillie, Beatrice seems more like the child, as though her mental development were arrested in her youth. She displays a childishly paranoid response to a world she sees as having rejected her and conspired to keep her down. This response is revealed in her inability to stick to a topic or plan; her mean-spirited revenge as Ruth tricks her into staying home, when she calls the school to leave an emotional message; her telling Nanny's daughter to take her mother back immediately; and her killing the children's rabbit. Nanny fits right in, as she is simply another social outcast, sent to live there by a daughter who does not want to have to tend her herself.

Unlike her mother, Tillie apparently has one person who believes in her, Mr. Goodman, her teacher. He has given her a rabbit to try to draw her out; encourages her in her scientific interest, helping her buy seeds for her experiment; and keeps an eye on what she is doing. This may be what makes the difference, for Tillie seems not to be affected by the teasing she gets from schoolmates or the criticisms fired at her by her mother and sister. She openly chats with both about her interests, helps out at home as much as she can, and calmly accepts most of her mother's outrageous demands. Her escape is science, which gives her a measure of self-esteem, success, and respect, as well as a perspective that helps her transcend the petty squabbles at home. Her science presentation is inspirational next to Janice's silly report on her cat. And her closing speech is far more persuasive than anything we have heard from Beatrice.

It is ironic that both Tillie and Beatrice are the ones accused of being crazy, as it seems that Ruth is the most unbalanced of the three. We later learn that this stems from her horror at discovering a previous lodger, Mr. Mayo, dead; she still has nightmares about this. She enjoys telling lies at school, tends to wear too much makeup (perhaps to cover up her insecurity), is self-consciously absorbed with how her family's behavior reflects on her, and behaves meanly to both her mother and her sister, feeling that her mental fragility justifies anything she says and does. Perhaps it does, for of the three she certainly seems the most damaged, which we see most clearly in the fragile state to which she is reduced by her convulsive fits.

The English play *A Voyage Round My Father* begins with an elderly, blind father asking his son to describe to him his garden. The action then reverts to the past as the son recalls his relationship with his father and various scenes from their lives. We learn that a gardening accident blinded the father and the son was sent to boarding school. The son has various conversations with his father, a barrister, about education, sex, the law, and nature. We follow the son's development from boy to man as he finds a wife and two careers: law and writing. The son tries to copy his father's style in court, but comes off ridiculous, yet finally wins a major divorce case, despite defending the less deserving half of the couple. He is proud of this, though his wife, Elizabeth, accuses him of becoming like his father in his too casual attitude toward life. After we hear the father tell stories to his grandchildren, he and his garden both deteriorate and die, and the son is left to mourn his loss.

The father here is not a bad man, but a complex human being to whom the son has spent a lifetime trying to get close. Partly a product of a more restrictive social period when men were encouraged to hold themselves more emotionally aloof and a woman's place and duty were still widely believed to be in the home, the father is totally dependent on his doting wife, yet treats her like a servant. Selflessly she provides for his every need and desire, with no affection or thank-you in return. His relationship with his son is no less distant, as implied by the play's title, which only allows the narrator to voyage "round" his father, never "toward" him or "with" him, which would imply a closer connection.

It is ironically not the father's lack of sight that separates him from his son, but his refusal to see, as implied by his utter disengagement from all other human beings. His refusal to even acknowledge his own blindness leads him to a solitary life, as he withdraws into his home and garden, only venturing outside to try a case, which he continues to do highly successfully. The father maintains his distance partly by his superior manner, but also by his refusal to become emotionally involved in anything, or with anyone. He also refuses to take life seriously and accept reality for what it is. He prefers to avoid anything he considers unpleasant, and discounts anything that gets too serious with a joke.

The father offers his son parental advice through the years on such matters as education, sex, career, the law, and marriage, but these are scarcely opportunities for connection or learning on the son's part. When he informs his son that education is useless, sex overrated, and the law a simple game, the father may be imparting grains of truth, but they are hardly what a father usually tells his offspring. The father's commentaries are largely contemptuous and dismissive, and it is hard for the son to gauge if his father means him to follow through on any advice so disparagingly offered. Yet the son continues to strive to emulate and please his father. At times he succeeds, at other times he fails, but neither success nor failure draw any clear reaction from his father.

Based on his father's advice, the son ultimately goes into law, though his attempt to emulate his father in court is a disaster. He works in his father's chambers, but receives such slight wages for his efforts that he is forced to moonlight at the Free Legal Centre to make more money. His father never intervenes to help, other than to advise him not to give up the law in favor of writing. Although the father had initially disapproved of the son's decision to marry a divorcée with children, seeing it as economically unwise, it becomes clear that he has grown to like his daughter-in-law and pays more attention to her than to his son. We also suspect that he loves his grandchildren as he entertains them with stories, despite his inability to openly speak of love, regard, or even respect.

A clever man, the father makes an ideal barrister, in some respects: he needs no personal belief in people's guilt or innocence to argue their case convincingly. But this ability comes at a price: it sets him apart from those who strive to believe in something, and suggests an empty inner life. Yet, through the play's natural imagery, Mortimer seems to suggest that his father has an inner life, one that is just well contained. The garden blooms while his father lives, but deteriorates as his father's final illness progresses. Nature is something in which his father believes, and it is something that cannot be restricted; hence his remarks about its persistence at the close of act one. Can this be read as a mute confession of the existence of his own natural love for his son? The son dutifully spends countless hours with his father, being his eyes, describing for him the garden and the scenery they pass on country walks. Together in physical proximity, they forge a bond without need of outward admission, which, on the father's death, leaves the son feeling lonely rather than relieved, grown up, or freed.

The Migrant Farmworker's Son begins with the death in the fields of farmworker Oliverio Santos. It swiftly moves on past a brief scene in which a father violently objects to his daughter singing to her baby brother in English, and then on to that baby, Henry, as a teenager in conflict with his father over the son's apparent lack of interest in Mexican American culture. The mother acts as mediator between the two, encouraging her son to go to college and learn better English, while asking her husband to lighten up and be a better provider.

Henry discovers a surrogate father in the more open and balanced Oliverio, who has returned as his guardian angel. Henry never learns that Oliverio is a ghost, showing how one can keep the older generation alive by respecting them and listening to their advice. The father loses their savings on a restaurant scheme and the family threatens to fall apart, until the mother pressures her husband into revealing their guilty secret: an older sister they have never told Henry about drowned in the canal, and the death has haunted both parents ever since because both had had harsh words with her just before she died. The release of this guilt allows the family to start afresh, each more tolerant of the others, and the play ends on a hopeful note.

Henry finds American culture more compelling and seductive than Mexican culture, of which he has no direct experience. But his every attempt to ignore his culture riles his father, whose own English is poor and who insists on calling him *Enrique* as a way to encourage him to speak Spanish at home. Henry prefers English and is fast losing his Spanish, he listens to rap, and he demands to be treated like an American child, with respect. Yet respect is a two-way street, and it takes Oliverio to teach him this. Henry disrespectfully ignores his father, wearing headphones when his father is speaking, or provoking him by arguing back. He even sprays him with beer, admittedly an accident, but a careless one that could have been avoided. He shows no gratitude for what his parents have done for him and only complains.

Henry does not initially understand Oliverio's lesson about the important connection between family members, cemented by what they sacrifice for one another. This ghostly father figure gradually leads Henry to understand that it is possible, and indeed preferable, to balance Mexican and American cultures, combining the best of each. Thus, a beautiful Spanish poem is rendered ugly when translated into English, yet America can offer great opportunities through a college education. The most important lesson Henry learns, however, is respect for what his parents have achieved, and the backbreaking work and sacrifices they have undergone to ensure that he gets those opportunities. He finally agrees to go to college, and offers to work in the fields for extra money to show respect for what his parents do. They refuse his offer, since they only do such work so he will not have to, but they appreciate the sentiment behind his desire to join them.

The father is not a bad man, just misguided. He has a good heart and has led a tough life, full of disappointment. Coming from an old-fashioned background, he feels his manhood and family position threatened by his inability to provide for his family, exacerbated by his wife having to work. He keeps his love of cooking secret, fearing it will make him less of a man. Likewise, he bottles up his guilt and sadness over his daughter's death, viewing these as signs of weakness.

Eager to be successful for his family, his trusting nature continually sets him back, such as when he uses Henry's college money to finance a restaurant and is cheated by his partner, Julio. He buys Henry a Nintendo to please him, teaches him how to fish the old peasant way, and is rightfully upset at his son's general lack of respect. However, he uses the cultural issue as an excuse to criticize Henry and cover up his guilt over how he treated his daughter. His first response to his children is the violent shouting we hear, directed at his daughter for singing baby Henry the English children's song "The Itsy Bitzy Spider." His anger, however, is less at the use of English than his response to the hurt he feels that she is growing away from him. Although he shouts at her, he also shows her affection, and his daughter evidently loved him back, despite his violent outbursts. He also loves his son, but cannot say so, and behaves harshly toward him, since that was how his father had treated him.

The father was himself beaten as a child whenever he displeased his parents, which is how he believes children should be raised. Henry tries to resist the violence, insisting that this is not how children are treated in America, but we see the danger of Henry following in his father's footsteps as he lashes out at his girlfriend in his frustration. Under the tutelage of Oliverio, he realizes his mistake and tries to help his father by offering to be beaten, while explaining that violence is no way to win respect.

It takes the admission of guilt over losing a daughter immediately after punishing her (she had drowned while trying to wash the dress he had shouted at her for dirtying) for the father to break the cycle and realize that using violence in raising children can only destroy or alienate them. He swallows his pride and tells his son of his misery, incapacities, and sorrow over his daughter's death, which allows his son to finally understand him and become closer to him, as indicated by their embrace. The father's love for his children is what gives him the strength to change his ways and attempt to better understand his son, shown by his listening to rap and recovering some of the money Julio took for Henry to go to college. Henry responds by speaking Spanish to please his father and showing him the respect he now deserves.

FURTHER SUGGESTED READING

Adams, Bert N. *The American Family: A Sociological Interpretation.* Chicago: Markham, 1971.

Anderson, Robert. *I Never Sang For My Father.* New York: Random House, 1968.

Gardner, Herb. *Conversations with My Father.* New York: Samuel French, 1994.

Gonzalez S., Silvia. *The Migrant Farmworker's Son.* In *Multicultural Theatre II: Contemporary Hispanic, Asian and African-American Plays.* Ed. Roger Ellis. Colorado Springs: Meriwether, 1998: 47–98.

Mortimer, John. *Clinging to the Wreckage: A Part of Life.* New Haven, CT: Ticknor & Fields, 1982.

———. *A Voyage Round My Father.* London: Methuen, 1971.

Shorter, Edward. *The Making of the Modern Family.* New York: Basic Books, 1975.

Wilson, August. *Fences.* New York: Plume, 1986.

Zindel, Paul. *The Effect of Gamma Rays on Man-in-the-Moon Marigolds.* New York: Harper & Row, 1971.

Religion (Christianity)

St. Joan by George Bernard Shaw (1923)
The Amen Corner by James Baldwin (1965)
Sister Mary Ignatius Explains It All to You
by Christopher Durang (1979)

Although there are considerations of many of the world's religions in modern drama, by far the religion most commonly referred to has been Christianity. However, the way in which this one religion has been approached is multifaceted. While some playwrights choose to examine theological differences and social relationships between alternative branches of Christianity, others are more interested in the role of religion itself as it pertains to human survival and happiness. Others choose to satirize organized religion, pointing out its potential strengths and weaknesses.

In the 1920s, George Bernard Shaw developed his theory of Creative Evolution, by which he stated that the Life Force can only keep evolving by the input of special individuals whose new ideas force people to develop and move forward. He viewed figures like Jesus, Mohammad, and St. Joan as such individuals: the new concepts they each embodied necessarily threatened the existing social order, which is why people in power tried to suppress and kill them. It is from this perspective that he relates the life and death of Joan the Maid in *St. Joan*. In a preface that is half the length of the play, Shaw describes Joan as "a professed and most pious Catholic," but "one of the first Protestant martyrs" (v). He goes on to explain his interpretation of Joan as a figure who forced the people of her time to confront the concepts of Protestantism and Nationalism, which are explained in scene four of the play by Bishop Cauchon and the Earl of Warwick.

In her belief that God spoke to her directly, Joan was seen as a danger to the Catholic Church of medieval Europe. If people insisted on interpreting God's will for themselves, rather than leaving it to the Church to interpret it for them, men like Cauchon honestly believed there would be religious and social chaos. The nature of Joan's belief, although within the bounds of the Catholic Church, had a distinctly secular aspect that emphasized individual conscience and would turn into the more democratic Protestantism, which would seriously challenge the feudal social structure of the time, just as Warwick suspects.

Moving from fifteenth century Europe to 1960s America, the action of James Baldwin's *The Amen Corner* takes place within an African American Pentecostal church of the period, in which all believers are referred to as "sister" or "brother." Central to the play is its insistence that love is a necessity in the family, church, and community. The play considers the best balance between religious and secular concerns. Sister Margaret has allowed religion to take over her life, at the cost of losing touch with the everyday world and those she loves, including her husband, Luke, and son, David. Faced with the loss of both church and family, she discovers a new strength and outlook that should, hopefully, allow her to be more tolerant in future.

In Baldwin's eyes, Luke is a better preacher than Margaret because he deals in reality. She cannot face her love for Luke until he dies (reflective of her love for Jesus), and she tries to prevent David from becoming a man, and so restricts his life. Her religion also restricts sexuality, which Baldwin sees as tantamount to restricting life itself. Luke, by contrast, realizes that David has to be allowed to grow up, and so teaches him how to be a man by embracing life in all its facets, explaining that despite what Margaret has said, this does not make a person ungodly.

Written in 1979, Christopher Durang's *Sister Mary Ignatius Explains It All to You* reflects a more recent skepticism toward the efficacy of the Church, as Durang exposes what he sees as the dogma and limitation of the Catholic Church in the 1950s. Representatives of the Catholic Church have at times demonstrated and succeeded in having performances of this controversial play canceled, denouncing it as in bad taste and guilty of distorting and misrepresenting Catholicism. But Durang's criticism is not so much of Catholicism as of how it is interpreted and taught by people like Sister Mary, a nun in the Catholic Church—people of limited understanding, sensitivity, and intellect. It is probably Durang's best-known play, and many have appreciated its satirical authenticity.

Sister Mary is not the Roman Catholic Church in all its complexity, but she represents a facet of it, which asks us to question the system that gives such people authority over others, especially impressionable children. The Sister's intolerance of human fallibility and her simple ignorance are conveyed through verbal irony, as her own words unwittingly expose her unsuitability as a religious teacher; she herself is never aware of this, but Durang ensures that the audience fully realizes how dangerous such people can be.

Saint Joan begins in France in 1429, as Joan the Maid requests a horse, armor, and soldiers from her local lord to take her to Charles the Dauphin. On her arrival at the Dauphin's court she sees past their attempt to fool her and test her abilities, and reports that she has been sent by God to drive the English out of France and crown the Dauphin king. He reluctantly gives her command of his army, and after she offers to pray for a wind, whose lack has kept the French fleet from attacking, her request is instantly answered. Meanwhile, both English and French, worried about the impact of Joan's opinions on the Church and social structure, conspire to compel Joan to abandon what they perceive as her heretical beliefs. Despite her victories, the French authorities grow tired of her control and hope she will return to her father's farm, but she is soon captured and ransomed to the English, who turn her over to the French Church for trial. In 1431 she is tried for heresy in Rouen, and because of her insistence that she is her own judge of what God has commanded, she is found guilty. Initially recanting to avoid death, she changes her mind and allows herself to be executed rather than face life imprisonment. Twenty-five years later, the Dauphin learns that Joan's verdict has been overturned. He is visited by specters who discuss Joan's impact, including Joan and a twentieth-century man who announces her 1920 canonization. Significantly, they all agree that it was best for everyone that she died.

The religious background of the play highlights what Shaw saw as the central differences between Catholicism and Protestantism, although Joan herself could not see this distinction, believing herself to be a devout Catholic and never fully understanding the charges against her. The Catholic side is represented by both secular and Church officials, while the Protestant side, unwittingly, is represented by a teenage French country girl, Joan. Shaw describes "the quintessence of Protestantism" as "the supremacy of private judgment for the individual" (xlviii), so it is fitting that it should be represented by the lowliest of people. Joan says she will obey the Church, but only within limits, since she must place God foremost, and the Catholic Church cannot accept this. It cannot accept Joan's claims without waiving its own authority or raising her to a level with the trinity, a height unthinkable for the Church to confer upon a living teenage girl.

Shaw upholds the fairness of the Church trial against Joan, insisting that the tribunal's decision was true to the law of the time, even though the Protestant Church has since used her death as evidence against the Roman Catholic Church. Even Joan declares that her trial was honest, albeit misguided, and the Church's mercy is depicted in its refusal to torture her, as would have been customary. The Church was already under threat from the early expressions of Protestant beliefs, and so had to quash Joan to silence this dissent and maintain its control. This is what Cauchon refers to as the "Will to Power in the world" (74), which not only threatens the Church itself but also endangers the social system. Warwick voices this concern when he explains how Joan's attempts to make the King "God's Bailiff" will reduce the authority of the nobles in the minds of the people, thus making her death a "political necessity" (101).

Shaw presents a world where God's presence is felt through Joan. Bluebeard
tells how Joan predicted the death of Foul Mouthed Frank, and she later predicts
her own premature death. She need only talk of praying for a change in wind
direction and it instantly occurs. But this is a world in which secular concerns
have already begun to outweigh religious concerns. When Joan insists that God
and the saints wish her to continue the fight, the others are reluctant to follow
her, and the Archbishop warns her that to believe in such a religious imperative
will lead to her destruction, which it does—not for religious as much as for
political reasons. She dies because she really is a heretic in terms of the prevailing system of thought, just as anyone who resists orthodoxy becomes a
figure for persecution, regardless of his or her own purity of spirit.

Belief in her own rightness leads Joan to talk down to others, be they kings
or Church officials. What she has done is miraculous, but she has been near
insufferable in the manner in which she did it. She displays the lack of social
grace of most zealots: contempt for anyone else's opinion, judgment, or authority. Proud and dismissively haughty, Joan has a distinctly negative side,
which Shaw allows us to see even as he makes her his heroic protagonist. It is
her sincerity, honesty, and simple faith that save her from being odious. Cauchon is enraged by the way she sets her country above the Church and acts as
if she is higher than the Pope. "She acts as if she herself were The Church"
(69), he exclaims, and he wants her to submit to the Church or be seen as an
agent of the Devil. But she sets God above the Church rather than herself, as
she truly sees herself as "a servant of God" (52). We excuse her manner in
such a service, although officials of the time could not.

In *The Amen Corner* religion dominates every aspect of Pastor Margaret
Alexander's life, leaving little room for secular concerns. However, such a life
makes her very narrow in her outlook, which her congregation find increasingly annoying. Discovering that she left her husband and that her son is
leading what even she would define as a sinful life, her congregation eagerly
becomes critical of Sister Margaret's life and family, turning against her and
trying to replace her with the virginal Sister Moore. The ensuing struggle,
against both her congregants and what she sees as her wayward son, David,
leads Margaret to initially fear that she has lost her calling. However, after she
speaks openly to her ex-husband on his deathbed, she has an epiphany that
renews her faith and commitment to God and the world around her.

Margaret not only runs the church, but lives in it, and the way Baldwin
describes the staging, the church dominates the set, taking precedence over the
home. Such is Margaret's life, as she declares: "In this home, Sister Moore, the
Lord comes first" (55), though at the expense of the whole family. Having
turned to God after the death of a child, Margaret left her loving husband,
Luke, deciding that God was punishing her for enjoying her life with Luke and
showing disapproval of Luke's way of life, with its sinful jazz music and drinking. In place of the freedom associated with jazz, Margaret adopts the strictures

of a very restrictive religious outlook. She has tried to raise her son as a devout Pentecostal Christian, having him play the piano at her services, hoping that he, too, will become a pastor, but instead, he is drawn to his father's less restrictive music and way of life.

David is a self-possessed eighteen-year-old who wants his independence and is sick of being told what to do by his mother. He has inherited his father's love of jazz and love of life, which, according to his mother's beliefs, makes him a sinner. It is no surprise that he feels he has lost his faith. Fearful of offending his mother by pursuing a music career that he knows she finds offensive, he has been lying to cover up his playing. This only makes him feel worse. Luke allows him to realize that it is not the music that is sinful; neither is love, be it of music or a person, no matter what his mother says. Luke stands up for David against his mother, showing him that such a thing is possible, and freeing him to live his own life. Luke may have lost his faith, but he explains that any loss of faith stems more from his loss of Margaret than from his pursuit of music.

At the opening Margaret had preached a message for her congregation to "set thine house in order" (23), and, ironically, it is a message that comes back to haunt her as she discovers her own house in disarray. Her strictness is absolute and is largely responsible for what occurs. She refuses to condone sex other than for procreation, and she rejects alcohol and anything connected to the alcohol trade (so she will not allow Brother Boxer to take the job he needs because it would mean driving a liquor truck). Essentially, anything that smacks of fun, such as reading the comics, she demonizes, suggesting that such activities distract a person from God and encourage the Devil. It is little wonder her congregants rebel and begin to object to her high-minded attitudes, resentfully feeling that she is lording her superiority over them.

Looking to overthrow Margaret, the members of the congregation accuse her of taking church funds because she has a new frigidaire, until her older sister, Odessa, explains that she paid for the frigidaire, and the money taken in on collections barely covers the church's upkeep. They consider her cold treatment of her erring but sickly husband un-Christian, and yet they condemn her for her association with men who play jazz and drink. Ironically, her own intolerant teaching is at the root of most of their complaints: they are scandalized by her inviting the Philadelphians to come to their church with drums and a trumpet. Margaret insists that the evil is not in the instrument but in what people do with it and what it leads them to. She means this as a dig against jazz, but she fails to see how this contradicts her refusal to allow Boxer to drive the liquor truck.

Margaret will not allow herself to love people—only God—and it will take the loss of both people she most loves, Luke and David, to get her to see the error of her ways. Luke had tried to get through, pointing out that they had done nothing wrong to lose their child. Margaret puts all her hopes into the life hereafter and suggests that she and Luke will "be together in glory," but

Luke insists, "I want to be together with you now" (92). He is more interested in life on earth and insists that she has been using religion to hide from feelings she is scared might hurt her. Near the start, Margaret bluntly tells Mrs. Jackson, whose child is sick and whose husband has lost his faith, to leave her husband, just as she did. Later on, after she begins to see her mistake, Margaret offers better advice after Mrs. Jackson's child has died and the woman declares that she too has lost her faith. Margaret tells her to go home to her husband and have another child, for she has learned how important family is, now that Luke is dead and David gone into the outside world.

Margaret had faced opposition when coming to her church, partly because of her gender; her fervor back then had won many over to a female preacher and displaced those still opposed to her. Now, she momentarily loses that fervor, as she realizes that it has been somewhat limited and misdirected, indicated by her inability to complete her prayers and her loss of vision. But after having confessed her love to Luke before he dies, she is revitalized, realizing that it is possible, and indeed preferable, to love both God and people. She castigates her congregation for their judgment of her conduct, insisting on their respect for what she has sacrificed for the Lord. Then she declares in a rush of insight, "To love the Lord is to love all His children—all of them, everyone!—and suffer with them and rejoice with them and never count the cost!" (126) as she decides to start life again, just as she had advised Mrs. Jackson.

Sister Mary Ignatius Explains It All to You begins with Sister Mary, an old-fashioned nun and parochial schoolteacher, lecturing on Roman Catholic principles concerning proper conduct in life and the promised rewards and punishments that come after death. With numerous digressions, which inform us about her own abusive upbringing, she continues to patchily explain doctrinal matters and answer questions supposedly submitted by her audience. Her young pupil, Thomas, satisfies her abrupt requests for refreshment. Four former pupils appear, Diane, Philomena, Aloysius, and Gary, and act out a Nativity pageant she has her classes perform every year, then reveal to her the horrors of their lives since school, lives for which her teachings had ill prepared them. The leader of the four, Diane, tries to force Sister Mary to admit to having deceived them, and pulls a gun. The Sister distracts her, then draws her own gun to shoot and kill Diane and Gary, warns Philomena to reform, and holds Aloysius at gunpoint until she decides to take a nap and leave Thomas in control, obediently holding the gun on the terrified Aloysius.

Sister Mary's lecture covers everything from heaven, hell, purgatory, and limbo, to the meaning of the Immaculate Conception and the question of Papal infallibility, although her opinions tend to be outmoded, lacking in insight, and rigidly orthodox. Despite setting herself up as a religious authority, her ignorance of even the Bible borders on the sacrilegious: she forgets or leaves out important details that alter the meaning and, on the question of Jesus's attitude toward adultery, is patently wrong, suggesting that Christ only protected the adulteress for "political" reasons and privately joined in the stoning of many such women. It is left to the audience to recognize her wrongness and excesses as she is egotistically blind to both.

Her frequent digressions suggest that Sister Mary has little of the usual humility associated with nuns: they indicate an egocentric preoccupation with herself. It becomes clear that despite her insistence on uncritical obedience and acceptance, she hypocritically resents the Pope's attempts to update the Church. Full of her own self-importance, she insists that students bow to her authority, even as we see more and more how psychologically unsuited she is to tell anyone how to live. One of the reasons she likes the Nativity play her student wrote is that it makes reference to her and supports her restrictive morality. Her students are only allowed to know what she tells them, to satisfy her authoritarian nature. Sadly, what she tells them is often self-indulgent, foolishly pious, and hopelessly inadequate to prepare them for the outside world. Her upbringing was admittedly harsh and oppressive, with an abusive, alcoholic father, twenty-six siblings, and a mentally unstable mother, which may account for some of her eccentricities but cannot condone her current inability to act compassionately or even humanely.

Her responses to the question cards from her audience vary from silence to terse monosyllables that brook no argument, to effusive detail regarding her strict and morally simplistic ethical outlook or her own family upbringing. Refusing to answer anything that questions God's goodness in the face of all the suffering in the world or asks the precise nature of the sins committed at Sodom, we soon become aware of her tremendous limitations. These parochial limitations are further highlighted in the ways she responds to her former pupils who come to challenge her teachings. All are evidently troubled, and struggling with consciences she has instilled, which only allow them to see things as sinful or pure—nothing in between. Thus they are filled with self-loathing for the people they have become, seeing only divine retribution for their sins rather than any possibility of forgiveness.

Between them, the former pupils represent most of the hot-button issues the Catholic Church has faced in modern times. Diane watched her mother agonizingly die of cancer and began to question the goodness of a God who could allow this. She also had two abortions after being raped twice—once by her therapist. Philomena is an unwed mother, after being taken advantage of by a married man. Aloysius is an alcoholic and abusive husband with suicidal tendencies. Gary is a homosexual, having been first seduced while studying for the priesthood. Instead of trying to understand why they have all suffered so, offer sympathy, or consolation, the Sister just lectures them further on proper Catholic values and practices. Diane accuses Sister Mary of deception, asking why she taught them that the world was ordered and good, when her every experience has shown the opposite to be true. But Sister Mary's simplistic teachings cannot explain why a benevolent God would allow bad things to happen to good people, and she is incapable of telling her.

Diane's desperation is proven by the gun she brandishes, but it is ironically the nun who shoots and kills. Sister Mary kills Diane rather than admit that she has taught anything wrong, and she shoots Gary because he had been to confession that morning, sending him to heaven before he can sin again. Intolerance and violence are what she offers instead of the compassion and forgiveness that true Christianity espouses. The damage she is doing to children by continuing her misguided teaching is highlighted by the way she uses Thomas at the close to hold her gun on Aloysius.

FURTHER SUGGESTED READING

Baldwin, James. *The Amen Corner.* London: Corgi, 1970.

Berst, Charles A. *Shaw and Religion.* University Park: Pennsylvania State University Press, 1981.

Durang, Christopher. *Sister Mary Ignatius Explains It All to You.* Garden City, N.Y.: Doubleday, 1981.

Eliot, T. S. *Murder in the Cathedral.* New York: Harcourt Brace, 1963.

Hill, Holly. *Playing Joan: Actresses on the Challenge of Shaw's* St. Joan. New York: TCG, 1987.

Miller, D. Quentin, Ed. *Re-Viewing James Baldwin.* Philadelphia: Temple University Press, 2000.

Osbourne, John. *Luther.* New York: NAL, 1961.

Pratt, Louis H. *James Baldwin.* Boston: Twayne, 1978.

Shaw, George Bernard. *St. Joan.* New York: Brentano's, 1924.

Thompson, Kenneth. *Beliefs and Ideology.* New York: Tavistock, 1986.

Weintraub, Stanley, Ed. Saint Joan: *Fifty Years After.* Baton Rouge: Louisiana State University Press, 1973.

Wellwarth, George. *Modern Drama and Death of God.* Madison: University of Wisconsin Press, 1986.

A Sense of Community

Our Town by Thornton Wilder (1938)
Lydie Breeze by John Guare (1982)
Two Trains Running by August Wilson (1991)

People's sense of community has changed greatly in the twentieth century. Yet there remains nostalgia for the idea of that smaller, supportive, physical community in which many people used to live and work. Reflective of this nostalgia, many dramatic explorations of community take the form of backward glances at how society used to be; some are attempts to understand and reclaim the strength of those social groups, and others are a warning about how limiting and limited such communities can be.

Inspired by the poem "Lucinda Matlock" in Edgar Lee Masters's *Spoon River Anthology,* Thornton Wilder's *Our Town* takes place at the beginning of the twentieth century. The play depicts the easy community of small-town America, as represented by Grover's Corners, New Hampshire—the kind of town where everyone knows everyone else, and the daily rituals of milk and paper deliveries evoke a simple but rich existence. Yet the simplicity and popularity of the play make us forget its fundamentally radical style and theme at the time it was produced.

In a period when realism dominated the theater, like Bertolt Brecht's plays in Germany and Luigi Pirandello's in Italy, Wilder sought a different means of presentation, stripping away props and scenery to encourage audiences to pay closer attention to the cast and what is being said on stage. But where Brecht and Pirandello sought to alienate their audiences, Wilder seeks to engage them both emotionally and intellectually. With its bare stage, *Our Town* transcends a particular time and place, presenting a universal vision of what Wilder saw as the meaning of life, lived from day to day, wonderful in the very details of its ordinariness. Thematically, at a time when America faced despair at the peak of the Depression, Wilder offers a gentle message regarding the essential benevolence of the universe, despite the pain and suffering of life.

John Guare's *Lydie Breeze* is the first in a tetralogy set in nineteenth-century America that centers on the fate of an attempted "ideal" community on the remote island of Nantucket, inspired by the verse of Walt Whitman and the desire to create a totally egalitarian society based on love rather than hatred or selfishness. The failure of this community to thrive is attributed to the misplaced greeds and passions of the individuals involved. No outside force doomed the ironically named Aipotu (Utopia spelled backwards); rather, the society's downfall came as a result of the corruption of the people who began the community, manifest in their individual ambition, sexual jealousy, and human weakness. The play seems to suggest that, given the unavoidably flawed nature of humanity, any community built on idealistic principles is bound to fail, just as the noble dream of a true democracy in America has been tarnished by the forces of unfettered capitalism and materialism.

By contrast, August Wilson's *Two Trains Running* considers the difficulties of forming and maintaining a sense of community in a beleaguered African American section of Pittsburgh in the 1960s. The play can be read as a compelling metaphor for many of the problems afflicting the whole of contemporary society. The characters we meet are by and large decent people, whose concerns and struggles are typical of those of us who struggle to survive in a world that often seems hostile to our needs and desires. The play illustrates, in microcosm, the evolution of a humanistic democracy, as the disparate personalities who come to Memphis's restaurant gradually band together to form a unified community. More brutally honest than the idealized community of *Our Town*, Wilson shows greater weaknesses and strengths within his troubled social group, yet his depiction is not as pessimistic as the rotten society witnessed in *Lydie Breeze*. The characters in *Two Trains Running* may often behave as self-serving individuals, but by the play's close they have also found the capacity to act, when necessary, as a mutually supportive social group.

Our Town offers a slice of small-town America over a period of twelve years, centered on the neighborly interactions of the Gibbs and the Webb families in Grover's Corners, amid milk and paper deliveries, town gossip and news. The Stage Manager leads us through these people's daily lives, sets each scene in detail to bring it alive in our imagination, and instructs various town members to contribute additional information about the town's historical and social background. The courtship, marriage, and loss of the young couple, George Gibbs and Emily Webb, lie at the play's center, from their early school days to Emily's ghostly return after dying in childbirth twelve years later. As a ghost, Emily restlessly longs to rejoin the living, but after reliving her twelfth birthday comes to see that the past is forever changed by the knowledge of what is to come and one cannot happily go back, but she also gains a new appreciation of the wonder of life itself.

With no scenery or props, Grover's Corners is vividly brought to life before us, indicating that the true spirit of any community lies in the individuals of which it is composed. Yet Wilder does not make his individuals complex characterizations but rather types, allowing Grover's Corners to stand for any small American township. As a community, everyone knows everyone's name and business, and together they celebrate the ups and downs of everyday life: the births, the marriages, the deaths. They chat as they eat string beans and attend choir practice.

These people's dreams are modest, unalloyed by materialism or capitalistic designs. Ninety percent of those born in town end up settling there, even when they go to college. Dr. Gibbs is content with a vacation to visit Civil War battlegrounds every other year; their son, George, wishes to be a farmer. Mrs. Gibbs longs to go to Europe, but satisfies herself making French toast and leaving the money set aside for the trip to her son. Mr. Webb runs the town's twice-daily newspaper; his wife spends her time canning vegetables for the winter, and his daughter, Emily, is also content to become a housewife.

Yet, despite the contented surface, there are aspects of Grover's Corners that jar the audience. Simon Stimson, the church organist and choir director, is unhappy with small-town life. He drinks, and restlessly prowls the streets at night until he commits suicide. To make him fully representative of the type of person who is never happy, we do not learn the specifics of his troubles, but he remains bitter even in death. We also might have seen Emily as a woman with a future; academically gifted, she assists George with his homework. Yet he is the one elected class president and she his secretary/treasurer. This foreshadows her marriage to him straight out of high school to become his helpmate and wife, rather than pursuing any career of her own. But this is 1904 and Wilder is not concerned with gender issues, but with what he sees as a larger scheme.

Emily is initially restless as a ghost, wanting to return to the world of the living, but the dead mostly want to forget life as soon as possible because it is too painful to remember, knowing it is gone. It matters not that their lives may be viewed as trivial, because to them, as they lived them, they were not. As Emily relives her twelfth birthday, she becomes horrified noticing the details she missed at the time and is overcome with a sense of loss. As the Stage Manager suggests, it is only saints and poets who come close to appreciating life's wonder while still living. But at the play's end, while night falls, life goes on.

Wilder recognizes the brevity of human life on a cosmic scale and the commonplace fact of sadness and suffering in those lives—so much so that they are in some sense a part of those lives and what gives them shape. From the start we know from the Stage Manager that many of these people will die. Emily and George have nine brief years of marriage before he is left to mourn her loss with his four-year-old son, but the fact is, they had nine years of happy marriage. Indeed, most of the town's inhabitants have been happy with their lives. What Wilder asks is that, along with Emily, we rediscover the simple joy of living—beyond pain, frustration, and failure—and relish the little details, because that is what life is about; their ordinariness is what makes them so special. It is a timely message for the Depression age, but its relevance has not diminished over the years.

Lydie Breeze depicts the sad repercussions of an attempt by a small group of idealists to form a utopian community on Nantucket Island. Founded by Lydie Breeze and three Civil War veterans—her husband, Joshua Hickman; Dan Grady; and Amos Mason—the community has disintegrated by the play's start; all that remain are Joshua Hickman and his daughter, Lydie. Lydie Breeze and Dan Grady are dead, and Amos Mason has abandoned the community in preference for a political life on the mainland. With the aid of their serving girl, Beaty, young Lydie Hickman keeps alive the memory of her dead mother; her sister Gussie has left with Amos to pursue a better life. On Gussie's return with Amos to visit her father, the community's sad history is retold. When Jeremiah Grady appears to avenge the death of his father, killed by Joshua, it seems as if many of the original community's mistakes are to be repeated. Truths surface, more people die, but the play ends with the promise of new bonds between family members and a reaffirmed hope for the future, as if recent actions had cleansed the community of past mistakes.

The play is an exploration of both the idealism that formed the community and the factors that caused it to break apart. In part, Guare sees the seeds of the group's destruction in the very idealism that sparked its formation: idealism is always unobtainable given the rotten nature of people. The play uses syphilis as a central metaphor for the corruption that eats from within all attempts to build an ideal community. The syphilis is transmitted from Ned Grady, who has an adulterous relationship with Lydie Breeze, then from Lydie Breeze to Dan's son, Jeremiah, with whom she perversely takes up after she loses Dan, and from Jeremiah to Beaty, whom he secretly seduces and abandons. The wrongful nature of these relationships is emphasized by the disease that has become part of each union. As Beaty and Jeremiah are discovered drowned together, just as Lydie Breeze had drowned herself, washed by the cleansing sea, there is the possibility that the spread of the disease (and thereby the corruption) has finally been halted.

The title character, Lydie Breeze, who had envisioned their society and named it Aipotu, destroyed her dream and herself through her misguided passion for Dan, her seduction of Jeremiah, and her own suicide, a final act of both despair and expiation for her sins. The loss of her lover and her dream of an ideal community, and the understanding that she was complicit in both, drove her to suicide. But it seems her actions live on and continue to poison the community—as Beaty teaches young Lydie to hate men and her own sexuality, and young Lydie exhibits a strained and suspicious relationship with her embittered father. Joshua had begun by believing in the possibility of Aipotu, but having both his optimism and his innocence destroyed by his own jealousy and spite, he became the self-pitying, bitter drunk we see. The intense hatred and murder to which he was led are clearly antagonistic to the life principles on which the community had been formed. Jeremiah carries on this negative tradition in his desire for revenge, and it is not insignificant that he has made his fortune playing the monster in a stage version of *Frankenstein*. Until the memory of Lydie Breeze can be viewed with love rather than hatred, no one on the island can move on. Jeremiah's intrusion, even when he decides to ask for forgiveness, only worsens matters, as Joshua realizes the apologetic suicide note his wife had left was not intended for him but for Jeremiah. But the close of the play—with Joshua reconciled with his daughters and reading with young Lydie the inspiring words of Walt Whitman that had first inspired her mother—suggests that a change has occurred. Lydie is also given new hope by the sympathetic and kindly Jude; Gussie, too, finds hope with Lucian Rock, a quintessential American inventor whose future holds more potential than the ruined Amos Mason.

But past events stay with us, and inevitably color the optimism that emerges at the close. Even though Lydie and Gussie look to more hopeful futures, there is no reason to suspect that they will be any more successful than the previous generation; they are just as prone to ambition, anger, and deceit as their parents had been. Lydie refers to herself as blind and wears dark glasses, even though it is clear that she exaggerates her injury, presumably for sympathy. Lucian Rock is tricked into taking Gussie with him, as she bandages her eye and pretends to be her sister Lydie, with whom Lucian has declared himself, from a brief past meeting, to be in love.

Part of the problem lies either in placing one's trust in the wrong people, or in looking with only partial vision, as Lydie pretends to do. Joshua felt betrayed by his wife and friend and has taken it out on Jeremiah, and then Dan himself. Beaty has been disillusioned into thinking it was Amos who had seduced her, when all along it was Jeremiah, yet Amos is ruined by her groundless accusation. Gussie placed her faith in the power and materialism she saw possible through Amos Mason, but she fails to see that his backer, William Randolph Hearst, only uses Amos as a front man to extend his own power and drops him at the first hint of scandal, and her too.

The whole tale has been told with an uneasy mingling of tragedy and comedy, symbolism and realism, and the final effect can be read as either optimistic or pessimistic. For Guare, nothing is ever certain. While he praises the human capacity for love and hope, he cannot dismiss the human capacity for deception, hatred, and despair. Our better nature might strive to create the perfect community, but our worse leanings are always present to ensure it will not survive.

The 1960s community of *Two Trains Running* is centered in a Pittsburgh restaurant owned by Memphis. The restaurant is about to be demolished to make room for a city council redevelopment project, and Memphis is unsure that he will receive a fair price for his property. His waitress, Risa, serves customers who include Holloway, a kindly busybody; West, the local funeral director; Wolf, a numbers runner; and Hambone, who goes to Lutz's meat market every day to demand (and fail to receive) his payment for having painted the owner's fence. Into this group comes Sterling, newly released from jail, looking to make something of himself. We witness the interactions of the group as they learn to recognize their own individual flaws and, more importantly, how to become a stronger community.

Despite hardship, we see a potential community from the start. Although Sterling is a newcomer, Wolf, Memphis, and Holloway all offer him helpful advice, and he is served food whether or not he can pay. They "look after" Hambone and the local savant, Aunt Ester, in the same way. We also see everyone willingly donate to community causes, such as bailing Bubba Boy out of jail. But living here is a struggle, and their community is under as constant a threat of disintegration as the buildings in which they live, buildings the council wants to tear down. Even Memphis's restaurant business has gone steadily downhill in recent years. The area's depression is a natural reflection of the lack of available work, but it is up to the area's residents to turn things around, for they cannot count on outside assistance.

Holloway is valuable as the community storyteller. His knowledge fills in the background details that explain the other characters. He observes the community, reporting back what he sees to improve people's understanding of each other, and helps build a stronger community. His explanation of Risa, as having scarred herself so that men will be forced to look at her personality and not take her for granted, is very insightful. He also has a clear vision of what Hambone's behavior signifies. He knows that Hambone fights for respect and esteem and cares little about the physical ham he seems to be clamoring for. It is Holloway who notices that Hambone is missing and takes the trouble to find out why.

What many of the other residents must learn is to accept more responsibility for their community. Memphis refuses to get involved, caught up in the loss of his property down South and unable to settle down. He is so wrapped up in himself that his wife leaves him, tired of being shut out and ignored. Refusing to display a flyer for the Malcolm X rally is an indication of his reluctance to join community ranks. By teaching him to accept his responsibilities, Aunt Ester changes his life. Demanding a high price for his restaurant, he receives it, which gives him the confidence to open up to his wife and win her back. He also decides to reclaim that Southern property. After Hambone's death, he contributes to buy flowers for the funeral, making it a communal gesture by having the card read that the flowers are from everyone who has striven, like Hambone, to be responsible. He then announces plans to open a bigger restaurant in the area, employing a dozen locals—an even more positive gesture of community responsibility.

West and Wolf are also isolated figures. West only connected with his wife, and since her death has shut himself off completely. Making his living from deaths in the African American community, he hires white men to guard the funeral home and repair his property. Thus, he profits from the community without giving anything back. However, he shows signs of a developing community spirit in his offer to bury Aunt Ester for free and in laying out Hambone without cost. Wolf's name indicates his tendency to be a loner. Despite notoriety and popularity as the community's numbers runner, he too is unable to connect with others. Wolf is alone, and no one will come to his funeral, especially not the women he boasts will show up.

Sterling has a background similar to Wolf's—broken family, few breaks, criminal activity—but displays a different personality, suggesting that character can determine fate. Though close to death and despair from an early age, Sterling chooses life and hope. Refusing to dwell on misfortune, he speaks of himself as a lucky man, as if to counter his bad experiences. He defines himself in terms of his community, which is something Wolf lacks the courage to do. Sterling initially seems self-involved, but soon joins the community in Memphis's restaurant, and becomes a leading force within that community.

What makes Sterling a good leader are his clear vision and willingness to share this with others. He instantly recognizes the unfairness of Memphis's constant commands and complaints to Risa, and speaks out against his treatment of the waitress. His first reaction to Hambone is to show concern that he does not have his ham, rather than dismiss him as an idiot. He befriends Hambone and tries to help him. He is a younger, more virile version of Holloway; neither can stay silent when they see injustice and both care for others. Sterling can also help others to dream, leading them forward with his infectious enthusiasm. Having been set apart in jail for five years, Sterling wants to be involved in the community, so he encourages everyone to attend the Malcolm X rally and borrows money to contribute to Bubba Boy's bail fund (including Hambone in his donation). Sterling recognizes the underlying importance of connection and seeks to create and maintain such connections.

Like Sterling, Risa has a good heart. She cares for others and seems able to understand them. She insists that Hambone eat, whether or not he can pay, and gives him a warm coat. She treats him as an equal, asking questions about his health and activities as if he were capable of answering more than, "I want my ham." It is she who insists that he be respectfully buried. Yet, even she is fearful of proximity to others and this restricts her. However, Sterling insists: "You in the world" (100), and advises her to open herself up. When she and Sterling embrace, both are strengthened by their connection.

Despite his small role, Hambone is central to this community, impacting everyone. His quest represents a desire for justice, and the others need to recognize this and offer support, as a community must work together if they wish to progress. Sterling leads them by taking a ham from Lutz to place in Hambone's casket. As the play closes, we are given a sense that this community is on the move, as Wolf reports the streets are filled with people. The previous evening there had been three thousand people at the rally. These people, as they come together at the play's close, display the spirit to keep going, struggling on despite the odds against them to claim lives of their own and a place for everyone in a truly democratic community.

FURTHER SUGGESTED READING

Bogumil, Mary L. *Understanding August Wilson*. Columbia: University of South Carolina Press, 1999.

Burbank, Rex. *Thornton Wilder*. Boston: Twayne, 1978.

Freedman, Morris. *American Drama in Social Context*. Carbondale: Southern Illinois University Press, 1971.

Haberman, Donald. Our Town: *An American Play*. Boston: Twayne, 1989.

Herron, Ima Honaker. *The Small Town in American Drama*. Dallas: Southern Methodist University Press, 1969.

Miles, Malcolm, Iain Borden, and Tim Hall, Eds. *The City Cultures Reader*. New York: Routledge, 2000.

Miller, Arthur. The American Clock *and* The Archbishop's Ceiling. New York: Grove, 1989.

Plunka, Gene A. *The Black Comedy of John Guare*. Newark: University of Delaware Press, 2002.

Shannon, Sandra. *The Dramatic Vision of August Wilson*. Washington, DC: Howard University Press, 1995.

Simon, Linda. *Thornton Wilder, His World*. Garden City, NJ: Doubleday, 1979.

Smith, Anna Deveare. *Fires in the Mirror*. New York: Doubleday, 1993.

Wilder, Thornton. *Our Town*. New York: Harper & Row, 1957.

Wilson, August. *Two Trains Running*. New York: Plume, 1993.

Sibling Relationships

The Three Sisters by Anton Chekhov (1901)
Dancing at Lughnasa by Brian Friel (1990)
True West by Sam Shepard (1980)

The special connection between brothers and sisters, whether supportive or antagonistic, has often been explored in modern drama, from the realism of Anton Chekhov to the mythic symbolism of Sam Shepard. Changing social conditions in the twentieth century impacted family structures, and sibling relationships were undoubtedly affected to some degree. Social and political upheaval, periods of intense impoverishment, and the alienation caused by ever-fragmenting personal relationships in an increasingly materialistic and profane society all affect the dynamics of the sibling bond and are reflected in the plays chosen for this chapter.

As an early proponent of the movement toward realism in drama, Anton Chekhov had a desire to write plays about "real life" as it is lived by ordinary people, so relationships between family members must have seemed like promising material to him. In his attempts to create realistic plays that still entertain, Chekhov has melodramatic events (like deaths) happen offstage and only shows their impact on the characters involved, thus putting the emphasis on feeling over action. His characters converse, often inconsequentially and even illogically, as real people do, and are rarely the stock representations seen in "well-made plays." His conclusions avoid triteness, usually seeming as messy as outcomes in real life.

Anton Chekhov's *The Three Sisters* looks at the relationship between three sisters and a brother from Russian aristocracy at the turn of the twentieth century. After his father went bankrupt and abandoned his family, Chekhov assumed responsibility for his siblings and was a father figure to them for the rest of his short life (he died at age forty-four). This is reflected in his plays by offspring who have usually lost one or both parents, and one of the siblings takes on a parental role. In *The Three Sisters*, it is Olga, unmarried at twenty-eight, who keeps the home together until she is displaced by their brother's new wife, Natasha. Even then, she holds the three sisters together in their idealistic dreams of a better future to counter the apparent misery of their actual lives, though the brother is left to deal alone with the horrors of living with his new wife.

Brian Friel's *Dancing at Lughnasa* looks at the relationships within a lower-class family—the five Mundy sisters and their older brother in rural 1930s Ireland—through the memory of a young relative. The play depicts the benefits of living among a large group of siblings, and the severe threat under which such family communities live. The unmarried sisters provide a supportive network of friendship and caregiving that shelters Chris, a single mother; Rose, who is simpleminded; and, on his return, Father Jack, the brother who has apparently lost his mind while performing missionary work in Uganda. Despite occasional squabbles, the sisters stick together until worsening economic and social conditions scatter them apart and destroy their spirit. None fare so well once the family is broken apart. Their lengthy service to each other, and the family's eventual breakdown and failure, are echoed in the missionary career of Jack. When he dies, so too does the family itself.

True West, by Sam Shepard, is more contemporary in its presentation of two brothers encountering each other for the first time in five years. Totally contrasting types, Austin and Lee are instantly at odds, yet each strives to understand the other and, for a time, even become the other. The exercise is futile, since they are who they are, and they end up in a tableau of eternal conflict. Shepard wants us to know that the sibling bond is not always warm and supportive, and can be as marked by jealousy and mistrust as any relationship; indeed, such feelings often run that much deeper between family members, whose very connection allows them to cause more damage.

Prior to *True West,* Sam Shepard's plays were mostly experimental, impressionistic collages of sound, movement, and image. *True West,* which is more consciously crafted, is closer to realism, and marks a turning point in the playwright's career. It represents a definitive statement by Shepard of his concern with family dynamics and the plight of the artist. Although ostensibly about two opposed siblings, Shepard uses their confrontation to express concerns about the dual nature of the self and America itself, especially the seductive myths of the West in which Americans often place their hopes to avoid facing reality. The play's title is taken from a defunct magazine that purported to tell true stories of the Wild West, but created a romanticized vision for its readers. In the same way, the brothers attempt to create a "true" image of the West, but cannot conjure up anything convincing beyond their own struggle, the reality of which they all, including the mother, fail to recognize as what the West has become.

In *The Three Sisters,* the Prozorov siblings walk a tightrope between their romantic illusions and the banal necessities of their lives, and they become both comic and pitiable in their efforts to maintain this tricky balance. While they long to return to the Moscow of their birth, this is shown to be an impossible dream as they become trapped by loveless marriages and exhausting jobs. Their father had encouraged them to become highly educated—all speak at least four languages, and Masha and Andrey are accomplished musicians—but it is an education none utilize. It is partly the father's fault, since he moved them to this provincial town far from Moscow and married Masha to a boorish schoolteacher, Koolyghin, who is incapable of original thought.

Their mother died when they were young, and their father has been dead a year when the play begins, so the Prozorov children are thrown back on each other for support. All feel deeply, but are unable to fully voice what torments them. When they try to express their feelings—Masha speaks about her desire for Vershinin and Andrey bemoans his former ambitions and current reduced state—the others refuse to listen, for they find such feelings messy and uncomfortable. If only they would listen, it might allow them all to properly connect and support each other; instead they resort to idealistic platitudes about future possibilities whose impossibility they completely ignore.

As siblings they profess to love one another and offer sympathy and encouragement for each other's dreams, but it is questionable how much they truly support each other. The three sisters seem proud of their brother's abilities, but once his professorial ambitions disintegrate, they offer him little comfort. These siblings are too self-involved and fearful of commitment to help one another emotionally or to offer any practical advice. Andrey finds himself in a loveless marriage, his young wife turned shrewish and unfaithful; he hates his job; and he is too scared of his sisters' teasing to admit to them his feelings of despair. Instead he resorts to gambling to fill the void, and impoverishes himself to the point where he has to mortgage their house, further alienating his sisters. All are frustrated, filled with unrequited longings—for others, for meaningful work, for personal achievement—and see themselves as trapped in a provincial town. The sisters long to return to cosmopolitan Moscow, and in some sense sustain each other through this common desire. Poor Andrey feels alienated from their union, and thereby more isolated in his grief. He eventually asks for advice from Dr. Chebutykin, who suggests that his best course is to walk away and leave Natasha, but Andrey is incapable of such decisive action.

The Prozorovs are like the dead tree Toozenbach sees in their garden: "It's all dried up, but it's still swaying in the wind along with the others" (321); they only play at life and never really live it—internally they are as dead as that tree. Masha is also unhappily married. She complains to her sisters about her husband (though not to him directly), whom she sees as vulgar, limited, and as offensive as the company he keeps and tries to get her to join. The only relief her sisters propose is the possibility of a summer escape to Moscow if they ever move back, which it becomes increasingly obvious will never happen. Desperately in love with Vershinin, Masha asks her sisters for help, but they refuse to even accept that her problem exists. Vershinin is transferred and she loses him, and her husband annoyingly offers to pretend that nothing ever happened.

Irena, meanwhile, seems incapable of actual love—she agrees to marry Toozenbach only as an act of duty and desperation, and this kills him, for he is murdered in a duel with a rival suitor the day before their wedding ceremony. Irena constantly speaks about the wonders of work, and how that will provide fulfillment and escape from a stifling life, but she should be warned by Olga's constant weariness and complaints of headaches that work may not be the answer she seeks. She tries working at the post office and for the council, quitting both jobs as too uninspiring, and plans by the end to follow teaching, the very job that exhausts Olga.

As Natasha takes over the family house, she displaces the Prozorovs one by one, and their old nurse, Anfisa, whom they have never had the heart to fire. Natasha even plans to move her husband and give his room to their daughter. She stops their socializing at home, canceling their carnival party with the excuse that her son needs peace and quiet. As she declares: "I do like order in the home, I don't like having useless people about" (296). She may stroke Olga's cheek in a gesture of affection, but it is only a gesture, for her intent is to displace her without compunction. Andrey is embarrassed by his inability to control her, but accepts whatever she does and follows instructions; his only freedom is the surreptitious gambling in which he indulges, but even there he has no luck and seems to have a constant losing streak.

Dr. Chebutykin gets angry at the family's tendency to ignore what is happening. He breaks the clock, frustrated at the way they pretend not to notice Natasha's infidelity. Unsurprisingly, even when challenged by the Doctor, they just continue talking as if he had never spoken, and refuse to acknowledge any reality that hurts them. Masha and Irena discuss their brother's decline since marriage but do nothing to help him reverse course.

What we see is a family affected by the degeneration of a formerly wealthy and respected aristocracy. Irena's declaration that she must work becomes as empty as the hopeful declarations about going to Moscow, and equally as unlikely. For all her talk about the beauty of work, she hates its actuality. However, despite this, all three sisters offer expressions of hope at the play's close, regardless of the nihilistic interruptions of Dr. Chebutykin. Their collective idealism seems born out of their boredom, but instead of trying to improve the present, they gaze into the future. Each has a dream that gets deflated by someone else.

Colonel Vershinin suggests to the sisters that their education is not wasted, since it will help them to create a better future. But, too wrapped up in their own disappointments, they make no efforts to disseminate their knowledge, beyond Olga and Irena's careers as schoolteachers, so this becomes yet another empty dream. Natasha is an intrusive force who kicks the others out, becoming rather melodramatic as the villain who hurts the good Prozorovs. She is animalistic in the amoral way she manipulates others, and, like an animal, her priorities are to preserve her children and satisfy her own needs. She survives, happily achieving her aims.

The sisters spend too long talking about life to really enjoy living it, and are shown to be too analytical and idealistic, while Natasha just gets on with it. Only a peasant, she can also be seen as a sign of the future, like the peasants in the upcoming revolution, who just want to be landowners, and who have the capacity to be cruel to those below them on the social ladder rather than changing the system.

Despite their evident intelligence, capacity for energy, and refinement, the sisters totally lack will and the power to combine these qualities into effective action, and are effectively paralyzed. By consistently living in the past and looking toward the future for hope, they cannot ever be truly happy in the present. The play ends with an image of support between the sisters as Olga holds Masha and Irena and tries to instill in them a hope for the future despite their current suffering, but this only shows their lack of progress, in its echo of her opening speeches.

In *Dancing at Lughnasa*, Michael Mundy narrates a memory of the summer when he was seven years old, living with his mother and her unmarried sisters in rural County Donegal. Besides relating his first impressions of his father, Gerry Evans, and the relationship Gerry had with Michael's mother, Michael also tells us about the sisters' ups and downs, which are punctuated by snatches of song and dance by which the family reaffirm their connection and raise their spirits. During this summer, their older missionary brother, Jack, having been sent home in disgrace from an African leper colony by the Church for "going native," returns to the family to die. As the sisters lose their livelihoods, the family breaks apart.

Dancing is the central metaphor of the play. In an age where honest communication has become increasingly difficult to maintain, these siblings resort to song and dance to display their love for one another, fierce spirits, and presence. The title refers to the pagan dancing of the Lughnasa festival, in celebration of the harvest via a Celtic god of fertility. It is a celebration of life, and it is the impetus behind the dances in which we see the sisters indulge, either to Irish folk music on the radio or to their own songs. They welcome the sense of connection and the release dancing offers from the mundanity of their simple lives. They dance as do the people in the leper colony, because they have little left to lose. The dance is tribal in essence, as no one dances truly alone, for even if they dance apart they are watched by the others and the experience is shared. They do not get to attend the festival, because Kate insists that they are too old for such revelry, but they dance together at the house, albeit Kate somewhat reluctantly, and apart, to relieve their frustration. Chris and Gerry also dance outside each time he calls to celebrate their relationship, as the other sisters jealously watch from indoors.

By the interesting parallels Friel draws between what goes on in Ballybeg and Uganda, he universalizes the play's impact. Jack draws comparisons as he describes the Ugandan festivals and dancing. The Mundy women become like the hens in their own henhouse, barren without a rooster. It is most likely Jack who killed their rooster, attempting to reenact a tribal rite, as a fox would have killed the other chickens. And it is Jack's return in disgrace that puts an end to Kate's job, which has been holding the family together. The wearer of the plumed hat, which significantly gets passed on from Jack to Gerry, is the metaphorical rooster of the household; but Jack is past his prime and Gerry mostly absent. Gerry becomes the African chieftain with his "preferred wife" (presumably the one he keeps in Wales with his other children), and the women of the Mundy family fawn over him, with Chris giving him a "love child."

In 1930s Ireland, times are hard, and the family shares the domestic chores, with Kate's job largely covering the household expenses. Together they try to protect Rose and raise young Michael. Together they survive. But when a group lives so closely, whatever happens to one affects the others. Families cannot live on love alone, and they soon discover that they are not yet at the bottom. The family is gradually stripped of every opportunity for income, and worn down by continual misfortune. Kate is unfairly "let go" from her teaching job because of her brother's disgrace. Agnes and Rose lose their knitting contracts when a knitting factory starts up nearby. Chris refuses to marry or ask for support from the unreliable father of her child. Jack, of whom they had originally been so proud, has lost his ministry and faith, and his health deteriorates until he finally dies. His return from a life of service, broken in body and mind, echoes the family's decline, but even before his death, the family has fallen apart, ironically, because of that regard they have for one another.

While Maggie and Kate struggle to avoid reality and keep things going, Agnes and Rose slip away to London so as not to be a burden, where they both die miserable deaths—Agnes on the streets of exposure, and Rose in a hospice. Political engagement to counter these misfortunes is shown to hold no answers, by the way Gerry's involvement in the Spanish Civil War is mocked, with him wounded falling off his bicycle. Neither down-to-earth Maggie nor the more refined Kate have the courage to leave Ballybeg, so they unhappily remain, despite having no future there. Chris reluctantly works at the knitting factory, and Kate tutors the children of a man she had once hoped to marry. What Michael remembers most clearly, and is haunted by, is the dance, the ultimate symbol of connection, but it is a ghostly legacy, just as he is clearly the last of his clan, and the only one who never dances.

At the start of *True West* Austin is house-sitting for his mother on vacation, when his brother, Lee, arrives from three months in the desert. Not having seen each other for five years, their conversation is uncomfortable. Tension mounts as they discuss their father, and Lee becomes increasingly threatening, mocking Austin's scriptwriting, talking about casing the neighborhood, and acting insulted at Austin's offer to help. Austin's producer, Saul Kimmer, is coming to see him, so he bribes Lee to stay away by lending him his car. Lee returns early with a stolen television, and arranges to play golf with Kimmer, so he can pitch his idea for a Western. He gets Austin to help him write this script after telling him he envies his life. Kimmer buys Lee's story, dropping Austin's script, which provokes Austin to drink, steal, and behave like his brother, even asking Lee to take him into the desert, which Lee agrees to do if Austin will help him finish his script. As they work together, their mother arrives, and her behavior provokes Lee to quit and leave, alone. In anger, Austin attacks him. Lee appears to be dead, but then springs back to life, and the play closes with the brothers circling each other warily.

As brothers, Austin appears to be the softer and more open of the two, offering to help his brother with money and a place in his home. He enjoys recalling their youthful escapades, and feels drawn to Lee's apparently unfettered existence, revealing that he finds his own existence empty. He helps Lee type his script, despite his skepticism about its authenticity, and when Lee confesses that he envies Austin's comfortable middle-class life, Austin is drawn to help further. Austin is intrigued by as much as fearful of his older brother, as evidenced by his attempts to become more like him by drinking and stealing. Ironically, it is he, rather than his violent brother, who makes the first direct attack, strangling Lee with a telephone cord because he is angry that his brother refuses to take him to the desert.

Lee, on the other hand, is threatening from the start, as he mocks and cajoles his brother and talks about burglarizing the neighborhood. He seems to enjoy disconcerting Austin, rejecting his kindness as insults, disrupting his nostalgic remembrances, and refusing to clearly answer his questions. He overturns Austin's life, edging him out with Kimmer by getting his script to replace the one Austin has been working on, and promising, then refusing, to share his desert existence. However, Lee is no less discontent with the life he leads than his brother is with his own life, although Lee is shaken out of his desire to pursue a middle-class lifestyle after witnessing his mother's automatic and mindless behavior.

In one sense, the brothers are two halves of the same person: Lee portrays the darker, more dangerous id, which Austin, concerned with placating the superego, has spent his life repressing. Thus, the play explores Shepard's belief in people's "double natures," whereby one side is repressed in favor of the other, which inevitably limits the whole. Austin is a well-groomed suburbanite, who writes television scripts for a living and likes to keep everyone happy. Lee is a scruffy criminal, who likes to drink and pick fights. Both envy the other's life to some degree, and on the surface they seem diametrically opposed, representing a whole series of apparent opposites: imagination/reason, anarchy/conformity, lowbrow/highbrow, emotion/intellect.

However, the differences between Lee and Austin become blurred as they each try to take on characteristics of the other, provoked by envy for the life each sees the other as leading, and in search of their own missing egos. Austin is drawn to the romantic possibilities of his brother's independent life out in the desert, just as Lee wonders what life would be like as a member of the steady middle class, making a living by the less dangerous process of writing about life rather than living it.

They attempt to switch lives, as Austin drinks and burglarizes the neighborhood while Lee writes a script. Both are utterly ineffective at what the other does. Austin ends up stealing toasters that he polishes up and uses to toast bread—a parody of a dangerous criminal—while, in frustration, Lee takes a golf club to the typewriter. Evidently, they cannot surmount their essential differences, by which Shepard suggests that the two sides can never be entirely reconciled, but must be accepted for their differences. The brothers' conflict will continue until both recognize this. When they work together, as Kimmer suggests, they progress, but each feels the threat of the other, which stops them from completing their script. The play ends, necessarily unresolved, with the brothers facing each other with homicidal menace, neither prepared to give way to the other.

A further cause of the brothers' antagonism stems from the fragmented state of their family, the parents lured away by a promise of freedom that is nothing more than a refusal of responsibility. The father, an alcoholic living in the desert, abandoned his offspring long ago. The mother similarly escapes by vacationing in Alaska and has become totally disassociated from her children. She shows no concern over her destroyed kitchen or her sons, as one tries to throttle the other in front of her, and she refuses to see what is happening. Such parents indicate what Shepard sees as the spiritual death of the American family, and into this spiritual gap the brothers seek to place an image of something that might sustain them: the West.

Both brothers struggle to write an authentic Western story, but both have trouble connecting the reality they understand with their dreams of the Wild West, largely created by popular culture. Lee has been there and knows the West has been wiped out by development, though Austin insists it has simply changed, becoming a land of freeways and stores. Yet Austin idealizes Lee's desert life, while Lee desires to live in Austin's pragmatic world. But Lee's tale of the West is utterly contrived, comprising every Western cliché he can conjure up, while Austin's vision of the West is denatured and unsustaining. What each creates is as artificial as their mother's plastic grass and as dead as her plants, and their struggle and relationship remain unresolved.

FURTHER SUGGESTED READING

Bottoms, Stephen. *The Theater of Sam Shepard.* New York: Cambridge University Press, 1998.

Chekhov, Anton. *Plays.* Hammersmith, U.K.: Penguin, 1951.

Cicirelli, Victor G. *Sibling Relationships Across the Life Span.* New York: Plenum, 1995.

De Maegd-Soip, Carolina. *Chekhov and Women*. Columbus, OH: Slavica, 1987.

De Rose, David J. *Sam Shepard*. New York: Twayne, 1992.

Elder, Lonnie, III. *Ceremonies in Dark Old Men*. New York: Farrar, Straus and Giroux, 1969.

Friel, Brian. *Dancing at Lughnasa*. Boston: Faber, 1990.

Gottlieb, Vera, and Paul Allain, Eds. *The Cambridge Companion to Chekhov*. New York: Cambridge University Press, 2000.

Leder, Jane Mersky. *Brothers and Sisters: How They Shape Our Lives*. New York: St. Martin's Press, 1991.

O'Brien, George. *Brian Friel*. Boston: Twayne, 1990.

Peacock, Alan J., Ed. *The Achievement of Brian Friel*. Gerrards Cross, U.K.: C. Smythe, 1993.

Shepard, Sam. *Seven Plays*. New York: Bantam, 1981.

Wasserstein, Wendy. *The Sisters Rosensweig*. New York: Harcourt Brace Jovanovich, 1993.

Substance Abuse

Long Day's Journey Into Night by Eugene O'Neill (1957)
Hatful of Rain by Michael Gazzo (1954)
The Connection by Jack Gelber (1959)

Although numerous drug addicts and drinkers appear in plays by pioneering modern dramatists Tennessee Williams and Eugene O'Neill, in the first half of the twentieth century few playwrights chose to consider such a potentially explosive topic as substance abuse in their work. It is an issue filled with pitfalls, given the public tendency to shun such topics for fear that any discussion of them may promote, or seem to condone, the taking of drugs or alcohol. But by the 1950s, attitudes had relaxed sufficiently to allow for a frank, yet sympathetic, presentation of the effects of alcohol and drugs on people's lives, although playwrights approached the question of addiction from differing perspectives. While O'Neill shows us drinkers and dope addicts desiring but unable to change, Jack Gelber presents addicts content with their addiction, and Michael Gazzo suggests both the desire and possibility of "kicking the habit."

The most common portrayals of drinkers or drug addicts in modern drama show people who drink or get high as a refuge from a world that they feel has somehow betrayed them. They opt to set themselves apart from others and their personal pain or demons by creating a protective cushion of alcohol or drugs. We see this in O'Neill's largely autobiographical *Long Day's Journey Into Night*. The characters, with their addictions, fears, and failings, are closely based on his own parents and elder brother; the character of Edmund is based on himself. Such personal experience allows O'Neill to present detailed and realistic psychological portrayals. He depicts a father and two sons who constantly drink to avoid feelings of inadequacy, guilt, disappointment, or fear, while the mother injects morphine as both solace and escape.

While we may sympathize with O'Neill's characters, we see their addiction mostly caused by their own weak will and inability to cope with whatever life has dealt them, and we see little hope for any cure; Gazzo's *Hatful of Rain,* by contrast, offers an alternative view. The play introduces us to a wider range of drug addicts, including a dealer, and centers on the troubled figure of Johnny Pope, who has been betrayed less by himself than by others. Johnny is not an addict by choice; he has a loving wife and a baby on the way. The play's impetus lies in his father and his wife discovering his addiction, then offering the support he needs in order to beat it.

Gelber is less concerned with excuses as to why someone takes drugs; for him the drug culture is more an unavoidable fact of life than a sad response to personal or social wrongs. In other plays dealing with the drug culture, the playwrights are concerned with offering sympathetic excuses for the addict. But Gelber suggests, controversially, that some people become addicted because they desire an alternative life to the materialistic nine-to-five grind of the rest of society, not because they need to heal some major rift in their life. The lives of Gelber's addicts are not necessarily happy but, unlike the addicts that populate O'Neill's and Gazzo's plays, they display no desire to change how they live. *The Connection* is as experimental in its style as it is in its subject matter: it neatly blurs the line between drama and reality in an effort to convey a sense that this is a true depiction of how addicts live.

Long Day's Journey Into Night recounts a bleak day in the life of the Tyrone family in which all their fears and guilts bubble to the surface and are swiftly reburied. As they alternately blame themselves and each other for the sad state of their lives, the men, James Tyrone and his sons Jamie and Edmund, drink to excess, and Mary, the mother, gradually recedes into a morphine-induced haze. We learn of Tyrone's lost career and penny-pinching ways, Jamie's wasted life and predilection for brothels, Edmund's experiences at sea and current ill health, and Mary's disappointments and addiction.

Mary refers to them all as victims of a past they cannot change. Her addiction grew out of a difficult birth with Edmund, and a doctor overzealous in prescribing morphine to soothe her pain. The Tyrones try to forget their pasts to improve their present, but it is a futile exercise, since the past keeps intruding. If they could only face what has happened, they might be freed of it and move forward, but they can only view it when under the soothing influence of drugs or alcohol, which does not allow them to deal with it honestly. They cannot come to terms with what they have collectively done or not done, so they allow their memories, or the memories of others, to destroy them, or enrage them to destroy each other. Although each one tries to blame the others, every Tyrone is partly responsible for his or her own destruction.

Mary prefers to live in an imaginary past. Although she begins the play drug free, as it proceeds, she keeps taking morphine to help her to slip into this past and avoid the unpleasantness of her present-day reality—currently the harsh fact of Edmund's life-threatening consumption. Even though it is clear by her occasional outburst that she knows the truth, she tries to believe that Edmund only has a cold, thus freeing herself from any need to worry or act.

The morphine assists her in this self-deception and offers her a life free of psychological pain, where she can blot out her unhappy marriage, her selfish husband, the death of her baby Eugene, and even her own addiction. As she explains: "It kills the pain. You go back until at last you are beyond its reach. Only the past when you were happy is real" (104). Her idealized past as an innocent convent girl from a happy home, tricked into a disastrous marriage, is a complete fabrication, but the morphine helps her avoid the reality of even that, as it totally fogs her mind. Mary ends the play in a narcotic dream in which she relives her past as if it were physically occurring in the present, and it seems like a dream to which she is destined to keep returning.

O'Neill depicts the Tyrones being gradually encompassed in darkness, as night closes in and their home becomes fog-bound. The fog is symbolic of the way in which each of them has become isolated and insulated—from each other and the outside world. They separate themselves off through embarrassment or disgust, then complain about their loneliness. Each is both victimizer and victim in an endless round of recrimination. The darkness at the close of the play is both external and internal; given their fears and insecurities, these people have no means of escape. Mary and Edmund both welcome the fog, grateful for the opportunity it gives for them to lose themselves; its opacity may be restrictive, but they see it as safe. Edmund's visions of the sea are as ethereal as Mary's drug-induced visions, and no more real. Edmund is very sick, but hides from this truth, as it rightly scares him, and his excessive drinking only exacerbates his condition.

No one in this family expects to be happy because all are consumed by real or imagined guilts. Tyrone feels guilt over Mary, because he has given her a shabby life and hired the cheap doctor who got her hooked on morphine. He feels more guilt over trying to send Edmund to a cheap sanatorium. These guilts stem from his miserliness, a habit he cannot break. Mary feels guilt over Eugene's death, since she had not been there to stop Jamie from infecting him with the measles, which killed him. She also feels guilty just for giving birth to Edmund who seems so unhappy. Also, her addiction makes her feel guilty because she knows how much they all want her to stop, and, unable to break her addiction, she feels inadequate as a wife and mother. Jamie feels guilt over his own failure in life, and for causing Eugene's death. He even feels guilt over Edmund's ill health, believing that his attempts to corrupt Edmund to make himself look better caused the consumption. Edmund feels the least guilt, but still sees his life as a waste.

Tyrone's actions are equally driven by his past, especially his lost chance at becoming a great actor due to his financial insecurity. Instead of extending his repertoire, he kept playing one popular role until he became so typecast that no one wanted him to play anything else. Tyrone pushes his sons to make something of their lives, but usually in the wrong direction, exploiting rather than assisting them. Also a chauvinist, he has always put himself and his career ahead of Mary. He loves her, and depends on her for emotional support, but has never really considered her feelings. He has had a hard life, having to support his mother and siblings from an early age after his father walked out on them, and it is this that has made him so penny-pinching. He tries to break free of this habit, agreeing to let Edmund pick his own sanatorium and promising to pay for it, but he cannot resist insisting "within reason."

Jamie's life of dissipation, with its prostitutes and alcohol, is born of a need for the guiding hand of a mother, having lost Mary to her morphine habit, and his own guilt at possibly having caused Eugene's death. Being the most drunk, he is also the one most aware of the truth, though it is a truth from which he desperately wishes he could hide. Pressured by his father, Jamie became an actor, but it is a profession he despises. He has no idea what he would do in its place, but takes out his frustration and dissatisfaction with life on himself. Jamie is an empty shell of man, a lost soul with no sense of selfhood. His lifestyle reflects his desperation—for love, direction, and happiness—all of which are precluded by such a lifestyle. Alcohol acts as a lubricant for confessions from Tyrone, Edmund, and Jamie, but the trouble is that they can do nothing to rectify their lives, so their only recourse is to drink some more until nothing matters anymore.

Hatful of Rain tells the story of Johnny Pope, who became addicted to morphine from his time in a veterans' hospital, in recovery from being tortured by his captors during the Korean War. He has tried to quit, but could not stay clean, and has started using again, which causes him to lose a string of jobs, give up attending night school, and get in debt to a local dealer called "Mother." Mother pressures Johnny for his money, giving him a gun and demanding that he rob someone, but Johnny's intrinsic morality prevents him from doing this. His brother, Polo, who has helped him in the past, sells his car to pay Mother, and Johnny's whole family helps to get him into rehabilitation.

The small apartment setting, with windows facing a brick building, conveys a sense of entrapment, visually depicting the way an unwilling addict must feel about his addiction. Johnny had gone into rehabilitation before with Polo's help, but when he returned to morphine, Polo had given him the money to pay for the morphine rather than see Johnny go through the pain of withdrawal again. Polo just wants to help his brother, but, as Celia explains, "When you love you have to be responsible to what you love" (381), and giving Johnny the money had not been in Johnny's best interest. Celia suggests that it would have been better to try to understand what caused the pain, and learn why he is using in the first place.

The cause of Johnny's addiction is complex. His father admires him for his innocence and his ability to believe in people, but these are qualities Johnny has had stripped away. His life has been a series of betrayals, from his father placing him and his brother in an orphanage soon after their mother's death, to his sergeant abandoning him to torture during his tour of duty in Korea, and the doctors and nurses pumping him full of drugs to keep him quiet while he was in the hospital. Johnny rightly feels betrayed by society as a whole, which has effectively caused him to become an addict against his will.

Although Johnny is reunited with his father, the father's unremitting favoritism toward Johnny annoys Johnny, since it is Polo who most desires the father's approval. While Johnny has not forgiven his father for abandoning them, Polo keeps all their father's letters and saves money to help him start a business. When Johnny and his father speak honestly, we see a breakthrough in their relationship, in which even the irresponsible father finally offers his support, and it is this, alongside the support he gets from Polo and Celia, that spurs Johnny to change.

Polo loves his brother, but he is angry at him for his weakness. He also worries about his own motivation in giving Johnny the money to buy more dope; might he have been trying to destroy Johnny because of his feelings for Celia? Knowing he can never have Celia, Polo initially refuses to supply any more cash, but does so in the end to save Johnny's life. Polo alone got Johnny through his last rehabilitation, but he does not have the strength to do it alone again. Fortunately, he does not have to, as both their father and Celia are ready to help this time around, and Johnny, managing to overcome his sense of shame, is willing to allow them.

Celia loves Johnny, but has found the way he has distanced himself from her since his return from Korea increasingly troubling. Knowing that his brother Polo desires her, she nearly turns to him for comfort, but both realize the mistake of that before anything happens. Even though she is pregnant, she declares her intention to leave, thinking that Johnny's neglect of her stems from his having lost interest in her and taken a mistress. When Johnny speaks honestly to her, sharing his feelings openly and admitting his addiction, their relationship takes on a new strength, just as his relationship with his father became stronger once Johnny opened up to him. Celia does not hesitate in her support once she knows that Johnny still loves her, and it is she who, with Johnny's consent, calls the police to have him taken in to get cleaned out. She emphasizes her married name when making this call to ensure that we know she will stick by him.

The play's title refers to a story from Johnny's childhood, in which he is told that people are rewarded for hard work, so he digs a hole while it rains and ends with only a hatful of rain for his trouble. This illustrates how Johnny's innocent faith in social rules betrays him—in a corrupt society, sometimes it takes more than faith in the system to survive. Johnny never betrayed his sergeant, even under torture, and it pains him to know that his sergeant betrayed him. Yet without some kind of faith, survival is equally impossible. Gazzo's answer is a belief in the power of community: when people help each other, rather than selfishly work alone, then progress is possible.

Johnny's problem is partly caused by having to live in what his father calls "the age of the vacuum" (321), in which people no longer believe in anything. Gazzo suggests that people without faith or hope are those most prone to becoming drug addicts. He underlines this by his depiction of other addicts in the play. The group who break into Johnny's apartment, sent by Mother to beat him up, are particularly vacuous. Doped up, they act selfishly, unable to trust each other, with no sense of time or purpose; they even keep forgetting why they are there. There is a sense of aimlessness as they talk, occasionally squabble, and try to decide where to go next.

The dealer Mother is an utterly immoral force who manipulates those who depend on him for drugs. Abusive and violent, he represents everything bad about the drug world. When Johnny cannot pay, he cuts off his supply, forcing him into painful withdrawal, and threatens his life if he cannot find the money. He has put Willy De Carlo in the hospital for nonpayment, and even threatens Polo. Were it not for Polo selling his car to raise the cash, Johnny would be dead. Mother fails in his attempt to force Johnny to commit armed robbery, but he got another addict, Church, to murder his own mother for her cash—less than $4—and then beat up his dog. But the strength of Johnny's family behind him is more than a match for Mother.

The Connection takes place in the apartment of Leach, a heroin addict who allows other addicts to use his place and connects them to dealers in exchange for a portion of their score. A group of addicts wait for their "connection," a dealer named Cowboy, and pass the time playing music, telling stories, and discussing various facets of their lives. They are supposedly improvising on themes provided by Jaybird, who has been living among addicts to see how they live. He was hired to do this by Jim Dunn, a television producer, who wants to cash in on the current interest in drugs by filming this group in action. The media depicts drugs as exotic and even erotic, but this will not be what we see here, to the disappointment of Jim and Jaybird, as they see themselves losing control. Jaybird and one of the cameramen are persuaded to try shooting up, there is the threat of a police raid, and Leach overdoses, nearly killing himself.

The Connection, coming five years after *Hatful of Rain*, is an open attempt to enter the world of the addict rather than simply to vilify it. Gelber humanizes his addicts; they take center stage and their lives and dependencies are the play's subject. With Jim trying to direct the action, we get a sense that we are watching the real thing; Gelber even has Leach shoot up on stage. The group of addicts we meet are predominantly passive, living for their next "fix" that will allow them to briefly feel alive. They do not see themselves as victims, just people who have opted out of everyday life. They do not hate society, they just do not wish to be part of it. One of the addicts, Sam, points out that what they do is not that different from what people do in regular society, suggesting that everyone is an addict in some sense—to work, money, clothes, vitamins—the only difference being that he is addicted to something illegal. They do not consider themselves better than "regular" people, but neither do they consider themselves worse, and we become increasingly sympathetic to that view.

Gelber's addicts are drawn to drug use for different reasons, and they are shown to be as varied as the rest of society, crossing boundaries of race and class, with Solly the intellectual; Sam the companionable storyteller; Ernie the misanthropic, self-deluded musician; and Leach the busy opportunist. None of them have any intention of quitting, and we do not expect them to. Gelber is careful not to paint them as heroes: what they do is not heroic, it is simply how they live. Every society contains addicts: this type is just more prone to crime and early death, but it is a life they choose. They are neither mentally unbalanced nor traumatized by events in their lives. As we watch these men wait and hope, we come to see them not only as addicts, but as representative of the whole human condition.

Solly lists contradictory reasons why addicts get high: for hope, to forget, to remember, to feel happy, or to feel sad, but they all do it by choice. He asserts, "You are your own connection" (37), invoking the play's title, to suggest that everyone chooses his or her own life and beliefs. A junkie's life exists in a delicate balance between life and death, and Solly's suggestion that most addicts shoot up in search of transcendence rather than escape hits a nerve in the ambiguous conversation the men have with the Salvation Army sister. Cowboy brings in Sister Salvation, with whom he is pretending to have found religion, to escape detection by the police. Naively, she is unaware that these men are drug addicts; while she thinks they are talking about religion, they are talking about drugs. Thus emerges another "connection," this time between drug use and religion, both being described as sources of salvation and joy.

While Jaybird had hoped for heroic figures warring against social expectations, and Jim for a freak show to market, both are disappointed; what they see are fellow human beings. Though men like Ernie seem more desperate and out for themselves, Sam, Solly, and Cowboy all stick by Leach when he is in trouble. These men have a community of sorts, with certain rules of conduct by which they mostly abide, and though Jim refuses to see this, suggesting that they should all die to give him a neat ending, Jaybird accepts the essential ordinariness of what they are doing: "No doctors, no heroes, no martyrs, no Christs . . . It's all yours now" (96). Throughout the play, Gelber constantly breaks the "fourth wall" by having characters speak directly to the audience and vice versa. By this he hopes to draw his audience into the play to the point where they see no real difference between themselves and the performers, and so make the addicts' experience an intensely personal one for every spectator.

FURTHER SUGGESTED READING

Barry, Sebastian. *Our Lady of Sligo.* New York: Dramatists Play Service, 1999.

Gazzo, Michael. *Hatful of Rain.* In *Famous American Plays of the 1950s.* New York: Dell, 1988: 313–84.

Gelber, Jack. *The Connection.* New York: Grove, 1960.

Gusfield, Joseph R. *Contested Meanings: The Construction of Alcohol Problems.* Madison: University of Wisconsin Press, 1996.

Hinden, Michael. Long Day's Journey Into Night: *Native Eloquences.* Boston: Twayne, 1990.

Murphy, Brenda. *O'Neill:* Long Day's Journey Into Night. New York: Cambridge University Press, 2001.

O'Neill, Eugene. *Long Day's Journey Into Night.* New Haven: Yale University Press, 1956.

Schrader, Paul. *Light Sleeper.* London: Faber and Faber, 1992.

Williams, Tennessee. *Cat on a Hot Tin Roof and Other Plays.* New York: Penguin, 1976.

Wright, James D., and Joel A. Devine. *Drugs as a Social Problem.* New York: HarperCollins, 1994.

War and Violence

Arms and the Man by George Bernard Shaw (1894)
The Plough and the Stars by Sean O'Casey (1926)
The Basic Training of Pavlo Hummel by David Rabe (1971)

Despite the patriotism that overtakes most nations during times of war, it is nearly impossible to find any drama that suggests that war is anything other than bad, although they assert this with varying degrees of intensity. George Bernard Shaw's *Arms and the Man* is decidedly comical in its satire of the ills of war. But assuming that some wars are inevitable, the play does not question the reasons for the war, and the soldiers involved are willing participants. Sean O'Casey's *The Plough and the Stars* is a mix of the comic and the tragic, just as the combatants are a mix of the willing and the reluctant, the cowardly and the heroic. Although O'Casey supports the reasons for the conflict, he clearly views the conflict itself as a blight on Ireland. David Rabe's *The Basic Training of Pavlo Hummel,* by contrast, presents a completely negative experience, bereft of humor, in which war is the result of unnecessary American macho posturing, and an indignity perpetrated on all those involved.

The differences between the conflicts in each of these plays are largely responsible for the playwrights' differing responses to the subject. Shaw's play takes place during a nineteenth-century war between Serbia and Bulgaria, while Sean O'Casey's focuses on the Anglo-Irish conflict that has continued into the twenty-first century. Rabe deals specifically with the American involvement in Vietnam. All try to explain the cost of war in terms of how it affects those directly involved and those who watch from the sidelines, as well as considering both the direct and collateral damage war causes.

Arms and the Man takes place during what was then a recent conflict between Bulgaria and Serbia, but it is not about that conflict. Rather, it deals with the nature of battle itself and how it is often wrongly perceived by society. Its central "hero," Captain Bluntschli, is a Swiss mercenary who fights on both sides of the conflict. Although a play like *Arms and the Man* is entertaining,

Shaw ensures that it is also thought provoking. In it he exposes what he sees as the dangerously blinkered old-order attitude toward war, fueled by social expectations that have been supported by rigid class structures and overly romantic ideals. *Arms and the Man* was Shaw's first commercial success and it encouraged him to continue playwriting. It also showed a shift in his work from his earlier propagandist plays that targeted specific social wrongs to plays attacking the more abstract beliefs and ideas behind them. Always the social reformer, Shaw had reached the understanding that he must first change attitudes before he could change social conditions.

We see plenty of national pride in Sean O'Casey's *The Plough and the Stars*, but that pride is depicted as dangerously overemotional and poorly organized. O'Casey is sympathetic to the cause of Irish freedom from British rule, but he is strongly opposed to furthering it by violent means. Thus, the play becomes an unflattering consideration of the Easter Rising of 1916 and a criticism of the fighting that destroyed so many. At its Dublin opening, the play caused riots outside the theater. O'Casey also draws our attention to the terrible conditions of the Irish slum-dwellers in his characterization of the consumptive Mollser, and the inevitable degradation of human nature in those forced to live in such conditions. This is depicted in the way the characters constantly argue, fight among themselves, and behave so selfishly. Despite comic moments, O'Casey intends *The Plough and the Stars* as a tragedy in its depiction of the destruction of lives by social conditions, war, and political blackmail.

Born in 1880, Sean O'Casey was the youngest in a large, impoverished Protestant family living in Dublin. By 1913 he was a secretary in the Irish Citizens Army, although he later resigned on a matter of principle. A strong socialist rather than a nationalist—O'Casey was not involved in the 1916 Easter Rising—he saw his first allegiance to the oppressed and suffering among whom he lived, rather than to any political or military causes. The character of Young Covey, with his insistence that economic change must prefigure any improvement in their living conditions, comes close to acting as the playwright's voice in this play. The plough and stars of the title refer to emblems on the Irish flag of liberation. The significance of the flag's design is that the farmer's plough is combined with the astral Plough constellation to show the heights to which hard work can take a people. What was originally a workers' flag has become a political symbol.

David Rabe has resisted calling his plays "antiwar," preferring them to be viewed as efforts to define what takes place during wartime, for himself and others. One of a trilogy of plays written by Rabe about the effects of the Vietnam War on American soldiers, *The Basic Training of Pavlo Hummel* is the only one to take the audience to Vietnam, although all three offer insightful analyses of the effect of Vietnam on those who served and those who stayed behind. The other two plays are titled *Sticks and Bones* (1969) and *Streamers* (1976). *The Basic Training of Pavlo Hummel* gives us a naturalistic view of various aspects of the soldier's experience, from basic training camp to active duty. On top of this are laid expressionistic elements that probe more deeply into the mind of the single soldier named in its title.

In *Arms and the Man*, the romantic idealist, Raina Petkoff, is engaged to Major Sergius Seranoff, a bold, though careless and conceited, cavalry commander. Both see war as a grand spectacle and an opportunity to perform heroic deeds. Shortly after a Bulgarian victory brought about by Sergius, Swiss mercenary Captain Bluntschli, a refugee from the fleeing Serbian army, takes shelter in Raina's rooms. The two argue because Bluntschli's more realistic view of war offends Raina, but she decides, with the help of her mother, to protect him. Four months later, an embittered Sergius has failed to get a promotion, Raina and her mother are trying to keep secret the aid they gave the "enemy," and Bluntschli arrives to return the coat he had been given for his escape. After a series of comical cover-ups, the truth comes out. Forced to see that Raina loves Bluntschli, Sergius challenges Bluntschli to a duel, but when Raina discovers that Sergius has engaged in an affair with her family servant, Louka, Sergius backs down and proposes to Louka instead, leaving the way free for Bluntschli to marry Raina.

At the center of the play is Shaw's attack on the false ideals of warfare and the soldier's profession, which were prevalent in the nineteenth century. British society, especially the upper classes, tended to see war as a noble pursuit and the men who engaged in it as courageous heroes, eager to die for their country. Plays of the time that dealt with military themes usually upheld such idealistic views and were filled with brave and virtuous soldiers who feared nothing in their mission to conquer the enemy. But Shaw rightly understood that this was mostly a civilian viewpoint, and not how soldiers generally saw themselves. He exposes this contrast in the opposition between Sergius and Bluntschli. Sergius is the Byronic idealized soldier, his inexperience making him oblivious to the true nature of war. He is full of grand gestures his own army cannot even sanction. By contrast, Bluntschli is the practical career soldier, who is more interested in survival than winning, who follows the rules and fully understands the potential horrors of war.

Shaw was no pacifist—he saw war as necessary in certain circumstances—but he wants the public to recognize war for what it is and understand the difficulties faced by its participants. In war, soldiers are often tired and hungry, afraid for their lives, and unsure about what to do. We are shown all of this through the character of Bluntschli, whose name echoes the bluntness with which he forces the true nature of a soldier's life upon Raina, whose romanticized vision of soldierly behavior is clearly unrealistic. The play satirically targets such unrealistic views, making those who hold them appear shallow, pretentious, and prone to deceit.

Under the guidance of Bluntschli's clear-sightedness, Raina gradually recognizes the impossibility of her ideals and modifies her expectations to realistic levels. Raina's initial repulsion at Bluntschli's apparently cowardly, ignoble action of running away and hiding in her rooms rather than fighting to the death is soon turned into compassion as she recognizes the reality of his hunger and desperation. Although she is partly motivated by her pretensions to nobility when she makes herself responsible for his safety, she is not above slipping a portrait of herself into his pocket as he leaves—a token for him to remember her by. While she tries to hide it, she is pleased at his return, rejecting her former fiancé in favor of this more practical man.

Sergius, who initially shares Raina's vision and helps to feed it, vainly tries to live up to the romantic ideals the couple has set. Yet he cannot escape the realization that war is not the glorious adventure he had believed it to be when he led his reckless cavalry charge against the enemy. He had acted without orders, but had luckily survived because the Serbians had the wrong ammunition for their guns. His unprofessional behavior may have won the battle, but it does not win him the promotion for which he had hoped. Resentful and bitter, he turns to the less demanding Louka for comfort, as Raina expects too much of him. His lack of true nobility is shown by the way he plays around with Louka behind Raina's back, and his readiness to duel with Bluntschli to prevent him from having Raina. It is only when Raina becomes disenchanted with him that he gives up the duel, though he has become disillusioned with life in general by this point and seems incapable of any action.

Sergius's main difficulty is that he never fully understands the problem. He despairs at his own inability to live up to the ideals he and Raina had envisioned, but Shaw wants us to see that the real problem is that people believe such impossible ideals to be possible. Sergius is foolish for ever believing in them, but it is the ideals that are wrong rather than he. Shaw supports an antiromantic view of life, shown through the practical efficiency of men like Bluntschli, who takes life seriously and refuses to be duped by romantic idealism. Although Bluntschli confesses to having a romantic streak that led him to run away from home and join the army, it is a romanticism kept firmly under control.

Bluntschli's army service is marked by his calm efficiency and professional understanding of the mundane details of warfare, such as the troop movements with which he assists Raina's father. His practical nature is shown by his pawning the coat the women gave him to get money for his escape, and by the fact that he never played Raina's romantic game by looking at the portrait placed in the pocket. He may have returned the coat in hopes of seeing Raina, but he only proposes once he discovers that she is both free and of marriageable age. It is little surprise that Bluntschli will switch professions from soldier to hotelier by the end of the play, and that he will bring the same skills to bear on his new profession, including an understanding of people's real needs, desires, and limitations.

While Shaw's main characters are drawn from stock military melodramas of the period—noble soldier, cowardly soldier, and beautiful lady—he turns our expectations around. The beautiful lady does not end up as expected with the noble soldier, and the noble soldier turns out to be not so noble, just as the coward is really not so cowardly, just practical. All of Raina's noble aspirations, the guiding ethos of those melodramas, are deflated by Bluntschli's measured responses, as Shaw forces us to see war as it truly is: an intensely wearing, unpleasant, destructive conflict, that, while necessary at times, should never be welcomed or entered into too lightly.

The Plough and the Stars is set around slum-dwellings in Dublin, in the period leading up to the Easter Rising of 1916. The neighbors argue among themselves and belittle Nora Clitheroe as too uppity in her desire to improve her surroundings. Nora loves her husband Jack but is unable to prevent him from taking a battalion of the Irish Citizens Army to fight the British, when he is offered promotion and a speaker rouses the local Irish to fight for their independence. Some months later the fighting has dissolved into a free-for-all, with the locals more interested in looting than freedom. Nora has unsuccessfully tried to find Jack and bring him home. He stops by briefly as his troops are being routed and ignores her pleas to quit the fight, sending Nora into a fragile mental state and causing her to miscarry their child. A few days later we get news of his death, as well as the death of young Mollser, a consumptive neighbor. The British have taken charge, tracking down the last few snipers. When Nora screams at the window for Jack, her neighbor, Bessie Burgess, pulls her out of the way and gets mortally shot herself. The play ends with Dublin in disarray and the British soldiers calmly eating the supper Nora had made for Jack.

O'Casey's plot can be viewed as both depicting the effect of outside events on domestic lives and showing how the conflicts of those domestic lives compare and contrast with the political conflict. Despite snatches of humor, there is throughout a general aura of approaching despair and cataclysm. The deaths are made to seem brutal, unnecessary, and random, thus underlining the terrible reality behind such undefined conflicts. Jack's sacrifice is pointless, and Captain Brennan's declaration, that "Mrs. Clitheroe's grief will be a joy when she realizes that she has a hero for a husband" (204), is deeply ironic. Bessie's death seems even more unnecessary, as she herself points out as she is dying. And while people die through the conflict, poor Mollser dies of consumption because of the poor conditions under which she is forced to live. As Covey observes, more people are dying of consumption than war, because the social system has remained unchanged despite all the fighting. Poverty is rampant, and nothing is being done to change that.

Nora sees the Irish Citizens Army going nowhere, so she had tried to keep Jack out of it. Thus, the play considers the conflict between domestic and political loyalties seen in the lives of a typical Irish couple. Jack succumbs to political pressures and is killed, though not without Nora trying to prevent this by burning the letter that conveyed the news of his promotion to Commandant. Although he had left the army on her account, this promotion flatters

Jack's pride and stirs his patriotism, so he rejoins. He is given one more opportunity to desert, but his fear of being called a coward overcomes his fear of death.

O'Casey sees it as sadly inevitable that the innocent suffer most in such wars, and he partly blames them for being misled by the rhetoric of politics and a spurious nationalism. The speaker outside the pub who incites the men to arms insists, "Bloodshed is a cleansing and sanctifying thing, and the nation that regards it as the final horror has lost its manhood" (162). He appeals to their virility and fear of being called cowardly, pumping them up into a frenzy by describing their cause in religious terms to invest it with a surpassing importance—one that Covey denounces. Covey points out that fighting now is pointless: unless they first gain economic freedom, any other gains will be meaningless.

Mollser can be seen as representative of Ireland itself—sickly, weak, and unable to help herself. Her inevitable death becomes emblematic of the death of Irish hopes, especially since it occurs when the Irish army has clearly been decimated. As Covey keeps suggesting, to strengthen Ireland they must first address the social conditions that produce such sickly children as Mollser; only then will they have the proper strength to fight. But as the British soldier who comes to collect Mollser's corpse points out, "A man's a man, an 'e 'as to foight for 'is country, 'asn't 'e?" (209). The call to duty sadly overrides all sense in times of war.

The play is dedicated to O'Casey's mother, who was reputedly hanging out washing and laughing shortly before her death, and it is the women in his plays who seem the strongest and most tenacious. If only the men were not so vain and easily led, he suggests, then Ireland might stand some chance. Nora has ambition and courage, but insufficient influence with her husband to prevent him from pointlessly sacrificing himself. Bessie, too, objects to the fighting, with a son fighting alongside the British in the trenches of World War I. She points out that to rise against the British at this point is like stabbing them in the back while they fight the Germans for everyone. More importantly, the British have artillery and organized troops against a ragtag collection of Irish fighters who are more concerned with how they look than with learning the principles of warfare.

The constant bickering and backbiting between the various residents of the tenement over religion, drinking, class, and what each considers to be correct speech and behavior should make us realize how unlikely it is that such people could ever present a united front against the British oppressors. The only time they unite is when they go out looting, a far cry from the noble endeavors of which the political instigator spoke. At the close we see the British defeat the Irish completely, having taken all the remaining men into custody while they ferret out any remaining fighters. Their bullets having just shot Bessie, they sit in her room eating the supper Nora had been making for Jack, in her refusal to accept his death. Outside we hear gunfire, artillery, and the British soldiers singing "Keep the Home Fires Burning;" no doubt an ironic commentary on the fact that Dublin is now aflame, and the whole uprising itself gone up in smoke.

The Basic Training of Pavlo Hummel begins at the end, with Pavlo Hummel picking up a grenade that has just been tossed into a Vietnamese bar. Before he dies, we are treated to flashbacks from his life during Army training, a trip home before his tour of duty, his battlefield experiences, and, finally, the ironic truth that it was not the enemy who threw the grenade but a fellow American soldier annoyed because Hummel had interfered with his seduction of a local prostitute. During this rerun of the formative periods of Hummel's life, he discovers the illusion under which he has been living and sees the true brutality of the Army life he had idealized.

Rabe's play conveys in graphic terms the experience of the realities of war in a series of moments from Hummel's life. The American soldiers he portrays serving in Vietnam are predominantly motivated by a desire for sex and survival, rather than by any noble calling. As we witness the way in which they have been trained, the reason they are like this becomes more understandable. Boot camp training is geared to validate extreme violence, along with stupidity, sexism, racism, and unthinking obedience. Hummel's company is ironically named Echo to show that they are trained to believe whatever they are told to recite through their call-and-response marching and training chants. It is the unthinking obedience that is echoed in Hummel's name, as he exhibits a Pavlovian response to all he encounters. This is in brutal contrast to the more caring side of his nature he has tried to suppress his whole life. Training camp teaches these men to reject traditional values and embrace, instead, the force of violence, supported by the weapons they constantly carry.

Even before Army life Hummel learned to suppress his individuality to try to make himself over into the fake tough-guy image of his missing father, an image he has been fed by his mother. In reality, his father had been a deserter (of both Army and family). Hummel pretends to have had sexual and criminal experience, to try to raise his status in others' eyes, but these experiences are pure invention. What is important is that if he were a more convincing liar, he would gain the status he desires, for he is right in his assessment of what counts in contemporary society. He has grown up admiring soldiers who are killers and is keen to become such a figure. While in Vietnam, he proudly boasts about his fighting ability and his girlfriend Joanna, back home. However, these are just more lies: Joanna had left him and was pregnant by another man even before he left America, and his combat experience mostly amounts to being shot at, although he did kill one defenseless Vietnamese farmer. It is evident that the reality of war is far more sordid than the noble images of fighting on which Hummel was raised.

As Hummel retraces his life, he invents a black soldier named Ardell, who is a projection of his inner and wiser self. Ardell helps Hummel to better understand why he has turned out as he has and confront the true human suffering and death faced by both sides in Vietnam. As Ardell explains to him, when Hummel is shooting the Vietnamese farmer and gets hit himself, the damage is mutual in such conflicts: as you shoot the opposition, it is as if you are shooting yourself. Hummel relates this experience to drowning, evidencing a sense of helplessness over what happens to him. After being shot, Hummel had hoped to return home, but he was awarded the Purple Heart and sent back, where this time he is killed, and by a vengeful fellow American soldier he has annoyed rather than by the "enemy." *The Basic Training of Pavlo Hummel* offers a disappointing reality to contrast with Hummel's earlier dream of heroic soldiers; war is shown to be neither noble nor heroic, just a lot of pointless killing. Brisbey, the soldier who has lost most of his limbs to a land mine, is emblematic of the reality of a soldier's reduced quality of life, and he pleads with Hummel to help him die.

Hummel was never truly comfortable with his fellow soldiers, and it is clear that they never fully accepted him. Fellow trainees Kress and Parker called him stupid and weird because of his attempts to fake being streetwise. But on a deeper level, they all suspect that he has the wrong temperament to be the obedient killing machine the Army requires, despite his admiration of Sarge Tinden's capacity for slaughter, and the brutal training and casual violence they are all forced to undergo. His assignment as a medic, rather than as a member of the infantry for which he had hoped, suggests the Army's understanding of that softer nature he tries to hide, a nature of intelligence and compassion that recognizes how dehumanizing army life truly is.

It is hardly a surprise to discover that Hummel has attempted suicide during basic training to escape what was happening to him. However, as at other times when he shows his opposition to the Army way by beginning to fight with his fellow trainees, his squad leader Pierce cuts in to apparently save him and restore order. However, Pierce intercedes less for Hummel's own benefit than to ensure that he is passively transformed into a soldier along with the rest of the squad, which is the true order Pierce requires. Hummel is made into a soldier and, in the process, loses his individuality entirely. This is shown by the clean uniform he is given at the end of act 1, displaying his new identity in all of its uniformity. Alongside this is Ardell's commentary pointing out the similarities between Army training and other social programming, such as the ways blacks are expected to subserviently treat white people. Both are self-negating, automated responses that have been instilled under the threat of physical abuse. Hummel has become just another piece of cannon fodder, as exemplified by his swift reassignment to active duty after being shot. Although he finally comes to recognize the truth of his own dehumanized position, it is sadly in his dying moments, and there is nothing he can do with this recognition to save himself or others.

FURTHER SUGGESTED READING

Alexander, Nigel. *A Critical Commentary of Bernard Shaw's* Arms and the Man *and* Pygmalion. London: Macmillan, 1968.

Bergquist, Gordon N. *The Pen and the Sword: War and Peace in the Prose and Plays of Bernard Shaw.* Salzburg: University of Salzburg, 1977.

Dukore, Bernard F. *Shaw's Theater.* Gainesville: University Press of Florida, 2000.

Kolko, Gabriel. *Anatomy of a War: Vietnam, the United States, and the Modern Experience.* New York: Pantheon, 1985.

Lowery, Robert G., Ed. *A Whirlwind in Dublin:* The Plough and the Stars *Riots.* Westport, CT: Greenwood, 1984.

Millay, Edna St. Vincent. *Aria da Capo.* New York: Harper, 1920.

Nhuong, Huynh Quang. *Dance of the Wandering Souls.* In *But Still, Like Air, I'll Rise: New Asian American Plays.* Ed. Velina Hasu Houston. Philadelphia: Temple University Press, 1997: 131–57.

O'Casey, Sean. *Three Plays.* London: Macmillan, 1980.

O'Riordan, John. *A Guide to O'Casey's Plays: From The Plough to the Stars.* New York: St. Martin's Press, 1984.

Rabe, David. *The Vietnam Plays.* 2 Vols. New York: Grove, 1993.

Reston, James, Jr. *Coming to Terms: American Plays and the Vietnam War.* New York: TCG, 1985.

Shaw, George Bernard. *Arms and the Man: A Pleasant Play.* New York: Dodd, Mead, 1926.

Shaw, Irwin. *Bury the Dead.* New York: DPS, 1936.

Zinman, Toby Silverman, Ed. *David Rabe: A Casebook.* New York: Garland, 1991.

Women's Issues—Current

for colored girls who have considered suicide/when the rainbow is enuf by Ntozake Shange (1976)
The Heidi Chronicles by Wendy Wasserstein (1988)
Oleanna by David Mamet (1992)

There was a decided shift in women's issues in the final quarter of the last century. Going beyond the questioning of the limitations imposed on women as mothers and homemakers, these plays begin to explore the future of women rather than their past. As women have begun to take a more prominent role in public life and the workplace, they have both questioned the quality of such advances and what they may have lost in the process. At the heart of many of these explorations remains the concern over a woman's relationship with the men around her and how this contributes to her self-definition as both woman and human being.

In *for colored girls who have considered suicide,* Ntozake Shange depicts the continuing difficulties of being both female and black in modern America, and offers the vision of a supportive network of women bound together by their pain to refocus on their life possibilities. The collaborative nature of the production is, to some critics, particularly feminine, but Shange's emotive mix of poetry, prose, music, and dance, which she terms a "choreopoem," creates a theatrical expression more closely related to African performance. Her text, however, is informed by the conditions faced by black women in a racist and patriarchal American society.

While Shange asks for women to recognize common bonds and help each other, Wendy Wasserstein, in *The Heidi Chronicles,* points to the unrealistic idealism of such a request, showing the intrinsic selfishness of many women even as they espouse community motives, and their essential isolation as they strive for true freedom. Wasserstein's play, despite its comic surface, exposes the fads and weaknesses of the women's movement in the latter half of the twentieth century, while simultaneously eliciting its true advances, which turn out to be more emotional and psychological than material. By the close of the play, Heidi wins what she has most desired all along, confidence in her own ability to choose what she does with her own life, regardless of social expectations.

Widening the focus, David Mamet's controversial *Oleanna* explores the effects of the women's movement on the relationship between men and women. Mamet's protagonist, John, considers himself to be an enlightened man, yet when he is systematically destroyed by Carol, a female student who accuses him of sexual harassment and worse, his response is primal and savagely "male" as he lashes back both verbally and physically. As much as John believes himself to be sensitive to women's equality and rights, his treatment of Carol is condescending and unnecessarily paternal, a fact she eventually forces him to recognize. Although Carol's revenge is justified to some extent, its harshness makes us feel uncomfortable. Through this ending, Mamet points out the potential dangers of feminine empowerment.

for colored girls who have considered suicide/when the rainbow is enuf is a series of poems written about a variety of black women, from youth to maturity, who relate stories of fear, pain, loss, and joy, through which they forge a triumphant, collective, black-female voice by the play's close, and thereby celebrate the resilience of black women. The play shows a variety of possibilities faced by black women, who suffer from abusive lovers who will not allow them to be themselves and a predominantly hostile environment. The women seek love and connection, and move toward the understanding that they can fulfill this need without the aid of untrustworthy men. Starting with a mélange of voices, naming a series of American cities and female adolescent concerns, the play separates into a series of individual characterizations that offer a variety of female experiences and responses to the world, society, and men, both in particular and general. The finale connects the women with nature, an intensely feminine symbol, and allows them to discover the power to transcend the difficulties of their lives with renewed self-esteem and the strength of their community.

The poems that make up the play can be grouped into five subcategories, the first of which is an exploration of female youth and early forays into love. We learn that being a young black girl can be filled with pain and misunderstanding; even at this age, men are predatory, as one girl loses her virginity after her high school graduation. However, these harsh images are balanced against a third poem told by a girl who is filled with joy over the possibilities of music and dance, which suggests there are alternatives. Dance continues to symbolize life and vitality throughout the play, as music serves to underline the characters' moods.

The second group of poems further conveys the possibility of rebellion against other unpleasant outcomes as the women grow older, but no more happy, in their dealings with men. One woman, disgusted by her lover's lack of commitment to their relationship, decides to put him out of her life for good, returning his plant, and another cuts herself off from others completely to pursue her art. Such rebels are counterbalanced by stories of how women can also be abused into submission through rape, often by close acquaintances, and forced to face the shame and physical pain of abortion. Shange uses obscenities at moments like these to force home the ugliness of such violence against women.

The third section presents a series of portraits that offer wider social commentary on the lives of black women, embracing both political and historical themes and images. We meet a defiant New Orleans dance-hall girl who sees herself as an Egyptian goddess despite the negative opinions of others. It is a lesson in self-esteem, one of the most difficult achievements in a group that has been so historically demeaned. Next comes a young dreamer who runs away from home with Haitian rebel Toussaint L'Ouverture as her imaginary companion, upset at not receiving the library prize she deserved. On meeting a real-life boy named Toussaint Jones, she decides to return home. This symbolizes how the exotic can be transformed into the commonplace to make it accessible to all. Then a woman who lures men to her bed, only to vengefully throw them out the next morning, implies that vengeance against men provides no relief, but the next poems suggest a better direction. The section culminates with a lady who comforts women who are victims of harassment, and three more women who set aside their rivalry over one man to bond together like sisters. The possibility of a supportive community is forming.

The fourth series asserts a woman's need for love and the heartbreaking search many follow in its quest, especially given the average men they meet. As they dance and sing together, it becomes obvious that the most positive love they might find is a mutual and supportive love of each other. The play's climax comes in the fifth series of poems, mostly about the price women have paid when they have opened themselves up to a man. One laments the loss of her possessions, taken away by a false lover; the group considers the misuse of the word "sorry" by unfaithful lovers; and we hear how Beau Willie Brown tries to persuade his children's mother to marry him by dangling those children out of a five-story window, but before she can answer him he drops them. Yet despite such mounting violence against them, the women find the resilience to end on an affirmative note. The colors in which they are dressed, which have come to represent differing aspects of their lives, combine to create the rainbow of the title—an apt symbol for the beauty and worth they have discovered within themselves.

The play is a purely feminist vision, as Shange makes no attempt to consider male difficulties. While some poems in the play come out of her own experiences, others relate to her studies in the mythology of women. Shange speaks to and for all women who see themselves as dispossessed, mistreated, or misunderstood, and she does not confine her stories to the black community, even though the play's language is a celebration of black English. She is somewhat idealistic in her suggestion that female empowerment rests in women's ability to form a community, but she successfully illustrates the unjust patriarchal past and the possibility of an improved nonhierarchical future. Balancing images of dirty, lonely cities and technological circumstances that oppress black women against images of natural beauty accompanied by song and dance through which women can become free of oppression and gain equality, Shange creates a world filled with ugliness and beauty, and asks us to choose which we prefer.

The Heidi Chronicles relates formative moments in the life of Heidi Holland as she grows from adolescence into womanhood. Through Heidi and her friends, Wasserstein encapsulates concerns, fears, and victories women faced through the developing women's movement from the mid-1950s through the 1980s. The play begins with Heidi in 1989, lecturing on the inequalities of "Women in Art," and then shows us how this self-assured woman was formed by depicting various occasions in her life from sixteen to forty. At her high school dance, she already shows signs of discontent with the expectation that a woman's main aim in life should be to secure a husband. While her friend Susan pursues this aim, Heidi meets Peter, with whom she forms a friendship rather than a relationship, based on their joint refusal to be categorized.

While Susan tends to bend with the wind of every feminist fad that comes along, from radical feminism, through life on a women's commune, to an executive position, Heidi is staunch in her focused ambition to bring neglected women artists to people's attention. She is correspondingly more successful, too; while Susan's feminism dwindles into a facile sitcom, through picketing, scholarship, and sheer determination, Heidi brings women artists into the public eye through exhibits, lectures, and publications. It is a focus she needs to learn to apply to her own life and, eventually, through the insistence and aid of her friend Peter, she does.

Peter is homosexual, meaning that he and Heidi can never be more than friends, but it is a friendship toward which Heidi is often neglectful. In her efforts to seek validation, Heidi frequently abandons Peter without warning as she moves to England or the Midwest in search of a better life. Ironically, she leaves behind what she sought, an honest connection to another human being, unaffected by gender, rather than the problematic romantic relationships she has with men and the facile mouthings of support she hears among the female gatherings she attends. From consciousness-raising rap groups to baby showers, it becomes clear that the women attending these gatherings, despite their words of solidarity and support, are only out for themselves; they are consumed by their own individual problems. It is not until she learns to value Peter's friendship and stop running away, that Heidi learns how to be herself. It is a lesson her friend Susan, forever consumed by the latest craze, fails to learn. Susan ends the play a successful businesswoman with a hit show, but she leads a shallow, unhappy, and intrinsically unfulfilled life.

Despite her reluctance to commit, Heidi is not adverse to sexual relationships. Her sexual awakening comes on meeting Scoop, an intriguing but inveterate womanizer. Despite her insecure reliance on Scoop to make her feel valuable, Heidi is as unable to permanently commit to him as he is to embrace monogamy. While Heidi, Scoop, and Peter appear on a television talk show as a cross-section of the sixties generation, they are intrinsically the same—each hurts, cheats on, and abandons others as they selfishly pursue happiness; gender, or even sexual orientation, has little to do with it. Scoop marries Lisa because, unlike Heidi, she will put up with his unfaithfulness, be the good little wife and mother, and restrict her own artistic abilities to illustrating children's books so as not to overshadow her husband. Lisa is the compromising woman Heidi refuses to be.

Since she was a teenager, Heidi was unhappy with the expectations imposed on her gender. She insists that men and women are not intrinsically different, despite gendered social expectations, but her attitude seems more humanist than feminist. She continuously asks throughout the play why everyone cannot be allowed to live up to their potential. Scoop offends Heidi by his outrageous confidence; she feels shortchanged by her inability to be so bold. She suspects that this lack of self-confidence stems from women being taught to be deferential and self-sacrificing. It takes her some time to overcome her need for a relationship to feel that her life is worthwhile. The 1970 meeting of Susan's "Consciousness-raising Rap Group"—although satirizing such groups with its stereotypes of the man-hating, aggressive lesbian, and nurturing, acquiescent housewife—is also a defining moment for Heidi, where she faces the inequities of her life and becomes a committed feminist. While Susan just plays at being liberated, Heidi truly lives a life of liberation, refusing to settle for an unfulfilling marriage, as so many women do, and refusing to be discontent with the single life women are expected to abhor.

Heidi is an intelligent, attractive woman who does not want the burden of a husband, but refuses to lose out because of that decision. Her choice at the close to remain in the city to support Peter whose partner has AIDS, and become a single mother by adopting a baby girl, are commitments with which she feels comfortable. She had felt a sense of betrayal from her fellow women, who talked about equality, yet never seriously believed in it as they settled for abusive relationships, or unhappy, unfulfilled lives, trying to live up to male ideas of what their lives should be like. She reveals her discontent in a speech she gives on "Women: Where Are We Going?" to her old school. Satirizing the picture of the perfect woman who has it all—important job, husband and lover, children, wonderful home as she works, cooks, and does charity work and exercise on the side—Heidi recognizes that this image is not only impossible, but ridiculous. Feeling the constant pressure from other women to compete to become the closest to this "ideal," she declares her intention to withdraw from the competition, seeing it as divisive rather than supportive, and fated to bring disappointment rather than contentment.

By the play's close Heidi has redefined her expectations and learned to be content with who she is and what she achieves, regardless of gender. Having reaffirmed her friendship with Peter, she no longer feels unconnected to the world around her and begins to look forward to the future; perhaps not her own, but at least that of her daughter. Scoop could not settle down with her, since he could never accept a relationship in which his desires did not come first. Heidi refuses to enter such an either/or relationship, in which one half of the couple sacrifices their ambitions for the other: she insists on the possibility of equality, in which everyone is encouraged to fulfill their potential, however great or small it may be, regardless of gender. Such is Wasserstein's message to her audience.

Oleanna depicts the mounting antagonism between a college professor, John, and a student, Carol, as they engage in an uneasy interplay of power and control. As a self-absorbed teacher, who hypocritically denounces the very system to which he pays court, John is forced to question his own actions and motives in his dealings with a student whose concerns he has tried to sidestep and whom he has consistently patronized. Carol is struggling in his course and needs answers, but John is too wrapped up in his own needs to give her the proper attention. As a male, he is too conditioned to being in the seat of power and refuses to see anything wrong in his behavior. Reading his words and actions from a feminist perspective, Carol charges him with sexual harassment, which jeopardizes his tenure, his new house, and, eventually, his job. At the play's close, John viciously attacks Carol, and reaches a momentary enlightenment as to why he is being so punished.

Mamet's epigraph from Samuel Butler suggests that this is a play about the dangers of accommodation. Women have long submerged their desires and needs to placate and satisfy the male expectation of dominance. The women's movement attempts to free women from self-restrictive bondage and offer them power to equal that of men. Mamet's question is whether women will become as indiscriminate in their abuse of men as men have so long been toward women. Carol initially feels subservient to John in terms of social, economic, and educational class, but gets the courage to challenge him partly from a women's support group.

Carol admits that she takes out her anger at all men on John, for she is sick of men's assumption of power over women. She empowers herself by attacking John: "You can't *do* that anymore. You. Do. Not. Have. The. Power. Did you misuse it? *Someone* did. Are you part of that group? Yes. You. Are. You've done those things" (50). She cares no more about John's thoughts or feelings than he cared about hers when he was in control. Sickened by his patriarchal behavior and his pride in lording it over women, she upbraids John as an example that such behavior is no longer acceptable. Carol's apparent lack of compassion and hatred are disconcerting, being qualities frequently accepted in men, but rarely exhibited by women.

Thus Mamet depicts an uneasy relationship between genders in light of the increased power granted to women through the women's movement, coupled with the unwillingness of men, so used to being the figures of power, to step aside. One can sympathize with John for losing so much, when all he seems to have done is try to help a student, but Carol also elicits our sympathy as we can see the hypocrisies behind so much of what John says and does, whether it be consciously or subconsciously. It is this double vision that makes the play so controversial.

John's office is a locus of patriarchal power: the place to which he summons his students, rules on their fates, and, if his treatment of Carol is typical, demeans and belittles them to maintain control. It is not just the way he repeatedly keeps Carol waiting while he talks on the phone, but how he rarely allows her to complete a sentence, consistently denigrates the education in which she firmly believes, and, instead of listening, insists that he knows what the problem is and tries to tell her what she is feeling. He is unwise to burden her with his inadequacies as he does, because, despite his assertions to the contrary, they are not alike; ironically, it is largely these "confessions" he offers to try to help her that she uses to bring him down.

John's treatment of women over the phone gives more credence to Carol's charges of sexism. He repeatedly reduces his wife to "Babe," insists that she allow their male realtor to take charge, and angrily screams "*screw* her" into the phone, when the woman whose house he is trying to buy refuses to be tricked into a lower price (39). Irony again creeps in, as his reaction to his realty deal echoes that of Carol toward education—both being in worlds they do not understand and responding with anger—but instead of gaining insight, John tries to deny Carol her anger, frustrating her further. Having brought her to the verge of tears, he puts an arm around her to comfort her. On the surface, this appears to be an honest attempt to calm her, but the casualness with which he touches her without consent implies an unspoken male prerogative that goes to the core of the system that Carol challenges.

By act 2, Carol has shattered John's complacency with a formal complaint, yet he remains oblivious to her needs. Instead of apologizing for his formerly blasé attitude, he responds with denial and threats, trying to coerce her into backing down. He *is* sexist and elitist, and there is nothing false in her report: she is simply expressing her perspective on his words and actions, a perspective that may not have been his intent, but one of which he should have been aware all along if he really believed in equality. His resort to physical force, as he tries to prevent her from leaving, allows her to extend her charges to battery and attempted rape, against which he will have no defense, since it will be his word against hers and she is now in control.

By act 3 the tables have been fully turned. It is now Carol who has the power and it is John's turn to feel impotent and frustrated as she cuts *him* off, says she understands *him,* and asserts her point of view, forcing him to listen to her as she lists his failings and hypocrisies. When she reprimands him for demeaning his wife, he loses control entirely; he knocks her down, curses her, and is about to hit her with a chair when he finally sees himself through her eyes and recognizes the "monster" she has seen all along. Saying, "Well," he sits at his desk, and she replies, "Yes, That's right" (80), and we see the first moment of recognition and understanding between them in the play.

FURTHER SUGGESTED READING

Albee, Edward. *Three Tall Women.* New York: Dutton, 1994.

Ciociola, Gail. *Wendy Wasserstein.* Jefferson, NC: McFarland, 1998.

French, Marilyn. *Beyond Power: On Women, Men, and Morals.* New York: Summit, 1985.

Hudgins, Christopher C., and Leslie Kane. *Gender and Genre: Essays on David Mamet.* New York: Palgrave, 2001.

Kane, Leslie. *David Mamet: A Casebook.* New York: Garland, 1992.

Lester, Mark. *Ntozake Shange.* New York: Garland, 1995.

Mamet, David. *Oleanna.* New York: Pantheon, 1992.

McDowell, Linda, and Rosemary Pringle, Eds. *Defining Women: Social Institutions and Gender Divisions.* Cambridge, UK: Polity, 1992.

Schleuter, June, Ed. *Modern American Drama: The Female Canon.* Rutherford, NJ: Farleigh Dickinson University Press, 1990.

Shange, Ntozake. *for colored girls who have considered suicide/when the rainbow is enuf.* New York: Macmillan, 1989.

Vogel, Paula. *How I Learned to Drive.* New York: DPS, 1997.

Wasserstein, Wendy. *The Heidi Chronicles and Other Plays.* San Diego: Harcourt Brace Jovanovich, 1990.

Women's Issues—Past

A Doll's House by Henrik Ibsen (1879)
Trifles by Susan Glaspell (1916)
A Man's World by Rachel Crothers (1909)

Throughout the nineteenth century, women were still very much viewed as chattels of their husbands—with the unmarried woman hardly registering at all on the social register—and we see such couples represented in many earlier dramatic works. But, by the turn of the twentieth century, early feminists were beginning to question the limitations imposed on women as passive mothers and homemakers, and the toll such narrow lives took on those women, and modern dramatists, both male and female, have been keen to explore these changing perceptions. Although playwrights like Henrik Ibsen and Susan Glaspell depict marriages within a contemporary society that expects wives to be submissive, they show how damaging such relationships can be. Rachel Crothers's depiction of women as independent, capable of holding down jobs outside the home, and running their own lives without the constant guidance of men in *A Man's World*, was considered shocking when it debuted—as espousing views liable to topple the very fabric of society. But Crothers, and other feminists, persisted in advancing such views, until women were given opportunities to live freer and more fulfilling lives. Although the prevailing cultural myth had been that men were "trapped by marriage," the feminist viewpoint brought to public attention that it is really the women who were thus trapped.

A Doll's House, by Ibsen, is an early depiction of a woman trying to break free of the restrictive, paternalistic relationship she comes to recognize she has with her husband. By today's standards Nora's rebellion may not seem so earthshaking, but in 1879 it was considered downright immoral to suggest that a woman might abandon both her husband and her children. By showing Torvald's romanticized marriage to be an empty dream, Ibsen was exploding the conventional, sentimentalized Victorian ideals of the "little woman" and the "angel in the house." Nora's leaving to pursue self-fulfillment challenged society's whole concept of the sanctity of marriage, and marks an early call for female emancipation. The fact that the law actually prohibited a woman from borrowing money without a male relative's consent is important to recognize. Nora lives in a patriarchal society that will not be easy to combat alone. It is an incredibly brave action she takes in leaving at the close.

Glaspell's *Trifles* depicts a poorer class of woman, who would be utterly trapped by her marriage, with no way out. An educated woman like Nora, coming from a moneyed background, would have found it slightly easier to remain economically viable in the outside world. Women like Minnie Wright were often forced to remain with either father or husband just to have a roof over their heads. The life of a solitary woman without male protection was not an attractive option.

A Man's World by Crothers is one of the earliest American attempts at what George Bernard Shaw had labeled a "Discussion Play," in that the argument within it is what keeps the play progressing, and the action becomes almost peripheral. The play's argument concerns the double standards by which men and women of the day were treated, by which men were allowed to be sexually irresponsible while insisting that their women maintain the highest standards of morality. Within the play Crothers depicts the "New Woman" of the period, who was attempting to live independently of men, and shows the sacrifices such women were often forced to make. Crothers herself was one of the most successful female playwrights of the early twentieth century, a period when a career in the theater was not seen as particularly respectable for a woman. Though often dismissed by critics as too conventional, Crothers consistently focused on such women's issues as the conflict between career and marriage or motherhood, the hollowness of many marriages, and the opposition faced by strong and successful women. *A Man's World* is one of her earlier and more daring dramas, and, for that reason, less popular at the time of its production.

A Doll's House depicts the marriage of Nora and Torvald Helmer. Torvald treats his wife as a plaything rather than a person, and when she acts independently, raising the money for him to recuperate from a bad illness, it changes their whole relationship. Nora had to forge her husband's name to get the money, and the man with whom she made the deal, Krogstad, discovers this and tries to blackmail Torvald. After meeting the widowed Mrs. Linde, an early love, Krogstad destroys his evidence and frees the Helmers to show himself worthy of his new wife. However, Torvald's reaction to events makes Nora rethink their relationship and decide to leave her husband to reclaim her humanity.

Initially, Nora deserves the incessant diminutives Torvald heaps on her. Nora's desire for macaroons ensures that we understand that she is still a child who needs to grow up; she is, after all, a willing "doll." She virtually twitters as she throws things around, leaving them for servants to pick up, coyly flirts with her husband, and childishly plays with her children: she is a "little lark," "a little squirrel," "a little featherbrain" (3–4). Her frivolous world is in stark contrast to Torvald's cautious, ordered world of business. He naturally prefers the sanctuary of his study or of work, merely using his wife as an occasional diversion or entertainment. The fact that he will not even allow Nora to read the mail, locking it in a box to which only he holds a key, shows how far he has kept her apart from the outside world so she will remain under his total control.

But Torvald's world is shown to be as remote and cold as Norway itself, a strict world of men and law in which women are allowed no footage. By contrast, as Nora develops, we see her being related to the warmer, more passionate climes of Italy. It is to Italy that she takes Torvald after showing some spirit in defying the male world and procuring the necessary funds. It is an Italian dance, the tarantella, that Ibsen uses to indicate her feminine growth and development into a woman. When Nora threatens to burst out as a woman while dancing the tarantella Torvald feels compelled to control her, though, to his consternation, his attempts are less than effective. It is a growth he will not be able to comprehend or prevent.

Nora wins our sympathy through her generous spirit and because of her domineering husband. Her generous nature is indicated from the start, as she overtips the porter and earnestly tries to assist her old friend, Mrs. Linde. Her spending is noticeably on others and not on herself. Even the crime she has committed was done to restore her husband's health. He had thoughtlessly refused to raise the money they needed for the trip the doctors recommended, preferring instead to risk leaving his wife and newborn child without a husband and father.

Nora's marriage has no pretense of equality; Torvald simply cannot envisage such a relationship. He selfishly runs their lives according to his own whims and does not feel it necessary to consider his wife's feelings. Nora is aware that their marriage is based on appearances and realizes that she may need something to keep Torvald's interest once her looks have faded. What Ibsen is telling us is that a true marriage needs a deeper bond than Torvald and Nora have managed to create. Nora has invested a great deal in her marriage, far more than Torvald realizes, but she has invested unwisely and will be forced to recognize this sad fact.

Mrs. Linde can be seen as a foil to Nora. While Nora married into an idealized dream of love, Mrs. Linde first married because she felt responsible for her family. She gave up her true love, Krogstad, for the financial security of a richer man who subsequently lost his money and died, leaving her to go out into the world and work to support her mother and younger brothers. Though harsh, this has perhaps been the making of Mrs. Linde; she has gained self-respect from her achievements. She is now a woman who can bind herself to a man she respects without losing that independence. Her misfortune has allowed her to tap her own hidden resources and she may be the lead Nora must learn to follow. In an interesting gender reversal, Mrs. Linde proposes to Krogstad, as she persuades him that they need each other equally—and we cannot fault the honesty of this assertion. Indeed, they exhibit the qualities on which a true marriage should be based: mutual honesty and respect rather than concealment and falsehood.

Torvald's image of Nora is romantic fantasy: no human being could really be like that. Nora finally learns to reject Torvald's "doll-like" image of her, as she comes to realize that this is the only way she can reclaim her humanity. Torvald helps her reach this decision by his reaction to her dealings with Krogstad: he completely condemns her, does not take into account her altruistic motives, and only considers how *he* will be affected. Nora realizes that she, too, has been the victim of a romantic dream—having expected her husband to stand by her and even nobly take the blame. She now realizes that such "a wonderful thing" is only fantasy (66). She needs to enter the real world so she can discover how it operates and forge an identity for herself. She admits her own fault in having allowed first her father and then Torvald to use her as a plaything, but feels theirs is the greater fault for expecting her to fulfill such a role and for not allowing her to be any more than that. Torvald does offer to change, but she rightly believes that that can only happen if she leaves.

In *Trifles*, we learn about the troubled marriage of the Wrights, which has culminated in Minnie Wright strangling her husband, John. Her neighbors, Mrs. Hale and Mrs. Peters, have come to the house to fetch Mrs. Wright clean clothes as she waits in jail to be charged, and they discuss her case. The men vainly look for signs of violent rage, but the women, with growing empathy, are able to recognize the signs of quiet desperation under which many women of their time were forced to live.

Although the occasion of the play is a murder, it is really a play about the condition of marriage in the nineteenth century and an exploration of the differing male and female reactions as they search for a motive. There is never any doubt that Mrs. Wright killed her husband, but the question is: why? Glaspell contrasts male and female perspectives throughout the play, and engages our sympathy firmly on the side of the women.

We are asked to witness Mrs. Wright's life rather than Mr. Wright's death, and we are shown that the true "crime" has been the way she was being subjugated and "destroyed" by her marriage. We never see Minnie Wright; we learn about her only through others' comments. This dramatic method serves the dual function of allowing her to avoid particularity and so serve as a symbol of all women trapped in loveless marriages, as well as ensuring that our attention is focused on the reactions of those others.

The play's opening firmly sets the scene. The gloomy kitchen is where Minnie Wright struggled to stay sane, and the domineering men immediately take charge while the women remain on the periphery. We learn that John Wright said little and demanded the same from his wife. We can also recognize that he is not so different from these other men, who clearly see women as a subservient group whose concerns hold little importance. Thus, in their search for hard evidence to convict Mrs. Wright, they repeatedly overlook the existing evidence that the women uncover, dismissing such evidence as mere "trifles" (9). Mrs. Hale's early defense of Mrs. Wright against the belittling comments of Mr. Henderson foreshadows her growing sympathy and complicity with the "murderess."

Once a woman marries, she loses her former identity, along with her maiden name, and she becomes subsumed by her husband; note how even the sheriff impersonally calls his wife "Mrs. Peters." The lives of Mrs. Peters and Mrs. Hale may not be as dreary as the life Mrs. Wright evidently led, but, as women, they are aware of the limitations that a patriarchal society has placed on their gender. Their husbands are a little more communicative, and both women have children to distract them, but their days are no less yoked to the home and the demands of those husbands.

Standing in the kitchen, the center of every farm wife's existence, Mrs. Hale and Mrs. Peters soon piece together the clues to events that continue to elude the men. Before marriage, Minnie Foster had been singing and full of life; placed within the confines of marriage, however—symbolized by the house she lives in "down in a hollow" where you "don't see the road" (21) and the concentric bars of the log cabin pattern of her quilt and the canary cage—she has had all the life strangled out of her. Her husband destroyed Minnie Foster, just as he destroyed her canary. Her revenge, knotting a rope around his neck while he slept, eventually appears just. Mrs. Hale leads Mrs. Peters to a full understanding of the situation as she removes the clues they discover, unpicking the erratic stitching in the quilt and putting the dead bird in her pocket.

Having known Minnie from the past, and being a neighbor who had neglected to visit for over a year, Mrs. Hale accepts her own guilt in not having helped Minnie. Both women now pay penance for this by removing evidence and lying to Mr. Henderson, the county attorney, about how the canary died. Mrs. Hale's final retort, "We call it—knot it, Mr. Henderson" (30), becomes layered with significance. The words themselves sound defiant against Mr. Henderson's facetious tone, and she mocks him with the evidence that she and Mrs. Peters have found, and that even now he continues to miss—the knot around Mr. Wright's neck being clearly related to such a quilting knot. The emphatic "We call it," further suggests the "knot," or bond, that has been tied between these women and Minnie against the men. Glaspell wishes us to recognize the potential strength bestowed on the women who forge such bonds— a strength that comes with unity. It is a strength that will allow them not only to withstand male subjugation but also, we hope, to begin to forge an independent female identity.

Despite its sympathy for the female characters, Trifles is not an antimale play as much as an attempt to awaken audiences to the dilemmas of womanhood at a time when women were still considered second-class citizens. Feminism was in its infancy, and even its supporters were at times ambivalent about where it might lead. The rebellion of Glaspell's women is consequently minimal; Mrs. Hale and Mrs. Peters protect Minnie, but they never speak openly to the men in her defense. Minnie ends up still locked in prison, even though there is a slim chance that she may escape punishment.

In *A Man's World*, the female protagonist, Frank Ware, is a promising writer, whose success her supposed friends insist she must owe to a man's influence. She has adopted the son of a ruined woman whom she befriended shortly before her death, and everyone assumes the boy must be her own child. Having fallen in love with Malcolm Gaskell, she is prepared to give up her independence in marriage to him, until she learns that he is the father of that child. Refusing to accept the double standard by which Gaskell would have refused to marry her had it been *her* child, yet he expects her to overlook *his* indiscretion, she finally rejects him for ruining this other woman's life.

The women characters offer different outlooks on the possibilities for women of the day. Frank, whose masculine first name also indicates her frank nature, desires the independence men are afforded, but is not sure she is willing to sacrifice love to maintain this. By the close she discovers the strength to reject Gaskell, to uphold her principle in refusing to accept the double standard he insists on. She repudiates Gaskell's claim that "nature made men different" (68), and condemns him for refusing to admit that both sexes should share equal responsibility for sexual activity. She is a talented writer, a loving adoptive mother to Kiddie, and a generous friend, as her support of Clara particularly shows. Though she loses her man, her life still holds the potential to be fulfilling in her professional work, her daring insistence on motherhood, and her volunteer work with the poorer women of East Side, by which she helps troubled girls better their lives.

Lione Brune, displaying the cattiness her feline name implies, is jealous of Frank's success at managing to blend aspects of both work and home into her life, and expresses her jealousy through malicious gossip. A committed careerist, Lione feels isolated, accepted neither in the male career world nor in the feminine world of married homemakers. She is no villain, though, and apologizes for her hurtful gossip when she recognizes the honesty of Frank's character. Her initial jealousy had been sparked by the thought that Frank was duplicitously attempting to hide a sexual relationship with Gaskell. However, unlike Frank, she accepts the double standard that operates as an inescapable way of life, and would not challenge it as Frank does: "What's the use of knocking your head against things you can't change?" (57).

Clara Oakes, in contrast to Frank and Lione, is an utterly dependent type, and since she is untalented and unattractive seems doomed to a life of unfulfilled spinsterhood, unable to have a career to support herself, as Lione does, or land herself a husband. She admits, "I'd marry any man that asked me" (52), as she is tired of trying to survive alone, but also acknowledges the unfair likelihood of that: "If I were a man—the most insignificant little runt of a man—I could persuade some woman to marry me—and could have a home and children" (53), but as a woman she will be allowed no such choice. Frank offers her accommodation and a job working at her women's club, by which she allows her some refuge and conveys the need for solidarity among women to ensure that those like Clara survive.

The sexism of the day is evident from the newspaper review of Frank's latest book: "Her first work attracted wide attention when we thought Frank Ware was a man, but now that we know she is a woman we are more than ever impressed by the strength and scope of her work . . . and the marvel is that any woman can see and know so much and depict crime and degradation so boldly" (7). Gaskell's praise is even more grudging, pompously insisting that a man would have written a better book, and that Frank's efforts to address female social issues is doomed to failure: "It's too big for you . . . this is a man's world. Women'll never change anything. . . . Man sets the standard for woman" (23). Secure in his superiority, and certain that Frank will fall into line as soon as she commits to a man, he refers, of course, to that double standard to which Frank so strongly objects.

All the men in the play staunchly believe in the rightness of the double standard, and are easily convinced that Frank's literary success must be based on male input. The one exception is Fritz Bahn, whose motherly attitude toward Kiddie and staunch support of Frank (whatever her past), show that it is possible for men to behave without sexism, although Fritz must turn down career opportunities, just as Frank turns down marriage, to maintain his principles. Fritz sympathizes with Frank's plight as a woman of intellect in a patriarchal society, but is powerless to do anything more than offer the support of his friendship.

FURTHER SUGGESTED READING

Abramovitz, Mimi. *Regulating the Lives of Women*. Boston: South End, 1988.

Crothers, Rachel. *A Man's World*. In *Plays by American Women 1900–1930*. Ed. Judith E. Barlow. New York: Applause, 1985: 1–69.

Durbach, Errol. *A Doll's House: Ibsen's Myth of Transformation*. Boston: Twayne, 1991.

Friedl, Betty, Ed. *On to Victory: Propaganda Plays of the Woman Suffrage Movement*. Boston: Northeastern University Press, 1987.

Glaspell, Susan. *Plays*. Boston: Small, Maynard, 1920.

Gottlieb, Lois. *Rachel Crothers*. Boston: Twayne, 1979.

Ibsen, Henrik. *Four Great Plays by Ibsen*. New York: Bantam, 1959.

Jackson, Robert Max. *Destined for Equality: The Inevitable Rise of Women's Status*. Cambridge, MA: Harvard University Press, 1998.

Makowsky, Veronica. *Susan Glaspell's Century of American Women*. New York: Oxford University Press, 1993.

Marden, Orison S. *Woman and Home.* New York: Crowell, 1915.
Shafer, Yvonne, Ed. *Approaches to Teaching Ibsen's* A Doll's House. New York: MLA, 1985.
Strindberg, August. *Miss Julie.* San Francisco: Chandler, 1961.
Waterman, Arthur E. *Susan Glaspell.* New York: Twayne, 1966.

Work

Waiting for Lefty by Clifford Odets (1935)
Death of a Salesman by Arthur Miller (1949)
Glengarry Glen Ross by David Mamet (1984)

Work has a special place in modern society, having taken on a different emphasis from the days when people simply worked to survive, and modern dramatists have been keen to explore these changes and their impacts on people's lives. Their central concerns have been the threat of dehumanization in the workplace in an industrial society increasingly uncaring of its workforce; the ways in which people are judged by the work they do, rather than by who they are; and the ways in which people allow their work to take over their lives. Of equal concern is the relationship between work and ethics, as capitalism threatens to eradicate the last shreds of compassion and humanity from the business world. It is perhaps this underlying brutality of business that makes the majority of playwrights who address the theme of work consider only male workers, rather chauvinistically protecting womenfolk from the dangers of the workplace. In the plays considered here, we see very few female workers, and those who do appear play only minor roles.

With his communist leanings, Clifford Odets wrote what is perhaps modern drama's best-known play about workers' rights. *Waiting for Lefty* has become the most definitive work of agit-prop in American theater. Agit-prop is a style of theater purposefully designed to incite its audience to political action. Its language and situation are usually simplistic, and designed to harangue its audience to an awareness of social abuse. Odets's drama relates the genesis of a taxi drivers' strike, and its cry for a workers' revolution has been heard around the world.

Grounded in a belief that honest work deserves to be rewarded with fair pay, *Waiting for Lefty* also explores ideas about freedom from prejudice and decent conditions (both physical and psychological) in the workplace during the time of the Depression. Odets emotionalizes and humanizes his message through a series of vignettes that reveal conditions at home and in the workplace, and show the difficulties of finding fairly paid, honest work in the 1930s, just before World War II began to revitalize so many businesses. The play's dialogue was innovative for its time, in its attempt to recreate working-class cadences; although the characters' speech may at times sound a little awkward, it consistently conveys the strong emotions of both workers and the playwright, as they try to bring down the "big shot moneymen" and create a more equitable society. Odets presents an extreme vision that allows for little debate, but that demands an immediate, active response.

Selling has become one of America's prime business practices, and Arthur Miller's tragedy *Death of a Salesman* contains a blueprint of the changing nature of salesmanship in America from the pioneering days through to the postwar boom. With such constant change, some people are bound to get left behind, and such a man is Willy Loman, who has become stuck in an old-fashioned and outmoded style of selling. His death is not just that of a human individual, but of a whole way of life.

Glengarry Glen Ross, David Mamet's exploration of a world where business comes first, can be viewed as an updated version of Miller's play. Salesmen continue to strive for success in a business where the rules keep changing, though Mamet's characters are more cutthroat, their language is fouler, and the outlook on life seems bleaker. Willy's counterpart, Shelley Levene, may not commit suicide at the close, but he faces prosecution and a ruined life, while the world continues on in its pursuit of wealth. The play introduces us to a collection of real estate salesmen, each with his own sales technique, each vying to be the best salesman of the group. Everyone is totally preoccupied with work and any semblance of private life has been eradicated—these men are defined by what and how they sell.

The vignettes of *Waiting for Lefty* are woven between scenes from an increasingly emotional taxi-drivers' strike meeting, where the men wait for their elected chairman, Lefty, to appear. We see the impoverished home and family of Joe, a typical driver; the contrasting problems a lab assistant faces in his work for an ambitious industrialist; the plight of a young driver, Sid, who is waiting to earn enough money to marry; and the firing of a doctor with socialist sympathies. The play ends with a call to arms for all workers to strike for freedom and a better world.

It is evident from the complaints of Joe and Sid that taxi drivers are getting a raw deal. The taxicab company takes such a large share of fares that the drivers are left with just $6–$7 a week on which to survive—barely enough to pay the rent. Joe worries about striking, since he will receive no pay while on strike and may lose his job once the strike is over, and there are no other jobs available. Joe is desperate: unable to pay his bills, his furniture is repossessed, and there is no money to feed and clothe his family. Edna, his wife, puts the children to bed early, "so they won't know they missed a meal" (8). She spurs

Joe on to strike by threatening to leave him if he does not at least try. It is Joe who first speaks out at the meeting, where the corrupt union official, Fatt, is trying to dissuade the men from striking. Sid cannot raise enough money to even start a home and family, and has been engaged to Florrie for three years. She loves him and is prepared to wait, but her family is pressuring her to give Sid up because he has no future. Out of decency, Sid offers to free her, but is glad she refuses.

At the meeting, Fatt displays his control over the union through the looming presence of a threatening Gunman who pressures the attendees to keep quiet. Fatt tries to assure the men that working conditions will improve if they are patient, but the men's skepticism is evident. They have heard this before and no longer trust those in power. But the country is still in the Depression, and, while jobs remain scarce, those who have them are easy to intimidate because they have few other options. What Odets wants the working classes to realize is that they *do* have options, and strength in unity. The bosses cannot exploit them if they stand together and demand better conditions and wages.

Fatt patronizes these hardworking men, calling their elected committee a "bunch of cowboys" (6). Using the national suspicion and uncertainty toward communism, he accuses anyone who complains of being a "red," trying to silence them and discredit whatever they say. He introduces Tom Clayton, supposedly a fellow worker, who speaks about his regret at being involved in a strike, warning them to hold off. But a heckler, who turns out to be Clayton's brother, exposes him as a company spy, paid to try to get them to back down. He works for an organization that supplies "scab" labor to replace the strikers. Thus the work climate truly sets brother against brother. The unions, formed to help the workers, are clearly not doing their job, as Agate Keller indicates when he speaks about his union button burning up out of shame.

In counterpoint to the taxi drivers' plight, we have that of Miller, a comparatively well-paid lab assistant at an industrial company. He puts up with the blatant racism of his boss, Fayette, but despite the hefty raise he is offered, he walks out on the job when its demands become morally repugnant. He feels bad that the company makes its money by producing poison gas for the military, despite Fayette's assertion that, "That's not our worry. If big business went sentimental over human life there wouldn't be big business of any sort" (15). But the clincher comes when his boss insists that he must also spy and report on his colleagues. The portrayal of Fayette is meant to show the corruption of big business in America, and its disdain for the workers who keep the companies afloat.

There is also Dr. Benjamin, a talented Jewish doctor with socialist leanings, who loses his position because of both his religion and his affinity for socialism. To show its disdain for the working class, the hospital pulls Benjamin from a charity-case operation, replacing him with an incompetent doctor who kills the patient. A sympathetic colleague, Dr. Barnes, complains: "Doctors don't run medicine in this country. The men who know their jobs don't run anything here" (27–28). He sees the very wealthy in control, but so isolated from everyone else that they are ignorant and uncaring of anyone's needs. Barnes feels too old and vulnerable to rebel—he has a dependent, disabled daughter—but he encourages Benjamin to challenge the unfair dismissal. Benjamin is an excellent doctor and had seniority, but he was the one the hospital board chose to fire when pressured by their wealthy trustees to reduce expenses.

What Odets suggests is that both blue-collar and white-collar workers are being exploited by the system. Honest work is not sufficient to put bread on the table, and things must change; if communism is the only means to effect that change, then communist principles should be embraced without compunction or shame. The only way to change the system is to rise up united against it, and demand fairer wages and greater rights. As this becomes evident, at Keller's instigation the workers begin to rise up in force, overcoming the opposition of sychophants like Fatt and his accompanying thug, calling for all to unite, from Edna to Barnes, in the fight for right and the freedom to better their lives. News of Lefty's murder pitches Keller into a greater fury as he exhorts everyone, including the audience, to join the strike. Although Odets's call for workers of the world to unite had a particular resonance in the 1930s, the cry remains applicable in any capitalist society that privileges the rich over the poor.

Death of a Salesman recounts the final twenty-four hours in the life of salesman Willy Loman. The story of his life is told in a series of flashbacks and remembrances to help explain how he reaches the point of desperation that causes him to take his own life. Central to his life is his relationship with his sons, and what he attempts to teach them, wrongly or rightly, about selling and how to become successful in society. As their name suggests, the "Loman" family represents the plight of so many of the "lower" class during the period of economic and labor-force changes that followed World War II.

Willy has witnessed major changes in the economic structure of his country. He experienced the sense of limitless possibility at the beginning of the twentieth century, a time when his father and brother both left home to pursue their fortunes. He lived through the wild prosperity of the 1920s, a period that convinced him he could become successful in his work, through to the 1929 Wall Street Crash, which marked the start of the Great Depression and saw his dream begin to fall apart. The Depression lasted through the 1930s, and Willy would have found his selling increasingly difficult, as people had little money to spend. With the economy jump-started in the 1940s by the increased market demands and industrial advances of World War II, Willy recognizes a renewed sense of vigor in the American economy, which creates much of the hope he places in the prospects of his two sons.

The play was written and is set in 1948, at the time when the forces of capitalism and materialism came to the fore and technology made an enormous impact on the lives of everyday people, and we see this in the lives of the

Lomans with their desire for household machinery and an up-to-date car. But Willy has an uneasy relationship with machinery, understandably, as it is the efficiency of this new machine age that is pushing him out of his job.

Through the generations of the Loman family we are given a history of salesmanship in America. It is a male history, as selling was a predominantly male profession up until the latter half of the twentieth century. Willy's father began as an itinerant peddler, who traveled from sale to sale, often with his family in tow. He personally produced some of what he sold, and Willy still recalls the sound of the flutes his father made. This personal connection to what a person sells has bled away by the time we meet Willy, and we never even learn what he sells, other than himself. He has modeled himself on Dave Singleman, an old-fashioned traveling salesman who got by on being well liked, but Willy is living in a far less sentimental age. Efficiency, productivity, and the hard sell are the contemporary workplace buzzwords, and Willy cannot keep up with such demands, just as he could never be sufficiently ruthless to do well in such a world.

Times have changed and Willy has been unable to change with them; the values he espouses, where deals are made with a smile and a handshake, are those of a bygone age. His brand of selling is now considered old-fashioned in an increasingly technological business world. Howard Wagner is the epitome of the new type of cold-hearted, exploitative businessman Miller saw succeeding in this new world—one who callously takes away Willy's job when he starts to lose business, without a thought to the man's financial obligations or years of service. Howard is only concerned with the bottom line: he is more interested in things than in people, as illustrated by his paying more attention to his tape recorder than to his employee. He foreshadows the businessmen who decimated their workforces as cheaper automation took over. Ben is another exploiter, who ignores family responsibilities in search of a fortune that he makes by taking risks and plundering the jungle. His advice to Willy is self-aggrandizing and essentially useless, for his success stems more from luck than from judgment, though his cold, calculating approach to selling allows him to survive until he finds his diamond mine.

Willy recalls his idealized past, both as an escape and as an attempt to discover what went wrong. Convinced that his current unhappiness is due to his failure in the business world, he searches for the answer to the question he has asked all his life: How do you become successful? Willy remains convinced that the answer is to be well liked, and he passes this belief on to his sons. But Miller makes it clear that being well liked has little to do with succeeding in the modern world. People usually get ahead by hard work (Charley and Bernard), inheritance (Howard), or by sheer luck (Ben).

It is unlikely that Willy's sons, Happy and Biff, will fare any better than their father did. Happy believes, to the end, that Willy's dream was right and plans to try to follow in his father's footsteps, and we know where they will lead. Biff recognizes what the business world has done to Willy, and though he tries to fit in by planning to create a sporting-equipment firm out of regard for his father, he quickly sees that it will never succeed. Biff has a chance at happiness, but only if he rejects everything his father has taught him, and turns his back on the business world in favor of a more modest dream of living close to the land out West. But this kind of pastoral existence is also under threat from predatory business interests, and Biff's plans may be no more realistic than Willy's.

Although characters like Howard and Ben embody a selfish and uncaring face of capitalism, Miller indicates that values of compassion, respect, and hard work still exist within the marketplace, as illustrated by Willy's neighbor Charley. Charley is satisfied with moderate success without feeling compelled to be the best, and he does not take shortcuts but relies on steady, hard work. He knows that winning the high school football championship is no guarantee of success in life, and that being well liked has little impact in the modern business world. He passes his values on to his son, Bernard, who is as caring and compassionate as his father, and a highly successful lawyer besides, showing the continuing efficacy of such values. Unfortunately, Willy chooses to admire men like Ben rather than Charley, and it is partly this misguided admiration that kills him.

Glengarry Glen Ross opens with a group of real estate salesmen in a restaurant talking about their sales techniques. In competition with one another to become the best salesman, even when the property they sell is rather dubious, they know that those who fail to produce will lose their jobs. This puts everyone under enormous pressure, especially those like Shelley Levene, who are in a selling slump. Everyone is obsessed with getting good leads for potential clients. While star salesman Ricky Roma makes a sale to James Lingk, Dave Moss plots to steal their firm's leads to sell to rival brokers. The second act shows the office investigating the theft of these leads, while Ricky, creatively but unsuccessfully, tries to prevent Lingk from canceling his transaction. At the close we discover that it was actually Levene who stole the leads, his arrest is imminent, and business for the rest goes on as usual.

These men are consumed by their work and will try to sell to anyone, regardless of a client's need or the quality of the property they sell. Duplicitous and desperate to make a sale at any cost, they lie, wheedle, and trick their clients in their efforts to close a deal. The conversation is constantly about land and travel, and yet we never see any land but only the narrow and rather sleazy world in which these salesmen live, in which no one really moves or goes anywhere.

The play's title refers to the illusory world of salespeople, a world that seems to force one to sacrifice truth and humanity in order to be considered successful. "Glengarry Glen Ross" is an illusion, showing how salespeople often offer their clients false images of whatever Promised Land they seek. The name sounds pretty, but it is made up of two worthless pieces of land without any merit, created by putting together the misleading names of the two main properties these people peddle, Glengarry Highlands (a place in Florida that has no hills) and Glen Ross Farms (a wooded area without any farmland). The "Highlands" are being sold by younger salesmen, like Roma, and represent the present, while the Farms, which Levene has been selling, are emblematic of the past, which is where Levene has been left, since selling property has become a young person's game.

The characters create illusions—not only for others, but also for themselves—to try to bolster their spirits. They constantly blame other things—poor leads, customers, land, and management—to cover up their own ineffectiveness. Levene and Roma, especially, like to play roles, and both feel no allegiance to the truth. Levene, who cannot accept the he is old and cannot sell any more, is constantly trying to make his next sale. Roma, meanwhile, explains the soft-sell illusion he creates, in which he pretends he is not a salesman and the land is not worthless, and comes close to believing his own sales pitch. The audience is also continually deluded, as Mamet misdirects them to believe the wrong man stole the leads, that Levene actually sells something, and that Roma's contracts have gone through.

Youthful and handsome, Roma is in a different league from his colleagues, with a personal style and flair that is attractive but insidious. While the others need to talk about past conquests and dream about increasing their current sales, he gets to work and makes those sales. His friendly chat with Lingk quickly turns to business, and he soon persuades him to invest in property. When Lingk comes to the office to cancel the deal on his wife's insistence, Roma tries every trick he can to prevent him from pulling out, resorting to a series of lies, including professing to Lingk that he values friendship over business. This is just a pretense of human compassion designed to allay Lingk's fears and keep him on board, and Roma nearly succeeds with it, were it not for the manager's unwitting interference.

When Levene pleads with the office manager, John Williamson, for better leads to help him recover from his slump, Williamson is unmoved. He is only interested in sales and not with the messy humanity of the people who do the selling. Indeed, we quickly realize that the business imperative necessarily cancels out the human response. All the men in the play begin with energy and enthusiasm, garbed in business dress, but as the play progresses we see their outfits become increasingly disheveled, and they take on a haggard appearance, as the pressures on them to sell mount.

Driven by an uninhibited competitive spirit that they see as key to democratic capitalism, these salesmen rationalize every deceit that might close a sale, distorting language and ethical principles to justify what they do. They are selling themselves as well as the land, manipulating people's obsession with the mythic dream of America as the Promised Land to generate more sales. Mamet wants us to know that such selling takes a heavy toll on the human spirit, and a total preoccupation with self-interest inevitably leads to an amoral society. When selling defeats them, people like Dave Moss and Shelley Levene resort to crime, and it is ironic that even here competition reigns, as Levene beats Moss to the leads.

The play's offensive language, which is so clearly exaggerated, is not an attempt at realism. Through such violent language, Mamet reveals both the intense desperation of his salesmen, trapped in an endless cycle of selling, and the negative influence that such selling exerts on their characters. The overly cluttered and drab office setting of the second act further underlines the barren spiritual state of these people. Rather than end with any epiphany after the crime has been solved, they continue their amoral routines as before, and Roma heads back to the restaurant at the play's close. Mamet has depicted not only a highly competitive, capitalistic world, but also the morally stultifying effect such a world has on business and the men it employs.

FURTHER SUGGESTED READING

Bigsby, Christopher. *David Mamet*. New York: Methuen, 1985.

Brenman-Gibson, Margaret. *Clifford Odets: American Playwright 1906–1940*. New York: Atheneum, 1982.

Deem, Rosemary, and Graeme Salaman, Eds. *Work, Culture, and Society*. Philadelphia: Open University Press, 1985.

Greenfield, Thomas Allen. *Work and the Work Ethic in American Drama, 1920–1970*. Columbia: University of Missouri Press, 1982.

Kane, Leslie, Ed. *David Mamet's* Glengarry Glen Ross: *Text and Performance*. New York: Garland, 2000.

Mamet, David. *Glengarry Glen Ross*. New York: Grove, 1984.

Miller, Arthur. *Death of a Salesman*. New York: Viking, 1976.

Miller, Gale. *It's a Living: Work in Modern Society*. New York: St. Martin's Press, 1981.

Murphy, Brenda, and Susan C. W. Abbotson. *Understanding* Death of a Salesman. Westport, CT: Greenwood, 1999.

Odets, Clifford. *Six Plays of Clifford Odets*. New York: Random House, 1939.

Rice, Elmer. *The Adding Machine*. New York: Samuel French, 1956.

Roudané, Matthew. *Approaches to Teaching Miller's* Death of a Salesman. New York: MLA, 1995.

Weales, Gerald. *Clifford Odets Playwright*. New York: Pegasus, 1971.

Worlds of the Deaf and Blind

Children of a Lesser God by Mark Medoff (1979)
The Miracle Worker by William Gibson (1959)
Molly Sweeney by Brian Friel (1994)

Few notable modern plays have been written that demand serious consideration of the condition of life without hearing or sight. All too often the deaf or blind person in a play, such as the blind figure of Susi Hendrix in *Wait Until Dark* (1967), is present to provide an interesting plot angle, rather than offer any insight into the worlds of people with hearing or visual impairments. Those plays that do address these worlds directly often present deafness and blindness as disabilities that need to be overcome. A rarer type accepts deafness and blindness, not so much as limitations but as conditions that need to be more socially accepted and understood. It is the latter on which this chapter is based.

Mark Medoff's *Children of a Lesser God* was the first play written about deafness and the use of sign language. Although the National Theatre for the Deaf had previously staged numerous plays using sign language, they did not explore the controversial issue of deafness and signing versus lipreading and speaking, as Medoff's play does; they had merely put on signed versions of plays originally written for hearing people. Medoff tries to dramatize the world of deaf people and its relationship to the hearing world in a play intended for hearing people.

Having met the deaf actress, Phyllis Frelich, who had been born deaf to deaf parents and raised with deaf siblings, Medoff was taken by the fact that she did not lip-read or speak as he expected, but relied entirely on signing. What also surprised him was that she had a hearing husband. Frelich commented to Medoff on the lack of roles for deaf players in the "hearing" theater; impressed by her evident acting skills, and intrigued by her situation, he wrote *Children of a Lesser God* for her to perform, and staged it with her real-life husband in the role of James. The 1986 movie version, adapted by Randa Haines, was very successful, but made integral changes by cutting the subplot of Orin's rebellion, and not having the protagonists actually marry.

While *Children of a Lesser God* provokes its hearing audience to reconsider their relationship to the deaf, William Gibson's *The Miracle Worker* is a more conventional depiction of the deaf. In this, the deaf-blind protagonist is depicted as needing the aid of the hearing and sighted (albeit partially sighted), in order to become accepted into their privileged society. The play's conventionality can be attributed to the fact that it is a much earlier piece. It was initially produced as a television drama in 1957 and made its way to the stage two years later.

The Miracle Worker is based on the real-life relationship between Helen Keller, who had become deaf and blind after an early childhood illness, and the woman who taught her how to communicate, Annie Sullivan. It is less about the challenges of being deaf and blind than about how a dedicated teacher can transform the life of her pupil through sheer perseverance, even against the overwhelming odds of severe disability. Gibson wrote a lesser known (and less inspiring) sequel to this play called *Monday After the Miracle* (1982), which takes up the relationship between Helen and Annie twenty years on, when Helen is attending college and Annie has become frustrated and embittered after having limited her own prospects by devoting her life to Helen.

The central protagonist of Brien Friel's *Molly Sweeney* is not deaf, but a blind woman. Friel insists that she be played authentically, requesting no groping or "blind props" like canes or dark glasses in the performance, since most people with impaired vision "look and behave like fully sighted people" (1). The play is a series of monologues presented by Molly, her husband, and her doctor, showing their alternative points of view regarding an attempt to restore Molly's sight. Friel's presentation of Molly is sympathetic, and he asks us to consider her blindness not as a disability as much as an alternate way of life, which well-meaning people almost destroy. Through this concept of blindness, Friel also asks us to explore how we perceive our existence and relationship to others. The play's epigraphs from Emily Dickinson and Denis Diderot emphasize this dual concern with perception and the clinical understanding of what it means to be blind, Dickinson invoking the idea of blindness versus sight as a metaphor for the way we perceive truth, and Diderot warning of the tremendous impact that sight must have on a previously blind person.

Children of a Lesser God begins with an intense quarrel between Sarah, a deaf woman who does not speak but uses sign language to communicate, and her hearing husband, James, who met her when teaching at a state school for the deaf and whom she has recently left. From this we travel back in time as James traces their relationship and tries to understand how they have come to this impasse. Each blames the other, and the play ends ambiguously, though hopefully, as they admit to a mutual love, but Sarah declares herself as yet unready to return to James.

The play expands the concept of deafness to embrace an exploration of communication on many levels, so its theme of deafness becomes more than a political statement, but a universal metaphor for the way people relate to each other. On this level it depicts a search for identity, a search that in the case of Sarah has been made all the more complicated by her condition. Deafness intensifies the problems between James and Sarah, but it does not create them. Their difficulty stems from their equal inability to accept the other as they are. Thus Medoff helps to humanize the condition of deafness, which is too often viewed as alienating and setting people apart.

Sarah is very intelligent and is wasting her life as a cleaning woman, but has been consigned to such a position because she cannot (and refuses to) speak. As an individual she does not want to conform to social expectation, and this alienates her from those who expect her to conform, like her mother and James. The play's title, taken from the poet Alfred Lord Tennyson, refers to the way people have a tendency to force others to conform to their own expectations. This is exactly what James attempts as he pressures Sarah to learn lipreading and speech to fit in better with the hearing world. But Sarah questions such a scheme, insisting that the hearing world should adapt itself to include her instead, and accept her as she is.

Sarah resists lipreading and speaking because she considers signing a genuine language. She views those who cannot sign as handicapped, and so places herself in a dominant rather than subservient position. To preserve this, she perhaps unfairly rejects James's largely pragmatic concern for her future, and James himself. However, her accusations do highlight a disturbing tendency in the hearing world to equate deafness with stupidity, and society's often unfair pressure on everyone to embrace a certain "norm," which frequently undermines our true selves.

James is a kind and loving man with the best of intentions, despite an initial difficulty in understanding his wife's perspective. Contrary to Sarah's accusations, he is not teaching her to lip-read and speak as a game or power play, but out of love and a desire to allow her greater opportunities in life. His intent is entirely altruistic. He has been attracted to her from the start by both her beauty and her intelligence, and he has not seen her deafness as any kind of obstacle that must be removed. He views her as a challenging equal, and not some charity project. Sarah teaches James (and the audience) a lot about the world of the deaf from the perspective of the deaf, so he becomes as much the student in their relationship.

The play not only educates its audience about the life of deaf people in general, but also about the communication options open to them, by having James and Sarah communicate in a combination of Signed English and American Sign Language. While American Sign Language spells out words letter by letter, Signed English uses a more pictorial approach, with signs for whole words. The latter actually predominates among the deaf and adds an interesting visual layer to the play. Rather than slowing down the action, the signing tends to more closely involve the audience, who find themselves focusing on every gesture.

Sarah signs throughout the play and speaks aloud only once during the performance. This "speech" tales the form of an incoherent rage against James's demands, which has no discernable language except that of its emotional charge. In some sense the audience's reaction to this is an attempt to turn the tables, by having them feel the restrictions of not being able to understand Sarah, and having to reconsider how they communicate, rather than always have her be the one who is expected to try to make herself understood. James, Sarah's fellow student Orin, and the school's supervisor, Mr. Franklin, all speak aloud what Sarah signs for the audience, and although this is unrealistic, it provides Sarah with additional ammunition in her charge that James is trying to recreate her in his own image, when she insists that he no longer translate for her, but let her "speak" for herself in her own way.

A subplot to the central relationship of James and Sarah is the rebellion of Orin, a student with some residual hearing who lip-reads, and who James has been helping to speak more clearly. As a campaigner for deaf rights, Orin may be overly militant, and he has a decided chip on his shoulder, but he does point to a number of valid inequities in the way the deaf are generally treated. He expresses resentment toward instructors whom he feels have chosen this profession merely for their own self-satisfaction and self-glorification in being viewed as helping the "less fortunate." He sees them as too keen to assume that they know better than their deaf students, just because they have full hearing. Wanting to change the system, he apprentices to become an instructor himself, and brings in a lawyer to complain before the Equal Employment Opportunity Commission to force the school to hire deaf teachers.

The Miracle Worker takes us from her parents' discovery that their daughter, Helen, is deaf and blind, through an indulgent childhood in which the undisciplined Helen behaves disruptively, up to her first experiences with Annie Sullivan, a partially sighted and newly trained governess. Annie perseveres through Helen's antagonism to teach her discipline, and to finally make her understand how language works, which will allow Helen to better communicate and expand her range of experience.

Having been raised by overly indulgent parents who have never tried to restrain her in any way, Helen is very temperamental and lacking in self-discipline. Because of this, she is thought to be mentally defective in addition to deaf and blind, though her father refuses to have her institutionalized. But we are made to see that young Helen, despite her wild appearance and behavior, has intelligence and an elemental understanding of the world she can neither see nor hear, when she performs such actions as taking the buttons from her aunt's dress to make eyes for her cloth doll. Also, her stubborn and initially successful resistance to Annie suggests something more complex than animalistic cunning, and makes her a worthy adversary rather than an abject figure of pathos.

Part of Annie's charm is her youthful enthusiasm. She is determined to teach Helen language, even though she knows what a challenge a deaf-blind child will be: "Words can be her *eyes*," she declares, "to everything in the world outside her, and inside too" (101). Although some of Annie's treatment of Helen may seem almost abusive—indeed, that is how Helen's parents see it— we know that Annie is a caring person who was much beloved by the younger students at the Perkins Institute for the Blind where she trained. Annie recognizes that before Helen can have any hope of learning to communicate with others, she must first learn to discipline herself. Annie sets out to do what Helen's parents should have done, but felt too guilty to do: teach Helen that there are rules and boundaries governing acceptable social behavior. Once Helen can learn to be part of society on a physical level, she can then begin the slow process of discovering how to join society on an intellectual level and communicate through sign language.

Partly out of a sense of guilt that they may have prevented Helen's condition, her parents have exacerbated her condition by being overprotective and not attempting to restrict her. Helen is depicted as an anguished child despite this apparent freedom, trapped in a dark world from which she has no means of effectively communicating with others. It is a world from which Annie's persistence will partially release her, by restricting her wildness to a level where she can begin to learn the discipline of sign language. Formerly, at mealtimes, Helen's parents allowed her to roam around the table, fingering other people's food. This is one of the first things Helen refuses to allow, although it sends Helen into a violent tantrum. However, despite Annie's youth and the objections of Helen's parents, Annie stands firm, insisting that Helen learn "reasonable" discipline. The two remain locked in the dining room where they physically and emotionally confront each other until Helen learns to better govern her behavior.

Helen's process of civilization does not occur instantaneously; it takes two weeks of isolation with Annie, as the pair move into the Kellers's garden house together, and Helen is tricked into thinking she is far away from her home and any parental refuge. After two weeks, the change in them both is evident; Helen appears neat and tidy, self-restrained, and apparently obedient, even able to crochet a little. By contrast, Annie is exhausted and frustrated.

Annie has taught Helen the signs for twenty-one words, but has not been able to get her to associate these with the things to which they apply, and thus to make Helen understand the basic concept of language. Annie begs the parents for more time, but they will no longer allow her to dominate their daughter in what they suspect is a pointless endeavor. It looks as if Helen will be allowed to revert to her previous behavior until suddenly, in one final confrontation with Annie, who has yet to give up, the title miracle occurs: Helen makes the connection between the sign for water and the thing itself. It is a virtual baptism as Helen excitedly wants to learn more, and signs m-o-t-h-e-r and f-a-t-h-e-r for the first time.

The play is filled with recurrent images of keys and locks, emblematic of the key of language Helen needs to acquire in order to free herself from the closed space of her deafness and blindness, and satisfy her previously restricted intellect. On Helen's first encounter with her teacher, she significantly discovers Annie's key and unlocks her suitcase to find the unexpected treasure of a doll Annie has brought her. So too will Annie unlock more treasures for Helen if she can only learn the self-restraint to embrace them. Unfortunately, after this initial unlocking, Helen chooses to reimprison her opportunity as she locks Annie in her room and throws away the key. Fortunately for Helen, Annie refuses to allow her to dismiss this opportunity so casually, and perseveres until Helen finally holds the "key" she needs to free herself: an understanding of language.

Molly Sweeney relates the experiences of Molly—blind since infancy—before and after an operation to restore her sight, from the points of view of Molly, her husband Frank, and Doctor Rice, who performed the operation. Molly nostalgically recalls her experiences as a blind woman and the resulting confusion that sight brings, which ends in a psychological condition the doctor calls "blindsight" in which Molly withdraws into her sightless memories and ceases to function in the real world. Alongside that we witness her husband's initial enthusiasm but subsequent loss of interest as her case goes awry and he deserts her for a another cause, plus the doctor's suspicions that somehow he failed his patient even as he managed to rekindle his own career.

Rice perceives at once that the Sweeneys are not well matched, and Frank only sees Molly as one in a series of causes, many of which he has embraced and dropped through the years; even Molly acknowledges that Frank married her less out of love than from a fascination with her blindness. Their very natures seem antagonistic, with Frank's ebullience a constant threat to Molly's calm equanimity, which is borne out by the fact it is Frank who pushes for the operation. When persuading Rice to take her case, he asks, "What has she to lose?" and answers himself, "Nothing" (6), but we learn that he is wrong. His limited perception blinds him to Molly's contentment with her condition, insisting that she has to wish to be able to see. He wrongly equates vision with knowledge, viewing his wife's blindness as a limitation that needs to be overcome. But it turns out to be sight that limits Molly, as it destroys her confidence and independence.

When Rice is reticent over their chances for success, Frank gets angry, insisting that Molly must gain vision to acquire "a new life for both of us" (17). However, it seems that he has little regard for what Molly wants: he just wants one of his causes to finally succeed and for his life to be changed, since he is incapable of staying content for long in one place. He continues to demand the miracle of perfect sight, even when the possibility of partial sight is the best that can occur; by constantly setting his sights so high, his constant failure becomes easier to understand, even while he himself cannot see this. His final abandonment of Molly to pursue a new cause in Ethiopia comes as little surprise.

Molly trusts Rice because he seems more understanding of her position than her husband is. Instead of quizzing her about what it is like to be blind, or telling her that she lives in a world of touch, as other doctors have done, he just asks if the idea of sight excites or frightens her, recognizing the possibility that a blind person may not long for vision. Rice understands the dangers of giving sight to a blind person, yet proceeds with the case, less out of a concern for Molly than as an opportunity to regain the prominent position he once held in the medical community. It is a position he lost through blinkered vision, concentrating too much on his work and neglecting his wife, who eventually ran off with a colleague who paid more attention to her, causing him to have a breakdown, abandon his career, and become a reclusive drunk. Molly has given him the motivation to reenter the mainstream of his profession, but it is through the sacrifice of Molly herself, and he knows this before he does the operation. He talks about the frivolous ease with which he and his former colleagues had pursued their careers, and little has changed, despite his time away.

Other perceptions constantly change throughout the play. Molly describes a childhood spent mostly in the sporadic company of an affectionate father, who taught her to recognize flowers by their scent and feel, and use her hearing to create a more detailed sensibility of her world, skills in which she delights. Her mother seems to have been either quarreling with her father, or hospitalized with a nervous condition, and had little relationship with her daughter. However, as events unfold, a new picture of the family emerges, in which roles are reversed. The father becomes the villain, empty of passion, refusing to allow her the benefits of a Blind School out of miserliness, and she begins to see her mother in a far more sympathetic light.

As a blind woman, Molly feels no self-pity or even resignation because she honestly feels no sense of deprivation. As she tells us, "I knew only my own world" (14), and she is content with that, deriving intense pleasure from actions like swimming, from which she secretly suspects she gains more pleasure than sighted people, innately knowing that seeing changes the experience. She only goes along with the operation to keep Frank happy. Even after the operation, all she asks for is "a brief excursion to this land of vision; not to live there—just to visit" (36), clearly out of curiosity not discontent, to increase her understanding with the knowledge of what things look like. Her disappointment is indicated by her reaction to the Baby Blue Eyes she buys—the flowers had held a special place for her when she was blind, but visually she decides they are not very pretty.

Rice speaks about sight being a chore for Molly that takes work. It is something Molly has to want enough to make the effort, or it cannot happen, and

it soon becomes evident that Molly does not want sight. She finds it too dazzling to accept and begins shutting her eyes for a while, until she feels calm
and has the courage to reopen them. But she will soon retreat entirely into her
sightless world.

Given the nervous period of reckless desperation, mood swings, and disori-
entation she goes through when trying to learn to use her sight, her regression
to blindsight may seem like a victory for Molly in some sense; she seems at
least content. But if we compare the descriptions we get of this motionless,
bed-ridden figure, scarcely able to communicate, with the Molly we hear about
from the party the night before her first operation—socializing with friends as
an equal, dancing a crazy hornpipe with, "No timidity, no hesitations, no fal-
terings" (24)—such a view is hard to accept. Rice's vision of Molly as a lost
soul, caught between the worlds of the blind and the sighted, now confined to
a psychiatric hospital, is more chilling and probably more accurate. In her
immobility, she has lost touch with the tangible world she once relished, and
her former existence, ironically, has been seriously reduced rather than expanded by the attempted acquisition of sight.

FURTHER SUGGESTED READING

Andrews, Elmer. *The Art of Brian Friel.* New York: St. Martin's Press, 1995.

Friel, Brian. *Molly Sweeney.* New York: Plume, 1994.

Gibson, William. *The Miracle Worker and Monday After the Miracle.* Garden City,
     NJ: Doubleday, 1983.

Kerwin, William, Ed. *Brian Friel: A Casebook.* New York: Garland, 1997.

Kleege, Georgina. *Sight Unseen.* New Haven: Yale University Press, 1999.

Knott, Frederick. *Wait Until Dark.* New York: DPS, 1967.

Lash, Joseph P. *Helen and Teacher.* New York: Delacorte, 1980.

Lowefield, Berthold. *The Changing Status of the Blind: From Separation to Integration.*
     Springfield, IL: Thomas, 1975.

Medoff, Mark. *Children of a Lesser God.* Clifton, NJ: J. T. White, 1980.

Nash, Jeffrey E., and Anedith Nash. *Deafness in Society.* Lexington, MA: Lexington,
     1981.

Index

SUSAN C. W. ABBOTSON has taught English for over 15 years, both at the high school and university levels. She currently teaches in the English Department of Rhode Island College. She is the author of *Student Companion to Arthur Miller* (Greenwood, 2000) and co-author of *Understanding* Death of a Salesman (Greenwood, 1999). She also contributed the drama section of *Resources for Teaching: Literature and Its Writers*.